CU000802945

PENGUI
STRANGERS

Sanjoy Hazarika was born in Shill...
He went to school at St Edmund's College there and later studied
journalism and printing at London. He began his career with *Himmat
Weekly* and later worked for the *Hindustan Times* and the *Associated
Press* before joining the *New York Times* for which he has reported
extensively out of the South Asia bureau since 1981. He published his
first book, *Assam: A Crisis of Identity* in 1980. He was the recipient of a
New York Times Publishers Award for his reporting on the Bhopal
gas tragedy in 1984. His second book, *Bhopal: The Lessons of a Tragedy*
(Penguin India) which was listed by the *Observer*, London, as among
the ten best science books released in 1988. In 1993–94, he was awarded
a fellowship to study the changes in US environmental law after the
Bhopal disaster at the Joan Shorenstein Barone Center of Press, Politics
and Public Policy at Harvard University.

Sanjoy Hazarika lives in New Delhi with his wife and daughter. He is
co-authoring two volumes of a study of the crisis before India with
T.N. Seshan, the Chief Election Commissioner.

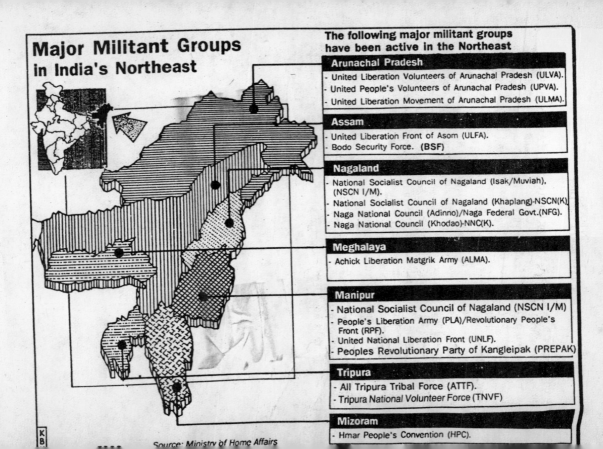

Major Militant Groups
in India's Northeast

The following major militant groups have been active in the Northeast

Arunachal Pradesh
- United Liberation Volunteers of Arunachal Pradesh (ULVA).
- United People's Volunteers of Arunachal Pradesh (UPVA).
- United Liberation Movement of Arunachal Pradesh (ULMA).

Assam
- United Liberation Front of Asom (ULFA).
- Bodo Security Force. (BSF)

Nagaland
- National Socialist Council of Nagaland (Isak/Muviah), (NSCN I/M).
- National Socialist Council of Nagaland (Khaplang)-NSCN(K)
- Naga National Council (Adinno)/Naga Federal Govt.(NFG).
- Naga National Council (Khodao)-NNC(K).

Meghalaya
- Achick Liberation Matgrik Army (ALMA).

Manipur
- National Socialist Council of Nagaland (NSCN I/M).
- People's Liberation Army (PLA)/Revolutionary People's Front (RPF).
- United National Liberation Front (UNLF).
- Peoples Revolutionary Party of Kangleipak (PREPAK)

Tripura
- All Tripura Tribal Force (ATTF).
- Tripura National Volunteer Force (TNVF)

Mizoram
- Hmar People's Convention (HPC).

Source: Ministry of Home Affairs

Sanjoy Hazarika

Strangers of the Mist

Tales of War and Peace from India's Northeast

PENGUIN BOOKS

Penguin Books India (P) Ltd., 210, Chiranjiv Tower, 43 Nehru Place, New Delhi 110 019, India
Penguin Books Ltd., 27 Wrights Lane, London W8 5TZ, UK
Penguin Books USA Inc., 375 Hudson Street, New York, NY 10014, USA
Penguin Books Australia Ltd., Ringwood, Victoria, Australia
Penguin Books Canada Ltd., 10 Alcorn Avenue, Suite 300, Toronto, Ontario M4V 3B2, Canada
Penguin Books (NZ) Ltd., 182-190 Wairau Road, Auckland 10, New Zealand

First published in VIKING by Penguin Books India (P) Ltd. 1994
Reprinted 1994
Published in Penguin Books 1995

Copyright © Sanjoy Hazarika 1994

All rights reserved

10 9 8 7 6 5 4 3 2 1

Typeset in Times Roman by Digital Technologies and Printing Solutions, New Delhi

This book is sold subject to the condition that it shall not, by way of trade or otherwise, be lent, resold, hired out, or otherwise circulated without the publisher's prior written consent in any form of binding or cover other than that in which it is published and without a similar condition including this condition being imposed on the subsequent purchaser and without limiting the rights under copyright reserved above, no part of this publication may be reproduced, stored in or introduced into a retrieval system, or transmitted in any form or by any means (electronic, mechanical, photocopying, recording or otherwise), without the prior written permission of both the copyright owner and the above-mentioned publisher of this book.

For my father and mother

Contents

Acknowledgements   *ix*
Note from the Author   *xv*

Section One   1

The Bangladesh Syndrome

From Dhaka To Delhi   3
Neighbours And Disasters   10
A Frontier State And Nationalism   41
The Gandhi Card   75
Nagaland: 1,000 Years In A Lifetime   86
The Hills Revolt   111

Section Two   135

The New Rebellions

The Boys In Business   137
The Rise and Fall Of ULFA   167
The NSCN Takes Wings   237
A Stepmother In Delhi   249
Neighbours, Secret Affairs   276

Section Three   317

A Search For Solutions

A Security Doctrine For The East   319

Section Four

Section Four   333

Appendices

Appendix A (I)   335
Appendix A (II)   338
Appendix B (I)   340
Appendix B (II)   343
Appendix C   346
Appendix D   349
Appendix E   355
Appendix F   357
Appendix G   359
Appendix H   362
Appendix I   365
Appendix J   368
Appendix K   372

Select Bibliography   381
Index   383

Acknowledgements

Of the many associated with this book, there are some who can be named but there are others, by force of their professions and requests for anonymity, who asked not to be identified. There are many more whose names may not figure but who have had a generic role in it: school friends, family associates, relatives, contacts in officialdom and politics and others who I have interviewed or met just once during reporting assignments to the area over more than twenty years but whose strength of conviction has remained a constant memory. This list, spanning all my life and the entire region from Nepal to Nagaland, Dhaka to Arunachal Pradesh and Bhutan, is far too lengthy to contemplate publishing.

This book would have been completed earlier but for events that disrupted millions of lives across India, including those of journalists: the demolition of the Babri Masjid at Ayodhya, by a Hindu mob on 6 December 1992 and the communal riots that followed across the country. In January 1993, the selective massacres of Muslims at Bombay and the devastating revenge bomb blasts there two months later led to extensive travelling and reporting for the *New York Times*. In addition, there was 'normal reporting': the Punjab, environmental, economic and political issues such as the billion dollar scam in the Bombay stock market, corruption charges and infighting that brought Prime Minister P. V. Narasimha Rao's government almost to its knees.

Thus, the forbearance of my publishers, especially David Davidar, who counselled ways the book could read better has been a great strength. Sudha Sadhanand was a cheerful editor.

I am grateful to the Nehru Memorial Museum and Library, New Delhi for giving me extensive access to the personal papers of Sir Syed Mohammad Saadulla, Gopinath Bardoloi and Bishnuram Medhi. I am also grateful to Lily M. Baruah, the Bisnu-Nirmala Trust and S. M. Sawoodulla for permission to publish extracts and material from the papers of Gopinath Bardoloi, Bishnuram Medhi and Sir Syed Mohammad Saadulla. The International Institute for Strategic Studies in London granted me permission to publish extracts from Adelphi Papers 262: "Environmental Issues and Security in South Asia" by Shaukat Hassan (Autumn 1991).

B.G. Verghese's book, *Waters of Hope*, is a source of inspiration and a bank of knowledge which no writer can do without. *Chai Garam!* by Arup Kumar Dutta was illuminating on the tea industry in Assam. Nirmal Nibedon's series on the Northeast were pathbreakers: *Nagaland, The Night of the Guerrillas, Mizoram, The Dagger Brigade* and *India's Northeast: The Ethnic Explosion*. Visier Sanyu gave generously of his time, ideas, advice and also permission to use excerpts from his unpublished manuscript on the oral traditions of Khonoma village and the Nagas.

I would also like to acknowledge my gratitude to the following for their patience, counsel and assistance:

In Delhi: former Congress President Dev Kanta Borooah, former Indian National Trade Union Congress President Bijoy Chandra Bhagwati, L.P. Singh, B.K. Nehru and M.L. Kampani, formerly of the Home Ministry, Arobindo Sarma for help with translation, C.D. Tripathi, B.P. Singh, former Minister of State for Home Affairs Subodh Kant Sahay, former External Affairs Minister Inder Gujral, Rajmohan Gandhi, Hemen Barooah, Minister of State for Food Processing Tarun Gogoi, Minister of State for Labour, Purno Sangma, Lieutenant-General Ajai Singh, George Fernandes, and Jaya Jaitly. Also, Bijoy Handique, Jayanta Rongpi and Satyen Brahmachowdhury, Members of Parliament. The Bodo leaders I met included the late Upendra Brahma and S.K. Bwasumatari. Others who helped in Delhi were the development economist L.C. Jain, Chakra Bastola, Nepal's Ambassador, Dinesh Bhattarai of the Royal Nepal Embassy, Sonam Rabgye of the Royal Embassy of Bhutan and Farooq Sobhan, the Bangladesh High Commissioner at Delhi.

In Assam: the family of the late Dr Bidyadhar Baruah, Pranab Baruah, Chief Minister Hiteswar Saikia, Home Commissioner Tapan Lal Baruah, former Chief Minister Prafulla Kumar Mahanta, former Home Minister Brighu Kumar Phukan, the late Pradip Das, the late Sushil Kumar Barooah, Ashok Saikia, Jones Mahaliya, Bapa Rao, M.S. (Muli) Oberoi and the family of Siba Ram Das; Dhiren Bezbaruah, editor of the *Sentinel*, Parag Das of *Budhbar*, Kartik Baruah of the Press Trust of India and Subir Bhowmick of the *Telegraph*. Dr Birendra Bhattacharyya and Dr Bhupen Hazarika also gave generously of their time. And from the United Liberation Front of Asom (among others) Sunil Nath, Tapan Dutta, Munim Nobis and Jugal Kishore Mahanta.

In Calcutta: executives of the Indian Tea Association, Gautom Baruah of MacNeil and Magor and Swapan Dasgupta.

In Bombay: Hemant Vyas of Prag Bosimi and Hari Mathur.

In Chandigarh: K.P.S. Gill, Punjab's Director-General of Police, who is an Assam cadre officer.

In Nagaland and Delhi: Chief Minister S.C. Jamir and former Chief Minister Vamuzo; Niketu Iralu, Mene Chandola and her brother, Tubu Kevichusa, and Rana Shaiza and her late husband, Lungshem.

In Mizoram and Delhi: the late Laldenga of the Mizo National Front, Brigadier T. Sailo, L.R. Sailo, Denghnuna, Chief Minister Lalthanhawla and Joseph Zokunga.

In Manipur: Rishang Keishing, R.K. Singh and Joychandra Singh.

In Tripura: Bijoy Kumar Hrangkhawl of the Tripura National Volunteer Force and members of the Shanti Bahini.

In Bhutan: His Majesty King Jigme Singye Wangchuk, and senior officials, including Foreign Minister Dawa Tsering, Home Minister Lympo Tshering, Planning Minister C. Dorji as well as Jigme Tsultrun, Chang Tsering and Sonam Tenzin.

In Nepal: Prime Minister Girija Prasad Koirala, Sushil Koirala, former Prime Minister Krishna Prasad Bhattarai, Nepali Congress Leader Ganesh Man Singh, Mayor P.L. Singh of Kathmandu, Kanak Dixit, editor of *Himal*, Tahir Ali of the United Nations High Commission for Refugees and Bhim Subba. Utpal Sengupta was a sparkling host at Kathmandu, along with his splendid staff at the Shangri-La Hotel; without Sarada Bista's vehicles, we surely would have been footweary if not immobile.

In Bangladesh: Mahabub Hossein and Atiur Rahman of the Bangladesh Institute for Development Studies; Ataus Samad of the British Broadcasting Corporation and Serajuddin Ahmed (Nafa).

In Europe, the United States and Canada: Gopinath Bardoloi's biographer and historian, Dr Nirode Kumar Barooah of Cologne, Germany; the late Angami Zapu Phizo and Kevi Levor; Astri Suhrke of the Chr.

Michelsen Institute in Norway; Jeffrey Boutwell and Annette Bourne at the American Academy of Arts and Sciences in Cambridge, Massachusetts; Professor Myron Weiner of the Massachusetts Institute of Technology; Sherman Teichman of Tufts University; Dennis Gallagher of the Refugee Policy Group; Peter Glieck of the Pacific Institute for Studies in Development Environment and Security; Vasant and Manisha Gandhi, then of Washington; Ashok and Meera Bhogani of Boston; Daniel Stephanos and Pradeep Srivastava of the Harvard Institute of International Development for their friendship; Marvin Kalb and the Staff of the Joan Shorenstein Barone Center on Press and Politics at Harvard University for their unflagging good spirits. Shaukat Hassan of Ottawa and Thomas Homer-Dixon of the Peace and Studies Program at Toronto University gave valuable insights.

Support from the Mahadeo Jalan Trust and the Magor Education Trust made extensive travel and research possible.

Ed Gargan, then South Asia bureau chief of the *New York Times,* was generous with schedules, enabling me to complete the book.

There are many others I cannot name: intelligence officials in the Northeast and Delhi, members of the armed forces, senior government officers, human rights activists, businessmen and executives, especially in the tea companies. They provided inputs which were integral.

Many relatives have lavished affection and more on me and on my brother, Sujoy, in Nowgong (now Nagaon), Shillong, Guwahati and elsewhere for years. They were always ready to listen to yarns, views and maintained an interest in my work—without expecting anything in return. Not that I had much to offer, anyway.

Closest among them to me are my grandmother, Amiya Baruah, and my brother, Sujoy. My grandmother, teller of stories and religious woman, has been companion all these years to her daughter—who also is my mother. Sujoy—cricketer, car engineer, artist, photographer and doctor—has been a friend, despite the physical distance between Delhi and Tura, the town in Meghalaya where he tends to people's bodies and spirits.

Minal, my wife, and Meghna, our daughter, have patiently handled carpenters, masons, exams, visitors and illnesses and borne my cantankerousness, long silences and absences stoically and with good humour. They will be relieved that their current ordeal is over.

Acknowledgements

A deep regret is that my father, Chaitanya Nath Hazarika, who died when I was barely fifteen, is not around to view this offering. Many people in the Northeast spoke to me for this book out of affection for him.

This book is dedicated to him and to my mother, Maya Hazarika, who has always been supportive.

Without them *Strangers of the Mist* could not have been written.

New Delhi
22 February 1994

Sanjoy Hazarika

'Our traditions are being destroyed. Soon, we will be the nowhere people, without a past or a future. I tell the young men, "Do not throw away your traditions. Not all of them were bad."

'In the ways of the new government, the new rulers, there is no love, there is no care. India has not done anything for us except after the Chinese aggression of 1962: it needed a shock to do something for the Northeast. Now at least, people are clothed, they are learning personal hygiene, they are getting educated, there are some health services. It may not be bad that some traditions are going. But we have to ask ourselves: where are we headed?

'The new officers, they sign files, they come to work for some time and go away without touching the lives or hearts of ordinary folk. These big officers and politicians, they have no knowledge of what is going on: they step in and out of big offices, cars, airplanes. Our boys are following their example. People have stopped doing things for the common good. Nowadays, the first thing that they want to know is what is in it for themselves.'

— *Village elder at Thankip village, Arunachal Pradesh.*

Note From The Author

India's Northeast, home to seven states and many more insurgencies, is part of a great tropical rainforest that stretches from the foothills of the Himalayas to the tip of the Malaysian Peninsula and the mouth of the Mekong river as it flows into the Gulf of Tonkin.

As the crow flies, it is closer to Hanoi than to New Delhi.

For me, as for millions of others, it also is home and sanctuary, where I grew up and which holds a special, magical attraction with its mist-clad hills, lush green forests and smooth valleys, the bewildering range of its languages and the rich, colourful mix of its people, ranging from former head-hunters to city slickers.

All this has changed in my lifetime. At times, dramatically; and other moments, covertly.

It has changed in every way: the shape of the Northeast—or rather its shape on the maps of the world—has been altered with new lines drawn to recognize new political and administrative realities. The names of these units have changed: the Naga Hills became Nagaland, the Lushai Hills changed to Mizoram and the North Eastern Frontier Agency, still known to many simply as NEFA, was converted to Arunachal Pradesh, the Land of the Rising Sun. I am sure that those who coined the last title meant no offence to Japan.

And if these frontiers have changed, so have attitudes among its people; so have the skylines of its cities and towns. So has the way people talk to each other, the things they talk about and in which they involve themselves and one another.

Its forests of pine, teak, sal and mangrove swamps are being maimed by plunderers. Yet, thick bamboo, coconut and banana groves, rubber and tea plantations, clusters of frangipani and bougainvillaea still dot the countryside. Its hills are terraced with rice fields. So are its steamy plains.

One image that endures is of wiry farmers with Mongolian features, balancing bamboo poles across their shoulders with cane baskets filled with vegetables, chickens or eggs at either end, walking jerkily to market.

Another image is of naked, cheerful children on water buffaloes, prodding the animals along narrow village tracks.

These images could be true of any part of this belt, which comprises a single geographical entity. Yet, under this postcard-like facade of calm and exotic locales, smiling faces and lushness lie deeper emotions: grief, terror, war and all the torments, tragedies and gore that accompany them. For decades, this jungle has seethed with unrest, rebellion and violence.

The jungles of Southeast Asia sweep down from Bhutan and Arunachal Pradesh across seven other nations—Bangladesh, Myanmar, Thailand, Laos, Kampuchea, Malaysia, and Vietnam—spanning political boundaries, irreverential even of physical frontiers. Ethnic coalitions, oral traditions and lifestyles based on respect for nature have mattered more in these regions than frontiers. Here men and women, with common origins but different nationalities, share a racial, historic, anthropological and linguistic kinship with each other that is more vital than their links with the mainstream political centres, especially at Delhi, Dhaka and Rangoon.

It is this affinity that has played a role in the unrest and insurgencies that have long troubled the Northeast of India. The embattled communities have been bonded by suffering and opposition to the brutality of government crackdowns against militancy and revolts.

Affinity and Identity. These, more than any other factors, represented the principal compulsions that triggered the Naga, Mizo, Meitei, Tripuri and Assamese affirmation of separateness from the non-Mongolian communities that dominate the Indian subcontinent.

India's Northeast is a misshapen strip of land, linked to the rest of the country by a narrow corridor just twenty kilometres wide at its slimmest which is referred to as the Chicken's Neck. The region has been the battleground for generations of subnational identities confronting insensitive nation-states and their bureaucracies as well as of internecine strife. It is a battle that continues, of ideas and arms, new concepts and old traditions, of power, bitterness and compassion.

Yet, it also holds warm memories.

Some of these are of the years in school: crisp mornings, the joy of friends and St. Edmund's School, run by largely-cheerful, occasionally sherry-laden Irish missionaries from the Christian Brothers. Cramming for exams, lunches from tiffin boxes brought by servants and served in the Great Hall (where exams were held three times a year for senior classes), cricket on the playing fields on Sundays and on the back lawn of the sprawling bungalow where we lived during my father's tenure as head of the Reid Chest Hospital, a treatment centre for tuberculosis patients. We broke more windows with our home cricket than I care to remember. There were picnics in the hills among pine trees and streams with relatives and school friends. Above all, the fresh aroma of pine in the air, the sight of golden and pink flowering orchids growing wild.

And the rains: steam rising from smartly macadamized roads with the first sharp showers of early summer, the wet, warm, sensuous smell of fresh earth washed by rain, so fresh that you could almost taste it.

In winter we gathered in one main bedroom around a crackling fire where we dozed in our chairs, munching on sweet oranges, throwing pips into the fire and listening to their sputter as they exploded in the heat. The fire also slowly baked the large sweet potatoes, placed under the iron grate, with a mixture of heat, embers and ash.

We were exposed too, to the power of nature. I remember watching with awe as a thunderstorm slammed into Shillong and crumpled our garage like a piece of paper. Then, as if in slow motion, the wind picked up the heavy asbestos roof and hurled it 100 feet away, spinning above the servant's outhouse into a vegetable patch.

In many ways, it was a carefree existence. But we were also aware of the turbulence around us.

During the 1965 war with Pakistan, all the windows of our home and of every home in Shillong, the capital of undivided Assam and located nearly 5,000 feet above sea level, were plastered with blackened paper to prevent any light from escaping and indicating our presence to the enemy (a flight of planes? A spy, perhaps?).

We went through air raid drills at school, flinging ourselves enthusiastically at the red, wet earth by the playing fields, ruining our sparkling, starched white shirts and grey flannels. There were mock drills but there was one which came late at night when we were at home.

'Out,' snapped Father, as he switched the lights off and opened the front door. We dashed to the nearby khud, flung ourselves face down on the grass and covered our heads with our hands as we had been trained to do. I was frightened and excited. And before the All Clear sounded, I broke discipline: I looked up.

Moving noiselessly and gently against the starlit sky, a small band of planes flew above us, their lights twinkling peacefully until they swept out of sight.

The Northeast has best been described as Asia in miniature, a place where the brown and yellow races meet and mingle. The oral history of the tribes of Mizoram, Nagaland, Manipur and other areas tell of ancestors from the shadowy past, from mountains steeped in mist and romance, from lands far away, of snake gods and princesses, epic battles and great warriors.

Its people have a fear of being swamped by 'outsiders', of lifestyles and histories being destroyed by modern nation-states that bother little about small communities but pay more attention to 'strategic' considerations such as the natural resources of the area, their exploitation for the national 'good' and the region's proximity to a friendly or inimical neighbour. Decisions for the little peoples of such regions—the historian Amalendu Guha describes as 'sub-nationalities'—are made by bureaucratic and political mandarins in national and state capitals, far removed from the realities of the customs and beliefs that govern the thoughts and lives of the indigenous peoples.

The women are pretty, the men handsome. The girls of Imphal in Manipur who ride cycles and scooters, resemble their Thai and Lao counterparts. They could easily be placed either in Bangkok or Vientiane. The seductively swaying Manipuri dances are similar to the gentle rhythms of the Khmers and Laotians as well as the Thais and Indonesians. The distinctive shawls of Nagaland, Manipur and Mizoram, each colourful strand proclaiming a tribe, a lifestyle and an identity, share a commonality with communities across the borders in Myanmar and Thailand.

That diversity was seen every day at school, located on a series of gentle hills several of which had been flattened to make space for playing fields, tennis and squash courts, and buildings. To them came Khasis and Garos, Assamese and Punjabis, Bengalis and Anglo-Indians, Bodos and Garhwalis; we were Christians, Hindus, Sikhs and Muslims and we were not infected by the viciousness of today's society.

Our friends, especially the Khasis, had delightful names. Parents gave their children the names of their favourite rock star or any other name that caught their fancy: there was Elvis Presley Lyngdoh, North Star Diengdoh and a politician named Hopingstone Lyngdoh.

The buildings were of sturdy wood, and had a rough-hewn attractiveness about them. The best classroom was the Senior Cambridge room, located above a stone porch and looking out over the front lawn. These days, the buildings are of ugly concrete; the senior classroom has been pulled down, the solitary date palm tree has gone too. Those days, a businessman, old man Goenka, would chug in every afternoon in his 1926 model Ford, lovingly polished and cleaned, to pick up his grandchildren. Now the narrow road leading to the school is packed with Marutis, jeeps and outsized Contessa cars as school ends to the clanging of the great bell, located above the water tower in the old wing.

The bell has remained constant in the midst of these frantic changes.

The physical transformation to the school reflects the larger changes in Shillong where pretty bungalows of wood and plaster are giving way to concrete and brick monsters, faceless, heartless, ugly and symbolic of the devastation that easy money and irresponsibility have wrought on the place.

These days, it is easier to walk from my mother's home, on the hill above the Fire Brigade, to Police Bazar, a distance of about three kilometres, than to travel by taxi or bus. The reason lies in the traffic of buses, trucks, taxis, private and government vehicles that swamp the roads.

Every winter, we travelled to Nowgong, home of our grandparents and lazy days of cricket, films, playing with the dogs, cycling and picnics. We would race our dogs and plunge in together into the smooth and gently flowing Kolong river, scrub the animals with soap and brushes, towel them down. Then would come the best part: as all of us, wet and happy, would sprint along the sandbanks, over the narrow lane home, each trying to outrush the other.

Home here was where my grandfather and his younger brother, a doctor, whom we affectionately called Da, lived. And it was at Da's clinic where my brother and I learned of the kaleidoscopic sweep of the ethnic mosaic of that little town: Muslim Mymensinghias, who seemed to complain the loudest, came to him; so did Lalungs, a major tribe, Kacharis and Assamese and Bengali Hindus. Da is a figure that perhaps exists in every family around the world: selfless, always prepared to attend to a call at any time of the day or night and ever patient with questions that all children ask. His sturdy Austin 16 car was a landmark in the district, the only one of its kind at the time.

But there was an anger below this placid surface of a society apparently at peace with itself that was always trying to get out.

My first glimpse of public anger was in my father's company one day, when while returning from school, we were suddenly confronted by a furious mob, waving clenched fists, shouting something incomprehensible. As we watched, the mob surrounded a city bus, forced all the passengers out and then with a great surge sent the vehicle toppling on its side. The bus was then set on fire.

'Go away from here,' said a bystander. As he spoke, my father swerved the car and took a safer route home.

The people of the Northeast are the guardians of its most precious asset: its uniqueness. Which other area has such beauty among its people and its environment? Which sees such a range of religions, creeds, communities, lifestyles and traditions? Which other area can match it in the sheer raw power of nature: whether it is the Brahmaputra that resembles a great sea during its rain-swollen, flood-hungry days; or the force of its gales and the grace of its waterfalls, the lushness of its forests and bamboo thickets. And the solitude of its spirit, found in the mist of the mountains.

But these days, those of the area are grappling with the changes that the modern age relentlessly brings. And it is these changes and alienation that are at the root of the militancy, the insurgencies, the desperation and the growing violence.

This book does not purport to be an analytical treatise on insurgency and the superiority of the political wing over the military arm. Far from it. It is largely a look at how little men and women have reacted to imperial, insensitive administrations, politicians and policies through their eyes and mine.

There are no Shangri-Las left. Perhaps it is just as well for the people of the region—ranging from Bhutan to Bangladesh and Nagaland to Nepal—as they confront each other and India, strangers in the mist, and span a thousand years in a lifetime.

SECTION ONE
The Bangladesh Syndrome

From Dhaka To Delhi

My search for a key to the crisis that is overwhelming the Northeast of India took me to a squalid slum in Delhi.

Ikram Ahmed lives here, in a basti at Nizamuddin in New Delhi, a short distance from the cloistered tomb of the Urdu poet, Mirza Ghalib. The tomb itself is surrounded by beggars and boon-seekers, armed with flowers, couplets and hopes. The flowers are from the flower-kiosks in the narrow lane that begins at a mosque near the famous Karim's restaurant. Ahmed's home is in a congested colony of ragpickers, rickshaw pullers, labourers and petty traders. They live in a sprawl of fetid lanes, one-room huts of cardboard, tarpaulin and, if they are lucky, tin and asbestos sheets. The swarm of settlers has overwhelmed a once-gracious sixteenth-century mahal of the Mughal era that is located near the mosque, itself a short distance from the tomb of the Emperor Humayun.

Welcoming a visitor to his newly-whitewashed small house—among the few brick buildings flanking the basti, which has expanded to the Nizamuddin flyover near the plush Oberoi Hotel—Ahmed beckoned to a young nephew hovering nearby.

'Go get the tailor,' he ordered in Hindi. And when the young man hesitated, the lord of the Nizamuddin basti and local Congress Party leader, barked: 'The tailor, that Bengali fellow, from Bangladesh, what's his name Basheer or Shameer.'

The young man walked quickly away as a blistering sun beat down on us, and Ahmed, a gruff-voiced man of indeterminate age, sporting a messy stubble but clad in the rumpled khadi homespun pajamas and kurta that politicians of all hues and strata wear in this nation, spat a few times and talked.

'We have people from everywhere, from Bengal, from Madras, from Punjab and even from Bombay. And there are many from Bangladesh, they've come in over the years,' he remarked as we waited in the lane outside his house. The battered wooden door leading to his courtyard creaked open in the warm, moist breeze. Ahmed, who described himself as a leader of the Congress Seva Dal (a band of volunteers whose main job is to organize obsequious receptions for visiting party bosses), talked about the dispute between a Hindu temple nearby—it blares mantras and pujas over loudspeakers—and his community. 'They're encroaching on our land and since the Bharatiya Janata Party has become strong, they're getting more aggressive.' The Bharatiya Janata Party (BJP) is seeking power in Delhi on the main ground that, in their own land, under successive Congress and Janata Party regimes, Hindus who are the majority have been discriminated against to appease Muslims. The party's leaders say they will remedy this, once in power: a tall promise, unlikely to be kept—or as likely to be implemented as the call to Garibi Hatao or Banish Poverty by Indira Gandhi in 1972.

Ahmed spat again and spoke of the Hindu-Muslim riot in that neighbourhood a few months ago. In the violence, police attacked the rioters with clubs, fired teargas and bullets at them, as they chased the crowd through the narrow lanes and entered homes to seize suspects. In his mind and in those of others who listened, the police were anti-Muslim. At least two persons were killed and a curfew proclaimed.

The bitterness of those days was still fresh in Ahmed's mind and on his tongue.

At this moment, a slight man in a lungi and a loose shirt came upto us and waited, unsure of himself.

'This is the fellow you should meet, reporter sahib,' scowled Ahmed. And, he said, there were many others like him.

The visitor gave his name as Sheikh Barah. He sported a stringy beard, and watched the reporter sahib with shifty eyes.

Yes, he was from Bangladesh, he said. He had come in 1971 with his wife; they were newly-married at the time. As he responded to questions, the flow of conversation became smoother despite a bunch of curious onlookers who gathered to listen.

A few months before the Indian army went into East Pakistan to liberate that unfortunate nation from the brutal repression of West Pakistan, Barah was a tailor in Dhaka, the capital of the eastern province. He lived in a tiny room with his wife. The uncertainty of their times, lives and of the country made them restive. Finally, Barah felt he could not take the tension any longer. He decided to leave and move to India.

'I never thought of going to Calcutta to live, I always wanted to go to Delhi,' he said. It was as if he wanted to go farthest from his homeland. The continuing brutal crackdown, one of the worst military repressions by any country on its own people since the Second World War, the disappearance of people, the constant rumours decided them. One night, he and his wife bundled up their meagre possessions—cooking utensils, a few clothes, an aluminium pitcher for water—and boarded a bus to the West Bengal border. Once there, they waited again for nightfall before slipping across the frontier. They did not meet a single guard.

From there, the couple travelled by bus, train and on foot to Calcutta, investing much of their savings of a few hundred taka on the journey. And on by train from the noisy Howrah station to Delhi.

At the time, he said, there were some friends and relatives in Delhi. He did not elaborate. He stayed with them for some time before learning that plots were being parcelled out in Nizamuddin, one of the oldest parts of the capital, near the majestic tomb of Humayun, second of the Mughal dynasty.

The Nizamuddin basti was not very crowded in those days. The ragpickers and rickshawwallahs who are its mainstay had just started coming. Sheikh Barah found work and, as the local politicians took the newcomers under their wing, found a place to live. They built their tiny shacks on their own with friends, relatives, and children helping. In the months and years to come, other things also became available: facilities such as ration cards for the family. Their sons studied at local government schools. But the best was yet to come.

In 1984, Sheikh Barah, who said he was about forty-five, received the stamp of authority on his illegal presence: his name was registered as a voter from the basti. Thus, to all purposes, Barah is now a legitimate Indian. He supports a lifestyle, income and advantages that many others in the country of his adoption lack, although his lifestyle is neither luxurious or even middle class.

But he is a survivor.

He enjoys these advantages without formally having filed an

application for citizenship, a process that takes years. He has not reported or been reported by local neighbours to a police station as an alien.

'We will never go back, there is nothing for us in Bangladesh, here we have a house, a regular income, schools where the children can study,' said Sheikh Barah emphatically, in Bengali, his native tongue. His wife and the boys help him with cutting and sewing when they are free.

There are tens of thousands more like him in New Delhi alone, fleeing the destitution and desperation of Bangladesh for a better life. Here they earn two or even three times of what they could have earned in the land of their birth.

One intelligence official told me that there could be as many as 3,00,000 Bangladeshi migrants in the capital. That means that illegal aliens number as much as three per cent of the total population of this ancient city that is sandwiched in time and culture, with overwhelming pressures outstripping efforts to give enough people enough land, drinking water, electricity and jobs.

Police talk of efforts to drive the migrants out. But this is just not happening. In early 1994 hundreds of settlers were reported to be leaving Delhi, complaining of police harassment under a BJP administration. The consequences of continuing neglect of this issue will be a terrible social and political price that the poorest and the most vulnerable in these areas may eventually have to pay, as has happened in the Northeast.

And they are only trail followers, not blazers. They are walking on a road cleared over decades by millions of settlers who came to Assam, little Tripura and West Bengal (I am leaving out the Western sector of India and Pakistan, where clear migrations followed the Partition but virtually ceased in its aftermath). They first came at the end of the last century, and then surged in the 1930s before growing again in the 1950s to 1980s.

The trend is inexorable.

Many, of course, do not travel thus far. It is in the nature of migration and refugee/migrant movements that people move to the places nearest them where there is a friendly environment and where they can work and survive. Millions have, therefore, slipped out of their villages to neighbouring towns and districts in Bangladesh. According to one estimate, one million people are displaced every year by extensive river bank erosion in Bangladesh.

Others moved across the border into India, as Barah did, smoothly. Some bribed border guards on either side of the manmade frontier that zigzags uncertainly and without logic over forest and vale, stream and river, paddy field and marsh.

The Bengali diaspora, especially of Muslims from impoverished East Pakistan, now Bangladesh, has spread across South Asia with nothing but contempt for the international frontiers that the British drew up, carving up two nations out of one, on the basis of religion. And where there were two nations, there are now three.

The outflow from East Pakistan, accelerated by the trauma of Partition, when Hindus joined the flood, drew sharp reactions from the host population. For example, the classic acquisitive figure in the Assam valley was described as a Mymensinghia, a Muslim from the district of the same name which is now in Bangladesh. The area is one of the poorest in that country.

As far back as 1921, C.S. Mullen, the Census Commissioner for Assam wrote in a census report:

Whither there is wasteland thither flock the Mymensinghias. In fact the way in which they have seized upon the vacant areas in the Assam Valley seems almost uncanny. Without fuss, without tumult, without undue trouble to the district revenue staffs, a population which must amount to over half a million has transplanted itself from Bengal to the Assam Valley during the past twenty five years. It looks like a marvel of administrative organization on the part of Government, but it is nothing of the sort: the only thing I can compare it to is the mass movement of a huge body of ants.

These days, a walk along the banks of the Jamuna in Delhi provides striking proof that a similar situation is developing in the capital of India. Bangladeshi groups have mushroomed here especially in the Shahdara belt, on the side of the Jamuna bordering Uttar Pradesh. They are industrious: they ply rickshaws, work as maids and day labourers at construction sites, sell fresh fish catches in the areas, often near the Nizamuddin Bridge that connects more affluent neighbourhoods in Delhi with their poorer cousins across the river.

These are enterprising men who go from house to house, neighbourhood to neighbourhood selling the beautiful, unmatched Tangail and Jhamawar saris, shimmering, exquisite pieces of crafts-manship renowned in South Asia and beloved to women who can afford to buy them.

It is not merely a question of throwing out a few million migrants and demolishing their homes, as right-wing irredentists seek, but the crisis in Bangladesh, an unending cycle of poverty, overpopulation and hopelessness that is fuelling these flows of people into India. This, as much as any other factor, is creating the social and economic storm which is tearing society apart in Assam, Tripura and other parts of Northeastern India. The results are insurgencies and endemic violence by groups seeking to protect and assert their cultural identity in the light of threats or perceived threats. These problems can be viewed within Bangladesh itself, where settlement of Muslims on tribal lands in the Chittagong Hill Tracts (CHT) has led to alienation and armed revolt.

The unabated influx into eastern India has created problems of law and order, confrontations between Indian and Bangladeshi security forces, led to a spurt in smuggling and transfrontier gang wars in West Bengal as well as domestic troubles in Bangladesh where, one Member of Parliament complains, Indian goods, especially consumer items like chillies and medicines, flood the local markets, crushing local enterprise and products.

Bangladesh also blames India for what its elegant High Commissioner in New Delhi, Farooq Sobhan, describes as 'turning the tap on and off' at its own whim. Sobhan was referring to the dispute over the sharing of Ganges river waters; Bangladesh says that India is diverting most of it for irrigation, cultivation, industrial use and to flush Calcutta port of silt. It accuses Delhi of not caring a bit for the devastation downstream in its lands, which are becoming desertified with growing salinity in the water of the river, which is also unfit for human or even industrial consumption. One fourth of all of Bangladesh's 120 million people depend on the Ganges for their survival.

The crisis in Bangladesh has the potential of triggering security and societal crisis all across India. One reason for the lack of violence in parts of India other than the Northeast against the settlers can be ascribed to the absorptive capacity of society and the need of developing industries and agriculture for more labour, especially cheap and hard-working workers.

But what happens when the industrious begin to displace local people—sons of the soil or others—from jobs, land and edge them out in competitive deals? That is when the absorptive capacity of any society ends, where tolerance is exhausted and the disruptive reaction of awakened and embittered local populations begin.

This is the Bangladesh Syndrome, the Malthusian nightmare that has stalked that country for decades and now is surely overwhelming that unfortunate nation: too many people on too little land. The classic overpopulation versus natural resource base conflict is best seen in Bangladesh. It is coming to India too where the pressure of numbers is fast outstripping resources and facilities, such as energy, water supply and sanitation. India cannot afford the additional numbers from Bangladesh.

In the ragpickers' colony in Nizamuddin, men and women sweat as they sift through piles of plastic bags, mounds of newspapers and old magazines, soft drink bottles and beer crates and even empty bottles of Martell. In the background, a male singer's voice crackles over an old tape recorder: the bard from Bengal sings soothingly in the messy slum of the lush green paddy fields of his homeland, its great overflowing rivers and the beauty of its women.

Neighbours And Disasters

More than any other nation in the world, Bangladesh represents the Malthusian nightmare: overpopulated, with a growing landless community, and not enough food to feed itself.

Or too many people on too little land. The latest estimates place the population at 120 million, growing at about 2.2 per cent per year. The population has doubled in the past thirty years and shows no sign of faltering in its inexorable surge into the twenty-first century.

Yet, a visitor to this nation can be taken in by the lushness of its greenery, the mathematically precise, mapped strips of paddy fields and vegetable patches that begin at the edge of its highways and country roads and stretch for miles in either direction. Nearly eighty per cent of the agricultural land is covered by rice. Despite its teeming fertility, its rivers flowing with fish, especially the carp that all Bengalis prize for its taste and flesh, its rich soil and wiry, hardworking people, Bangladesh is one of the poorest nations in the world.

According to an account in *Time* magazine (2 August 1971): 'Unexpectedly lush and verdant beauty, whose emerald rice and jute fields stretch over the Ganges delta as far as the eye can see . . . . The soil is so rich it sprouts vegetation at the drop of a seed, yet that has not prevented Bengal from becoming a festering wound of poverty. Nature can be as brutal as it is bountiful.'

It has a per capita income of less than 170 dollars per year. This was exactly half of India's per capita income in 1991, before the drastic devaluation of the rupee.

What was once described as the 'basket case of Asia', also scores in a series of dubious firsts.

Bangladesh is the world's most densely populated country, with a density of 969 per square kilometre. In the rest of the world it is sixty-three per square kilometre. The Bangladeshi figure has soared from 624 in 1981, the last census year, to 969 in a single decade. Its family planning programmes have slowed: the government wanted to reduce the annual population growth rate from 2.4 per cent to 1.8 per cent in the third Five Year Plan (1985–1990). It has gone down but to 2.2 per cent. Every year 2.8 million Bangladeshis are added to the national population, increasing the pressure on health services, education systems, land, food, water and the rapidly-diminishing commons.

Prime Minister Begum Khaleda Zia says that the population boom will have 'disastrous consequences', if unchecked. The number of landless families in the nation rose from 5.7 million in 1976, five years after the Liberation War waged by Indian troops and the Bangla freedom fighters, the Mukti Bahini, that routed Pakistani forces, to 7.8 million in 1990.

A staggering seventy million Bangladeshis, or about sixty per cent of the population, live below the poverty line these days, compared to twenty-five million in 1963–64.

The country survives on foreign aid: between its inception in 1971 and 1990, Bangladesh received about 20.69 billion dollars worth of loans and grants. The huge size of the international assistance leads to a vicious cycle of paybacks: according to one estimate, Dhaka uses thirty-eight per cent of its export earnings to repay loan instalments and interest on foreign loans. The external debt was estimated at 10.7 billion dollars in 1989.

Clearly there are major flaws in Bangladesh's development strategy. A system of patronage and power has bred corruption on a scale that is matched only by Bangladesh's own extreme poverty.

Accounts of investigations launched after the nine-year rule of army strongman, H. M. Ershad, alleged that he and his relatives profited immensely from major domestic and international contracts awarded for development work. This has meant that money that should have gone to benefit people—in building roads, health centres, flood control measures—has lined the pockets of corrupt politicians, bureaucrats and groups close to them in the military.

Bangladesh is also the fourth largest peasant society in the world but its landlessness is rising at a faster rate than its population growth, forcing migrations that will spill over into India.

11

More than simply a delight for demographers, statisticians and researchers, Bangladesh represents one of the most hopeless statements on the human condition. An undignified life of penury is the lot of the vast population that resides in the fertile basin of the Brahmaputra and Ganges rivers. They are hardworking but to little avail. The fruits of development funding have reached only a handful of the population.

PATRIARCH AND PENURY

Some of these problems were reflected in a conversation with Mugha ul-Khand, a bearded old patriarch, who lives in the village of Modhupur, about 140 kilometres north of Dhaka. His home is set in a small enclave flanked by coconut trees and groves of betel leaf trees. In February of 1991, when I visited Modhupur in connection with a study on environmental degradation and migration from Bangladesh into Northeast India[*], its fields were dry and parched.

Mugha-ul-Khand's story is a clear example of the trauma that accompanies the exhaustion of existing land frontiers. In normal times, these fields would be filled with the sound of humming diesel pumps pouring water across wheat fields. When I visited, the fields were emptied by a diesel drought caused by the Gulf war between the United States and its allies against defiant Iraq over oil-rich Kuwait.

Mugha-ul-Khand has four sons; they have four wives and fourteen children between them. One son had sold some land because he was unable to make ends meet. 'In Bangladesh, we do not think of the future or even of tomorrow, we think of surviving today,' he remarked.

'When my father died, he divided his land between me and my brother. We received twelve bighas [one bigha equals 2.5 acres] each. I have divided the land equally among my sons: they have two bighas each. What can anyone grow on two bighas? And then they have more sons, the land will be further divided and ultimately it will be so fractured that no one will be able to sustain crops or life,' said the old man, as he sat in the shade of his handsome mud and thatch home. His sons and

[*] See, Sanjoy Hazarika, "Environmental Degradation, Migration and Ethnic Conflict: Bangladesh and Assam", Cambridge: American Academy of Arts and Sciences, Peace and Conflict Studies Program, University of Toronto, April 1993.

grandchildren gathered a short distance away, eyeing a visitor with curiosity. On the lane, a farmer clad in a loincloth drove a group of bullocks to a shallow pond. Chickens and ducks strolled and cackled in the background—it was a languid setting for a painful story.

'Our children, our people will be prepared to go anywhere they will get food, work, land, even to Assam,' the old man said. 'But will the people of Assam even have them?'

The whispers and tremors of hostility toward Bengali immigrants had reached Mymensingh district, where Modhupur is located, more than 100 kilometres from the nearest border with the Northeast.

'The economic viability of Bangladesh has long been in question because of its over-population, poor natural resource base, vulnerability to natural disasters and undiversified economy dependent on the production of two crops, rice and jute[*],' says Dr Mahabub Hossein of the Bangladesh Institute of Development Studies in Dhaka.

Alternately blighted and blessed by nature, Bangladesh appears to be perpetually moving through an unending cycle of floods, cyclones, devastation, death, drought and famine. Marauding rivers burst their banks and change their courses with impunity, heavy silting raises the level of river beds and increases the size of the flood plains, wiping out entire villages and reducing even the moderately affluent to penury overnight.

Despite adverse economic conditions, Bangladesh has struggled to increase its per capita income and improve the condition of its poorest. According to Hossein, half of the population had inadequate energy intakes by 1986 and fifty-eight per cent of rural children and forty-four per cent of urban children suffered from chronic malnutrition. The infant mortality rate is about 110 per thousand, among the highest in the world; adult literacy is less than one-third, and although 'three-quarters of children in the relevant age group enrol in primary schools, two-thirds of them drop out before secondary school.'

The traditional methods that are used across South Asia to prevent

---

[*] See Mahabub Hossein, "Briefing Paper on Bangladesh", London: Overseas Development Institute, 1990.

floods—embankments or low walls to protect villages and crop lands from high water—turn out to contribute to the degradation of the soils. The flood water that overflows these walls gets trapped inside the bunds or walls, making cultivation difficult even when the flood season is over. The digging of a widespread network of irrigation canals, started in the 1970s under the late President Ziaur Rahman, led to an increase in foodgrain production. But it also meant that during the annual flooding, the flood waters rushed through these canals, spreading their destruction over wider areas.

Thus, the monsoon rains which begin in May and continue in surges through September-October every year, swell the Brahmaputra, Ganges and Meghna to peaks in August and September. Their combined flood wave passes through one single outlet, the lower Meghna river, to empty into the Bay of Bengal. When their peak seasons and flows coincide, the Bangladeshi cup of misery—to use a cruel pun—flows over. And as tide levels increase in the Bay, the discharge capacity of the lower Meghna river drops, causing greater flood misery and greater salinization of ground water and croplands.

The annual storms between April and June and again between September and December have enormous capacity for destruction. The cyclone and tidal waves of 1987, carried away not less than 40,000 persons, including entire island communities at the mouth of the Ganges.

These crises caused by weather are therefore important to the economic conditions in Bangladesh. They hurt fisheries and fisherfolk as well as export earnings, in addition to devastating farmlands. Fish cultivation contributes about five per cent to GDP and about nine per cent to export earnings. Agriculture accounts for forty per cent of GDP and employs fifty-five per cent of the entire work force.

Foreign aid financed nearly sixty per cent of total investment in the country. Yet, there are pleasanter figures. These are rare examples, like the Gramin Bank, held out to the world as an example of a small bank reaching out to the poorest especially women and helping them grow. The bank's policy of giving small loans has enabled a growing number of borrowers to become self-sufficient.

Another success story was the way Bangladesh stood up, virtually single-handedly but with public support and the backing of its health department and its professional medical set-up, to pressures from multinationals to diversify its strict regime on drugs. Under the drug policy of 1982, Bangladesh announced that it was increasing the production of drugs at home and eliminating harmful and useless medicines. It announced a public distribution system for such essential drugs and the use of generic instead of brand names. Multinational corporations were told they would not be allowed to produce vitamins and antacids, two of their staple medical products for the country. The government said this would leave them free to concentrate their efforts and resources on those items not so easily produced by small, national companies. Cough mixtures, gripe water and alkalis were banned. According to the World Health Organization (WHO), as many as 4,000 drugs were sold before the 1982 policy. Nearly 1,700 of these were branded as 'useless or harmful'. The new list contained just 150 items, of which twelve were used by village level workers to treat common ailments.

This affirmative action naturally drew an outcry from the international drug companies. But Bangladesh went through with it, all the same[*].

Prominent Bangladeshi scholars say that the combination of environmental degradation and increasing destitution force people like Sheikh Barah, now of Nizamuddin basti, to flee their country.

Talukder Maniruzzaman, in an essay titled "The Future of Bangladesh"[**], speaks of the deprivation in his country, decries its dependence on foreign aid and its failure to boost modern methods of farming.

In 1951, Maniruzzaman says that Hindus accounted for twenty-two per cent of the population. The 1961 census showed their proportion of the total figure at 18.4 per cent. Their numbers have dropped with every successive national census.

---

[*] See, Sanjoy Hazarika, *Bhopal: Lessons of a Tragedy*, Delhi: Penguin Books India, 1987.
[**] See, Talukdar Maniruzzaman, "The Future of Bangladesh", in A. Jeyaratnam Wilson and Dennis Dalton, *The States of South Asia: Problems of Integration*, London: C. Hurst & Co., 1982.

'Any time there is political insecurity or communal trouble such as riots against Hindus, Bengali Hindus leave immediately for India,' said one Home Ministry official in Delhi. 'They go back only if things improve; otherwise they stay on, slipping into the cities and countryside.'

Another prominent Bangladeshi scholar who has investigated the linkages between environmental degradation and demographic displacement is Shaukat Hassan, Assistant Professor of International Relations at the University of Dhaka.

In a paper prepared for the International Institute for Strategic Studies in London[*], Shaukat pointed out that a collapse of the environment would lead to economic decline, a crisis in social cohesion and destabilize national politics.

He declared that such an overall decline would lead to a fall in job opportunities in the country afflicted. This in turn would cause demographic displacement within a country and across international borders. This is true of other countries facing situations similar to Bangladesh, even on a lesser scale. Mexico, for example, sends waves of migrants to the fields of California and New Mexico to work as under-paid labourers.

Shaukat takes a wider perspective, looking at migration from India into Nepal's Terai region where the population growth in less than three decades is a staggering 250 per cent. He warns that this can not only lead to tension between neighbouring countries but also cause political disorder, civil strife and insurgency and aggravate a potential conflict. We have the example of Bangladesh to drive the point home: India went to war with Pakistan in 1971, citing an acceptable basis for military intervention—the flood of ten million refugees that crowded into its eastern states after the Pakistani Army launched a brutal crackdown in East Pakistan.

Shaukat gives a rare and candid insight by a Bangladeshi scholar into a problem that has plagued relations between communities in India and Bangladesh for decades. He describes it as an 'uncontrolled migration', especially to Assam and Tripura, and that the migration appears to be unchecked despite Dhaka's strong denials. 'Historically, the relatively

---

[*] See, Shaukat Hassan, "Environmental Security in South Asia", London: International Institute for Strategic Studies, 1990, Adelphi Paper, 262.

unpopulated state of Assam has long attracted Bengali Muslim migrants in search of land,' he says.

Overall land and water degradation has led to a decline in the quality of life at home.

Forests have been among the first victims of uncontrolled population growth within Bangladesh. The hunger for *maati*—land—and survival has caused a sharp fall in tree cover in that nation and across South Asia. While the universally accepted minimum level of tree cover is twenty-five per cent of a country's total land area, in Bangladesh it is a mere nine per cent. 'Of the total available hill forests, 40 per cent have been converted into plantations, 11 per cent have been set aside for the rehabilitation of the 16,000 tribal families made homeless by the construction of the Kaptai reservoir [in the Chittagong Hill Tract and one of the causes for the anti-Dhaka insurgency there] in 1963 and almost 48 per cent have fallen to human encroachment,' says Shaukat Hassan. He adds that major reasons for the loss of forests in Bangladesh are 'illegal logging to satisfy burgeoning demands for timber and firewood, and salinity intrusion.'

The security of Bangladesh, according to Hassan, is inextricably linked with the question of flood and drought control. India's inflexible position seeking bilateral solutions to what is clearly a multilateral problem—for some of the rivers that flow into India and Bangladesh originate in Nepal—is unacceptable.

India does not want Nepal involved in its discussions with Bangladesh, preferring to deal with its neighbours separately. Its sheer size and political skills gave it a ready advantage and its officials have shown little compunction in driving these advantages home and conceding as little as possible.

THE ROOTS OF DISASTER

A prominent Indian writer, B.G. Verghese, says[*] the problems of Bangladesh have their roots in its geography and that of the

---

[*] See, B. G. Verghese, *Waters of Hope*, Delhi: IBH, 1991.

Ganges-Brahmaputra-Barak river basins. The problems of Bangladesh, this and other studies point out, cannot be viewed in isolation. They flow out of the social, economic, cultural and environmental impact of the great flood plains that begin at the foothills of the Himalayas in West Bengal and Arunachal Pradesh and roll through Assam, the plains of Bengal, Meghalaya and into Bangladesh to the mouths of the Ganges. The Ganges is joined at various times along its long route by the Kosi and the Gandhak from Nepal; the Brahmaputra is fed by the Subansiri, the Dibang, Kameng and Luit in Arunachal Pradesh and then by the Barak and the mighty Meghna. According to one estimate, the Ganges-Brahmaputra-Meghna system carries and dumps a staggering load of 2.9 billion metric tons of sediment into the Bay of Bengal every year.

The Himalayas which straddle the borders of India, China and Nepal, cause problems in all three nations but the most affected perhaps is Bangladesh, which has no control over the rivers that begin at the mountain range but thunder through its flatlands, gaining in power and size with every passing kilometre. Bangladesh is a child of the billions of tons of silt that are brought down by these rivers—not less than fifty large and small rivers flow into Bangladesh from India. One estimate placed the undersea fan of sediment brought down by the Ganges and Brahmaputra rivers and deposited in the Bay (of Bengal) at 1,000 kilometres wide, over twelve kms in depth and 3,000 kms long and extended south of Sri Lanka.

Salinity too is a problem and is caused by a drop in freshwater supplies in the Ganges as it flows from India. The Ganges is controlled by the Farakka Barrage on the Indian side that uses the water to flush silt from Calcutta harbour and upstream by farmers, industries and government projects in Uttar Pradesh and Bihar, lowering the level of the river in the lean weeks of April, when it is most needed by farmers in Bangladesh.

According to B. G. Verghese:

The Ganga-Brahmaputra-Barak basin has all it takes to be a granary. Its agricultural record has however been disappointing. Malnutrition continues to tell on morbidity and productivity . . . . Many regions have witnessed a migration of population either within national boundaries, or a movement of

18

Malthusian refugees across international borders. This erosion of human resources, often of able-bodied men or the most venturesome among the populace, has further undermined agriculture in the exporting areas even as it has aroused sensitivities in the importing regions.

The flatlands of Bangladesh, fertile though they are, are no longer able to sustain the people who live on them. During the annual floods, the country is divided into different regions, each with the waters of an angry river as its natural frontier. The Meghna, Brahmaputra and Ganges divide the eastern, northern and western sectors during the flood season better than any manmade boundary.

Floods cover the countryside like a vast sheet, often a metre or two of water. One estimate says that one-third of Bangladesh is covered by floodwaters every summer. It is impossible to grow even tall paddies in such high water, forcing people and livestock to migrate. To higher ground. To neighbouring, higher, better-protected villages and towns. To regions inside the national frontiers where land is available and across the international border. Those who migrate are not interested in agriculture, says Verghese, but in jobs that give them an income, a basis for survival. 'It is not simply jobs or more land that migrants want but more income,' he adds.

Bangladesh's population growth will have a disastrous effect on the cropland available in the future: one study in *Scientific American* (February 1993) pointed out that because of the exploitation of good agricultural land, the area that could be available will be slashed in half per capita by 2025. This data further concluded that 'although the contextual factors of religion and politics are important' to the exodus to neighbouring states in India, 'they do not obscure the fact that a dearth of land in Bangladesh has been a force behind conflict.'

Yet, despite the annual loss of lands to marauding rivers and the social displacement and trauma that they cause, floods are recognized in Bangladesh—and many other low lying parts of the world—as a necessary evil.

In Bangladesh, more than one million persons have been killed by floods since 1961. And the 1988 floods, the worst in recent years, reduced rice production by 1.6 million tons and caused 1.3 billion dollars worth of damage to roads, railway tracks, homes, offices and industrial machinery.

The scale of flooding is vast. According to B. G. Verghese in his *Waters of Hope*:

> A monsoon flood discharge, draining over 1.5 million square miles in five countries straddling both sides of the Himalayas and containing far and away the highest rainfall density zones in the world, funnels into the sea through the Bangladesh nozzle comprising barely 7.5% of the total basin. No other country anywhere faces a flood problem of the nature and magnitude that Bangladesh does.

The raw power of nature is best seen when rivers deviate from their traditional courses, slashing through soft soil and forging a new trail of devastation. In 1966, one account says, just downstream of Faridpur on the combined Ganges and Brahmaputra, the river moved laterally in the northward direction by 1,500 meters (1.5 kilometres), eroding the bank and digging a new channel fifty metres deep. This amounts to about 100 million tons of sediment moved per river mile.

The Centre for Science and Environment (CSE), one of India's strongest lobbying environmental groups, said in a 1991 report[*] that the fragile seismic structure and ecosystem of the Himalayas is one of the biggest factors causing downstream floods and natural disasters. As the youngest mountain range in the world, with occasional earthquakes that kill hundreds of people, destroy property and cause enormous silting as well as its fast-flowing streams and rivers, the Himalayas are 'inherently primed for natural disasters.' It suggested, controversially, that floods will remain a permanent feature of the plains whether the upland mountains and hills were forested or not. It pointed out that the Himalayas were battered by storms and rains of an intensity that few other mountain systems face and this aggravated top soil erosion and downstream flooding.

Water and silt move out of these mountains in explosive waves. Floods and the shifting of river courses are inevitable, according to CSE, and deforestation could worsen the problem but afforestation could not

---

[*] See, "Floods, Flood Plains and Environmental Myths", Centre for Science and Environment, Delhi, 1991.

end it. Major floods take place during 'intense and prolonged rainstorms, when the watershed gets saturated and interception [catching of rainwater by trees and bushes] and infiltration [entry of rainwater into the soil] are minimized.'

The Brahmaputra is often cited as an example, for the river flows through far more densely forested areas in its upper regions than in its southern belt. The northern slopes have steep slopes, shallow and braided water channels and coarse sandy beds. They carry heavy silt loads and are prone to cause flash floods. Natural factors such as earthquakes have played a critical role in determining the geography of the area, dwarfing human efforts to control the waters.

Thus, the great Assam earthquake of 1950 changed the course of major tributaries of the Brahmaputra and raised the bed of the main river and its tributaries by several feet. The low water levels of the main river at Dibrugarh town rose nearly ten feet, causing widespread devastation. These days, thick embankments have been raised all along Dibrugarh's battlefront with the river.

The floods damage settlements and encroachments on the flood plains at the outset. In the valleys, the natural drainage systems have been wilfully blocked, embanked as in Assam and Bangladesh or dammed. Natural depressions and wetlands have been encroached upon and reclaimed for intensive pisciculture or agriculture. Embankments which are designed to keep out floods become hostile to the engineers and workers who have designed or built them: they trap flood water in vast areas for months, making both cultivation and settlement of lands impossible. Road construction also has changed the landscape. Often, roads are the only high ground in low lying areas. Building them involves moving millions of tons of soil. Such extraction of earth deposits makes low lying areas more vulnerable.

Bangladesh is so starved of good rock and stones for its road-building that it imports millions of dollars worth of rocks of specified stones from the quarries of Bhutan.

Bangladesh must also contend with high tidal waves that regularly sweep the southern coast between April and December, soaring twenty feet high at times and smashing storm shelters, villages, bridges and killing thousands of people. Specialists say that global warming could make this much worse in the future. Experts agree that with sea level rise and major climate changes, large sections of Bangladesh's coastline could be submerged by sea water, raising the spectre of millions of homeless people, seeking shelter and food.

According to the Jehangirnagar University in Dhaka eighteen to nineteen million people are affected by flooding in Bangladesh every year. And Atiur Rahman* of the Bangladesh Institute of Development Studies described them as 'the most wretched of the landless poor.' He further said that they are so poor that donor countries care little for them and have done nothing to develop policies to assist these groups.

At his office in Dhaka, Rahman, an earnest-looking academic, told me that these displaced persons represented no political constituency and had been neglected by local politicians and administrators except during calamities. This was a reason, he said, for the lack of interest in one of Bangladesh's most vulnerable groups by foreign aid agencies which have rushed to help only in areas that interest them. One such project being prawn fisheries (solely meant for export) which are developed at the expense of mangrove swamps in the Sunderbans, causing soil salinity and degradation of the land. Most Bangladeshis believe that the only people who benefit are the international experts and their local co-ordinators.

'Those who have profited are rich farmers, politicians, village headmen and army people,' said Serajuddin Ahmed, a prominent Bangladeshi reporter. 'They have destroyed the forests and the natural beauty of the place and hurt the traditional economy of the area—when sea water comes in, agricultural lands go to waste.'

Overall flood plains management across the subcontinent is weak, depending on traditional devices such as embankments that can be as hazardous as they are a security. Few agencies have studied and developed ecologically sound management systems. In the mid-1980s Bangladesh had as many as 8.28 million hectares which were vulnerable to flooding. Of this, less than one-third was protected by embankments. Managing these plains is made doubly difficult by the high population densities and widespread landlessness, particularly in Bangladesh. Clearly, the need is

---

* See, Atiur Rahman, "Impact of Riverbank Erosion: Survival Strategies of Displacees", Dhaka: Bangladesh Institute of Development Studies, 1985.

to live in harmony with nature, adopting self-sustaining strategies with regard to natural resources and working toward a marriage of big and small technologies, including dams, modern engineering skills, traditional water harvesting and usage patterns as well as plain commonsense.

However, geographical factors alone do not determine the crisis that is overwhelming Bangladesh. Political pressures and inequalities spread over several decades have also played a central role in shaping the country.

A prime reason lies in the inequituous relationship between the two halves of what Mohammad Ali Jinnah, the inspirer and founder of Pakistan, called a 'moth-eaten' nation.

From the time of independence, on 14 August 1947, when the Union Jack was lowered and Governor-General Lord Louis Mountbatten and the thin, sickly Qaid-i-Azam watched the raising of the green crescent and moon flag of Pakistan, till the violent wrenching of Bangladesh out of East Pakistan in December 1971, the two halves rarely saw eye to eye in matters of culture, dress, language, politics or economy.

During Pakistan's brutal suppression of a campaign for autonomy in its eastern wing in 1971, a Punjabi military officer put the Islamabad perspective squarely: 'In the West, we wear the pants, here they let their women wear the trousers,' he told a Western reporter, deriding the lungis that the Bengali men wear.

The creation of Bangladesh was the result of a combination of shrewdly-timed political moves orchestrated by Prime Minister Indira Gandhi as well as brilliant generalship by Indian military leaders. On the converse side, Pakistan's military-political leadership collapsed, softened by years of power, baubles and corruption.

EAST AND WEST

East Pakistan was carved out of the former East Bengal, with a referendum deciding the way the large district of Sylhet, formerly in Assam state, was to go. A Muslim-majority district, it voted largely for Pakistan to the great relief of Congress Party leaders in Assam, who rarely missed an opportunity to make their animosity to the Bengal-dominated lobbies known.

After the first flush of freedom waned, the people of East Pakistan realized that they were little more than second class citizens, despite being more populous than the western sector.

'East Bengal sends out goods in return for which she gets nothing,' said Professor Muzaffar Ahmad of Dhaka University in an essay. 'It means a continuous economic drain of a magnitude and dimension unknown in any civilised country. East Bengal is being sucked dry of the life blood of her economy.' Documents of the time indicate that these remarks were not far off the mark. While sixty per cent of all Pakistanis lived in East Pakistan, the Central Government spending on this section varied from a low of twenty-eight per cent in 1950–51 of the total budget to a high of thirty-six per cent in 1969–70. Most of Pakistan's export earnings—the figures are placed at fifty to seventy per cent—were the fruit of eastern exports of jute, hides and skin. Yet, the east's share of foreign imports was a bare twenty-five to thirty per cent.

In addition, smuggling of rice, jute and consumer goods to neighbouring India, undercut the local economy, creating artificial shortages and pushing local prices up. It was good business for a handful of smugglers and their networks but bad economics for a nation constantly teetering on the edge of survival. Law enforcers from both sides, instead of curbing crime, are still assisting both in smuggling and allowing an illegal flow of people across into India.

Partition also crippled the economics of the entire region: the East Bengal plains and the hills of Assam as well as neighbouring West Bengal had been natural markets for each other's goods for decades, if not centuries. Commerce, river transport, barter and the movement of people into each other's marketplaces were the ways in which business and trade had been conducted all these years.

Suddenly, the Garo Hills of what is now Meghalaya—there are Garo tribespeople in Bangladesh's Mymensingh District, a cry back to the days when the Garo Rajas ruled these lands several centuries ago—found themselves without access to the lowlands of Mymensingh. Vegetables and other perishable commodities were ruined. It has taken many years for the peoples of the hills and plains of this single geographical unit to adjust financially to the political boundaries of 1947. Yet, secretly and illegally, this trade continues whether it is from across Mancachar, a major smuggling and business centre on the Indo-Bangla border, or elsewhere. The natural ways of economy, of man's ingenuity to bypass rules, allied to the geography of a region, have a way of triumphing over the best of administrative schemes and skills. Each border post virtually commands a price—on either side of the border—and the officers, cooks, sentries and sepoys get a regular, monthly income from the illegal profit that passes through the areas, a share that is sent to them by the dons of the transborder smuggling and crime gangs that flourish and function with impunity.

During the years of a united Pakistan, this illegal trade added to the burdens on the east. In addition, there was the transfer of resources from the east by businessmen.

In every area of public life, the East Pakistanis were shut out of the power structure: they had a handful of top civil servants, a small bunch of senior army officers and a few judges or powerful lawyers.

In the army, East Pakistanis were never more than thirty per cent of the total strength at any level and rarely above the five per cent figure among army officers alone.

In development terms, the growing economic divide between the two sectors of this doomed political animal can be seen in the following figures:

	West Pakistan	East Pakistan
	1947-48 to 1966-67	
cotton textiles (production in million yards)	350 to 6,836	508 to 550
increase of	1,853%	8.26%
cement production (in thousand tons)	305 to 1,934	46 to 75
increase of	534%	63%

The story was virtually the same in every sphere, making a volatile base for economic, cultural and political divergence. Even in the matter of fish, which the Bengalis love to eat in different forms, curries and breeds, West Pakistan outstripped the east. Their production figures for fish rose by 273 per cent between 1951–52 and 1966–67, while that of the east edged up by a mere forty-eight per cent.

Governments in the province were dismissed by the dominant

western wing. Before the Liberation War of 1971, there were only two elections to the state assembly and the national assembly. In the first, in 1954, the Muslim League, Jinnah's party, was routed by the Awami League and a United Opposition Front led by Husain Shahi Suhrawardy formerly Premier of Bengal before Partition and Maulana Abdul Hamid Bhashani, former chief of the Assam Muslim League and a radical peasant leader, who had led the Muslim immigrant movement for greater rights in Assam.

The origins of the struggle for independence lie in the 1951 uprising to protect and preserve the Bengali language against the imposition of Urdu from the West. February 21, 1951 is still remembered as the first shot fired in the liberation movement. This was a critical psychological and political victory. From Jinnah's time, it was made amply clear that the West would not tolerate any deviation from its own viewpoint with regard to culture and politics. Thus, the movement for Bengali as the lingua franca of the East was strongly opposed and deeply resented.

Several students were killed in police firings on the Dhaka University campus and a large memorial stands there today in their honour. The upsurge was uncontainable—the beginning of the eastern drive for eventual autonomy and bloody separation—and the West grudgingly conceded the Bengali right to their language.

The West smarted from this setback and Islamic radicals were irked by the knowledge that Bengalis loved the music and songs of Rabindranath Tagore and other great Bengali Hindu composers, whose works transcended the artificial barriers that the British drew across the map of South Asia.

The widening chasm between the two sides finally became unbridgeable in 1971, when the Awami League, under Sheikh Mujibur Rahman, campaigning on a platform of provincial autonomy won not just the elections to the East but because of its massive mandate (160 of 162 seats there, of a total of 300 to the national assembly) gained the right to form a government in Islamabad.

To the generals, bureaucrats and politicians of the West, long-used to control over struggling East Pakistan, this was unacceptable.

Under the prodding of Zulfikar Ali Bhutto, leader of the Pakistan Peoples Party (PPP), which won a bare eighty-one seats of 138 in the

West, President Yahya Khan ordered a brutal crackdown across the country to nullify the results of the national election.

Responding to the turmoil, President Khan gave an order that would destroy his nation and create an unending cycle of migration and human suffering that buffets societies across South Asia.

On 29 March 1971, Pakistani troops attacked Dhaka University, opened gunfire on unwary East Pakistani riflemen. They sought out and murdered hundreds and thousands of intellectuals, professionals and ordinary people.

'What is happening in Dacca is not a football match. When one fights, one does not throw flowers,' Yahya Khan snapped at a reporter.

NEIGHBOURS AND MIGRANTS

The flood that flowed across the borders of East Pakistan into India in 1971 began with Hindus fleeing their homes and villages. The Hindus of East Pakistan, as in the earlier disturbances of the mid-1960s that sent more refugees to Tripura and West Bengal as well as Assam, were the first targets of the Pakistan Army. They were suspected of backing Sheikh Mujib and the Awami League—not without basis—and prosperous Hindu businessmen were believed to donate large funds to keep the party and its agitation going. The flood of refugees swelled into a vast tidal wave that engulfed Tripura, the border districts of West Bengal, outnumbered the local residents of Meghalaya and entered Assam in a steady stream.

One of the most poignant descriptions of this tragic exodus came from *Time* magazine (2 August 1971). 'Over the rivers and down the highways and along countless jungle paths, the population of East Pakistan continues to haemorrhage into India: an endless, unorganized flow of refugees with a few tin kettles, cardboard boxes and ragged clothes piled on their heads, carrying their sick children and their old.'

An early estimate at the time said that of the first seven million refugees, at least six million were Hindus. Marcus Franda, Director of International Affairs at the University of Maryland who lived in India for more than ten years and worked with the American University Field Staff programme, talks about the 'deadly accurate' accounting of the Indian relief officials. Based on his interviews with relief officials in India and across the border in Bangladesh (after independence), Franda said that

6.8 million refugees were listed as camp inmates and another three million lived with friends and relatives.

The 'outside' refugees were provided rations and medical assistance by the relief organization led by Colonel P.N. Luthra, the man who ran 896 camps. After the initial flow of Hindus, Bengali Muslims also started fleeing the crackdown as the Pakistani Army became increasingly brutal and indiscriminate in its assaults. But it is clear from reports of the External Affairs Ministry of the Indian Government that the fleeing groups were overwhelmingly Hindu until late 1971. An External Affairs Ministry report of 1 August 1971 showed 6.97 million Hindus, 5,41,000 Muslims and 44,000 others.

The refugee camps were packed to overflowing and, as with any other calamity, human greed asserted itself: cases began surfacing of relief officials selling blankets and other camp material meant for the refugees in the black market. Some of the refugees did likewise.

Despite the mess, the camps were certainly safer than conditions in East Pakistan where terror, rape and murder ruled.

When the Indian Army moved in for its swift December campaign, they were welcomed as heroes by the oppressed Bengalis. Fighting alongside them were the Mukti Bahini, a force of Bengali civilians, army officers and policemen who had revolted against Pakistan.

It was the worst military defeat that Pakistan had tasted and it destroyed for good the political idiocy that assumed that two nations—for that was what Pakistan was even at the best of times between East and West—could live as a political unit under the banner of Islamic nationhood, separated as they were by distance, language, culture and politics. In the process, West Pakistan lost its most profitable colony, one that it kept in permanent deprivation while exploiting its immense natural resources.

As the leaders of the newborn nation returned to take over and renew a shattered society, India decided to close its refugee camps and send the inmates home.

Official figures available point out that by early March 1972, only 2,00,000 refugees remained in the camps. Another 8,17,000 continued to live with friends and relatives in West Bengal, Assam, Meghalaya and Tripura. Thus, in a magnificent effort that is not yet fully appreciated, Col Luthra and his men had succeeded in packing off more than nine million of the Bangladeshi refugees within three months of Dhaka's liberation.

But Marcus Franda, in his *Bangladesh: The First Decade**, pointed out that 'the last million may turn out to be much more difficult to repatriate than the first nine million.'

Ominous words. But they ring true.

LEBENSRAUM

As mentioned earlier, a considerable chunk of this earlier migrant population was Hindu. My travels in Bangladeshi villages as well as accounts on both sides of the border and available documents bear this out. The documents include the census reports of Bangladesh after 1974, which indicate a drop in the growth of the Hindu population nationwide. Of course, the situation in West Bengal and Assam, as of now, indicates that after 1971 the Muslim migration continues unabated. The current migrants or aliens are largely Muslim, who flee for simple economic reasons: land scarcity, drought, flooding, penury and debt. The Hindus left because of religious persecution, riots and fear of insecurity and threat to life and property.

It is the new Bangladeshi attitude to migration that has added an edge to the political and social problems that flow from it. A former diplomat in Dhaka spoke of the need for an International Demographic Order with the people of his country having the right to find a *Lebensraum*, a haven. Although this was originally targetted at the developed countries, it is quite clear that such a suggestion will be dismissed outright by Western nations. They certainly do not want boatloads and busloads of dark-skinned, impoverished 'foreigners' in rags rushing into their clinically clean spaces, seeking jobs.

The case of the Chinese migrants to the United States, who tried to come to the promised land, on their overcrowded, illegal ships in 1993, is a good example of this.

Clearly, the *Lebensraum* is to be the Northeast of India and other eastern states, setting up areas of potential conflict over natural resources, such as water, food, land and competition for jobs in government programmes and private enterprise.

---

* See, Marcus Franda, *Bangladesh: The First Decade,* Delhi: South Asian Publishers, 1981.

THE BEGUM FIGURES

In two little-known studies of migration, a meticulous researcher in Dhaka turned up the first semi-official acknowledgement of the massive outflow of refugees from Bangladesh into India. In the studies, the researcher, Sharifa Begum analysed data from Bangladesh records and came up with a figure of 3.15 to 3.5 million people leaving for India between 1951 and 1961[*]. Begum has worked at the Bangladesh Institute of Development Studies at Dhaka, one of the best think tanks in the country.

Begum placed the outflow from her country between 1961 and 1974 at 1.5 million. This is clearly a conservative estimate for it does not take into account the ten million who fled Pakistani repression in 1970 and 1971 before an Indian military victory enabled most of the refugees to come home. But an estimated one to two million refugees are accepted to have stayed on, having moved in with relatives and melted into the countryside, moving to distant villages, towns and cities—as far as Bombay.

The importance of 1961 and 1974 lies in that they were the years when national censuses were held in Bangladesh. A simple addition of these three figures—the Begum statistics plus the 1970 refugees—gives us a tidy sum of not less than six million in twenty-three years.

Using the Begum figures as a base, one can come to another set of statistics: the outflow of 1.5 million between 1961 and 1974 works out at about 1,10,000 migrants annually. If that level of migration was maintained between 1974 and 1990, then the out-migrants from Bangladesh could not be less than 1.76 million. This would make a total of not less than 7.6 million migrants and perhaps as much as 8.6 million.

This is, remarkably, almost the figure by which the population of Assam in 1991 exceeds the natural growth rate set in the 1950s. Assam has, in other words, seven million more people than it should have had if the 1950s' growth rate had been naturally adhered to.

Myron Weiner, who is regarded as an authority on migrations and their political impact, noted as far back as 1978 that the population of Assam in its present boundaries—which is one-third of what it was before

---

[*] See, Sharifa Begum "Birthrate and Deathrate in Bangladesh, 1951–74", Dhaka: Bangladesh Institute of Development Studies, 1979.

the smaller states were carved out of it in the 1970s—was 3.3 million.

Had Assam's population increased at the same rate as the rest of India from 1901 to 1971 (130 per cent), her population would now be 7.6 million rather than fifteen million, a difference of 7.4 million. Actually, the proportion of migrants and descendants is substantially greater since large-scale migrations into the state commenced in the middle of the nineteenth century. If we accept the 1891 census that one-fourth of the population of the Brahmaputra Valley was then of migrant origin, we can estimate that the migrant population and its descendants in 1971 was more like 8.5 million, against an indigenous population of 6.5 million . . . . Between 1961 and 1971 the population of Assam increased by 34.7 per cent as against 24.6 per cent for India as a whole[*].

Security officials say that an average of 2,00,000 persons slip annually into West Bengal State alone. This is in itself nearly two times the figure that the Begum statistics indicate, and that too with regard to a single state. Clearly, the number of migrants is higher these days as pressures increase at home.

Of course, it would be naïve to believe that the entire surge in population in the Northeast, especially Assam, was caused by illegal migration from Bangladesh and East Pakistan. While this constituted what appears to be the largest chunk of new settlers, there were also large numbers of people who had moved in from Nepal, West Bengal and Bihar.

In a 1990 paper[**], Sharifa Begum declared that though there were no statistics for migration after 1974, 'there is no valid reason why migration will suddenly cease in the years after 1974.' She added: 'There are indications that Bangladesh during this period (1974-81) has lost substantial proportion of population during migration and the famine of 1974-75.'

---

[*] See, Myron Weiner, *Sons of the Soil: Migration and Ethnic Conflict in India*, Princeton: Princeton University Press, 1978.
[**] See, Sharifa Begum, "Population, Birth, Death and Growth rates in Bangladesh: Census Estimates", Dhaka: Bangladesh Institute of Development Studies, 1990.

Clearly, those fleeing natural disasters will not try and get away to the Middle East or the West. They will go as far as their resources will take them and to a place where they will be assured of a reasonable welcome. Those places, at least until the 1980s, were to be found in Assam and the Northeast, and in the decade of the 1990s, in West Bengal and Bihar. This represents several hours' journey to the border or, at the most, a couple of days' travel by bus and train.

Marcus Franda, the expert on South Asia, says that migration levels actually increased from Bangladesh after its creation, instead of dropping. He once quoted police officials as saying that 200 Bangladeshis were entering Assam every day by train in 1975 while more slipped in 'via obscure village paths.'

In May 1975, migration into Tripura was estimated at more than 2,000 per day. and in the first seven months of 1975, an estimated 60,000 Bangladeshis entered Nadia in West Bengal.

The question that arises here is: how many of them went back?

After talking with security officials and ordinary people in Bangladesh and in the border districts of the Northeast as well as politicians in both countries, it is quite clear that few, if any, have actually returned to their blighted homes.

In 1974 and 1975, Bangladesh was devastated by a famine that affected millions of people and sent the most resourceful to seek shelter wherever they could, within and without their national frontiers. The migrations into Tripura followed the pattern of the 1940s and 1950s and even the 1960s: most of the inflow were Hindus.

The Demographic Yearbook published by the Registrar-General's Office, which supervises census operations in India, said in its 1981 report that as many as four million persons, resident in India that year, had reported their birthplace as Bangladesh. This excluded figures for Assam where the census was not held because of an anti-foreign nationals agitation.

It was, however, not possible to identify these individuals either as old or new migrants. There was no overwhelming hostility to them, as was experienced later in the 1980s.

Asok Mitra, the demographer from Calcutta and one of the country's most renowned data analysts, remarked that the Assamese must have 'welcomed them with open arms, settled them on waste lands they could not cultivate and reached heights of colonisation and productivity they could never hope to achieve.'

For India and Bangladesh, the issue remains contentious and unresolved, spilling over these days into charges of aiding and abetting insurgencies directed against each other from their respective territories. They trade accusations, especially from Dhaka's viewpoint, about New Delhi controlling the flow of water into Bangladesh during the dry winter months and diverting the flow from the Farakka barrage to flush out Calcutta port. Dhaka says this deprives Bangladeshi farmers in the north of much-needed water for their winter crops. In addition, 'Illegal migration remains the unfinished agenda at every discussion, it's really a dialogue of the deaf: we tell Dhaka these are illegals coming in: Dhaka says they're Indian smugglers or citizens returning after illegally visiting relatives or friends in Bangladesh,' said one Indian diplomat at Dhaka.

The influx follows a tradition that was set at the turn of the last century, particularly into the lightly-populated valleys of the Brahmaputra and the Surma, and then given a powerful political impetus during the controversial years of Sir Syed Mohammad Saadulla as Assam's Muslim League Premier in the late 1930s and 1940s.

Thus, the pattern for Assam's political milieu was set by these developments, decades ago. As B.P. Singh[*], an official with wide experience of the area, has pointed out: ' . . . in the forseeable future the tribal factor, the relationship between Assamese Hindus and Bengali Hindus and between Assamese Hindus and Bengali Muslims will dominate the cultural equations and politics of north-east India.'

The changes were speeded up by Lord Curzon, then Viceroy, and his controversial decision to partition Bengal in 1905. That one move was as much responsible for developing Assamese hardline attitudes to Bengalis as anything else, and especially toward migrants from neighbouring East Bengal. East Bengal was predominantly Muslim and the other Bengal was predominantly Hindu. That religious division holds good even today.

But Assam was, without much thought, dumped into East Bengal. Following an outcry, especially by Bengali Hindus, the British annulled the partition, reunited the two provinces in 1912 and then declared that

---

[*] See, B. P. Singh, *The Problems of Change*, Delhi: Vikas Publishing House, 1989.

Assam would be a separate province under a Chief Commissioner. It would be larger than its original size, with the British tagging on Muslim-majority Sylhet District and the Bengali Hindu-dominated district of Cachar. These frontiers remained unchanged until the partition of the subcontinent in 1947.

BRINGING IN LABOURERS

The attachment of a reluctant Sylhet onto Assam meant that the Assamese Hindus found themselves walking a demographic and political tightrope, with the population finely balanced between the communities. Furthermore, Sylhet was a poor district and needed to be sustained by funds generated by the bounty of the Brahmaputra Valley, an issue that made the appendage even more irritating to other parts of the new province.

In addition to the Bengal developments, there were other factors that played a role in fanning Assamese hostility toward Bengalis.

At the beginning of the century, the British began extending the railway lines into the remote and poorly-connected Northeast to link it to other parts of the 'Jewel in the Crown' as well as to improve communications within the sprawling, sweltering region. Apart from accessibility to markets and enabling better trade and exports, the new railway lines were to help officials, traders and others to move more easily and swiftly between towns in a land where floods covered large parts of the valley for several months in a year.

Labourers from Mymensingh, Sylhet, Rangapur and other districts of Bengal and later East Bengal were shipped to Assam to lay these tracks and build the townships that sprang up along the tracks. New villages were created of immigrants along the railway lines, villages that have grown over the decades. From the railway lines, the migrants struck inward. The workers were followed by a wave of agricultural labourers seeking larger lands and better incomes.

Migration into Assam was encouraged by the British, who had begun developing the tea estates that now run on either side of the highway linking lower and upper Assam. Local labour was scarce because the Assamese did not deign to work on lands other than their own. As a result, the other great migration of the nineteenth and twentieth century into Assam took place: tens of thousands of labourers were drafted from Bihar and Orissa, essentially from the Chota Nagpur region, to work on the tea gardens. In addition to picking and carrying bundles of tea leaves from plantation to factories, they helped to build the roads and towns that grew around the estates.

CHAI GARAM!

Over the years, the workers from the greater tribes of Central India—Santhals, Oraons and Mundas—developed into a tightly-organized community that now numbers four million and speaks a patois that includes words from all three languages as well as Assamese, the local dialect of the district, and Hindi. They have a strong trade union and have sent representatives to Parliament and the state legislature and have found berths in state cabinets as well.

Their conditions remained abysmal for generations. Descriptions of exploitation speak of thousands being killed by cholera and malaria, hustled into steamers and trains by 'coolie catchers' who drew them aboard with dreams of high pay and light work and left them to die on their way to the promised land. In many cases the agents kidnapped villagers from Chota Nagpur and others from Bihar and Orissa, obtained their thumb impressions on contracts after forcing drink down their throats.

The tea industry developed in a major way after the British took over Assam. Earlier, the plant grew wild but was used to make a brew by the Singpo and Khamti tribes, communities that came—as did the Bengalis and tea garden workers—from another land. The tribes were originally natives of northern Myanmar and crossed over into northern Assam and what is now Arunachal Pradesh centuries ago. Significantly, they came from a part of Asia that is part of the ancient tea-growing and exporting routes.

Arup Kumar Dutta[*], who has studied the origins of the tea industry, says that the planters described coolie recruitment in the nineteenth century as pimping and that they were totally indifferent to these migrants, treating them 'just like cattle.'

---

[*] See, Arup Kumar Dutta, *Chai Garam*, Delhi: Paloma Publications, 1992.

An industry that now brings large amounts of foreign exchange to India's hard currency-starved economy was thus built literally on the bodies of its most wretched labourers, who lived in miserable impoverishment, often hungry and sick. Packed into trains and boats like cattle, their lot was described by a Congress Party leader in 1899 as a 'wretched and downtrodden slave population.'

One of the pioneers of tea planting in Assam said in 1928 that 'mortality on the gardens was of a very high percentage, and the sanitary arrangements were nil.' Women who went by steamer found their vessels had no toilets and were expected to ease themselves by the side of the boat. It is a shameful chapter of British rule that can be compared to the African slave labour which was imported into the United States to work the cotton plantations in the southern states, a practise that led to the American Civil War and the end of slavery.

A.K. Dutta talks of the high casualty rates ranging from '10-15%' on a single passage but which sometimes 'ran as high as 50% . . . . Of the 84,915 workers who landed in Assam between May 1863 and May 1866, 30,000 had died by June 1866.' British and Indian managers mercilessly overworked the coolies; laziness was made a punishable offence. Authorities were vested with sweeping powers including the right to arrest 'absconders' without warrants. Yet, often planters took the law into their hands, detaining runaway coolies and publicly flogging them in defiance of new rules aimed at protecting the coolies.

It was not until the late nineteenth century that civil rights violations began to ease, under pressure from administrators. Under new recruiting system, the gardens appointed their own recruiting agents, known as sardars, instead of relying on freebooters from Calcutta. And with time and better managements coming into power, workers were provided housing and other facilities: schools for their children, scholarships for the brighter ones and better wages. But conditions, despite these improvements, continue to be harsh in many gardens, especially smaller and medium-sized ones where new entrepreneurs took charge in the 1960s and 1970s.

In the 1930s, a local socialist leader from Assam wrote to Jayaprakash Narayan (popularly known as JP), the then secretary of the Congress Socialist Party (CSP) attacking the miserable conditions. Pabitra Roy said in a letter in 1938 that the condition of the tea plantation workers 'beggars description.' 'No protective laws give them security. Economically they are half serf of the Middle Ages and half wage earner of our modern epoch. To organise them is the most difficult task not because they are unwilling . . . but because the law of the company does not allow them to do this.'

The story of tea in Assam began after the British learned of tea from Maniram Dutta Barua, the Dewan (or agent) of the newly-formed, British-owned Assam Company. He was also the Chief Minister to Purnadhar Singha, the last of the Ahom kings, member of a Thai clan that arrived in Assam in the thirteenth century. Maniram Dewan, as he is popularly known, was a man of great wealth and influence. He developed two tea estates after learning of the British interest in the shrub and recognizing that tea was the future cash crop of Assam. His plantations flourished despite the open hostility of the British, whose service he had left after learning the basics of tea planting and manufacture.

Maniram Dewan was arrested in 1857 for his alleged role in a conspiracy against British rule, tried in a kangaroo court and hanged. His lands were confiscated and sold to British planters who had steadfastly opposed his presence in the tea business, as the first private tea planter in Assam.

But well before his death, the export of what continues to be one of India's biggest foreign exchange earners had begun. The first tea boxes to England went out in 1838 and men like Charles Alexander Bruce extensively toured areas where no white man had ever set foot to look for suitable land.

The tea industry passed through a financial crisis in the 1860s after something that can only be compared to the gold rush that swept California in the first half of the nineteenth century. Hundreds of Britons gave up lucrative jobs in administration and business to invest in tea companies and wend their way to the jungles of Assam after the success of the pioneering companies. They were encouraged by the colonial government which liberalized land rent laws, providing for the lease of land for ninety-nine years on easy terms. This was further liberalized later.

The British planters and buyers of land in Assam became the biggest landlords in the region, dispossessing poor peasants who were unable to afford the taxes on their lands.

Significantly, the large group of immigrants from the Chota Nagpur belt—it is almost as large as the immigrants from Bengal—has rarely been looked upon as a cultural and economic threat to the Assamese as has the Bengali incursion. There are sound reasons for this: the chai garden workers did not confront the Assamese on sensitive issues. For example, few Assamese Hindus were interested in working in the gardens as hired hands. Those who went into tea were either owners or managers. Second, the tea workers were not interested in seizing land. They were, fortunately or otherwise, disinterested in doing more than working in the plantations. A reason for the lack of Assamese workers on the plantations was not because they were, necessarily lazy, as different historians have sought to paint the dominant Hindu Assamese. Rather they did not like to work on tea estates for they were not 'only easy going, but also a proud race, loath to labour manually for the invading aliens.'

But this pride ultimately turned into a mindset that shackled the community and allowed its leadership to be hijacked by cultural agitationists, who tried to replace economic development with strident emotional campaigns.

OPIUM AND THE BRITISH

In addition to the slave labour, the British also encouraged the use of opium. Farming of poppy plants, which produced opium, was banned but the British allowed the sale of non-Assam opium. This sleazy practice destroyed Assam's poppy cultivation and increased the dependence of local addicts on imported opium. It also increased its sales and the excise department in Assam collected hundreds of thousands of rupees from opium sales. Some Assamese demanded a total ban on opium, but such a move was opposed by the British.

It was not till the 1920s and 1930s, when the Congress Party launched its anti-British agitations that the opium or *kania* (lazy) shops, a common sight across Assamese towns, were finally shut.

The British attitude to opium cultivation in Assam was similar to their strategy in China when the East India Company sought to destroy the Chinese trade in opium by importing the drug from India. The British drive touched off protests in China and the ensuing repression triggered the Boxer Rebellion.

Another major group which flowed into Assam in the nineteenth and twentieth centuries was the Nepalis from the Himalayan kingdom and the areas around the Duars in northern Bengal. This community went into the small services sector: as labourers in the construction, transport and agricultural sectors. They became the *guhals* or milk suppliers for local communities for they kept small herds of milch cattle, a role they continue to play today. Many Nepalis have used the milk trade as a stepping stone for larger businesses and some have also entered politics. In fact, the first president of the Assam Provincial Congress Committee in 1921 was a Nepali, Chabilal Upadhyaya. Today, his grandson is a Member of Parliament from Assam to the Lok Sabha.

Others who came to this virgin nation also seized the opportunities. The Marwaris from Rajasthan captured the high ground of commerce and trade as well as moneylending. Some Pathans settled in the hills, basically as moneylenders where they duped poor tribals, lending money at usurious rates of interest, ranging from twenty to thirty per cent, ensuring the indebtedness of their client and his inability to escape the debt trap. A small group of industrious Punjabis also developed, honing their engineering abilities in the transport and business areas, while a community of Sikhs, whose forefathers had come over in the eighteenth century, with Guru Teg Bahadur, are now Assamized: they speak and write the local language and are primarily farmers in Nagaon district.

Of these groups, the most aggressive in terms of asserting their economic status have been the Bengalis, both Hindus and Muslims. The Muslims cultivators or *miyahs* took advantage of the lethargy of the local Assamese populace, especially the zamindars and large landholders who had been content with a single crop from their large estates.

Never loth to lose an opportunity, the migrants first began as cultivators who would share their produce with the owner. Often the landlord was an absentee owner, leaving the lands in charge of a family retainer. Over the years, the immigrants consolidated their position, building up their economic strength, working hard in the fields and gradually gaining both the economic clout and the political sustenance that enabled them to buy land both from the owner as well as neighbouring plots.

Often, this was in violation of the law. In the district of Nagaon, senior politicians recalled how revenue officials had colluded with immigrants in the 1940s and 1950s, giving them *pattas* or land deeds for small sums of money. Objections by local people were brushed aside. What made the violations worse were that those most hurt were poor tribal groups, like the Lalungs of Nagaon, the Mechs and Cacharis of Goalpara and other similar, small communities. Under special laws enacted by the British, these groups and their holdings were technically protected from encroachment by non-tribals under a system that developed tribal belts and blocks across the state.

The line system came into existence in 1921. It was simply a division of the land into three parts. One was an area where the immigrants could settle freely; a second where they were banned from entering and finally a line either on a map or on the ground: they were entitled to live only on one side of this line. There were not less than thirty-seven lines or blocks which were constituted after independence under what B. P. Singh calls the 'advice of a perceptive indigenous leadership.' This advice was consolidated into laws: the aim was to stop outsiders from grabbing tribal lands and the plains' tribals from being pushed off their traditional home areas. But human greed and inventiveness have never found laws a barrier.

Immigrants offered cash for the lands; the nominal owner continued to be the tribal. But the de facto owner was a Bengali immigrant, invariably a Muslim peasant from Mymensingh. The Hindu immigrant from East Bengal/Bengal and later East Pakistan and Bangladesh was predominantly a petty trader. The better off were professionals, such as teachers, doctors and lawyers.

A Frontier State And Nationalism

The reasons for the influx into the Northeast from East Bengal and Pakistan were not far to seek.

One was the abounding richness of the soil and the near-perfect conditions for crops like rice and jute with torrential rains, humidity, as well as the rivers, teeming with fish. Another was the abundance of empty lands and a meagre population, compared to other parts of the country.

For more than 100 years, Assam has been India's frontier area, not merely in the literal sense as a border state touching Myanmar, Tibet, Bhutan and Bangladesh but, as Myron Weiner points out in *Sons of the Soil: Migration and Ethnic Conflict in India,* 'also as new land attracting millions of settlers from other regions of the subcontinent.'

Before that, the Assamese of that area, an Indo-Aryan agricultural community in the plains of the Brahmaputra Valley, and hill peoples under the control of the Ahom kings had lived independently of the rest of India. They were neither vassal states nor conquered by any invading Indian power from northern or central India. They remained independent until the absorption of the area into the British Raj in the nineteenth century.

The Ahoms were of Shan origin, a group which conquered the area in the thirteenth century and adopted the culture and religion of the country (Hinduism) and community they had conquered.

The Shans were broadminded and married into the local Assamese community. Their administrative setup was smooth, their revenue collection just and their council of ministers efficient. One of their Prime Ministers or Bargohains, the respected Atanu Bargohain, once responded to a demand that the kingdom's soldiers pursue raiders from hill tribes by asking if 'an elephant can enter the hole of a rat?'

THE NAMGHAR

Hem Barua, one of Assam's best-known political figures in the post-independence era, said that the Ahoms were so impressed by the natural abundance of their conquered state that they called it '*Mung dum chum kham*' or Land of Golden Gardens.

In one the best-known works on Assam and its people, *The Red River and the Blue Hill**, Barua outlined the key elements of Assam village life. One was the *namghar* or congregational prayer hall, which he described as the base of rural life. Apart from being used for Vaishnavite chants and ceremonies, it also doubled as a village meeting place and social centre. The *namghar* is still built in traditional ways: it is a rectangular-shaped building, open on all sides but one. The structure is supported either by tall bamboo staves or by strong wooden beams and is covered by plain tin sheets or a thick roof of thatch placed over bamboo lattice.

Even these days, Assamese villages retain a flavour of the old times. Many homes are of mud, bamboo and thatch; other cottages are of thick bamboo with wooden rafters and tin roofs. Their floors are freshly plastered every day with a cooling paste of mud and cowdung. Most homes have little courtyards and, often, a tiny gate, announcing the individuality of the household.

The cottages are usually surrounded by groves of leafy fern and bamboo, palm and banana trees and the ubiquitous betel leaf clump and areca nut trees. People across the Northeast carry their *tamul*-paan (areca nut and betel leaf) with them. Any time is paan time, the leaf often laced with tobacco and a dab of lime.

The other eternal element of life in Assam is the broad Brahmaputra, which the Ahoms called *Nam-Dao-Phi* or River of the Star God.

The Brahmaputra is to Assam what the Hwang Ho and the Yangtse Kiang are to China, the Nile to Egypt and the Mekong to Laos, Kampuchea and Vietnam. It is both life-giver and life-taker. An entire culture, spanning socio-economic and political systems, has grown around this great sheet of water.

It provides work and life to communities who live along its banks,

---

* See, Hem Barua, *The Red River and the Blue Hill*, Guwahati: Lawyers Book Stall, 1954.

with its fish and rich soil sediments that make for intensive cultivation in the winter months when the water recedes.

Immortalized through songs, plays, poems and ballads, the power and pain of the Brahmaputra has been a constant theme in Assam.

Village life in Assam, especially in the Hindu hamlets, has its roots in the fifteenth-century Vaishnavite resurgence led by Sankardev. He preached a cleansed Vaishnavism that sought to wipe out the corruption of the declining Buddhist hold where sects like Ratikhowa Sampradai (creed of night enjoyment) existed. Sankardev's creed was based on bhakti or pure worship, and was marked by secularism.

His followers included people from the Naga, Garo and Mikir tribes as well as one prominent Muslim. It was Sankardev whose simplified Hinduism appealed to the Assamese because he combined preaching and chants with folk theatre, song and dance. It was he who conceived of and developed the *namghar* as the central theme of an Assamese village.

The *namghar* was part of an organism that Sankardev planned: of *satras* or monasteries, which are virtually a federation of villages commanding the religious loyalty of the villagers. There were weekly *haatis* or marketdays which also provided a meeting point and forum for discussion. The *namghars* did more than merely function as a plane for religious discourses, gathering and village assemblies. At one time they tried offenses by local villagers and their rulings were usually inviolable.

The *namghars* and Sankardev's teachings continue to shape Assam's rural social structure. One of the key elements in his teachings was a scorning of ritualism for the sake of tradition. A revolt against the pretensions of the priestly class, it fiercely opposed idol worship. Under its reformist leaders, the new faith propagated the worship of One God—Krishna—through bhajans and prayers, often involving the entire village community. Sankardev's campaign brought him into conflict with the ruling Ahoms, whose sexually permissive ways he opposed through his new creed that emphasized discipline and morality.

Assam's history too has developed differently from the rest of the country. Between the thirteenth and nineteenth centuries it was built around the Ahoms, their successes and failures. They held out against outside invaders for virtually all these 600 years except for three specific

43

periods. In the first, Mir Jumla, the great Mughal general, routed the Ahom army and river fleet but was forced to come to a peace: his troops threatened to mutiny after many of them were felled by the unhealthy climate and tropical diseases.

The Ahom grip over the empire loosened in the latter part of the eighteenth century as also in the nineteenth century after a succession of weak rulers and fierce Burmese invasions which shattered local society. But the Burmese overreached. They entered territory controlled by the British East India Company in search of fugitives. As a result, retribution was swift.

The British routed the Burmese in a series of military encounters. They were pushed out of Assam and ceded all rights to the area in 1826 by accepting the Treaty of Yandaboo. The Ahoms, softened by decades of easy living, were swiftly taken over by the British who turned their attention to exploiting the natural resources of this abundant land.

The British encouraged migrations that changed the face of Assam's society. They filled vacuums left by the brutal Burmese killings that depopulated many villages; the low population density also was attributed partly to recurring epidemics of malaria and the plague which wiped out entire communities.

The migrants came, reported census officials in the 1921 report, on 'almost every train and steamer.' And, it was noted that 'it seems likely that their march will extend up the valley and away from the (Brahmaputra) river before long.'

As British officials watched this inexorable long march, the economy of Assam also changed rapidly because of colonial interests exploiting oil and tea resources. On the political front, the state was awakened by occasional anti-British movements and then a sustained civil disobedience drive launched by the Congress Party.

Yet in the decades to come, the Congress Party's growth in Assam was based on a social and political compact between the Assamese middle class and bourgeois and the early immigrants from East Bengal. The alliance, reflected by the Congress, was based on a simple understanding: the Bengali *miyahs* would adopt the Assamese language, report themselves as Assamese speakers in the census, educate their children in Assamese schools and play what B.P. Singh calls 'a subservient role to caste Hindus in the agrarian sector.'

In this politically sophisticated equation, one that lasted, not without pain and challenges, for more than seventy years, the Assamese view of themselves is important. B.P. Singh describes it thus: 'The Assamese view themselves as a nationality with the Brahmaputra Valley as their homeland, Assamese as their language and Hinduism as their religion.' There is even an Assamese national anthem that speaks repeatedly and glowingly of "the beloved country", meaning Assam. One of the long-standing threats to this local concern about Assamese interests has been viewed as Bengali domination. The difficulties faced by the British colonialists in governing the State were aggravated by the resistance of the ruling class. As a result, the British imported Bengali Hindus, who were educated in English and could help administer the place.

Within a few years of the conquest of Assam, Bengali became the language of the courts and remained the official language until 1873. Assamese was passed off as a poor relative. The schools were in Bengali and in the race for jobs, the Bengali had a major advantage: his home state, the first to be colonized by the British, had English language schools and colleges. The first college in Assam did not start until 1901.

It was not easy to get Assamese reinstated as the prime language. A sustained campaign by Anandaram Dhekiyal Phukan, among others, and American Baptist missionaries were the key to the overturning of Bengali language as the lingua franca of Assam.

The Baptist missionaries, especially a man named Miles Bronson, prepared the first Anglo-Assamese dictionary and later published the first Assamese language newspaper, *Urunodoi*. Their activities moved Judge Andrew Moffat Mills to remark in 1853 that Britain had 'made a great mistake in directing that all business should be translated in Bengali and that the Assamese acquire it.' His recommendation that Assamese be reinstated did not happen for another twenty years. Therefore, it is hardly any surprise that this suspicion and resentment of the Bengali community prevails among most Assamese, no matter how educated or sophisticated. Given the Bengali record of active collaboration with the British in suppressing Assamese, it was not surprising that Assamese-Bengali discord was stoked fiercely during more recent agitations.

The upsurge against Bengalis in the nineteenth century paved the way for other nationalistic movements and agitations. There were revolts against tenancy laws and agricultural taxes, leading to occasional use of force by British troops against the agitators. In places, villagers or groups of villages set up *Raaj Mels* or peoples assemblies in defiance of British authority.

RISE OF NATIONALISM

Thus, the ground for nationalist ferment under Mahatma Gandhi and Jawaharlal Nehru had been laid in Assam. First there was the Assam Association and the Sabajanik Sabha of Jorhat town. Members from the Association and the Sabha went to meetings of the newly-formed Congress Party in other parts of the country, to ventilate local and national grievances. After the partition of Bengal was annulled in 1912, Assam became a separate area under the control of a Chief Commissioner, assisted by a Legislative Council of twenty-five members.

Younger Assamese, weary of masterly inactivity, began exerting pressure on the older, sedate leadership of the Assam Association to act more in line with the nationalist trends elsewhere in India. These included Tarun Phookan, Nabin Chandra Bardoloi, Gopinath Bardoloi and Kuladhar Chaliha.

Phookan had taken an anti-British stance as far back as 1918 and demanded self-government for India. Things moved quickly in 1920. Between October and December that year, the Assam Association virtually buried itself and was reborn as the Assam Provincial Congress, after adopting the national Congress resolutions seeking swaraj and advocating non-co-operation with Britain.

In 1921, the fledgling party was given a boost when Mahatma Gandhi came there for the first time to preach his gospel of civil disobedience, freedom from the British yoke and how his party was the best to campaign for it. Assamese of all hues, Hindus and Muslims, backed him and came in tens of thousands to attend his meetings. The British did everything in their power to harass Congress and its leaders, denying permission for meetings in open grounds during the Gandhi visit. But some of the wealthy leaders like Phookan held the meetings in their sprawling private grounds. Phookan's home was the site for the first meeting by Gandhi in Gauhati (now called Guwahati).

Gandhi was overwhelmed with the response.

The convention of the All India Congress Committee (AICC) in Guwahati in 1926 marked a turning point in Assam's involvement in the independence movement. Phookan became the first Assamese to be elected to the Congress Working Committee (CWC), the party's powerful central decision-making body. But the divisions here reflected those at the national level. Gopinath Bordoloi, later Premier of Assam in its most crucial, formative years, opposed the Lahore Congress resolution seeking resignation of Congress members from the state and central councils. So did another firebrand, Rohini Kumar Choudhury. Phookan too opposed the Lahore declaration but he and the others found themselves in a minority.

The divisions sharpened further as men like Phookan advocated entry into state and central legislative councils. He founded the Swarajya Party in Assam and yet continued to be president of the Assam Provincial Congress Committee. This was opposed by some Congress members and Phookan quit.

Bardoloi backed the old guard, resigned his presidency of the Guwahati District Congress Committee (GDCC). Nor did he participate in other civil disobedience movements, such as the campaign against the Salt Tax.

Younger Congressmen like Bijoy Bhagwati were opposed to the Phookan-Bardoloi position. 'He became totally isolated and Bishnuram Medhi became PCC President,' said Bhagwati, then a student leader. A contemporary of Bhagwati recalled how the latter was incensed by the sight of Bardoloi playing tennis in the Guwahati Tennis Club when, within eye sight, students picketed schools and colleges to oppose a British circular that sought to control political activity. There were clashes with the police, lathi charges and many young men and women were arrested and beaten badly.

'In fact, he was quite unpopular because he stayed away from the movement,' said Bhagwati, now eighty-four, of Gopinath Bardoloi. Bhagwati, a man with gentle eyes and a constant smile, still lives simply, wears the homespun khadi popularized by Gandhi and does not even own a personal car, unlike other 'freedom fighters' who now lead ostentatious lives, flaunting their wealth and corruption.

Angered by the dissension in the Assam Congress over ways to oppose the Salt Tax, a stocky young Assamese student at Calcutta set out for Gujarat to join the Mahatma. His name was Liladhar Baruah, an elder brother of my grandfather, and he came from north Guwahati.

After briefing Gandhi of developments in Assam, Liladhar returned to his home state to confront the old guard. Supported by a handful of students, he embarrassed a reluctant Phookan at a large meeting in Guwahati where the older leaders spoke in favour of staying away from the civil disobedience movement. At the meeting, Liladhar challenged these moves and called for salt-making.

The anti-Salt Tax agitation in Assam, as elsewhere, was marked by brutal assaults on students, repression in defiant villages and widescale arrests.

As the civil disobedience movement picked up tempo, many political workers ignored Bardoloi who turned to practicing law in the Guwahati courts to support himself and his family. He stayed aloof, without leaving Congress, a dormant figure until his moment came. The national elections of 1937 provided him a platform to return to active politics as Bishnuram Medhi, the most prominent Congress leader and later Chief Minister of Assam, chose not to contest. It was clear to Bardoloi that too many years in the wilderness would damage him irreparably. He sought and won a Congress nomination from Guwahati and was elected from his constituency.

Summoning his formidable talent for organization and identifying a vacuum in the local Congress leadership, Bardoloi became the party's unchallenged leader.

Gopinath Bardoloi's role was crucial to the relationship between Assam and India and for the legacy that Congress left the Northeast. This relationship and legacy has been inadequately recorded in India's independence movement and in the rich literature that exists of the country, post-independence.

Bardoloi was an impressive man, physically: he was tall and

broad-shouldered. Nirode Barooah[*], one of Assam's most eminent historians, described Gopinath Bardoloi as interested in 'English, drama and literature, in music both classical and modern, in theatre, in games like cricket and tennis, in shooting and angling,' and as a person who had a 'taste for good food and good clothes.' Like many of his contemporaries in Congress, Bardoloi was a lawyer, who studied history and law at Calcutta University.

Later, the power of Mahatma Gandhi weaned him toward anti-British struggles and a more disciplined life. He turned to spinning and wearing khadi and his spartan lifestyle was sharpened by several prison terms during which he wrote books for children about the *Ramayana* and the Bhagavad Gita. He also organized daily meetings in Jorhat jail with four other contemporaries including Fakhruddin Ali Ahmed, who later became President of India. Bardoloi's arguments were brief and blunt. But his discussions sometimes lacked the sophistry of his main rival, Sir Syed Mohammad Saadulla, knighted by the British imperial family.

The struggle between these two men dominated the politics of the region for the crucial years between 1937 and 1947, when they headed as many as five ministries between them.

BARDOLOI-SAADULLA FEUD

Bardoloi's conflict with Saadulla did not stem from a personal rift. It reflected a broader division: the ideological battleground between Congress and the Muslim League and the politics of the times. The British saw Saadulla as the ideal foil for Bordoloi and Congress.

Saadulla was a tall and fair Assamese lawyer from Golaghat who had settled in Guwahati. His father was a maulvi at a mosque in Nagaon. Saadulla had an indifferent law practise in Calcutta and later joined the Muslim League in the late thirties.

Saadulla also was quite a ladies' man: charming and elegant, he would throw parties that were hosted by his daughter, Betty, as he was a widower. In Shillong, the romantic hill station in the Khasi Hills that was

See, Nirode Barooah (ed.), *Gopinath Bardoloi: Indian Constitution and Centre-Assam Relations*, Guwahati: Publications Board, 1990.

known for its attractive women, archery contests, horse racing, golf and crisp climate, the gossip was about his relationship with another elegant and attractive Khasi woman, who later became a member of the assembly and a ministerial colleague.

But tea parties and gossip aside, Saadulla had a much sharper confrontation at hand.

The battle between him and Gopinath Bardoloi was the stuff of real drama. Their first major clash was in 1937 during the voting to the provincial legislatures across the country which was contested by the Muslim League, Congress and a range of other parties. While Congress won convincing victories in a majority of the provinces, the League captured a handful. In Assam, the situation was fluid, for no party had emerged with a clear majority.

The British wanted Saadulla: in their assessment, he was pliable since he did not command a majority on his own. He depended on the British and Indian tea planters as well as tribal members for a tenuous majority.

Sir Robert Reid, Governor of Assam, described Saadulla once as 'decidedly perturbed' and told the Viceroy in a message in 1939 that 'the story is long and complicated, mixed up as it is with personal intrigues, and tergiversations and all the miserable business of attracting a handful of votes here or losing a handful there.' Later, Reid was even more scathing: ' . . . his present idea is that he may have to buy the support of the Surma Valley Hindus . . . the price is a ministership.'

These, then, were Assam's men of destiny in the 1930s and 1940s, handsome men who wielded power and influence as if it were their birthright, who commanded and sought unflinching loyalty from their followers and who were prepared to face severe tests for their convictions. They were divided by perception, ideology, religion and lifestyles. But the decisions they took in those critical years continue to shape developments in Assam and the Northeast.

BARDOLOI: A MAN FOR HIS TIMES

The elections to eleven provincial legislatures was just over in 1937 and the Congress had won handsomely in several, the Muslim League in three but Assam's situation remained unclear with no party winning a majority. At the time, of course, there were Separate Electorates and constituencies for Hindus and Muslims. The inclusion of Muslim, Bengali-dominated Sylhet district in Assam created a delicate imbalance, for its Muslim voters were a solid vote bank for the Muslim League.

Under Gopinath Bardoloi, Congress had captured thirty-five seats of the 108 in the legislature. This was equal to what all the Muslim parties put together had won in the state. The Muslim League got only seven seats on its own. The others were made up by smaller groups, including Saadulla's own Assam Union Muslim League which later merged with Muslim League.

Governor Michael Keane's immediate concern was to prevent Bardoloi from fashioning a coalition with support from the tribes and the Christian factions. He began in this endeavour by offering Saadulla the premiership of Assam for the first time in 1937 but the latter was hesitant. He wanted more time to make up his mind, he told Keane. The Governor, a friend of the legendary big game hunter and conservationist Jim Corbett, was getting worried as the days went by and the situation in the legislature remained as fluid as ever.

Congress had easily formed a government in five provinces. However, personal rivalries and jealousies surfaced during the ministerships, with Congressmen clearly preferring office within the empire to agitating against the Raj. There was talk of corruption and nepotism, especially in the Central Provinces, in the Mahakoshal (Hindi-speaking) region and political strategies, attacks and counter-attacks within the government and the party led by Brahmins like Ravi Shankar Shukla (the father of Vidya Charan and Shyama Charan Shukla) and Dwarka Prasad Mishra.

Internationally, the Nazis under Adolf Hitler had completed a stunning rise to power in Germany and were making threatening noises about smaller nations in Europe and the Jews. Japan was the rising star in the East and Russia sprawled, monolithic, terror-filled by Josef Stalin's ethnic purges, across Europe and Asia. In China, warlords and the Kuomintang under Generalissimo Chiang Kai-shek carved out areas of control for themselves. Waiting in the wings were Mao Tse-tung and Chou En-lai, preparing to take the world's most populous nation and convert it to Communism.

But everywhere, Britain ruled its colonies and the United States was a developing great power, recovering from a disastrous Depression and bracing for President Franklin Roosevelt's New Deal.

At home, the times in the Northeast were as colourful and tense as the people who dominated them.

At the time Saadulla was in Calcutta, where he had a practise as a "not-very-successful" lawyer. He was reluctant to return in haste because he was being considered for judgeship of the High Court there. Eventually, he was not asked to join the Bench but was picked instead as a junior Government Pleader at the court. That was not good enough to hold him and he returned to a second summons, this time from Sir Robert Reid, who had succeeded Keane as Governor.

'The general opinion is that he is the only person who can be fairly, safely be relied upon to form a stable government,' Reid declared. But he added later that should Saadulla fail 'we shall be in a very difficult position.' Keane and Reid ran the administration for three months after the legislative elections in the absence of a government, under the vast powers that a Governor of a frontier province enjoyed. This gave Saadulla enough time to cobble together a majority and, finally, take office.

He was assisted by the special constitutional provisions for Assam that gave the tiny European population of 3,000 as many as nine seats in the legislature. This contrasted sharply with the four seats that were allotted to the tea garden labour force, at that time numbering nearly one million. Needless to say, the Europeans voted religiously with and for Saadulla. At one point, he was saved by the vote of one European legislator who was rushed from hospital to cast his ballot for the government during a bitter no-confidence motion.

The first Saadulla ministry was sworn in on All Fools Day, 1 April 1937. A Congress legislator reacted by snapping that 'the country has been befooled.'

Eight months later, Reid described the government's position in the legislature as 'disquieting' and laid bare his concerns in a passage referred to earlier. Here he describes the manoeuvring that Saadulla resorted to, including buying the support of 'the Surma Valley Hindus . . . the price is a ministership.'

The equation is depressingly familiar. It has been played out hundreds of times in post-independence India, both at the national level as well as state and district level politics.

For more than eight months after these activities, Saadulla managed to stave off defeat and edge his way around no-confidence motions. But his government finally fell in August 1938 when Gopinath Bardoloi moved a no-confidence motion and was supported by Saadulla's own party legislators and ministers.

Saadulla's personal characteristics and failings had much to do with his rise and fall, time and again, as well as his flawed politics. A man of meticulous habits who kept an account book but no diary, his accounts, scribbled on loose sheets of paper, in regular notebooks and available in the form of bank statements, show a stern, almost unbending side of the man who entered the cost of daily purchases of eggs, milk and bread as well as of hair oil, shoe polish and the cost of tickets to the Irish Derby sweepstakes.

Saadulla lacked conviction about the infallibility of the Muslim League and its leader, Mohammad Ali Jinnah. It was this dithering as well as his inability to assert himself strongly in the face of Bardoloi's sustained campaigns, to battle it out during the years in opposition and his failing health that made him a loser. He was parsimonious with money but was secretly supported by powerful businessmen in Calcutta, although he was reluctant to do anything for his benefactors when he came to power in Assam.

This is clear from the angry letters that a person named Faiz addressed to Saadulla from Calcutta in gracious, modulated but still furious English.

The correspondence took place over more than one year and has little in response from Saadulla in it. But Faiz of the elegant signature, obviously a businessman of influence in Calcutta and one of Saadulla's financial benefactors, said in one letter that the politician had failed to write 'a single line to me as to what arrangement you propose to make to discharge your obligations to our mutual friend Debi who has done so much for you and your party in the last two years.'

The mysterious Debi, obviously a Hindu businessman, had pumped money into the coffers of Saadulla and his party, and was calling in his dues. 'I am sure,' continued Faiz, ' that you will have the fairness to admit that he was not actuated by philanthropic motives alone when he went out of his way to help you and your friends. In the interests of all concerned . . . I strongly advise you to settle matters with Debi before he is compelled to show his teeth and expose you and your party before your opponents.'

Clearly, here was an indication that Saadulla should pay back his dues in the form perhaps of profitable government contracts to 'Debi'. Whether he did or not, we have no way of knowing but there is a letter from Faiz in February 1940, the last letter of this fascinating correspondence, where he denounces Saadulla in sharper terms.

Describing Saadulla's silence as 'puzzling,' Faiz snapped in a letter that he titled 'Secret and Strictly Confidential' that he was 'really sorry that I allowed myself to get mixed up in this dirty business called politics. It was understood from the very start—I am sure you will have the fairness to admit—that you would be able to make adequate return for what Debi had done for you during the last two years. To the surprise of all . . . You completely changed your attitude as soon as you found that your position was secure in your own province. You did not even take the trouble of conciliating or humouring one who had secured large amounts of money for you and your party funds in order to strengthen your position in Assam politics.'

Nor could Saadulla postpone defeat in the legislature for long. A series of embarrassing setbacks had begun in the very first session of the new assembly: Saadulla's nominee for Speaker was defeated by a senior Congress leader, Basanta Das from the Sylhet Valley. The Premier staggered on until September 1938 when he lost his majority and resigned without facing a spate of no-confidence motions. Fiercely besieged and unable to cope with strikes and agitations in the oil fields, coal mines and tea gardens as well as allegations of packing local Town Boards with his nominees in the teeth of furious objections, Saadulla found his options had closed. *The Statesman* of Calcutta had asked him several months earlier to resign gracefully since his own supporters often backed the opposition: 'A government which cannot control its own supporters and is continually humiliated by defeats carries little authority and should either reassert its authority or resign.'

Saadulla's defeat created a dilemma for the Congress. While Gopinath Bardoloi and other senior Congress leaders in the province wanted the party to take charge of the government, there was division a the Central level. Maulana Abul Kalam Azad, then in-charge of eastern provinces, barring Assam and Bihar, travelled to Shillong to assess the mood. He opposed the formation of a coalition ministry. But to Bardoloi's rescue at that time came Congress Party President, Subhas Chandra Bose. In a response to Bardoloi's call for help, Bose and Sardar Vallabhbhai Patel, one of the most powerful national leaders at the time, agreed to a coalition. 'If Sardar Patel had not come to my rescue, Moulana Sahib would not have supported my viewpoint . . . at the [Congress] Working Committee meeting at Delhi. In that case, there would not have been a coalition ministry in Assam,' said Bose[*] later.

B.R. Tomlinson looks at it slightly differently. In his book, *The Indian National Congress and the Raj: The Penultimate Phase 1929–1942*[**], Tomlinson points out that 'Bose regarded Assam as part of his personal sphere of influence and it was his insistence, combined with the advice of Patel and Gandhi, which removed the initial opposition of Azad and (Rajendra) Prasad to the formation of a Congress coalition ministry in that state.'

Azad's feelings on the issue were not recorded in his book, *India Wins Freedom*[+]. But there is a significant passage there, although this is in a much later setting, where he refers to 'certain leaders from Assam . . . (who) were possessed by an inexplicable fear of Bengalis.'

Bardoloi's first ministry and Assam's first Congress government did not make much headway. It inherited a financial mess from Saadulla and chronic labour unrest. In addition, floods wreaked havoc across the Brahmaputra Valley, destroying villages, eroding banks, sweeping away people and livestock, crops, roads and railway lines.

According to Bijoy Bhagwati, the strike in the Digboi oilfields in 1939 involved several thousand workers demanding wage increases and a forty-four-hour week. Conciliation efforts failed; there were police firings, the British management of the Assam Oil Company refused to co-operate with the government and, to cap it all, the Second World War

---

[*] See, Leonard A. Gordon, *The Nationalist Movement, 1876–1940*, Columbia: Columbia University Press, 1974.

[**] See B.R. Tomlinson, *The Indian National Congress and the Raj: The Penultimate Phase 1929–1942*, London: Macmillan Ltd, 1976.

[+] See, Maulana Abul Kalam Azad, *India Wins Freedom*, Delhi: Orient longman, 1988.

began. With the start of the war, the Central Government declared the oil belt a protected area and cracked down on the workers. The Bardoloi government was helpless and unable to check the assault.

More than 3,000 workers were sacked; senior union leaders were expelled from Assam. And finally, bowing to the Central Congress leadership, the Bardoloi government resigned—not over its failure to protect the oil workers but as part of the overall Congress opposition to Britain dragging India into a war in which it did not believe.

Yet, Bardoloi did not quit office immediately on the Working Committee's demand of October 1939. According to Mahatma Gandhi, Subhas Chandra Bose, who had assisted in the birth of the ministry, was opposed to its resignation because he thought 'Assam's was a special case.' Gandhi later said that Bardoloi had made a mistake by quitting: 'Although I was the author of that scheme of boycott, I said Assam should not come out, if it feels like it. But Assam did come out. It was wrong[*].'

Bardoloi did hold onto office until the middle of the next month, partly because he believed that Assam's peculiar position could not be helped by abandoning ship at this stage. But he lacked the all-India stature to battle the High Command singlehandedly. He also knew that the war would come closer to the Northeast, whose rich natural resources were as much a source of envy and lust of Japan as it was a reason to be defended by the British Raj.

Ultimately, it was the frontier districts of Nagaland and Manipur that faced the wrath of Japan and were able to turn the tide of history and the war. On the tennis courts of the Deputy Commissioner of Kohima, the capital of the Naga Hills, are rows of neatly-arranged gravestones, some marked, others without a name.

It was here that the Japanese dreams of a giant Asian empire crumbled. And here now stands one of the most moving epitaphs to courage, one that never fails to touch my spirit, and tug at it.

Near the graves is a simple memorial which says:

When you go home,
tell them of us
and say:

---

[*] See, D.G. Tendulkar, *Mahatma: Life of Mohandas Karamchand Gandhi*, Bombay: Vithalbhai Jhaveri, Vol. 7, 1953.

For your tomorrow
We gave our today.

Gopinath Bardoloi's resignation cleared the way for Saadulla's return to office. Within two days of Bardoloi leaving the top post, Saadulla was reinstalled as Premier of Assam on 17 November 1939. This term was to last two years; and after a brief interruption, he continued from August 1942 to February 1946.

It is no surprise that Saadulla, a man who did not trust others and in turn was deeply distrusted by his political colleagues, not to speak of his business supporters, survived best in office when the Congress was not physically around to needle him and make him trip. Or when, as part of a strategy, the Congress helped him form a coalition (with its support from outside) and then pulled out when it suited it.

The years of Saadulla's reign coincided with several national events concerning the Congress. For one thing, he formed his second government immediately after Bardoloi quit following the Congress party's opposition to the war. His third government came into existence soon after the bulk of the Congress leadership at the national and state level were arrested for moving the Quit India resolution against the British. It got a fresh lease of life with a coalition government that was the brainchild of Bardoloi and which he used strategically to demolish Saadulla as well as the Muslim League's bid to absorb Assam in East Pakistan.

Saadulla was pro-war and, to ingratiate himself with the British, organized fundraising efforts for the British military campaign. It was his pro-British bias and failure to champion local causes that led to the fall of his second government.

But there was sharp infighting within his own coalition with groups and individuals lobbying for themselves and their interests and against each other. The manoeuvring began within hours of Bardoloi's resignation and continued for weeks.

Amjad Ali, a legislator from Goalpara district, wrote in a letter, of 27 November 1939 that 'If our loyalty and faithfulness have any meaning we must be rewarded . . . how long to wait.' He also lashed out in the same letter, 'No Government either of yours or of Gopinath Bardoloi can or is willing to do us any good.' Another Muslim leader, writing against an immigrant leader, described his foe as 'mad after being a minister.' One whining letter from a ministerial aspirant complained of Saadulla's 'apathy and indifference . . . heedless of all the selfless service' by him and his associates and irritated by the fact that 'many unworthy and revolting members were long before consulted.'

The war years also saw the rise of a political group that continues to influence Assam: the students. A student movement in 1941 was preceded by widescale arrests of Congress members involved in the civil disobedience campaign. Those held included Gopinath Bardoloi, in December 1940. He was arrested at Guwahati, close to the very place where, ten years earlier, he had ignored the satyagrahis and earned their ire by playing tennis. Other groups followed suit and were detained and released in batches. In December of 1941, all satyagrahis were released under orders of the British Government, as the war took a turn for the worse and the Axis powers battered the Allied forces in Europe, Northern Africa and Southeast Asia.

The release from jail of its members was also important to Congress leaders, who were concerned about the way the Saadulla ministry was encouraging immigrants from East Bengal to pour into Assam. Saadulla had announced, in July 1941, a Land Settlement Policy that opened the floodgates to immigrants, allowing them to settle on government land anywhere in Assam and enabling them to seize as much as thirty bighas of land and more for each homestead.

This was a step that was to bring both prosperity and ruin to Assam.

In a 1945 letter, Saadulla boasted to Liaquat Ali Khan, later Prime Minister of Pakistan and then M.A. Jinnah's second-in-command in the Muslim League, that 'In the four lower districts of Assam Valley, these Bengali immigrant Muslims have quadrupled the Muslim population during the last 20 years.'

As a result, Congress prepared to battle Saadulla in the legislature. But unexpectedly students took the initiative and the struggle went onto the streets, out of the hands of Bardoloi, without his advice, consent or involvement.

In December, students protesting against a government pro-war exhibition were beaten by police. More than 200 were injured, many of them badly. The government denied opposition charges of brutality and said that a senior police official was hit on the head with a stone. The assault provoked widespread resentment against an already unpopular government, and lawyers and labour unions joined the agitation. There was support from Bengali students as well. The capital, Shillong, was shut down by a strike led by school and college students who converged on the legislature.

Saadulla remained adamant but was shaken when his Hindu Minister for Education, Rohini Kumar Choudhury, resigned when a no-confidence motion was tabled against the government. Gradually, several legislators abandoned Saadulla. The motion against him was carried without a single supporting ballot for the Premier. Finally, Governor's rule was declared in Assam.

It had taken exactly six days for the students, from the time of the police assaults at Guwahati, to force Saadulla to his knees.

Assam had seen the birth of a new political force which had won its first major victory over a despised foe. It was to be the first of many. Decades later, the same strategy worked with as many as four separate state governments as students and their followers took to the streets in 1979.

Because of a decision to boycott the legislature and Congress involvement with the Cripps Mission that sought to develop the theme of self-government after the war, Governor's rule continued until August 1942 in Assam. Saadulla waited in the wings, meanwhile, biding his time and licking his wounds.

His turn came immediately after the Congress approved the Quit India resolution of August 1942, calling on Britain to leave India. The entire Congress leadership, both at the Central level and in the provinces, was picked up by the police.

Within days of their arrest, Saadulla was back in the saddle as Premier. And in a bid to strengthen his tenuous hold on Assam's politics, he openly encouraged immigration from East Bengal, helping Jinnah when he sought to claim Assam for East Pakistan.

And for the following years, he was to rule Assam virtually without opposition, as his principal foes were in prison, and inflict on it a situation, borne out of the migrations, that had no solution.

Lord Wavell, the new Viceroy, remarked that Saadulla's slogan of 'Grow more food', supposedly for the war campaign and to feed the tens of thousands of Allied troops who had descended on Assam and Bengal as well as the Assam hills, was quite misleading. 'The chief political problem is the desire of the Moslem Ministers to increase this immigration into the uncultivated Government lands under the slogan of "Grow more food," but what they are really after is "Grow more Moslems"[*].

As Saadulla continued his short-sighted ways, Gopinath Bardoloi was honing his political skills and strategies—in Jorhat Jail.

Unlike Saadulla, Gopinath Bardoloi kept few accounts but he maintained an occasional diary, wrote often to his wife, children and friends, as well as political contemporaries and leaders. In fact, some of his best and most graceful writing took place in jail for participating in civil disobedience movements against the British. His writing, luminous yet spartan in English, stilted in Assamese, are a "Discovery of Assam", limited to his people and province and lacking the epic canvas that Jawaharlal Nehru painted in his *Discovery of India*. But there are poems and stories, letters of love and respect, notes on philosophy and Gandhi. But, most significant of his written work was his summarizations of discussions with fellow political prisoners on the future role of Assam in India, the detailed breakup of the administrative structure, the role of Muslims, education, land revenue, control over natural resources, such as oil and minerals, and the need for states to develop their policies autonomously, free of direct interference from the Centre.

With the help of close friends and political colleagues, he developed a concept for governance in Assam on the basis of daily discussions in prison. He also was concerned about providing money for his family while in jail. He asked his wife to sell the family car. Apart from writing regularly to his family, Bardoloi attempted an Assamese biography of Mahatma Gandhi, filled a bunch of loose sheafs of paper with poems, wrote two long essays on the need for a university in Assam and the development of policies toward the hill tribes.

Bardoloi's relationship with Gandhi was not always smooth. In the initial stages, when he wrote to the Mahatma on an issue apparently related to municipal elections in Guwahati (Bardoloi won his seat by a whisker),

---

[*] See, Penderel Moon, ed., *Wavell: The Viceroy's Journal*, London: OUP, 1973.

Gandhi wrote back, describing it as a 'domestic matter which the local people should settle . . . . You can act up to the formula that I have presented—he who has the least chance should retire.'

What Bardoloi thought of this advice, rendered in October 1934, is not known although he was not destined to play an active role in Congress politics until 1937.

The two became closer after Bardoloi formed his first ministry in 1938; at that point, Gandhi backed the Bardoloi-Bose coalition plan over Maulana Azad's objections. The period in prison cemented this relationship into one of mutual respect and affection. Later, Bardoloi travelled to Wardha, where the Mahatma stayed at the Sevagram Ashram, to consult him on satyagraha, policies in Assam, opposition to Saadulla and even setting up women's literacy cells in the state.

The Mahatma suggested in one of the letters that Bardoloi and his colleagues should learn Hindi and Urdu because a national language was essential for the future, united and independent India. As he prepared quietly and secretly for one of the most stunning political coups, Bardoloi cited Gandhi's advice to fellow legislators to speak fearlessly, operate openly and never in secret.

He was aware of the ignorance of other Indian leaders about his people and the Northeast region. He often despaired of even improving their level of knowledge.

In one of his entries in his private diary of 17 March 1941, Bardoloi remarked: 'I am astonished to know that even C. Reddy, the Vice Chancellor of the University in Andhra Pradesh thinks that Assam is a Muslim-majority state. There is no one (in Assam) to explain to the general mass of Indians that Assam is not a state to be incorporated into the League's concept of Pakistan.'

These are to be seen in his minutes of the meetings, jotted in a thick diary and the issues that these discussions tackled in 1940 and 1941 included the boundaries of a future Assam state, its relationship with neighbouring states and the rest of India, the need to control the income from taxes on natural resources and its internal problems.

He opposed special exclusion zones for the remote tribes on the frontier, many of whom had no concept of India and whose relationship with the outside world depended on trading with neighbouring villages or, at the most, a rare visit to the Assam Valley to sell produce such as cotton, ginger, chillies and fruit. According to Gopinath Bardoloi, while Christian missionaries had done good work in many distant areas by bringing education, medicine and hygiene to these communities, they too inducted an alien culture to the hills.

Bardoloi agreed that the simple hillfolk needed to be protected from mercenary traders and mourned the lack of knowledge about these people in his own state as well as in other parts of India. He and his colleagues wanted these groups to develop according to their own traditions and genius yet extend the democratic experiment of representative government to them so that they could slowly enter the modern age.

But his sharp denouncement of the Excluded Areas and areas which were described as Partially Excluded drew suspicion from tribal leaders. These descriptions need a little explanation:

In 1936, the tribal areas of Assam were divided into Excluded Areas including what is now Arunachal Pradesh, Naga and Lushai (Mizo) Hills, and North Cachar Hills. These areas were under the direct control of the Governor; the cabinet and legislators had no role here, not even to advise the Governor or create laws for the administration of these areas.

The Partially Excluded zones included the Garo Hills, the Mikir Hills of Nagaon and Sibsagar districts and part of the Khasi and Jaintia Hills in what is now Meghalaya.

These areas had a few representatives in the state legislature but discussions and legislation pertaining to them could be held and passed only at the Governor's discretion. Bardoloi and his colleagues regarded this as an anomaly for it deprived the people of the benefits of direct representation and forced them to rely on the whims of an all-powerful figure and his aides.

Bardoloi was paternalistic toward the tribes, if not assimilistic. In this, he perhaps followed a tradition set by David Scott, the Viceroy's Agent in Assam in the nineteenth century, who helped extend the frontiers of British influence in the region and established control over the different tribes, factions and communities.

On the crucial issue of oil revenues and mineral resources, the Bardoloi minutes felt that the Centre's 'shabby' financial treatment of the state should end. ' . . . there must be sufficient scope and powers in the province to be able to develop it without interference from the Centre.'

The group was clear that the Centre had no right over income from natural and mineral resources, including petrol, 'the financial control of which should rest in the provinces.'

Here was a clear advocacy of Central non-interference in state matters and for provincial autonomy, concepts which would have benefited mineral-rich states like Bihar and Assam, instead of making them perpetually dependent on the whims of the Centre and its insensitive bureaucrats and politicians. And in the process, impoverishing them. For the investment that has come from private enterprise and the public sector in either state is not commensurate with the outflow of resources and their value from the state.

Gopinath Bardoloi made similar points to the Cabinet Mission, entrusted with devising a political settlement for the Indian subcontinent in 1946, and Lord Wavell, the Viceroy in Delhi. '(Assam) was a Province with considerable resources, but the Government of India by absorbing the royalties on oil had taken a great deal of money out of it. About 200 million lbs. of tea were produced every year, 90% of which was exported, but the export duty was realised by the Government of India in Calcutta, and the revenue lost to the Province,' said the official account of that encounter. ' In return, the Province, though one of the poorest, got only 30 lakhs subvention from the Central Government. To enable Assam to utilize its resources in its own interest, he felt that the fullest possible autonomy should be given to it.'

This state of affairs continues, without fail, without correction. One of the main reasons for the Centre's continuous neglect of the Northeast is based on the country's ignorance of the region and its people. Leaders and people of the Northeast continue to be mistaken as foreigners in their own land, and are rooked in the badlands of Delhi and elsewhere by taxidrivers, hotel touts, the lot.

These may seem small incidents and examples. But this has happened to friends and relatives, just because they happen to have features that are slightly more Mongolian than the 'normal' North Indian.

There was one incident involving a Chief Minister of Nagaland checking into a five-star hotel in Bombay and being asked to show his passport. Such incidents can be repeated thousands of times. They only go to expose the hollowness of the so-called 'mainstream' of Indian society and its total and incurable neglect and interest in areas outside of its dusty, heat-battered borders. These places, such as the Northeast, are rich in their vegetation, have more educated people and treat their womenfolk honourably. Yet, these peoples and regions find themselves without a voice in Delhi because of the overwhelming numbers of the Hindi heartland and the total ineptness of their own leaders. Nagaland is confused with a Southeast Asia nation, and few have heard of Mizoram, fewer still of Meghalaya. Assam and Guwahati and, to some, Shillong are the only familiar names.

India's Northeast remains a peripheral area, drawing attention only when violence erupts, when massacres, riots, curfews and agitations spiral out of control. This is unfair and reflects the total insensitivity of the brown babus tightly ensconced in a power-sharing embrace with pajama-kurta-clad politicians.

BARDOLOI'S COUP

Gopinath Bardoloi knew that Saadulla's Land Settlement policy would be disastrous for the Assamese, especially the caste Hindus who comprised the political base for Congress. Uppermost in his mind was the unspoken fear that these migrations were laying the foundation for a demand by Jinnah for Assam's inclusion in a future Pakistan, by emphasizing the size of the Muslim population and its close links with East Bengal.

The Assamese caste Hindu power block felt most threatened by the migrations, fearing a loss of political power and economic and cultural dominance by the immigrant Muslims. On top of it, the issue touched old suspicions of domination by Bengalis in the nineteenth century. Those memories still rankled.

In 1945, after his release from prison, Bardoloi realized, better than anyone else, that the Congress had become sluggish. It needed shock treatment. His view was shared by Gandhi. Both men were perturbed by Saadulla's pro-settlement policies. Gandhi's concern was translated into a ringing call to the Assamese people, a statement recorded by his faithful diarist and secretary, Pyarelal. This statement has been completely ignored so far in Assam, perhaps because it is so little known. It reflects the Mahatma's anguish and frustration over the issue, to the point where he advocated the repudiation of non-violence.

The statement is simply called "A message to the People of Assam" and was issued from Panchgani, a hill station in Maharashtra in July 1944.

The Mahatma was blunt: 'If the people feel that the present policy of the Government on settlement and immigration is oppressive and anti-national, let them fight it non-violently, or violently, if necessary.'

A few days later, Gandhi sent another message expressing helplessness: 'I have no message of hope for my Assamese brothers and sisters but I send my deep sympathy for them. May God bless you all to come out of the ordeal successfully.'

Taking a cue from these messages perhaps, Bardoloi devised a brilliant strategy to counter Saadulla and his pro-land grab, pro-Muslim policies. In consultation with other Assamese Congress leaders and Rohini Kumar Choudhury, then leader of the Nationalist Independent Group (later the Assam Nationalist Coalition Party) in the legislature, he decided to hit at the very heart of Saadulla's campaign.

In many ways, it was nothing short of a coup.

Bardoloi recognized Saadulla's weakness for power and his willingness to compromise because his position in the 108-member assembly was shaky, especially with Congress back in force in the opposition and angry noises emanating from his fractious Muslim Leaguers and their supporters.

So he made an offer that Saadulla just could not refuse.

In a letter of 25 March 1945 to Liaquat Ali Khan, Jinnah's immediate deputy, Saadulla described his 'extremely tenuous' majority: 'The defections of one or two spells disaster for the ministry,' he said, referring to close shaves in the same month when he scraped through with just two votes.

'For some reason which I cannot fathom, the Leader of the Congress Opposition whose strength in the House is 32 and the leader of the Nationalist Independent Group with a following of 17, who always voted against Government, started parleying with me to form a stable Government,' he said. The Premier said that consultations with his coalition party and his own League followers were positive and as a result he had formed a new coalition.

Bardoloi insisted that the crucial Revenue portfolio, which controlled land disbursement, taxes and settlement, go to Rohini Kumar Choudhury, a right-wing Assamese Hindu parochialist. Saadulla appealed to Liaquat Ali Khan and Jinnah to allow him to bring his friend, Mavis Dunn, back into the cabinet as a Christian member. This, he said, would tilt the balance in his favour.

He tried to assure Khan that there would be no change in the migration pattern although he conceded that he had made 'maximum measure of concessions' on the issue, to Hindus and plains tribals. 'It is no use discussing greater concessions for which I could not obtain sanction of the legislature,' Saadaulla said, adding that the interests of Muslim immigrants were 'safe in my hands and settlement with them is going apace.' As mentioned earlier, he boasted that 'In the four lower districts of Assam Valley, these Bengali immigrant Muslims have quadrupled the Muslim population during the last 20 years.'

Liaquat Ali Khan, surprised by the turn of events, tried to stop the changes but Saadulla went ahead with them anyway.

It is now clear why Bardoloi bargained the way he did. The war had ended with the defeat of the Axis powers and elections were coming. Congress, if it was to ensure Assam's future role in India and not in Pakistan, had to have clear issues in the bag to appeal to voters.

In the most brilliant stroke of all, he kept the Congress out of the new coalition, assuring it of support from outside. By this strategy, Bardoloi was able to manipulate the new government at will, pressure and harass it as he wished, without getting any of the public opprobrium that it would draw for failing to implement its policies. Such dissatisfaction would work to the advantage of Congress, whenever elections were held, he reasoned.

Bardoloi demanded other concessions from Saadulla, driving home his advantage. Apart from whittling down the Land Settlement policy, he sought the release of all political prisoners and an end to the official ban on political meetings and processions.

The land settlement was redefined to mean that landless persons were those with a land holding of less than twenty bighas (for a family of five persons) and people holding less than this would be entitled to apply for the rest of their due. This was to be made applicable to indigenous people and immigrants who came to Assam before 1 January 1938. Migrants who had settled in forests were to be evicted.

Four months later, Bardoloi accused Saadula's government of failing in all areas of the agreement and said that immigrants were 'desperate and lawless' and 'violently trespassing in the reserves and private properties.'

He said that Saadulla's Muslim colleagues appeared disinterested in implementing the changes in the Land Settlement policy. The government, he declared, should not therefore expect further support from Congress.

Saadulla was furious. He had fallen into a trap and found his position untenable.

In a blistering rejoinder, he accused Bardoloi of not using 'common sense' by rushing 'into print prematurely.' He said that his foe was welcome to take 'whatever course your conscience dictates. I never relied upon any support from you or your party, for the simple reason that you are not free agents and that whatever is ordered by your High Command, you have to obey it implicitly.'

Such words ring true fifty years later with pliant Congressmen bowing to the all-powerful High Command in New Delhi, whenever called to heel.

Saadulla struggled on until February 1946, when elections to the provinces gave Congress a resounding majority in Assam. It captured fifty-eight seats, including all general seats. The League had to be satisfied with just thirty-one, a sharp drop from the fifty-nine members it had in the earlier assembly. Rohini Kumar Choudhury's party was wiped out.

Clearly, there was no political space for two Assamese nationalist parties, only for the Congress.

In its manifesto, the Congress declared among other things that the political boundaries of the state must be demarcated on political maps on the basis of the Assamese language and Assamese culture for without it, 'the survival of the Assamese nationality and culture will become impossible.' It stressed its opposition to migration in categoric terms, pledging to stem the flow when elected. Decades later, it reversed these very policies: 'The inclusion of Bengali-speaking Sylhet and Cachar (plains portion) and the immigration or importation of lakhs of Bengali settlers on wastelands has been threatening to destroy the distinctiveness of Assam and has, in practice, caused many disorders in its administration. For an appropriate solution and redress . . . the Congress Party should be installed as the majority party in the Assembly.'

Meanwhile, Bardoloi savoured his victory: at last, he had come into his own.

Saadulla had been outflanked and defeated. It was to be the last of his major defeats at the hands of his bitterest rival.

The coup had succeeded. But now Bardoloi was to face his severest test: to save Assam from being sold out to Pakistani interests.

The Cabinet Mission was travelling to India to develop a plan for a united, independent India comprising both Congress and Muslim League governments. It was a time when Bardoloi virtually stood alone, with the moral support of Mahatma Gandhi, as other Congress leaders like Nehru and Patel tried to force Assam into a corner and fall in line with Muslim-dominated Bengal.

A NATION DIVIDED

The struggle to ensure that Assam remained in India was not going to be easy. Things had been complicated by rumours that the Government of India and His Majesty's Government at London had planned to carve out an independent state by joining the Hills of northern Myanmar with parts of the hill regions of Assam and what is now Arunachal Pradesh. The idea apparently was that, in the event of India attaining independence, the Raj would still have its officers keeping an eye from across the borders. But the placement would be so strategic as to look into five nations: India, East Pakistan, Myanmar, China and Tibet.

Gopinath Bardoloi fired off telegrams to Congress President, Maulana Azad, denouncing this harebrained scheme. He also apparently suspected some leaders in the Bengal Congress of having a hand in the mischief, for he declared that 'Assam would under no circumstances agree to go to Bengal in order for that a province with linguistic and cultural basis in terms of the Congress manifesto may be formed.'

He drew support from a British educationist, G.A. Small, who blasted the concept in a letter to a British parliamentary delegation.

Such a New British Province or Protectorate said Small, who had worked in education in Assam for twenty-four years, would mean that the Surma and Sylhet Valleys, abutting on each other, would go to Bengal and the Assamese 'linguistic and cultural identity must inevitably be swallowed up by Bengal.' He was very sharp about European and American missionaries who had travelled to the Northeast to convert, teach English and the Lord's Prayer. He described the American Baptist Missionaries, active in the Naga, Mikir and Garo Hills, as members of a mission who 'knew nothing about education, but only wanted to send home sufficient return of converts to guarantee their salaries.'

The suspicion of foreign missionaries ran deep in several Congress leaders of Assam, especially Bishnuram Medhi who later succeeded Bardoloi as Chief Minister. This dislike of outside faiths and their proselytizers, the inability to fathom the proud mind of the hill and plain tribes, to handle their concerns with sensitivity was to cost Assam and the Northeast very dear—and continues to bleed the region.

The Second World War destroyed not only German and Japanese dreams of world dominance, but also hastened the end of Empire, speedened the independence of India and created a New World Order with the United States and the erstwhile Soviet Union as the main powers. Other nations played second fiddle and a growing number of independent nations unsteadily stepped into a globe for which they were little prepared.

For the new British Government of Clement Atlee, Indian independence was a priority. To establish its bona fides as well as to assist in the task of the creation of a new nation, London sent out a Cabinet Mission, comprising the Secretary for India, Lord Pethick-Lawrence, Sir Stafford Cripps, the President of the Board of Trade, and A.V. Alexander, the first Lord of the Admiralty, in March 1946.

After a series of interviews with Congress, Muslim League and leaders of other parties, both provincial and national, the Mission organized a meeting at Simla of India's political barons to try and hammer out a constitutional settlement fair to all communities and parties. It failed to bring about a rapprochement between Congress and the Muslim League, each bitterly resentful and openly suspicious of the other, accusing each other of mixed motives, bias and untrustworthiness.

Two months after it arrived at Karachi, the Cabinet Mission announced its own Plan for the subcontinent.

It said that the provinces of India should be grouped into three Sections: A, B and C, which were to include provinces such as Bombay, the Punjab, the Northwest Frontier, Bengal and Assam, states that had a mixed religious composition. The Mission clubbed Muslim-majority Bengal and Assam together.

The Sections were to frame the constitutions of the provinces in their groups. Then, they were to assemble together and draw up a Constitution for India.

The Mission's announcement was basically a three-tier form of government. At the top was proposed a Central Government, to be followed by a Group Government (if the provinces in each group wanted it) with an executive and a legislature and a government for each province in each of the groups. According to Anuradha Dutta, 'A province could opt out of a group if the people of the province so wished, but only after the new constitutions had been framed and inaugurated.' [*]

'Further, Britain was to transfer power to India soon after the Constituent Assembly had framed the Constitution. Meanwhile, the administration of India was to be carried on by an Interim Government composed of representatives of the Indian political parties.'

The outcry was instantaneous and furious, across the country, especially in the Punjab and Assam. In the Punjab, the Sikhs and Hindus protested because their total population was far less than that of the Muslims and they would have had little say in conducting their own affairs. In Assam, the reason was similar yet different.

For one thing, the Assamese suddenly realized that Bengal would again play a dominant role in the relations between the two states. Bengal was dominated by Muslims from East Bengal and of the total number of sixty representatives that it would send to the Constituent Assembly, the Muslims would have as many as thirty-three. Twenty-seven were in the general or non-communal sector. Assam had a bare ten seats in the Constituent Assembly with three Muslims and seven general seats. Thus, for Section C, the balance was close but clear: there would be a total of thirty-six Muslim lawmakers to thirty-four of the general side. Predictably, most of the 'general' representatives would be Hindu.

The potential pattern was clear: with a simple majority, Bengal could over-ride Assam; and not just that, the Muslim members, with their slight

---

[*] See, Anuradha Dutta, *Assam in the Freedom Movement*, Calcutta: Darbari Prokashan, 1991.

but decisive edge, could ensure that the Constitutions of the provinces reflected their views.

According to Nirode Barooah, the Cabinet Mission Plan was aimed at satisfying the Muslim League. 'Instead of conceding Pakistan as such, a half-way house was created by grouping the provinces in such a way that at least two Muslim-predominated areas would emerge, representing the Muslim "Nation." It was precisely because of this that the Council of the All India Muslim League accepted the Plan declaring (6 June 1946) that the "germ and essence of Pakistan" was there.'

The news angered Assam and the Provincial Congress.

Bardoloi was in Delhi at the time and opposed the grouping scheme calling it 'sinister.' The Provincial Congress fired a salvo at the High Command, speaking of 'apprehension and misgivings' among the people of Assam. Bardoloi warned the Central leaders that his state would regard it as a 'great betrayal' if they went along with the scheme.

Although Nehru and Maulana Azad initially expressed their support for the Assam Provincial Congress Committee (APCC) position, they later began to waver and even hold Assam responsible for distancing them from power.

This was the time when Azad viewed the position of the Assam leaders with not a little exasperation. 'Jawaharlal agreed with me that the fears of the Assam leaders were unjustified and tried hard to impress them,' recalled Azad in his memoirs. 'Unfortunately they did not listen to Jawaharlal or me, especially since Gandhiji was on their side and issued statements supporting their stand[*].'

Sardar Patel also backed the Assamese at the outset. He wrote to Cripps at one point that the structuring of the grouping was 'a betrayal . . . (the British) interpretation means that Bengali Muslims can draw up the Constitution of Assam. Do you think such a monstrous proposition can be accepted by the Hindus of Assam[**]?'

Later, falling in line with the others, Patel sang a different song.

Assam's leaders took the position, and here it can be argued that they were

---

[*] See, Rajmohan Gandhi, *Eight Lives: A Study of the Hindu-Muslim Encounter*, Delhi: Roli Books, 1986

[**] See, Maulana Abul Kalam Azad, op.cit., p.55.

legally flawed, that a province need not join any of the groups and should be able to form its constitution independently of Central interference. The Muslim League said that this was ridiculous, that the whole concept of the groups meant that they would frame the Constitution and that later any province, dissatisfied with its lot, could opt out.

This sounded easier than it could be. Life, as all of us know, has a rather nasty way of becoming more complicated than we would wish it to be.

But Azad acknowledged that legal semantics apart, the League's approach was flawed morally and politically. 'Nobody can understand why the League placed so much emphasis on the question of Assam, when Assam was not a Muslim majority province. If the League's own criterion was to be applied, there was no valid reason to force Assam to join Bengal[*].'

Meanwhile, bloody Hindu-Muslim riots exploded in Calcutta as Jinnah, smarting at what he believed was Nehru's betrayal of the Cabinet Mission Plan, called for Direct Action Day on 16 August 1946 to demand Pakistan. The Muslim League rejected the Plan, within a few weeks of accepting it and also declared a boycott of the Constituent Assembly.

Lord Wavell, the Viceroy, summoned Jinnah in an effort to improve relations between the two major parties. While Congress could not set up a Constitution without the Muslim League, Wavell also told Jinnah that he was being unfair by trying to push Assam into a group with Bengal 'against their consent.'

The British Government, in desperate efforts to bridge the chasm, called Nehru, Jinnah, Liaquat Ali Khan and Baldev Singh, the Sikh leader and later Minister for Defence, to London to resolve the impasse. It failed and that December, London declared that the Cabinet Mission Plan was an indivisible whole and 'no party could accept one part of it rejecting the other.'

It also pronounced that in the Sections of Provinces proposed, issues could be settled by a simple majority of votes.

For Assam, this would be a total disaster. It was precisely what Bardoloi had feared and his concern overwhelmed him when he realized

---

[*] See, Transfer of Power Papers, Delhi: Nehru Memorial Museum & Library and the India International Centre, Volume IX, Document No. 52, 19 November 1946.

that Congress leaders in Delhi, so close to independence and power, saw him and the Assamese movement, as well as Gandhi's opposition to the group, as exasperating irritants.

Nehru, from saying things like 'in no event are we going to agree to a Province like Assam being forced against its will to do anything,' and that Assam could not be forced simply because 'Assam will not tolerate it under any circumstances,' began barking at Bardoloi for being so stubborn.

Bardoloi decided to confront Nehru and the powerful Central leadership head-on, as well as snub the Muslim League.

Knowing that his bastion of support, the Assamese caste Hindus, were as concerned about losing their lands to immigrants as going to Pakistan, Bardoloi decided to implement earlier government resolutions to evict migrants from forest reserves and other places where they had no business to be. Lakhs were turned out and Lord Wavell sent a message to the Secretary of State in Britain saying that this drive 'may well lead to retaliation against the Hindus in the Surma Valley.'

Sardar Patel, who had been so supportive of Bardoloi, told a group of Hindu Congressmen from Bengal that he was prepared to accept the British statement of 6 December which gave provinces in a group the right to control the destiny of smaller states by a simple majority vote.

The Intelligence Bureau (IB) got wind of this conversation from the Governor of Bengal who sent word of the meeting to Lord Wavell.

These are crucial passages of history for they indicated that the entire Congress leadership, barring the Mahatma and the Assam leaders, were prepared to sell Assam out to the Muslim League and Pakistan.

The intelligence report quoted the Governor as saying that 'this was definitely a climbdown on the part of the Congress; but for the good of the people of India, principles have sometimes to be swallowed for the sake of expediency. In a political game, compromises have to be made . . . surely the whole of India cannot be plunged into a civil war for the sake of Assam.*'

When the same AICC members met Nehru and asked whether he was not letting down Assam after giving 'high hopes to the leaders of that

---

* See, Nicholas Mansergh and Penderel Moon, eds., *India: The Transfer of Power 1942–1947*, London: Her Majesty's Stationery office, 1980.

73

province,' Pandit Nehru gave a curt reply saying that Assam could not hold up the progress of the rest of India. Support to Assam would mean refusal to accept the British Prime Minister's statement of 6 December and 'letting loose the forces of chaos and civil war.'

But Bardoloi was not going to give up that easily. He had one final card, apart from the unflinching loyalty of the Provincial Congress.

And he played it: the Gandhi card.

The Gandhi Card

In December 1946, Mahatma Gandhi was camping in Noakhali district, putting his dharma of non-violence to one of its severest tests as hatred, suspicion and bloodshed enveloped Bengal.

Gopinath Bardoloi, anguished by Delhi's double-faced stance and under pressure from the Assam Congress as well as outspoken organizations in the Brahmaputra Valley—including the students and lawyers—turned to a handful of trusted aides. ' . . . in Bardoloi's perception the only way open to Assam was to revolt against the Congress itself,' said a contemporary historian of Assam.

He was still the most clear-headed of the Assam leaders and that is where the significance of his opposition to the League policies of settling Muslim landless peasants in Assam lies: he saw in it the basis for a future demand for Pakistan. That fear was finally coming true, through the Cabinet Mission's proposals on Grouping and Sections.

To two of his lieutenants, Bijoy Bhagwati of the crinkled smile and gentle face and Mahendra Mohan Choudhury, short, cheerful and enthusiastic, he entrusted the most delicate and difficult of missions: to find the Mahatma, brief him on the Congress leadership's perfidy and seek his support for Assam.

Earlier in the year, another group, led by Dev Kanta Borooah and Pushpa Lata Das, had been entrusted the task of alerting Congress units and leaders in other states, especially West Bengal, of the potential danger in the Central leadership's moves.

The Bengal Congress leaders, on the whole, wanted to keep Assam in Section C to try and 'upset the Muslim majority there,' said Nirode Barooah[*], the historian. But Subhas Chandra Bose's brother, Sarat

---

[*] See, Nirode Barooah, op. cit., p. 49.

Chandra Bose, and Dr Syama Prasad Mookherjee, who founded the right-wing, pro-Hindu Jan Sangh later, backed them fully.

Other leaders were sympathetic in the United Provinces and (now Uttar Pradesh) in Bihar although Jawaharlal Nehru's sister, Vijayalakhsmi Pandit, was described by Borooah as 'positively angry with Assam's stand and considered it against the interest of the nation.'

This was scarcely surprising as she was, after all, parroting the line of her elder brother.

Another group led by Assam Congress leader, Mohammed Tayyebulla in Delhi met strong assurances from Central Congress leaders such as Sardar Vallabhbhai Patel and Maulana Abul Kalam Azad that they would back Assam's position. But they began, as we have seen earlier, to back off.

Bardoloi then got the Assembly to pass a resolution binding the ten Assam representatives to the Constituent Assembly (including the three belonging to the Muslim League) to take part in discussions on the framing of Assam's Constitution, to abstain from any meeting of a Section or group, oppose moves to set up a group constitution and take part in Constituent Assembly proceedings to frame a Union Constitution.

The League had no option but to oppose the move. And from then things began to fall apart very quickly for the British Government's pre-ordained plans of how India should become independent.

At the time, Nehru had taken over from Azad as Congress President and also had assumed office as interim Premier of a Central Government that included the Muslim League, with Liaquat Ali Khan holding the crucial portfolio of Finance. Liaquat Ali used his clout in this ministry to frustrate and shoot down Congress policies and programmes that originated from Patel, the Home Minister, and other ministers. All this led to a souring of relations between the two sides, which was not helped by the riots in Calcutta and the boycott of the Constituent Assembly by the League.

Bijoy Bhagwati, the Secretary of the Assam Congress, and M. M. Choudhury, the Secretary of the Assam Congress Parliamentary Party (ACPP) and among Bardoloi's trusted younger aides, travelled by rail, road and ferry to reach Gandhiji, then at a tiny village called Sewrampore.

Bhagwati, now in his eighties and well-preserved, smiled his crinkled, charming smile as he recalled: 'We sought time with Gandhiji and we were told to go with him on his walk at 3 p.m.' But they could hardly get a word in as the Mahatma walked and talked with 'a Sikh' they did not know. Then it was time for his bath and massage. But Gandhi summoned them to his *kutir* (hut) in the evening and read the short letter that Bardoloi had sent, briefing him on the developments on Grouping and the positions of the Central and state Congress leaders.

'We told him that this was the biggest test of our lives,' Bhagwati recalled.

The conversation[*] is best told in a transcript of the times that was published by the Assam Congress and used to back the state's case against the League and the Central command.

The Mahatma urged Assam to defy both the Central leadership of the Congress as well as the Government of India and what can now be seen as a clear call to secede, if not from India, then certainly from a paternalistic Central Congress. 'If Assam keeps quiet, it is finished. No one can force Assam to do what it does not want to do. It is autonomous to a large extent today. It must become fully independent and autonomous. Whether you have that courage and grit and the gumption, I do not know. But if you can make that declaration, it would be a fine thing . . . for the independence of India, it is the only condition. Each unit must be able to decide and act for itself . . . . It is an impertinent suggestion that Bengal should dominate Assam in any way.'

He advised Assam against going into the Constituent Assembly under the Grouping and Sections scheme. 'It should lodge its protest and retire from the Constituent Assembly. It will be a kind of satyagraha against the Congress for the good of the Congress.' Further he declared that Assam had made a mistake by following his dictates on the resignation of Congress ministries across India to protest India's involvement in the Second World War. It should have stood its ground, he remarked to Bijoy Bhagwati and M.M. Choudhury, and abided by Subhas Bose's advise that Assam was 'a special case.' ' . . . Although I was the author of that scheme of boycott, I said Assam should not come out if it did not feel like it. But Assam did come out; it was wrong.'

He then proclaimed his testament on Congress and dissidence: 'I have said that not only a province but even an individual can rebel against the Congress and by doing so save it assuming he is on the right. I have

---

[*] The complete text of Gandhi's remarks and his conversation with the Congress leaders is reported in Appendix B (II) of this book.

done so myself. Congress has not attained the present stature without much travail,' he remarked, pointing to how he had moved the non-co-operation resolution at a provincial meeting of the Congress Party in Gujarat in 1918, thus pre-empting and forcing the Central leadership to go along with his views later.

'Revolt!' was the Mahatma 's message. The original rebel against imperialism was calling on his wavering ranks to unite and battle their own leaders.

Gandhi's message irked the Central leaders, who were under greater pressure from Gopinath Bardoloi, once the news of the Sewrampore meeting came out. Younger Congressmen in Delhi from the state carried copies of the statement to newspapers and leading journalists.

Number 4, Feroze Shah Road, the flat where Bardoloi was living, became a hub of rebel activity.

Gandhi refused to back down from his stand. Leaders of the High Command visited Sewrampore to dissuade him. Nehru and other Congress Working Committee (CWC) members held three days of talks but he stood his ground and encapsulated it in a more generalistic statement of advice to the Congress with regard to constitution-making.

'It must be clearly understood that it is open to any Congress individual or his unit to declare his or his Group's or Province's secession from the Congress stand which the Congress should be free to accept whilst still openly guiding the seceding elements. This will be in accordance with the Cabinet's proposition that they will not compel any group or Province.'

The confrontation grew. So did the agitation against Assam's grouping in Section C within the state itself. Even non-Congress leaders of the hills of the state, such as the Reverend J.J.M. Nichols-Roy of the Khasi Hills remarked that the Centre was completely ignorant of the attempt of the Muslim League to capture the hills and plains of Assam. 'We know what the policy of the Muslim League is in Assam,' Nichols-Roy said. 'Even now the Muslim League in Bengal wants to send thousands upon thousands of immigrants to Assam and take possession of the land of Assam. That is feared by everyone. The people of the hills are afraid of the immigration and say they will fight it to the last,' Nichols-Roy added.

Gandhi's resounding advice, his refusal to bend to pressure and the spirited opposition of the Assam Congress, united under Bardoloi, and other regional parties representing other religious and ethnic interests, forced the Congress to ultimately change its stand.

More important, it forced the Muslim League to reconsider its position with regard to the Grouping Scheme and the Cabinet Mission's Plan to push it through the proposed Constituent Assembly.

The Muslim League and the British Government realized that the plan was unworkable.

But it was not for want of trying on the League's part in the province. Saadulla, under pressure from his associates, agreed to lead a anti-Bardoloi agitation, based on the anger and fear among the immigrants over their evictions from agricultural land as well as from reserved forests and common grazing grounds.

The non-co-operation movement by the League in March 1947 created tension in several areas but lacked the drive and momentum of an enthused campaign. Saadulla seemed lukewarm over the whole thing, describing his irritation over the fact that he was hustled into the agitation in strong words to Jinnah. 'The position is hopeless from any point of view,' he wrote. Expressing his annoyance at not being consulted, he also pointed out that the people were not prepared for the movement. He said that virtually all sections of Assamese society had revolted against the 'Muslim immigrants from Bengal' and warned that a 'vigorous civil disobedience movement will surely mean much loss of innocent lives and destruction of property.'

Saadulla was thus, slowly but surely, distancing himself from the Muslim League's campaign. His words to the Qaid-e-Azam could not have been palatable for he remarked that it was immaterial if the Assam legislature and the province were intransigent and refused to be bracketed with Bengal in the Group and Sections. For, he declared, with communication being so tenuous, Bengal would continue to 'have a whiphand' over Assam.

Saadulla and Bardoloi sought to strike a deal on the Muslim movement against evictions, seeking a lowering of the communal tension in the Brahmaputra and the Barak and Sylhet Valleys, especially to investigate complaints about harassment on evictions. But it failed to get underway because of police firing on a mob of immigrants at Mancachar, near the India-East Pakistan border, in which ten persons were killed, and Moinul Huq Chowdhury, the secretary of the League's youth wing, was also arrested.

Chowdhury, one of the prominent votaries of Pakistan and opponents of the Assam Congress, later quit the League, joined Congress and rose to positions of power in Assam and later in Delhi, where he was Minister for Industrial Development in Indira Gandhi's Cabinet.

The League's agitation fizzled out.

Among those who were unable to drum up support was one of its most formidable leaders, a maulvi from East Bengal who had migrated to Goalpara district in 1928, Maulana Abdul Hamid Bhashani. He later rose to be the chairman of the Provincial Muslim League, a man whose rabble-rousing abilities combined with spiritual fire made him a powerful political figure—and to Congress and Gopinath Bardoloi, an implacable foe. His influence was strongest among Muslim peasants. His rustic background and mass base were viewed by the landed Assamese Muslim leadership, such as Saadulla, as a threat to their traditional role as representative of the Muslim community.

Bhashani campaigned for migrations into Assam and even had a settlement, Bhashani char, named after him. He was a bitter opponent of Saadulla, an Assamese Muslim; Saadulla often wasted no time in criticizing what he described as the greed of Bengali Muslim peasant leaders, driving out Assamese Muslims and tribespeople from their lands. The Maulana dismissed these accusations with contempt and was among the fiercest opponents of the Line System, which protected the indigenous communities from the onslaught of the land-hungry migrants.

But even he was unable to draw support for the civil disobedience movement: Bardoloi arrested him before he could get up to any mischief and when Partition came, Bhashani went to East Pakistan.

In April 1947, exactly four months after Gandhi had helped the Assam Congress to hoist the banner of revolt, Viscount Louis Mountbatten had a meeting with M.A. Jinnah. The Viceroy was blunt: Jinnah, he said, could not expect Assam in East Pakistan. 'In the east, I pointed out that he would get the most useless part of Bengal, without Calcutta, and if he wished it he could have Sylhet back from Assam.'

Earlier, the British Government officially announced the burial of the Grouping plan by declaring that the Hindu-dominated and the Muslim-majority parts of Bengal and the Punjab would meet separately to decide whether the province should be partitioned.

Final doubts were cleared by Mountbatten's remarks to Jinnah.

Assam was left to its devices barring a clause that a referendum be held in Sylhet, should Bengal be partitioned, to find out if it wanted to stay in Assam or go to East Pakistan. The outcome was rarely in doubt even though Gopinath Bardoloi and other Congress leaders accused the League of widescale fraud and intimidation of Hindu voters in the July 1947 referendum.

Thus, one month before India and Pakistan gained independence, Sylhet voted for Pakistan by a convincing margin.

The first major battle for Assam's integrity had ended.

Others were to follow.

After independence, Bardoloi's time was taken in helping to draft the Constitution as member of the Constituent Assembly, which also forced him to spend more time in Delhi, and in coaxing Delhi to understand Assam's problems better. He focused on its financial problems but found himself rebuffed by Delhi's political and bureaucratic mandarins even at that early stage.

Thus, as the drafting committee discussed the financial provisions of the Constitution, Bardoloi wanted a constitutional provision that would allow oil-and kerosene-producing states like Assam to get back seventy-five per cent of excise duties collected by the Union Government to make it part of the state's revenue.

This was rejected.

He sought another article that would enable Assam and other tea-producing states to earn seventy-five per cent of the net proceeds of export duty on tea.

This too was turned down.

However, he did win special assistance in the form of grants-in-aid to the state with regard to the administration of the tribal areas and the Scheduled Tribes. He succeeded in winning approval of a special committee that he headed to chart the future of plains' tribals and the Excluded Areas of Assam as well as of the Northeast Frontier (now

Arunachal Pradesh). The financial, legislative and administrative powers of autonomous councils to be set up in these regions, that included the Naga and Lushai (Mizo) Hills, the Khasi and Jaintia Hills and two other tribe-dominated districts were determined by Bardoloi's group.

But it bore within itself the seeds of revolt and bitterness that sprouted in the next decades, with demands for greater powers and separation from Assam by the Bodos, the Karbis and Mikirs.

Yet, the determination of the Central leaders to control the resources of the states meant that Assam, like mineral rich south Bihar where its impoverished tribes live, would always be resource-strapped. Thus it is that the sub-nations that make up India, because of the flawed ideological temper of Pandit Nehru and his contemporaries, riding roughshod over the appeals of state leaders, go with a begging bowl to seek alms from potentates in Delhi. Yet, it is these sub-nations that contribute the natural wealth and resources that make up the national kitty.

Bardoloi failed to win special status for Assam during these years as an underdeveloped state. Yet, in his struggle on this front, he won support from an unexpected quarter: Sir Syed Mohammed Saadulla.

The Assam's Premier's old foe, picked to help draft the Indian Constitution because of his legal acumen and brilliant craftsmanship—as well as his mastery of English—backed Bardoloi. Saadulla knew from personal experience that without special financial assistance and an understanding of the special problems that afflicted the Northeast, Assam would never become financially viable.

However, his appeal to colleagues on the drafting committee was turned down. It was perhaps the last time that the two men would agree on anything.

Bardoloi remarked in his diary in 1948, after Jinnah's death, that at a meeting of the state legislature at Shillong to mourn his passing, all those who spoke 'except' Saadulla made remarks of a 'non-controversial nature.' Yet one victory he must have savoured was the dissolution of the Muslim League in Assam in 1948 when Saadulla and his associates met at Guwahati and declared that in the changed political circumstances, their party had no role in Assam.

Meanwhile, Bardoloi's health was failing and time and again in his diary and letters there are reflections on death, on financial arrangements to make for his family and the need for medicines. On visits to Delhi, he was afflicted by sharp chest pains and always travelled with a doctor, who also was a good friend.

As a result, he offered to resign and wrote to Nehru that he had told the State Congress that he would not be contesting the next elections and that he should be 'relieved from my present responsibilities as early as the State Committee considered desirable.' Needless to say, it refused his request.

In the midst of bad health and losing battles to Delhi's new masters, Bardoloi found the time to let his free spirit roam. Instead of confining himself to debates and discussions in closed rooms, he once went to see a film on Marie Antoinette at a Delhi cinema. With a few friends, he drove to the holy Hindu pilgrim centres of Rishikesh and Haridwar and wrote about these places with awe. The Ganges was 'bunded' by 'huge dams', and the fields were criss-crossed with many streams and irrigation channels.

He was so exhilarated by the sight of the Ganges flowing free and fiercely at Rishikesh, near the Lakshman Jhoola bridge, that he wrote: 'I felt like rushing the heights where we were.'

In an undated poem, found among his many personal papers, Bardoloi wrote movingly of life coming inexorably to an end:

> *My last Arati, a song of resignation*
> *Will be at Your feet,*
> *An offering of sacrifice*
> *Sublime*

Till the end, Bardoloi remained an unqualified opponent of immigration from East Pakistan. Letters to Nehru and Patel denounced the continuing influx and urged a permit system for Assam—such as exists in Nagaland, Mizoram, Manipur and Arunachal Pradesh—to control people coming into the state.

This was rejected.

He even pointed out to Nehru that border authorities, which were Central forces, were so lax that in 1949, the Chief Secretary of East Pakistan and his family, accompanied by the Deputy Commissioner of Sylhet, visited Shillong and stayed there without formal permission.

Still, he found the Central leaders, especially Nehru, casual in their responses.

These disappointments aside, Bardoloi, who handled the Education portfolio himself, established Assam's first university at Guwahati, its first medical college as well as its first engineering, agricultural and veterinary colleges.

It was a burst of administrative and political zeal which was rarely seen again in Northeastern India. His last days also were troubled by the growth of the Assamese-Bengali divide with riots over the language issue after Bengalis in Cachar opposed the government's move to make Assamese the state language. These riots set the tone for future violence in the 1960s between these communities on this and similar issues.

Yet, after all, where else can Assamese be the state language? Surely not in Bengal.

Gopinath Bardoloi collapsed and died of a heart attack in Shillong in August 1950. There was widespread mourning for the man who had, virtually single-handedly, saved Assam from going to Pakistan. The Assamese called him 'Lokpriya' or 'People's Beloved.'

Into his shoes slipped his long-time associate: Bishnuram Medhi, the little man with a sharply pro-Assamese bent of mind, a figure who was perhaps unknowingly responsible for letting loose some of the forces of suspicion and division that now sweep the Northeast.

Within days of Bardoloi's death, Saadulla announced his plans to join the Congress and bring Muslims into its fold. But this did not last long. The suspicions that Medhi and the others harboured against the former Premier were too deep to overcome.

Saadulla was nominated to the Lok Sabha by Congress but he himself realized that it was a ploy by the party to banish him to Delhi. He turned down the nomination, citing bad health, medical advice and announced his decision to play a role in Assam's politics.

After a series of frustrating meetings and clashes with Congress leaders, Saadulla snapped his association with them, urged other Muslim leaders to oppose the party and fight the general elections and state legislature poll as independent candidates.

The story had a pathetic ending.

Saadulla's nomination papers were rejected by the returning officer as improperly filled. Most of his followers were soundly routed at the hustings. And the former Premier spent his last years in relative loneliness, in poor health, shuttling between the sprawling Saadulla Castle in Shillong and his home in Guwahati before he died in 1955. With Saadulla's death, a chapter in Assam's political history too closed.

By that time, Assam and the Northeast had begun experiencing the stirrings of insurgency, of mutinies by little men and women on the frontiers that would shape the region's destiny and its relationship with New Delhi.

The first shots of the first rebellion were fired in the Naga Hills by the followers of a wiry man named Angami Zapu Phizo.

Nagaland: 1,000 Years In A Lifetime

According to Naga legend, a person named Koza came from the east and after reaching Mekroma in Manipur rested for some time and pondered which way to travel. Ultimately, he prayed to his god for guidance. Suddenly a bird flew by and alighted on the horn of his mithun (ram) and then flew off in the direction of Khezhakenoma. In order to doubly check this guidance from above, he placed his walking-stick on the ground and the stick fell down, pointing in the same direction towards which the bird had flown. Koza took this to be direct guidance from the Spirits to continue his journey ... upon reaching his destination ... Koza found that a frog had brought a grain of rice and left it on a stone where it multiplied into two. After settling in the village with his cattle and presumably his wife or wives, Koza fathered several sons. A sacred stone where the sons scattered rice to propitiate and thank the gods, became a bone of contention between the young men who began disputing their turn to scatter the rice. Koza's wife then 'lit a great fire' under the stone which 'exploded with a mighty sound like thunder and the Power of the Stone left it and went to Heaven.'

As the number of Koza's descendants multiplied, they sought new land where they could settle. 'The people spread out in different directions and formed the different Naga tribes[*].'

In 1972, I was eighteen and living in London where I studied journalism and printing—a callow, uncertain youth—when one of my acquaintances, a young Naga named Kevi Levor, invited me to his home for dinner.

I blanched at the suggestion. For Kevi's father was Angami Zapu

---

[*] See, Visier Meyase, *Essay on the Oral Traditions and History of Khonama Village, Nagaland* [unpublished].

Phizo, the legendary chief of the Naga underground movement, and they had a home in Bromley, Kent. Kevi and I met at various functions and chatted sometimes about the Naga cause and his fear that New Delhi and the Indian Army would crush his people. He was studying international trade in London University and rarely talked about his father.

Therefore, when the invitation came, a literal bolt from the blue, a few days before I left London for India, it took me some hours before I could muster up enough courage to say 'Yes.' Would it be regarded as anti-national, I wondered, as I considered the meeting. Would it embarrass my relatives, especially those in national and state politics, who were nationalists to the core? Would Indian intelligence agents monitor our meeting?

The last was probably the most ridiculous of my worries for Indian agents learned only far too little and too late about Phizo's activities.

So, summoning what little courage I had, I boarded a train from London to Bromley. At the station in Kent, Kevi, who was in his mid-twenties at the time, met me in a small car, and drove me to a pleasant semi-detached cottage.

It was a small house, with little ostentation or show. After entering, Kevi said that his father was waiting in his study and showed me the way.

I walked in with some trepidation, not knowing what to expect: a fierce, tall man with a hatred of India and Indians perhaps?

The man who ran the most powerful insurgency in India at the time and whose people continue to defy India's military and political might nearly half a century after the first bullet was fired, was a little man, hardly more than five foot four or five inches tall, impeccably dressed in a dark, three-piece suit, sitting in an armchair and surrounded by what seemed to be thousands of books.

A photograph of a handsome and much younger Phizo, in traditional Angami tribe attire, looked down from one of the walls.

Virtually every inch on the walls was taken up by heavy, thickly-bound books. There were some Naga artifacts, such as spears and shawls. And surrounded by this cocoon of knowledge and study, the legend of Nagaland sat quietly, watching me.

Another striking thing about him was the paralysis on the left side of his face. Phizo was very conscious of this and took great pain, in most of his appearances and photographs, to be seen with the non-paralyzed side.

From that little house, Phizo had lobbied British Parliamentarians, businessmen and newspapers. He got support from the Observer group of newspapers that wrote extensively about human rights violations in Nagaland by Indian security forces and also about the right of the Nagas to form their own sovereign nation, free from Indian domination and interference. He lobbied the United Nations too from here and kept in touch with events back home through an intricate network of informants and agencies that stretched from Britain through Europe, Pakistan, (West and East at the time), Myanmar and of course, New Delhi and Nagaland.

I do not remember all the details of the conversation but parts of it still stand out. We spoke for nearly three hours in his library and over dinner, where his daughter, Adino, who took care of him, spoke bitterly against Indira Gandhi: 'We cannot trust her,' she said.

But Phizo did say then to me that Assam, like Nagaland, did not belong to India. 'How many Assamese are there in Britain?' he wanted to know. I hazarded a guess at several hundred. That was probably still too high a figure but his reaction was instant: 'That is an army!'

'The Assamese must get out of India: what has Delhi done for you? It has exploited your resources and one day they will turn their soldiers and guns against you as they have done to us,' he said. 'Assam and Nagaland must be together, otherwise they will suffer separately. Together we can face India.'

I gave the common response, because I knew little better at the time, that the Northeast would remain an integral part of India, especially Assam, because of traditional bonds and the power of the Indian State. Many years later, I am not that sure any more.

Phizo could speak some Nagamese and talked of that as one link between Assam and Nagaland. Nagamese is a pidgin language, a cheerful, rough and ready lingua franca for the hill peoples and their plains counterparts, to communicate, however crudely with each other. Thus, as a dear friend from Nagaland said to me some years ago in an illustration of Nagamese, '*Moin theng mari* Kohima *loi jaam*.' Literally translated this means a bewildering and funny 'I will kick my way to Kohima.' What he meant was that he planned to walk to Kohima. In Assamese, it would be '*Moin* Kohima *loi khuj karhee jaam*.'

At dinner, Phizo spoke with respect for Bimala Prasad Chaliha, Chief Minister of Assam for thirteen years who had negotiated with the underground as far back as 1956 as a leader of the state Congress. Chaliha who had recently died, was also one of the three-man Peace Mission of the 1960s, comprising Jayaprakash Narayan and the Reverend Michael Scott, who tried to bring about a reconciliation between the Indians and the Nagas. It failed, not because of lack of trying, but because of Scott's open siding with the rebels and the government's growing impatience with the mission's ineffectiveness.

'Mr Chaliha understood us, he was a man of honour,' said Phizo, dismissing the other Indian leaders and politicians from Assam as figures of little stature and with little understanding of the Naga imbroglio.

Phizo was a man of great passion—for the cause of Naga independence—and bitterly opposed even the thought of Indian dominance in any sphere of the life of his people. That later his Naga National Council (NNC) was sidelined by the heavily armed and ideologically separate National Socialist Council of Nagaland (NSCN) did cause him concern and bitterness.

A description of the man by Nari Rustomji, one of the truly great and unassuming administrators of India, a Parsi who gave the best years of his life to the far-flung reaches of the Northeast many thousands of kilometres from the warm shores of Bombay and home, is among the most faithful sketches of this sense of mission. Rustomji himself loved the hills, although he now lives with his wife and daughter in Bombay, recuperating from a stroke.

'What struck me about Phizo was his extraordinary thoroughness and pertinacity. He was around with neatly typed, systematically serialised copies of all documents relevant to the Naga problem and he gave the impression of carrying, single-handed, in his little briefcase, the destinies of the Naga people.'

The United Liberation Front of Asom (ULFA)) and its acolytes were not even conceived at the time. Assam had just been reorganized with Meghalaya being carved out of the Khasi, Jaintia and Garo Hills to placate the simmering grievances of those hill communities for a separate state; Manipur had been converted into a full state from a Union Territory; the former North East Frontier Agency (NEFA) had been renamed as Arunachal Pradesh with a legislature and the status of a Union Territory in an effort to bring it out of the "Stone Age" to modern times.

The Naga campaign for independence ebbed and flowed; the Mizo demand for independence continued to trouble the Lushai Hills pinning down thousands of Indian Army and paramilitary soldiers.

Yet there was no hint of a demand for secession in Assam, the mother state of the Northeast.

But Phizo was far-sighted. He knew, instinctively, better than anyone else in India, leave aside the Northeast and his fiefdom of Nagaland, that such a time of turmoil would come to the Northeast when the 'mainstream' community—the Assamese—would finally look to the Naga example as a way of drawing national and international attention to its condition.

I was an impressionable teenager with some knowledge of the area and of national and international politics. For some days, I turned this concept of alliances between ethnic groups in the Northeast over in my mind. Later, after reflection, I dismissed such co-operation as not possible, simply because of the deep distrust that divides communities.

The co-operation did not take place at the ground level but it is now increasingly happening, despite tribal differences and disputes over money and arms, among the insurgent groups of the area.

To an extent, if one looks at the troubled Northeast these days, Phizo's assessment was certainly better than mine. So was his analysis, if it is taken across India.

Witness the growing demands of the indigenous, aboriginal people for control over their own affairs, to carve out their own states, whether it is Bodoland in Assam, Jharkhand in parts of mineral-rich Bihar, Madhya Pradesh and Orissa, Vidharbha in Maharashtra and Uttarkhand in the hills of Uttar Pradesh.

There is one memory of that meeting that remains particularly sharply etched. Phizo delighted in taking his visitors unawares. Suddenly, in the middle of the meal, as I was sampling the salad, he looked up and asked: 'What is the Assamese name for cucumber.' It was so surprising a request—perhaps it was one of the vegetables he was especially fond of—that I was caught totally off-guard. I mumbled something before collecting my thoughts and responding with the right answer.

I never met Phizo again. He remained in the news and never let go of his commitment to a free Nagaland. This came through particularly in his brief and famous meeting with Prime Minister Morarji Desai in London in 1978. Desai, a puritanical nationalist who succeeded Indira

Gandhi after voters threw her out for the authoritarian internal Emergency (1975–1977), met Phizo and rebuffed him fiercely. At one point, a purported tape of the encounter had the Premier as saying, 'Yes, I will exterminate all the Naga rebels. There will be no mercy.' Recordings of the ill-prepared, ill-fated meeting reached the Naga Hills in their thousands.

It was an unpleasant confrontation but one that was fated to happen.

Eighteen years after our meeting in the quiet cottage in Kent, Phizo was dead. His body was brought to Kohima where it lay in state at the main stadium, near the state assembly buildings.

Tens of thousands of mourners filed by the coffin of India's first great rebel. The entire Cabinet, top officials of the state, *gaonburas* (village headmen), relatives, supporters and friends stood and watched this spontaneous outpouring of support and grief. There were few dry eyes in Kohima on that day in 1990.

Phizo's daughter, Adino, and son, Kevi, sought to claim the mantle of leadership that he had worn unchallenged for many years, until his one-time aides turned against him and split the Naga National Council to form the National Socialist Council of Nagaland. Yet, Adino and Kevi too faced opposition from within the NNC, including fellow exiles in London.

In his death, Phizo won the dignity and honour that was denied to him all his life by the Indian Government. It was a fitting irony.

His body was brought from London in a commercial flight and taken in a slow, dignified procession to the local stadium, covered by the NNC flag. It was in death, finally, that Phizo attained the position, even unwittingly in the eyes of the government, that he had always had in the hearts and minds of his people: that of a head of state, a sovereign ruler.

But he would hardly have been surprised: after all, the key ministry that dealt with Nagaland for decades was *not* the Home Ministry of the Government of India but its External Affairs Ministry. Men like T.N. (or Tikki) Kaul lorded it over the distant Northeastern tracts, ranging from the borders of Tibet to Nagaland, formulating policy, devising strategy, meeting leaders, doling out funds and recommending changes. The

Foreign Ministry's views on the Northeast often irritated the Brahmaputra Valley leaders who felt that the parent state was being ripped apart.

Till the end, Phizo maintained that the Nagas were not an Indian or subcontinental community, that their roots lay in Southeast Asia and beyond.

The scholar, Visier Meyase, also from Phizo's ancestral village, Khonoma, and a member of the powerful and mobile Angami group says that the Nagas are probably a wandering community of Mongolian—probably Chinese—origin that migrated from China in the pre-Christian era and wended their way from Southeast Asia across the Patkai range that curves across Myanmar's north and west and into their present abode.

He traces too their origin to one common village, Khezhakenoma, and points out that many major tribes such as the Angamis, Chakesangs, Semas and Lothas have branched out from this original home.

Another prominent scholar from Nagaland, H.Horam remarked that from 'their myths and legends one gathers that there is a dim relationship with the natives of Borneo in that the two have a common traditional way of head hunting; with the Philippines and Formusa (Taiwan) through the common system of terrace cultivation; and with the Indonesians, as both use the loin loom for weaving cloth.'

In visits to Laos and Vietnam in the mid-1970s, Meyase found similarities in dress and food habits among the hill peoples of those countries and some Naga tribes. There are magnificent stories, as befit these proud people, of their origins.

These tales and strong oral traditions have a resonance of other nationalities and cultures. To my mind particularly springs a comparison with the stories of the native Indians of America, the Lapplanders of Scandinavia and the aboriginal peoples of Australia and New Zealand. There is a sweep in the tapestry, a swirl of strength, divinity and earthy humour and common sense that gives these tales a universal relevance.

Myth, legend and history merge beautifully into a spell of oral storytelling, for Meyase's relatives and clan-people in Khonoma, a historic, sturdy village strategically straddling a belt of hills and dropping steeply along terraced ricefields into a deep and small valley. It is an ideal location for conducting both guerrilla warfare and for defensive action: it has been used for both in recent and earlier times.

Khonoma is virtually impregnable because the village has good sources of water and food that are normally unreachable by an alien force. An unrestricted view of the heights give warriors in Khonoma a good look at anyone approaching their stronghold.

These days, it is connected by a narrow road to Kohima, the state capital. As one enters Phizo's territory, there are memorials to Naga 'martyrs' who fought Indian troops on the roadside as well as forests of silver oak and alders that clothe the hill slopes.

The most prosperous and powerful of the tribes were the Angamis, Phizo's community, which had a tradition of fierce independence allied to sophisticated agricultural and water use practices. This reduced hunting to a supplementary activity, not the main, and settled agriculture gave them a strong economic base to build their suzerainship over other tribes. They sought and often received tribute from other tribes. Refusal to pay tribute was met with sharp retribution: villages were razed, villagers were enslaved, property was confiscated.

One strong group that the Angamis were often at war with were the Dimasa Kacharis, the forerunner of the Bodo tribe, who were among the earliest settlers of the Northeast. The Kacharis conducted an extensive empire in Assam with their capital at Dimapur, the major trading and transport centre for Nagaland these days, a sprawling, messy, crowded, corrupt town that abuts the Assam plains.

War and peace between the Angamis and Dimasas with either group raiding each other's territories and capitals, extracting tribute, taking prisoners, continued intermittently over many years. Yet they intermarried as well and learned from each other's military and administrative skills and strategies.

The Nagas clashed too with the Ahom Raja Sukhapa, who came to Assam, via the Naga hills in the thirteenth century. They were routed by the invaders who later established themselves in the Brahmaputra Valley, ousting the Dimasas and other smaller kingdoms, unifying much of present-day Assam and extracting tribute from the Naga Hills and other groups on the edges of the valley.

The Angamis and the other Naga communities were thus never under any direct Indian ruler's control or jurisdiction. They developed a rudimentary but effective form of democracy with headmen ruling on local disputes after discussing the problem openly. The form of governance was light and almost unstructured, giving the village a right to an open and free life, but had a fountainhead of authority, under the all-powerful chief and his *goanburas*.

Young men and boys attended *morungs*—as do adolescents and young males in the tribal belts of central and western India; these are traditional institutions and dormitories where the young are taught the virtues, culture and traditions of the tribe and clan by village elders. At festivals and special occasions, the village's history is narrated and discussed.

The British, after their conquest of Assam in 1826 and the Treaty of Yandaboo with the Burmese king, decided that they would not allow the tribes from the hills to continue with one of their favourite pastimes: raiding and looting plains' villages and outposts.

The first British contact with the Nagas was in 1832 when an army of 1,500 men, including 800 coolies, led by two English army officers, visited the Angami region. The Angamis resisted, fearing conquest, but the British managed to explore the area, fending off attacks with their superior weaponry.

When the former Ahom king, Purandhar Singha, gave a grant of land to the British East India Company that bordered the Naga region, the British used it as a base to launch more expeditions over the next fifty years.

A temporary truce was arrived at with some Angamis and the Nagas agreed to pay tribute. But the British desire for full control was unfulfilled. It took the massacre of a group of Indian sepahis or sepoys in 1847 to touch off a renewed campaign against the Nagas.

But again the British were divided on the issue of non-intervention with the tribes. An expedition to avenge the killing of an Indian representative and the soldiers led to the fall of Khonoma after a prolonged siege.

The policy of non-interference was invoked again and Lord Dalhousie, the British Viceroy of the time, called for the withdrawal of troops and declared that New Delhi should 'not meddle in the feuds and fights of savages; encourage trade with them as long as they are peaceful towards us' and cut off trade relations as soon as they become 'turbulent or troublesome.'

This policy was overturned by a British officer, Colonel Johnstone, who defied instructions from his government and drove a strong campaign through the heart of the hills into Kohima, which was taken without much of a fight and settled as the administrative headquarters of the Naga Hills.

But the Angamis still refused to give up.

They were insulted by the British demand that Nagas carry the luggage and provisions of various expeditions. The Naga attitude was simple: 'This is our land and we need not help you or be paid for our help by outsiders.' At gunpoint many were forced to help in mapping and geographical expeditions. But the resentment burned deep at being used like coolies. All it needed was a spark to ignite that anger.

The spark came soon in the anger felt against being forced to pay taxes to an alien race whose ruler they had not even seen.

The final battle was to be fought by Phizo's ancestors and began at Khonoma where the Angami clans gathered to 'send back the White Man back to where they belonged for once and all.'

Khonoma struck first and drew blood. A British official who went there to collect taxes was killed. His escort of eighty soldiers was badly thrashed, suffering thirty-five dead and nineteen wounded. It was not for several days that the survivors managed to reach Kohima and give the news.

The British were enraged and summoned forces from all outposts in Assam to muster for an assault on Khonoma.

The insult had to be avenged.

Meanwhile, the victors at Khonoma too were preparing to attack Kohima. They had been hugely encouraged by their swift win in their home fortress. But they delayed the attack, losing crucial days in feasting, celebrating their victory and burying their dead.

Had the Nagas not wasted those two weeks, they could have changed the course of their history and that of the Northeast.

They did finally attack on 23 October 1879, surrounding the British garrison at Kohima, frightening their enemies with war cries and howls, staying out of firing range yet advancing surely and slowly by erecting barricades and digging trenches. The Angamis snarled their scorn at the defenders. One amongst the British recorded their barbs: 'We had come here and occupied their lands, we had cut their trees, bamboos and grass. We wanted revenue from them and made them coolies . . . what will happen now.'

The Nagas would have overwhelmed the vastly-outnumbered force cowering in Kohima had it not been for the arrival of British troops from

Manipur under the ubiquitous Colonel Johnstone. The Nagas retreated to Khonoma where they made their final stand.

The second battle of Khonoma was bitter and bloody and the Nagas were defeated. The villagers were dispossessed of their homes and farms and reduced to the 'condition of homeless wanderers.' Many died of sickness and lack of food. The village itself was destroyed and many of the resisters were summarily punished and imprisoned.

To the Nagas, the battles of Kohima and Khonoma remain an inspiration. A century later, descendants of those warriors honoured their forbears at a special ceremony at the village:

It is one hundred years now since they fell. But they are not forgotten. Their names are still remembered and cherished and their deeds talked about and sung in ballads. . . . our heroes . . . made the supreme sacrifice in defending their fatherland and our honour, the heroes who died so that we might be free.

That call to freedom, that spirit of liberty endures in the homes and terraced fields of Khonoma even today. No matter how hard the Indian Government and its lackeys try, that spirit, embodied in Phizo's vision, cannot die.

Khonoma's people have rebuilt and renewed their village twice. Once after the British destroyed it. The second time after Indian security forces, searching for Phizo and his supporters, sacked and ravaged it.

The village is dominated by a magnificent church, of great stone slabs, built by the villagers. It stands above the main lane of cottages, its spire soaring into the sky, a symbol of reverence, defiance, of the integrity and inner strength of its people.

When the Indian soldiers attacked, to crush the pro-independence revolt, Khonoma's inhabitants—as those of hundreds of other Naga hamlets—were forced to flee the crackdown in the biting cold of winter.

The refugees included our historian from Khonoma, Visier Meyase, and his family.

Nari Rustomji[*] who single-handedly administered the North East

---

[*] See, Nari Rustomji, *Imperilled Frontiers: India's North Eastern Borderlands*, Delhi: OUP, 1983.

Frontier Agency, an area of 50,000 square miles, in the 1950s, describes the period of the crackdown as a 'dark and senseless' part of India's history. There was extreme brutality, first from the Indian Army side because the soldiers were ordered to soften up the Nagas. Their opponents retaliated strongly and 'it was not long before it was a matter of doubt as to who was softening whom.' The crackdown followed nearly ten years of hesitancy and uncertainty in the relationship.

In the mid-1940s, Phizo had returned to his homeland after a stint in Myanmar with the Japanese where he had worked with the invading army, hoping it would throw off the yoke of British control and give his people freedom. In him, the Nagas had found their spokesman and Phizo championed their cause ceaselessly, fearlessly, almost fanatically, some would say. He edged out the moderates in the Naga National Council and placed his men in control of the organization. His nephew, T. Sakhrie, was the cool, level-headed secretary, competent and articulate, an ideal foil to the blustering Phizo.

Phizo led a delegation to Delhi in 1947 to meet with Mahatma Gandhi and press the Naga claim for independence. His account says that Gandhi backed him and opposed any force in securing the loyalty of the Nagas to India.

During this period, as Gopinath Bardoloi and his colleagues were struggling to keep Assam in the Indian Union, Sir Akbar Hydari, the Governor of Assam, took a step that deepened the controversy about the Nagas.

Sir Akbar signed a nine-point accord with the Naga National Council which recognized the right of the Nagas 'to develop themselves according to their freely expressed wishes.' It looked at all areas of governance, including judicial matters (all cases were to be decided by customary Naga courts), sought to control laws passed relevant to the Naga Hills either by the state of Assam or the Centre, to levy taxes and to hold all land with the Nagas.

The last clause was the most controversial: after ten years of the agreement's implementation, 'the Naga National Council will be asked whether they require the above agreement to be extended for a further period, or a new agreement regarding the future of the Naga people arrived at.'

Yet, despite this accord, Phizo and the NNC wasted no time in embarrassing the Government of India: they proclaimed Naga independence on Pakistan's independence day: 14 August 1947. Ostensibly, New Delhi did not take much notice of this slight but it would not forget the incident.

A look at the accord shows that the language leaves little room for doubt. It is very specific: either the agreement is renewed or there will be a fresh one after ten years regarding the future of the Nagas. No such accord, embracing all the Nagas, has been negotiated. Only piecemeal accords have been signed with one insurgent faction or another.

And even if the Government of India and the Nagaland state government renounce the Hydari agreement as non-binding, they cannot wish away the fact that to many Nagas it remains a solemn pledge that remains to be fulfilled.

On 9 July 1948, Phizo was arrested for his anti-India campaign and taken to Calcutta. He was released after his wife was injured and his infant son killed in a car accident.

A few months later, Sir Akbar Hydari died of a massive stroke and with him the Naga accord that he had negotiated. It was repudiated by Gopinath Bardoloi; his position was that the Government of India had not formally accepted the NNC-Hydari accord. He certainly was not taking the ten-year-period as one after which Nagaland would be allowed to go its own way.

But Phizo was undeterred. Step by step, he consolidated his influence and his network. In 1950, he was unanimously elected President of the NNC.

He and the party conducted a referendum where Nagas were asked whether they wanted to live in India or resume their separateness. The vote, according to Phizo, was ninety-nine per cent in favour of independence.

The Nagas boycotted the Indian general elections of 1952, in response to a call from Phizo. In the meantime, Sakhrie, Phizo's aide and nephew, alienated by his uncle's headlong rush to a confrontation with India, warned that the Nagas were ill-prepared for such a clash.

All this time, the Government of India kept repeating its formula for peace: maximum autonomy within the Constitution. It was a formula it would use with other rebellious communities across the Northeast and other parts of India.

As the days passed, the divisions between Sakhrie and Phizo began to flare openly and Sakhrie quit the NNC.

At a critical meeting in Khonoma, Phizo confronted Sakhrie and attacked him bitterly. 'You do not deserve to live,' he roared. It was Shakespearelike in drama—the story of the Archbishop of Canterbury and the King of England, who asked his nobles: 'Will no man rid me of this troublesome priest?' The first prominent moderate among Naga nationalist leaders was seized when he went to meet his lover at a village near Kohima. Sakhrie was tortured brutally and then killed. But, till the end, Phizo denied any role in the death.

After Sakhrie's death, Nehru ordered the army to the Naga Hills to crush the revolt. Phizo fled, first to East Pakistan—having been smuggled out of his beloved Angami Hills in a coffin* —and then turned up in Britain under a Peruvian passport.

He was never to return to his native hills, except, ironically in the very way that he left Nagaland: in a coffin.

Visier Meyase is a tall, handsome professor of history, with the most unprofessional air that I know. He could easily pass off as one of his students. Like many other Nagas and hill people, he has an uncreased, ageless look about him.

For decades, he has remained trim, despite fathering three children and, like many of his people, he does not openly show the scars of pain and deprivation that they suffered as children.

In 1956, when Phizo declared independence, the Government of India sent in its troops and one of its first military targets was Khonoma.

Many families fled before the village was overwhelmed. They included the clan of Visier Meyase, then a child of five. The families had little to ward off the biting chill of winter. They had little food, too, and often boiled roots and grass to keep hunger and starvation at bay. Rice was a luxury, given to them by other Naga families. Fistfuls of it were boiled with what little vegetables were found and then served out of a common bowl. The youngest ate first—and the most. The elders added

---

* See, Nirmal Nibedon, *The Night of the Guerrillas*, Delhi: Lancer, 1978.

salt and onions to their own quota to make up for the lack of other vegetables.

They fled by day and rested at night, often in secluded jungles and rock heaps where they could hide from their pursuers.

Visier tells the story without bitterness and rancour. But life in those days was a story of near-misses and frightening escapes.

One night, they were resting at a lonely spot, protected, they thought, by a cluster of high rocks. But Visier's aunt was woken by a persistent dream of pursuit and danger. She woke the others, most of whom dismissed her dream as unimportant. They were very weary, this pitiful band of seven, ill-clothed and undernourished, led by the tall and dignified Theyievizo, Visier's father, and the place appeared safe enough.

But the woman was insistent. They must move, she said. 'There is great danger here, we are in great danger,' she whispered urgently. The others gathered themselves up, complaining all the time, and reluctantly left their refuge. They went to a nearby grove of trees. Within minutes, soldiers overran the place that the fugitives had just left. The military men had been drawn by the pool of clean water which was available there.

After that the little sub-clan took their dreams and nightmares a bit more seriously.

After months of flight, the group learned that the confrontation had eased; they decided to trek home. The place had been sacked and burned as had many other proud homes of wood and stone. Visier's parents and relatives set to rebuilding their homes in the company of other villagers, log by log, frame by frame, slab by slab. As had their ancestors after the British sacked Khonoma seventy years earlier.

Today, the village is whole again.

And its renewal is symbolized by the great church of stone, logs and glass that towers over it.

Yet, the fires of independence still burn fiercely. Kevi Dolie, a cousin of Phizo, told me at the family's ancestral home that he still believed in separation and that the Nagas 'were not and are not part of India.'

Visier is now a scholar and historian of his people, having crafted a remarkable essay on the oral traditions of Khonoma and its Angamis, where he describes the republican character of the Naga villages.

Visier himself is of two clans: the Meyase and the Sanyu, both of Khonoma and among its early settlers. They practised terrace cultivation, far more sophisticated than the jhumming or scorch and slash, crop cultivation of tribes in nearby valleys and hills.

War in the hills followed Sir Akbar Hydari's ill-fated nine-point accord with the Nagas, Phizo's interpretation of it and Nehru's rejection of the predominant Naga view. And month after month, year after year, guerrilla fought Indian soldier.

Unlike today's modern fighters, who specially prey on women, make extortion their way of life and money their god, the Nagas were honourable guerrillas. They rarely molested women or looted ordinary people. That special virtue was left to the Indian Army and the paramilitary forces to display in full force. The rare attacks on civilian targets by the insurgents such as massive bomb blasts on trains and railway stations in Assam signalled a resumption of the fighting by the extreme elements in the 1960s.

Churches were burned, villages were razed, aircraft were used to bomb and harass the Nagas. Women were raped and continue to be molested even these days by troops, nearly forty years after the first shots of the Naga uprising were fired.

In the 1960s and then in the 1970s, a series of ceasefires were announced and then violated. In many cases, they just broke down as political leaders from either side failed to make any progress during their negotiations.

The army respected and even feared the little men in the jungles, experts in the art of ambushing convoys and patrols. 'You never knew where the shots would come from,' said a Sikh politician who saw action in the Naga Hills in the 1960s as an army officer.

As the years went by and Phizo's dependence on Pakistan grew, fissures began to grow among the men of the underground. These took a distinctly tribal turn with the Semas turning against the Angamis, Phizo's tribe, and capturing the main armoury of the Federal Government of Nagaland.

The bloodletting went on as guerrilla fought guerrilla and the government's intelligence agencies as well as its administrators nudged the suspicions and divisions forward.

Delhi's policy in the 1960s and 1970s was controlled by a handful of men and women. Prime Minister Indira Gandhi directly met with leaders of the underground when they visited New Delhi for negotiations. And one of her principal aides on the issue was M.L. Kampani, later intensely disliked by the Nagas.

Until the 1970s, the Naga problem was handled directly by the Ministry of External Affairs, and clearly perceived as a domestic as well as an international issue. Dinesh Singh, then Minister of State in that department (and Minister for External Affairs in 1993), often met with the Naga leaders during the talks.

Three prominent neutralists, Jayaprakash Narayan, a leading follower of Gandhi, the Reverend Michael Scott from Britain and Bimala Prasad Chaliha, the Chief Minister of Assam, led a Peace Mission to Nagaland to try and end the conflict. Their efforts failed after Scott went too openly toward the Naga cause and Chaliha found himself in an impossible position when Naga extremists attacked a train and a railway station in Assam in quick succession in 1967.

In the late 1960s, Indira Gandhi sent a cousin, Braj Kumar Nehru, to the Northeast as Governor of Assam and Nagaland. There were only these two states at the time: the others were union territories.

B.K. Nehru was a sophisticated Kashmiri Pandit who had worked in the United Nations and had been the Indian Ambassador to Washington. He told his cousin that he was not interested by the offer of the Northeast. But Indira Gandhi was insistent and he went.

When I met him, Nehru was still a handsome man of eighty-two. He was nearly blind and had to use powerful glasses to read ordinary script. 'I knew nothing of the place and it all seemed so strange, all these little groups wanting their own states and countries, I decided I wasn't going to have anything to do with these demands,' he recalled.

At a function on the lawns of Kohima's Raj Bhavan, Nehru was installed as the new Governor of Nagaland. After the ceremony, he was told that several underground leaders wanted to see him. The delegation shuffled in and presented the new Governor with his first problem: when was the Government of India going to call them to Delhi for negotiations? It was a legitimate question for until then, they had been shuttling between peace camps and the jungle as well as New Delhi where they were hosted by the Ministry of External Affairs at Hyderabad House, the sprawling government palace for visiting foreign dignitaries. Nehru was irked by the red carpet treatment they received and especially irritated by fellow Kashmiri T.N. Kaul, then Foreign Secretary and Adviser to Indira Gandhi on Naga affairs. Nehru resented Kaul's meddling.

The famous Nehru temper exploded.

As the Nagas, including Z. Ramyo, a Phizo aide, watched in stunned silence, B.K. Nehru declared that there were to be no more talks with Delhi over his head. If the underground wanted, they could negotiate with him or with the Chief Minister. Otherwise, there would be no more talks and the Nagas would face the full wrath of the Indian security machine, he added, slamming his fist on the table in front of him to emphasize the point.

Nehru won the support of both Indira Gandhi and the Home Ministry, pushed Kaul out of the negotiating line and placed New Delhi on a firm path of collision with the rebels.

The conflict continued relentlessly, even after the fall of Bangladesh to Indian forces in 1971 and the rout of the Pakistanis, the main supporters of the Nagas after China had thrown its support to the guerrillas in the 1960s.

THE LEGEND OF MUIVAH

The China front was opened by Phizo's trusted secretary, Thuengaling Muivah, a handsome man, who had also initiated the Kachin connection in northwest Myanmar. Muivah is central to later developments in Nagaland and, was a major figure even at that time.

In 1966, Phizo picked Muivah, then his chief aide, and sent him to the Kachin Hill Tracts to establish contacts with the Kachin Independence Army (KIA). The KIA had already been fighting for freedom from Rangoon's yoke for more than twenty years and Muivah was to establish 'diplomatic relations' with the Kachins en route to Peking, where he would be seeking greater support from the Chinese.

Two brothers, Zawtu and Zasein, controlled the Kachins at the time although they were later purged by a nationalist group for deviating towards Maoism and leftism. But Phizo, ever the long-term strategist, knew that China's support to the Nagas would last as long as Peking and Delhi were hostile to each other. It appeared that this diplomatic freeze would continue for many years but the old man of Nagaland was shrewd and realistic enough to know that the military, economic and political pressures on the Asian giants would compel them to abandon hostility and develop better ties. The Kachins agreed to assist Phizo's Federal Government of Nagaland with weapons and training for its cadres in return for money. That early contact between Muivah and the Kachins held good for many years and especially for Manipuri and Assamese groups in the 1970s and 1980s.

Muivah was a true trail-blazer of Asian insurgency. A student of St. Anthony's College at Shillong, he was among the few Naga rebels to have studied and understood Marxism and Maoism. Yet, nationalism and Phizo's mesmeric appeal drew him relentlessly to a destiny that made him, after Phizo, the most important of the true Asian rebels in the Eastern India-Bangladesh theatre of war and insurgency. And among its most feared.

On 5 May 1966, the then Prime Minister of the Federal Government of Nagaland, Scato Swu, sent a letter to the President of the Peoples' Republic of China that would transform the history of the Northeast and turn a battle between two unequal sides into an international arena of espionage, insurgency and conflict.

Swu appealed for help from the Chinese and their 'great and strong country' for the Nagas, he felt, could not fight the power of India unaided any longer. 'We look to your government and your people for any possible assistance in any force so that we may properly safeguard our sovereignty through the liberal hand of your people.'

The man chosen as the Naga Ambassador to China was none other than T. Muivah, described as a "plenipotentiary" in the official missive. Thinsolie Keyho, then a Brigadier in the rebel forces and later promoted to General before his capture by Indian troops in Bangladesh during the Liberation War of 1971, led the military wing of the delegation.

In those days, there were no direct air connections to China. It was still the forbidding giant of the East, going through the disastrous Cultural Revolution. Nor were there ways in which the rebels could fly to Singapore—as the ones of today travel—and then take a connecting China Airways flight to a destination of their choice on the mainland.

Muivah did it the hard way, through a great long march that took his people through the thick jungles of Arunachal, past Khonsa, into the territory of S. S. (or Robert) Khaplang, a Konyak leader of Burmese origin. Khaplang had set up the Eastern Naga Revolutionary Council (ENRC) in the 1950s at Phizo's beckoning. The concept was evolved by the Angami leaders and it helped develop the theme of the Nagas being a nation. Even these days, many Nagas—whether underground, middle ground, former underground or just plain Indian Naga—refer to Naga-dominated parts of Myanmar as Eastern Nagaland.

At each step of the way the Naga delegation was given an armed escort by the ENRC of Khaplang and then by the KIA, to protect them against Burmese government fighters. Nirmal Nibedon said they had to 'pay through their noses' for KIA protection and guidance and part with most of their guns before stepping into China.

The footslogging, the leeches, the dangers of the tiny jungle trails, the rainsodden nights were finally worth it. Three months after starting out in October 1966, across 1,000 kilometres of terrain uncharted by any other guerrilla band in the history of the region, Muivah, Keyho and their brave band of 300 men reached the Yunan province and Chinese border patrols in January 1967.

They were the pioneers of wars that have not ended.

The Chinese received them warmly, taking Muivah and Keyho to Peking where they met with other rebel groups, including leaders of the KIA. The military instructors at Yunan, where the bulk of the training was carried out, passed on more than knowledge of arms and guerrilla tactics. They spoke of revolution, Maoism, Chairman Mao's thoughts, a classless society. Many Nagas were appalled by the Chinese rejection of Christianity although others were attracted by the materialism of Maoism and studied it seriously.

Later, Muivah went to North Korea and North Vietnam where he met leaders of the respective communist parties and watched their training programmes in sabotage, infiltration, exfiltration, developing local intelligence networks and conducting guerrilla wars.

In addition to his pioneering work in laying the trail to Peking and Kachin, Muivah was a superb draftsman, skilled in the arts of diplomacy and negotiation. But he could also be absolutely ruthless, said his critics, ordering the elimination of opponents without compunction.

Such is the legend of Muivah that he can probably walk around the markets and roads of Dimapur, the largest Naga town, and other towns in Nagaland and Manipur—as he has done—without being challenged by police officials or others. Intelligence officials say that most armed personnel posted to the area do not even know what he looks like.

But there is a dark side to the legend. Critics of the Naga leader accuse him of authorizing hit squads to execute political opponents in Nagaland and Manipur, and also of vendettas.

As a living legend, the power of Muivah has been far more difficult to tackle for the Indian Government than that of Phizo, who is dead and gone.

B. K. Nehru's approach to the Northeastern problems, especially those of its small communities, was unequivocal. He was against fragmenting states into smaller sub-states, into conceding by small ethnic groups, seeing in such concessions the death of New Delhi's control and power.

In one incident, he recalled, a young leader of a tribe that Nehru had not even heard of came to call on him. Upon being asked to identify the community, the young man replied: 'The Hmars.' The Nehruvian response was predictable. 'Hmars! Hmars! Never heard of them,' the Governor snorted. 'Well, what do you want?'

The young man patiently explained that his people were entitled to a separate district, not a state, because they were not getting adequate attention from Assam or Nagaland.

Nehru was irritated when he heard that the Hmars numbered only in their tens of thousands. 'That's not enough for a district, go and try and resolve your problems with the different governments and the local MLAs,' he snapped.

These days, the Hmars have been organized by the Hmar Peoples Convention, recognizing a decade-old truth that Delhi pays attention only when the ante of revolt is raised. The Hmars, including scores trained by the NSCN, have conducted raids in the North Cachar Districts, seeking greater autonomy and some even want a separate nation.

The unrelenting pressure of the Indian troops and the harsh life in the jungles in East Pakistan and then in Myanmar forced many insurgents to reconsider their aims. They needed time, a breathing-space and peace in which they could review their lives and their future.

At that time, Assam's Governor was Lalan Prasad Singh, a former Home Secretary of the Government of India, a tall, cavernous-looking man who enjoyed his pipe and wore a donnish look. L. P. Singh received word that a faction of the underground wanted to come to Shillong and negotiate peace. But they made one condition: that M.L. Kampani, the

Home Ministry's point man for the Northeast would be kept out of the negotiations.

L. P. Singh describes Kampani, a former army officer, as a 'blood and iron sort of chap' who had always advocated a tough line against the Nagas. The insurgents, led by Biseto Medom Kehyo, I. Temjenba, Z. Ramyo and Kevi Yallay, Phizo's brother, agreed to accept the Indian Constitution, lay down arms and return to a life in Nagaland, away from the jungles.

Crucial to that accord were the mediators, the Rev. Longri Ao, M. Aram of the Gandhi Mission and Lungshim Shaiza, who was married to Phizo's niece, Rano Shaiza. Kampani was used, L.P. Singh chuckled, as an errand boy to send messages to Delhi.

The capitulation by a group of the Naga underground—or 'hostiles' as they were described unsympathetically by Indian newspapers—in 1976 followed earlier convulsions in the movement.

In one major development, a group of middle ground leaders—or men who had been long associated with the revolt and also played a role in negotiations but had not been active in combat—decided to confront the might of the Indian State on its own turf, on its own terms: join an election to the state assembly, put up candidates and try and capture power.

The move, led by a sober, simple man named Vizol, electrified the Naga Hills and alarmed the Phizo group which tried to prevent a fracturing of ranks. But their pleas fell on deaf ears: the Vizol camp also was encouraged by the presence of men like S.C. Jamir, a former Parliamentary Secretary to Jawaharlal Nehru, who maintained contacts with Phizo during his years in power, and later switched to the middle ground. Jamir, Vizol and their new United Democratic Front (UDF) made simple but telling points:

For years, if not decades, the Nagas had not been properly represented even in their own state by people who mirrored their genuine aspirations. They had been deprived not just of power, and thus rendered impotent in the face of an onslaught that parties like the Congress actively supported, but also of economic facilities that would improve the standard of life in the hills.

There had been too much bloodshed; it was all very well to talk of a war without end but the practicalities of life under New Delhi Raj was somewhat different, the UDF realized.

Therefore, the UDF went to the polls in 1974, calling on Nagas to vote for it and that it would seek to bring about genuine reconciliation with the Indian Government.

The results were a cliff-hanger: there was no clear winner. Seven independent legislators switched their support to Vizol, prompting him to meet the Governor, L.P. Singh, and stake his claim to form a government. He now had a clear majority in the sixty-member assembly.

As L. P. Singh prepared to swear into office men who had at one time pledged to fight India, he was summoned to the phone. A call from the Home Ministry in Delhi, he was told. The message was clear: the UDF should not be allowed to form the government; it could lead to a political catastrophe—they could work against the interests of the country, they could openly support the insurgents, anything was possible.

L. P. Singh refused to be brow-beaten. To his credit, he realized that this was exactly the sort of thing that would undercut the UDF's trust in him and the Constitution. It would reinforce their suspicions about the Home Ministry and boost the hawks in the underground. The moderates would be destroyed by Delhi's errant stupidity and the political initiative would go to the radicals again.

He decided to call Vizol for a private meeting before the swearing-in ceremony. There in the Raj Bhavan, the Governor's House in Kohima, the pipe-smoking representative of India talked firmly but graciously with a man who had been closely associated with the rebellion against New Delhi. L. P. Singh said he was being pressured by the Centre not to allow Vizol to form the government. However, he added that he was inclined to back the UDF because it had a legitimate majority. And, he pointed out, that Vizol and his colleagues would have to take the oath of loyalty to the Indian Constitution.

The response was unambiguous: the UDF would take the oath of office, swear loyalty to the Constitution and pledge to do right by the people who had elected them. They would not create problems for Singh or embarrass him in any way.

A few minutes later, the first opposition government in Nagaland was sworn in. It did not last long and the government collapsed after defections engineered by the Naga Nationalist Organization (NNO), a pro-Congress outfit that was controlled by Delhi. J.C. Jasokie, a new NNO

Chief Minister, was sworn in. But within a few weeks, the UDF struck back—it engineered defections in return and grabbed a clear majority. This time, S.C. Jamir sought to form a new government as the UDF chief. The situation was becoming impossible and L.P.Singh proclaimed President's Rule, giving him virtually unlimited powers over the state, ignoring Jamir's request, in an effort to bring some stability around.

The Nagas had shown that they could play the politics of defection, chicanery and corruption—stories floated of legislators being 'persuaded' or 'induced' to join one group or the other—as well as the plainsmen. Vizol even accused his opponents of kidnapping several of his followers.

L. P. Singh also wanted to use his own persuasive powers with the underground and reached out to an earlier offer from Zashi Huire, a top underground leader. That offer had been made through church leaders to Vizol.

A few months later, Indira Gandhi imposed an internal state of Emergency and Indian forces were ordered to launch a fierce crackdown on Naga insurgents. The pressure began to tell—as did the part-success of the UDF experiment.

Offers from the underground to negotiate with the government came again. Early discussions led to a full-fledged meeting with L.P. Singh and his aides in Shillong in November 1975 and the signing of the Shillong Accord.

The accord was denounced by Phizo and Thuengaling Muivah. The latter called the agreement a betrayal and the signatories traitors. No one had the right to resolve the Indo-Naga issue, he said, on their own and that too within the framework of the Indian Constitution and nation.

But the Shillong Accord did achieve what Delhi had been seeking for decades: it sharpened simmering differences between the different groups in the underground. As a result, Muivah and Isak Swu, a close compatriot, eventually broke away from Phizo in 1980. Using Muivah's contacts of nearly fifteen years they established links again with the Kachin Independence Army and secured bases and support as well as arms and training facilities with the Burmese guerrillas.

This tieup had become necessary after the Chinese assured India in 1978, when the then External Affairs Minister Atal Behari Vajpayee visited Beijing, that they had stopped armed support to the Nagas and other insurgents in the Northeast.

Muivah and Swu established their National Socialist Council of Nagaland on Burmese soil. What one intelligence officer described as the 'mother of the northeastern insurgencies' had been born.

It swiftly ousted Phizo's group from positions and areas held for many years. With a harsh campaign of armed force and intimidation, it gained control over many Naga-speaking areas of western Myanmar. Differences among the NSCN groups led to another faction led by S.S.Khaplang called the NSCN(K). Both groups continue to have links with New Delhi and Khaplang's group visited the Indian capital in November 1992 on a secret trip to see if India was prepared for a deal.

The negotiations failed although the NSCN (K) indicated their interest in an Indian suggestion to act as scouts and trackers against the rival group as well as the United Liberation Front of Asom, the Assamese rebellion, which was showing signs of revival in collaboration with the Muivah faction. But India cannot come to a formal agreement with Khaplang because he is not an 'Indian' Naga; he is from Myanmar, and was born and brought up there.

The Hills Revolt

Ten years after Angami Zapu Phizo's men raised the banner of armed revolt against New Delhi, came the turn of the Mizos, natives of what was then known as the Lushai Hills. This area was even lesser-known than the Naga Hills, although during the Second World War, Allied forces used the route between Silchar in southeast Assam and Aizawl, a tiny hilltop hamlet, to transport troops, weapons and provisions to the war front.

That was one of the first exposures of the Mizos to the perils of modern civilization. But years later, the district slumbered on, under the paternalistic eye and benign neglect of successive Assam administrations. A few Mizos entered politics, associating with regional groupings such as the Mizo Union and the Eastern Indian Tribal Union, to promote the interests of highlanders. But their voices were few and muted in the face of political power which remained in the hands of plains-dwellers.

It took a natural disaster unique to the Mizos to break the cycle of neglect and lethargy.

THE MIZOS AND MAUTAM

Every fifty years, there comes to Mizoram a flowering of its vast bamboo forests which sprawl over its hills and valleys. The flowers heighten the rugged beauty of the landscape. But they are also the harbingers of starvation and death.

The flowering, the Mizos knew from bitter experience, meant that a crisis known as *mautam* was to follow: the flowers attracted rats like honey draws bees. Millions of rats swarmed the jungles and rice and vegetable fields of the district, devouring everything in their wake. Feeble efforts by local administrators to repel the ravenous hordes proved useless.

Mizo leaders appealed to the Assam government in 1959 for help:

the condition of the people was desperate, they said—the crops had been destroyed, foodstocks devastated, there was starvation because, with the loss of their crops, they had no cash to buy even the bare minimum for survival. Famine stalked the land.

Exasperated by the Assam government's failure to rush assistance in time, the Mizos formed a few famine-fighting squads. The most prominent of these groups was the Mizo Famine Front (MFF), launched by a young bank clerk named Laldenga. Laldenga was a man who took part in regular political discussions in Aizawl, a one-street town those days, which functioned as the capital of the district. He too dreamed of a strong and vibrant nation of his people, who had been lightly administered by the British in the nineteenth century and until independence. But, unlike Phizo, who made no secret of his vision, Laldenga kept his dreams to himself until he saw his chance in the famine.

To the Mizos, as also to other indigenous communities living in the hills and plains, land was their greatest and often their only asset. The failure of the land to produce, to feed them, was akin to death. And the Mizos, as much as any other community, loved their lands with an almost obsessive possessiveness.

The suffering caused by the *mautam* lasted two years, long enough to scar the kindliest of men. In order to help his people Laldenga developed a network of workers and supporters who distributed food and travelled to the remotest villages with relief and a message. The message was simple: the state and Central Government did not care for the Mizos and this was shown in its shoddy response to the famine; that the Mizo District Council, the main political forum, had failed to rally support at a time of crisis and was now unrepresentative of Mizo aspirations; that the area was integrated into Assam as late as 1898 under a political officer who acted as a representative of the Viceroy; and that the Mizos, like the Nagas,were a nation and deserved a place of their own, away from India.

The response was electrifying. Although older Mizos were worried about the possible consequences, Laldenga was unconcerned.

Eventually, the Mizo Famine Front was converted into the Mizo National Front (MNF) with independence as its goal. But the Indian Government did not take its threats seriously, believing that Laldenga had little popular support.

It could not have made a worse mistake.

All this time, Laldenga planned in secret, meeting with younger

Mizos, inspiring them and painting a broad canvas of struggle as he appealed to their fighting traditions. Arms were collected surreptitiously; the first group went to East Pakistan for weapons and returned under Laldenga's command. It was intercepted and Laldenga was captured in 1965.

Assam Chief Minister, Bimala Prasad Chaliha, aware of the sensitivity of the Mizos and battling the Naga conflagration at the same time, ordered Laldenga's release. He got little gratitude in return.

On 28 February 1966, Laldenga struck simultaneously at several places with Operation Jericho. Well-trained, young Mizo guerrillas overran Aizawl: the Treasury, the radio station and the police station fell into their hands. Lungleh, the other major town, was also swamped and the guerrillas had the run of the entire district. There was no resistance.

A stunned nation heard the news of the MNF's triumph over radio. And it was not for more than a week that Indian Army troops were able to break the rebel hold on Aizawl; it took another week to reach Lungleh and regain that little hamlet.

The Indian Defence Ministry retaliated with absolute fury, especially because the debacle came so soon after the 1965 war with Pakistan and the disastrous border failure with China in 1962. Air raids were ordered, for the first time in free India's history, on rebel holdouts within the country. Helicopters moved soldiers across jungle and vale in swift counter-insurgency operations.

India had suffered vast embarrassment and Laldenga was ecstatic. His men melted away into the jungles and hills of their homeland after the initial surprise to continue their fight.

Then came the move that has contributed as much to the alienation of the Mizos as any other single decision: the regrouping of their villages into virtual concentration camps by security troops under order of officials in the Home Ministry in Delhi. This meant that villages and hamlets, some little more than a cluster of four or five homes on bamboo stilts, were given two or three days and, in some cases, a bare twenty-four hours to pack their belongings and transported to unfamiliar terrain where they were dumped along the main road and told to set up new homes. Bamboo and thatch was provided and in many cases corrugated tin sheets for roofs. The aim was to establish new villages that would be under the control of troops but more important, to deny access to food, water and shelter to the rebels.

Tens of thousands of persons were uprooted and moved, within a radius of about twenty to fifty kilometres, to a settlement. The old buildings and homes were either torched, demolished or left to rot.

The destruction of this symbiotic relationship between the land and its people had predictable consequences. More younger Mizos, both men and women, joined the MNF, swelling Laldenga's legions and sharpening the outcry against Indian control. But it went deeper than increasing the number of rebels: it destroyed the structure of society among the Mizos.

Independent communities now found themselves dumped with scores of other families in a common village. Water, always a problem in the hills, became scarcer. The Mizos resented the permit system: all inmates of the camps or regrouped villages had to carry identity cards at all times, to clock into the village and to leave it. And they complained that the troops did little but harass them, often in a language—Hindi—that they did not understand.

Yet this did not stop the guerrillas from carrying on with their strikes. In one episode that shook the Indian Government—as well as regional officials—one of the top MNF marksmen walked into a meeting of top police officials at Aizawl, shot them and escaped in a waiting car.

Violence was met with greater violence and, although as in the Naga Hills, the Mizos followed a code of conduct by not harming innocent civilians or even the families of civil and military officials, the same was not true of their opponents.

Stories of atrocities: rape, extortion, destruction of property, damage to churches and illegal detentions abounded. The entire district was not under the control of the state government of Assam but under virtual military occupation, with little to prevent the troops and their officers from doing much as they pleased.

This part of India's wars against its own people has not received adequate publicity nor is there a large enough audience that knows enough about it. Suffice here to quote Nari Rustomji, the pioneering administrator of the region, on the violence let loose by either side. For, although he was speaking of the Naga tragedy, it is valid for the Mizo crisis, the Manipuri problem and the difficulties in Tripura and, later, in Assam. ' . . . this was one of the darker chapters in the history of the Naga hills . . . Fierce and relentless revenge was the main motivating force during this slack and senseless period. And when at last, from sheer exhaustion and the realization of the utter futility of it all, the curtain was lowered, there was no applause for either side. The seeds of hatred sown during this era of mutual brutality . . . have borne in the years that followed and up to this date the only to be expected fruit of deep-rooted bitterness and mistrust.'

I confronted that bitterness at my first meeting with Joseph Zokunga.

At the time, in 1970, Joseph led one of the best-known pop groups in Shillong. They were in great demand at school fêtes, senior class parties and at major musical evenings. With his beautiful baritone, this little, unhandsome man who always trotted, never walked, had girls swooning and men cheering.

One day, we happened to sit next to each other in a bus en route to Guwahati, where we caught a train to attend a students' conference near Bombay. We talked of general things and for some reason the conversation veered to his family and what they did.

At that time, Joseph was an intense, sullen young man and spoke gruffly, as if he resented speaking at all. But the words flowed out and I listened in growing horror and shame.

His father, Joseph said, had a little radio repair shop back home. He was uninvolved in politics but when the revolt exploded in 1966, along with thousands of others, the older man was taken captive.

For some reason, the soldiers who had seized him decided to force him to speak about his supposed underground connections. The frightened Mizo kept telling them he knew nothing, that he wanted to go home to his family.

And then came the sheer barbarity of it all.

'They pushed him to the floor and then they stamped on him with their boots, they kept kicking and stamping for a long time, and he kept screaming for help,' Joseph said, expressionless. They sent him back to his family after that, a cripple.

The entire family was, like thousands of others, thrown out of their village and forced into a regrouped settlement which Joseph likened to a concentration camp, with searchlights and soldiers on watch towers, armed with machine-guns.

The whole scenario was out of a Second World War film except that it had happened to this bitter man sitting next to me and his beloved father.

'Even now his body shakes and trembles, he cannot do anything properly,' said Joseph.

There was no Amnesty International those days to back the complaints of the Mizos, no Asia Watch to document the horror, however flawed and biased that documentation may be, no human rights groups at home to speak for the Mizos and their tragedies.

But men like Joseph conquered their hatred. They emerged bigger than the men who had tortured and fought them. And these days, he is the Director of the Music Academy at Aizawl, putting his magnificent voice and musical skills to teaching a new generation of Mizos the joy of song.

There are few experiences as touching, inspiring or moving as listening to Joseph singing the Prayer of St. Francis of Assisi, that extraordinary saint and philosopher:

> *Lord, I pray Thee*
> *Make of me*
> *An Instrument*
> *Of Thy Perfect peace*
> *Where there is hatred*
> *May I bring love*
> *Where there is darkness*
> *May I bring light.*

Men like him have gone through much tragedy; to hear them speaking of love and conquering hate is evidence that that they have found a secret that many seek but rarely find: the power of forgiveness.

They did not forget—but they did forgive. And it is in the telling of this story that I remember my reaction to it: a horrified, shamed silence. It is in the stories of people like Joseph that lies some hope for the Northeast and, in a broader sense, for our wretched, cruel, venal world.

In the meantime, Laldenga and his aides had been busy. They visited China and held meetings with Chou En-lai and the Communist leadership. They received word of support and the first bands of Mizos wended their way through the leech-infested jungles of Myanmar's Kachin Hills into China's Yunan province. The Chinese saw in the Mizos and Nagas an excellent opportunity to embarrass and destabilize their old enemy, India, as well as to keep the Northeastern ethnic cauldron boiling, bogging down thousands of troops in senseless conflicts that had no victors or losers.

As the years passed, China and Pakistan agreed that having the Mizos in East Pakistan for their bases and training would be a far more sensible arrangement than their long, dangerous treks, which lasted four or five months.

There were as many as seven battalions of the Mizo National Army, or about 7,000 men and women, heavily armed, most of them based in the eastern wing of Pakistan.

They were virtually given a free run, well-supplied with weapons and food by the Pakistanis. Laldenga lived comfortably in exile in Dhaka with his family and bodyguards.

One of his security officers was young Sangliana, the son of the only Mizo army officer who rose to the rank of Brigadier in the Indian Army and later led a fledgling regional party to victory: Thenphunga Sailo.

But the freedom that the Mizo rebels enjoyed in Pakistan was abruptly destroyed by the Indian Army's brilliant triumph in the 1971 war. The Nagas too lost this base for decades, until one of their leaders came to reclaim it in the 1990s. But for the Mizos, the Indian victory meant a more difficult struggle, especially as Laldenga and his family were forced to flee to West Pakistan instead of sheltering in Myanmar, as the Nagas had done.

The Mizos made it barely in time, on a small group of motor boats that roared desperately out of East Pakistani waters in the Chittagong Hill Tracts (CHT) into Myanmar. An Indian force, sent specifically to intercept the Mizos, missed them by a few minutes. The Pakistanis evacuated them later to Islamabad.

Laldenga survived but his power and influence over his people in the movement and at home, in the hills of the Mizos, began to wane. He was sufficiently concerned by this—and realistic enough to recognize it for what it meant: the end of the road. He agreed to talk with Indian intelligence officials at Frankfurt in 1975, having flown there from Islamabad.

In 1976, Laldenga decided to return to India and open talks with Indira Gandhi and her emissaries. From then, until the late 1980s when he signed an accord with Rajiv Gandhi, accepting the Indian Constitution, laying down arms and joining India's political life as a democrat and not an insurgent, he lived in a neat bungalow under, ironically, Indian Government protection, a short walk from Parliament House in Delhi.

Laldenga lacked Phizo's vision, charisma and unswerving dedication and integrity. But he was a shrewd manipulator and survived attempted coups by disgruntled MNF leaders, angry with his peace moves.

When he realized that he could not hold out against the might of the Indian military machine any longer, he did the obvious thing: struck a deal. He became Chief Minister of Mizoram in 1987 under the terms of an agreement with Rajiv Gandhi that enabled him to supervise elections to the legislature. Naturally, the MNF won handily and Laldenga retained his chief ministership.

But it was not long before there were accusations of corruption, favouritism, nepotism and inefficiency. Aizawl, like the other hill towns of the Northeast, was being defaced by thousands of ugly tin and concrete shacks that passed for houses. This was the legacy of 'modernization': former guerrilla allies of Laldenga raked in the profits as middlemen, contractors, builders and politicians.

Some turned against him, like Sangliana, the son of the saintly-looking Brigadier Sailo. 'I nearly gave my life for this man, I saved him so many times and now I wonder whether it was worth it all, worth all the sacrifice,' Sangliana pondered one evening at his father's official residence at Aizawl as the peace talks stuttered along.

In subsequent elections to the state assembly—for Mizoram had been proclaimed a state after the MNF agreement—Laldenga lost and his MNF has been in opposition for several years. And, ironically, Laldenga's elected government was brought down by a series of defections to the Congress Party: his jungle savvy and years of fighting against the Indian State did not quite prepare him for the astuteness of his Mizo foes.

There was one thing that jungle battle-worthiness had not prepared Laldenga and his boys for when they returned: how to adjust to life in peace. There were many cases of MNF cadres falling into acute depressions because they could not adjust to normal life and turned to drugs and liquor. Others went to the other extreme, collecting all the material goods they had been deprived of during the years in the jungles with a vengeance.

Few were able to maintain a balance.

And strangely enough, although the lives of Laldenga and Phizo did not run on parallel lines, they were fated to die within a few months of each other.

Yet, there was one crucial difference: Phizo, even in his death, continued to inspire Nagas to rise against the Indian State—hopeless though the fight seemed, and no matter how aware the rebels were of being outflanked, outgunned and outnumbered. On the other hand, the MNF's uprising against the Indian system died with Laldenga.

MANIPUR: THE MEITEIS ALSO RISE

It is said that the short and expert horsemen of the Manipur valley were the inventors of horse polo. Others dispute this, saying that the game originated in Gilgit, a mountainous spur in northwest Pakistan.

But Manipur, fenced by hills on all sides, is also a land of languorous dances—known as the Manipuri, where men and women enact the romance of Krishna, the divine cowherd, Radha and the gopis of Hindu legend—and of vigorous holi revelry, where people throw coloured powder and water on each other, as a further play on the Krishna theme.

Yet under a calm surface of lush green valleys and rich rice fields, of the sangai, the unique swamp deer that is on the world's list of endangered species but which, thanks to good conservation, is making a comeback, of elegant women in the sarongs and blouses of Southeast Asia cycling to work, Manipuri society has been riven for years by primordial hates and violence.

For more than thirty years, young Manipuris, especially the plains-dwellers of the Imphal Valley, known as Meiteis, had dabbled with Communist politics. There were revolutionary cells and students once even set up a group called the Revolutionary Government of Manipur. The radicalization spread even to the paramilitary wing of the state government with members of the Manipur Rifles revolting against their officers and the government before being subdued.

With the growth of the radical movement, came the questions that men like Phizo and Laldenga had put before their people: who are we? What were we before we became what we are now?

A movement against the Vaishnavite cult that had an ardent following in the Imphal Valley, the most heavily populated part of

Manipur, culminated with the open rejection of the faith by many young Manipuris. They called themselves Meiteis, as they were known before embracing Hinduism 200 years ago. Also rejected was the Bengali script which the natives said had suppressed their language and culture.

As with Laldenga, the Meiteis began organizing quietly. They began by seizing weapons from security troops, leading to larger ambushes of soldiers and more hit and run assaults. The soaring unemployment and the widely-held belief that much of the Central funds that poured into the state lined the pockets of politicians and bureaucrats fed the anger among younger Meiteis.

The first major rebellion was launched by another little man—with a difference. Unlike the Nagas and the Mizos, and even the Tripuris who proclaimed their platform as one of ethnic identity—this young man, who used only one name, Biseswar, did nothing of the sort.

Biseswar declared himself the Chairman of the People Liberation Army (PLA) and injected Marxism and Maoism into the movements of the Northeast, giving his campaign a larger canvas than those of his predecessors on the battle trail. He described the Indian Government as a bunch of bandits and called upon Nagas, Mizos and Meiteis to forge a common front and co-ordinate their military and political strategies.

According to Nirmal Nibedon[*], he pushed the Maoist line that revolutionary peasants should first be organized and then besiege towns and 'lead the whole people to a revolutionary war and to train them through a violent war.'

But Biseswar, as had Phizo before him, suffered from excessive vanity. He could not stomach opposition. A challenge from a factional leader in the PLA met with a hail of bullets from Biseswar's troops.

These differences aside, Biseswar propagated the classic Marxian theory that Indian workers were allies but the government at Delhi was the true foe of the PLA. It did not quite carry conviction, even within his organization, and the Manipuri rebel denounced even the erstwhile Soviet Union as the main betrayer of the Communist Revolution.

Biseswar's campaign drew the usual response from Delhi: curfews and troops, assaults on villagers and others suspected of harbouring the guerrillas. By this time, the Indian military machine was familiar with

---

[*] See, Nirmal Nibedon, *The Ethnic Explosion*, Delhi: Lancer, 1987.

ways to deal with armed insurrections in the Northeast.

But such was the fear generated by the PLA and another guerrilla group, the Peoples Revolutionary Party of Kangleipak (PREPAK), across the state with their ambushes and propaganda, that security troops patrolled Imphal by day and night on trucks with gunturrets, holding light machine-guns at the ready. The traffic thinned by early afternoon and government offices shut early. By the evening, the streets were empty and a pall of fear and suspicion hung over the city, broken occasionally by the crackle of gunfire.

The PREPAK group had different priorities: it spoke of no ideology but Meiteism and demanded an ouster of all outsiders from the state. Frightened settlers began to flee with their families, despite assurances from the state government and authorities in New Delhi.

Posters and handbills appeared in Imphal and other towns ordering all *mayangs* (outsiders) out of the state. Around the same time, a similar campaign was launched in Mizoram, sending convoys of shaken Bengalis, Assamese and others down the narrow highway linking Aizawl with the rest of the country.

The scare abated after some time but it was the precursor of a greater movement in the Northeast that was to change the face of the region.

Biseswar was captured by the Indian Army in the early 1980s when it raided a camp where the PLA Chairman was sheltering. At the time, Biseswar was indoctrinating his cadres in the subtleties of Maoism: the East Wind shall prevail over the West Wind and other assorted couplets that made pleasant reading but were drawn more from China's historic contempt for the outside world rather than any dialectic genius.

Although the PLA continued to function despite the arrest of its chief, it was never the same force again. PREPAK too suffered heavily in clashes with Indian troops and both the PLA and Meitei insurgents took shelter in Myanmar, in Kachinland where they received weapons and training in return for money from the Kachin Independence Army (KIA). But their views on Communism were vague. An American traveller who visited one of the KIA camps where he met with Thuengaling Muivah, as well as PLA leaders, said that the Manipuris appeared to have 'little knowledge' of either Marxist or Maoist theory or even jargon.

The PLA had to wait for another decade to get back its old

influence—though this time it developed a new image and identity, cloaking its separatist demands in Hindu religious garb. And Biseswar, who was once a fiery advocate of Maoism, turned away from Chairman Mao's Little Red Book during long years in jail.

In fact, he even contested and won an election to the state assembly as an independent candidate but did little of note during his tenure. Later, he apparently 'rediscovered' Vaishnavism and launched a campaign to protect Hindu rights and privileges in Manipur.

Although the Manipuris had fired the first shots in the Imphal Valley, it was in the hills around and in the distance where insurgents confronted Indian troops and one another.

Here lived the fiercely independent and tough Tangkhuls, the Kukis—also known as the Chins or Kuki-Chins in Myanmar—the tiny Anal tribe, the Maos, the Hmars and the Haokips.

Thuengaling Muivah, himself a Tangkhul, of the National Socialist Council of Nagaland (NSCN) decided to use the Tangkhul-dominated area of Ukhrul district as both base and resource area. His men levied taxes on villagers and sought recruits to their cause. There was initial reluctance because of Muivah's pro-leftist leanings. The NSCN attacked security columns and ambushed officials. Posters went up placing rewards on the heads of NSCN figures; these were pasted in the main towns, with photographs of the fighters.

There were attacks on Rishang Keishing, the Chief Minister at the time and a Naga, who barely escaped a hail of bullets from the NSCN guns, though many of his securitymen were not that lucky. An intelligence official later described the ambush as one of the most brilliant he had seen with the guerrillas firing a few shots early on to distract the guards and then, as the cavalcade came to a major turning, opening up with everything they had, neutralizing the main security cars before raking Keishing's vehicle with automatic fire.

Across in Myanmar, clashes erupted between pro-and anti-Muivah groups of Nagas over tax demands. In one incident, an entire village swamped the NSCN men and beheaded most of them. The incident invited retaliation with the insurgents attacking and killing more than 100 villagers in turn.

It is a cycle of violence and revenge that continues.

In Myanmar, as in the Naga and Manipur theatres of war, Naga rebels fought, fled and regrouped using Mao's classic theory of guerrilla warfare :

When the enemy advances, we retreat
When the enemy camps, we harass
When the enemy tires, we attack
And when the enemy retreats, we pursue.

Yet, these formidable soldiers, who fought thousands of troops, better-armed and better-equipped to a standstill, hitting and hurting and suffering in the process, went into battle with one phrase on their lips: '*Kuknalim*!' Roughly translated, this means 'Long Live the Land' or even 'May the Lord be with you.'

TRIPURA: LOSING BATTLE

The former kingdom of Tripura is host to an unenviable statistic: it is one of the few places in the world where, in the twentieth century, an indigenous people has been transformed from a numerical majority and ruling community into a minority, dependent on the goodwill and largesse of immigrants who have seized economic and political influence.

The only other place where this phenomenon has taken place in India is Sikkim, where the once-ruling Bhutia-Lepchas have been displaced by Nepalis, including settlers from Nepal and India.

Tripura, a small thumb of land that juts into Bangladesh from Assam's southeast, has been swamped by waves of Hindu refugees and migrants from Bangladesh. These waves have rolled in, one after the other, since the 1950s.

Once dominated by nineteen tribes, which share characteristics with ethnic groups in the Chittagong Hill Tracts in Bangladesh, and across the hills in neighbouring Myanmar, Tripura is now controlled by Bengali Hindus. The indigenous communities are Buddhist, Christian and include some nature worshippers.

Attacks on Hindus in East Pakistan in the 1960s led to many refugees settling in Tripura. One estimate says that 600 persons fled to Tripura every day after the assaults.

The scale of the migration can be seen in the following figures: in 1947, ninety-three per cent of Tripura's population of 6,00,000 comprised tribespeople. By 1981, they had been reduced to a pathetic minority of 28.5 per cent of a population of 2.06 million.

In 1980, the impatience of the indigenous communities manifested itself in the Tripura Volunteer Force (TVF) led by a man called Bijoy Hrangkhawl. The TVF, later the Tripura National Volunteers Force (TNVF), snubbed the 'mainstream' tribal groups accusing them of selling out local interests and latching onto the apron strings of Congress.

The pent-up anger found release in a series of bloody incidents that summer. The worst of them was a massacre of Bengalis at Mandai Bazar, near the capital of Agartala, a town overwhelmed by a cloying sense of decay. Several hundred Tripuris and other tribal communities descended on unsuspecting Bengalis and slaughtered them at Mandai Bazar. At least 300 were killed.

I reached the scene of the attack soon after it had taken place. It was the first time that I saw a senior army officer break down as he surveyed the carnage. The hatred of the attackers was clear: a two-year-old-child had been split in two and laid on either side of its mother.

The only living creature in that village that day was a dog, barring the army officials, reporters and photographers who were led to the site.

An army intelligence official later estimated the death toll in the state in that single burst of violence at more than 1,000.

Hrangkhawl and his followers based themselves in the Chittagong Hill Tracts bordering Tripura and also moved about in the villages of their state, close to the frontier with Bangladesh. Their targets were security forces, from whom they seized weapons, and Bengalis, whom they killed to strike terror into the community.

Others on their hit list included members of the Communist Party of India (Marxist) [CPI(M)], which ruled Tripura between 1978 and 1988 before surrendering power to the Congress and then regaining it in 1993.

In a reaction to the anti-Bengali campaign, a pro-Bengali movement sprang up, Amra Bengali, apparently with Congress backing. This group attacked tribal groups wherever they were small in number but never became a major threat.

And although the TNVF was feared, it never confronted the security forces head on. With only about 400 men and women under arms, it was too clever to risk a conventional clash.

But as in Mizoram, life in the jungle can get tiring. And in 1988, soon after the Mizos embraced the Indian Constitution, Bijoy Hrangkhawl and his family were flown secretly to Delhi, booked into a suite at the Claridge's Hotel, a five-star hotel in the heart of the capital, and presented to the press after signing a peace accord. The content of the peace accord was similar to those forged with the Nagas and Mizos although there was one significant clause not in the other agreements: that the government would make sincere efforts to identify and deport illegal aliens from Bangladesh and distribute lands illegally settled upon among landless tribespeople.

This accord remains a paper document although Hrangkhawl, now nattily turned out in two-piece business suits, is chairman of a rehabilitation committee that administers funds and projects for former rebels. Wherever he goes, a burly government security guard accompanies him.

Most of the rebels, he says, want land and a honourable place in society. But the TNVF remains committed to the deportation of illegal migrants and says that little has been done on this front. Hrangkhawl also says that not enough land has been distributed among the dispossessed tribespeople. 'If this state of things continues, then people will take to arms again,' he says.

Indeed, another rebel group—supposedly with links to the CPI(M)—has attacked troops and Bengalis in recent years in much the same way as the TNVF had done in the 1980s. But intelligence officials in Tripura say that the main group, the All Tripura Tribal Front (ATTF), is basically using its firepower to secure good jobs and land for its members. 'There is nothing revolutionary about them at all, this is the bottom line for them, not independence, not separation,' said one official. 'They want a deal, they want to be secure.'

TROUBLE IN ABODE OF THE CLOUDS

If Bengali migrants were a key factor in the Tripura uprising, then Assamese irredentism led to the creation of Meghalaya, the only state of the Northeast, barring Arunachal Pradesh, that has not seen a full-fledged insurgency.

The Khasis of the Khasi Hills and their fellow tribes, the Jaintias and Garos, were exposed to Christian missionaries in the nineteenth century. And over the decades, under the benign eye of successive British governors, a network of Christian missionary schools and hospitals as well as colleges were set up, among the best in the country.

The Khasis thus had an advantage over the Nagas and Mizos and, of course, the Tripuris in terms of education. It was also not as if they had accepted British suzerainty without a fight. Several Khasi leaders resisted the British but were seized, imprisoned and killed. And when the British decided to make Shillong, amid the pine trees of the Khasi Hills, their capital, with an eighteen-hole golf course, horse racing on Saturdays and cricket and church services on Sundays, they introduced a way of life that was alien and distant to the hill people of the area.

The two stayed at a distance from one another. And although Christianity's spread did lead to the breakdown of traditional indigenous practices here—as in other parts, such as Nagaland and Mizoram—it also created a ruling élite that sought to emulate the ways of the British, no matter how foreign they were.

In the Khasi Hills, the indigenous people follow a matrilineal society where women are influential and the youngest girl in the family inherits the property. Husbands go to live with the families of their wives and children take the surname of the mother, not the father.

Shillong drew entrepreneurs from Rajasthan—the slick Marwaris; traders from Sind and Bombay followed. Tea planters took welcome breaks from the monotony and difficulties of their routine there; so did British officers and their families.

The good school system was a further attraction as well as a factor in preparing the indigenous communities of these areas for outside influences, far more than their counterparts in Nagaland, Mizoram, Tripura and Manipur for that matter.

But the highlander here had as much affection for the people of the plains as his contemporaries in the other hill districts. Which was virtually nothing at all.

And the smooth way in which men like the Reverend J.J.M. Nichols-Roy, a Khasi religious man and politician, was able to side with Sir Syed Mohammed Saadulla of the Muslim League in one administration and still retain his place in a cabinet of Gopinath Bardoloi,

Saadulla's inveterate enemy, showed how well they were able to balance their political convictions.

Nichols-Roy later helped draft the Indian Constitution, particularly those sections relating to the tribes of the country, especially in the Northeast.

But in the years after independence, the Khasi and other indigenous leaders of the tribes felt let down by Assam.

Different groups, cutting across party and tribal lines, supported a hill state for hill tribes, separate from the plains of Assam. There was a brief truce, when tribal leaders joined the Assam cabinet, but when their demands were not met, the ministers quit and relaunched the drive for a separate state.

Divisions crept in among the tribes and the Mizos broke away from the All Party Hill Leaders Conference (APHLC), reducing that group to tribes limited to the Khasi, Jaintia and Garo Hills. Opposition to Assamese irredentism grew with the Assam government announcing that all communities in the state would have to learn Assamese. Strikes were followed by agitations and riots over the issue.

After nearly ten years of negotiations, the hills around Shillong were handed over to a fresh state: Meghalaya, which means the Abode in the Clouds.

Years earlier, Stanley D.D. Nichols-Roy, son of the Rev. Nichols-Roy, and a strong campaigner for a hill state, had told Jawaharlal Nehru that they could not co-exist with the Assamese because they were treated as 'second class citizens.' However, both sides showed forbearance and statesmanship that prevented the confrontation from degenerating into large-scale violence and armed rebellion.

The new leaders of Meghalaya proclaimed that theirs would be the state that would set a moral example for the rest of the country. They would show how to get work done and not just push files from desk to desk in the Secretariat. There would be no corruption or favouritism. Within months, these ideals lay in tatters after ministers and other politicians and bureaucrats plunged into bribe-taking, gift-taking and corruption of every kind on a grand scale.

These days, Meghalaya is a leader on these fronts for the rest of the Northeast. But, despite some hiccups with the involvement of several young men in arms training and the discovery of the presence of anti-Indian groups, however peripheral and small, it has been spared the pain of large-scale rebellion that the other states have suffered.

But the state remains a tinder box in other ways: every year, almost without fail, there are anti-Nepali and anti-Bengali riots in Shillong, particularly around the Hindu festivals of Durga Puja in the autumn months. Curfews last for days and in one such riot in 1992, I found that I could visit my mother only for a few hours. The taxi driver from Guwahati would not stay longer because of the risk.

Decades after its creation, although they have avoided the path of insurgency, Meghalaya's ethnic communities, especially those in Shillong, have yet to learn how to live with each other. This poses as much of a danger to the state's stability as does the threat of an armed insurrection, assisted by rebel groups from other parts of the Northeast.

CHANGES IN THE MIST

Few places in the world, perhaps, have seen such profound changes as the highest belt of the Northeast, straddling the Himalayas and looking down into the Assam plains, and which is now known as Arunachal Pradesh.

In the past, it had been officially called Tribal Areas and then, for a long time, the North East Frontier Agency (NEFA) and, after 1972, Arunachal Pradesh.

Since China claims it as part of its territory, Peking lodged a protest with New Delhi when Arunachal was proclaimed India's newest state in 1987, along with Mizoram.

This was the war theatre in 1962 for China and India that saw the humiliating rout of Indian troops, outclassed, outgunned and outgeneralled. The Chinese Army inexplicably withdrew as it approached the rich plains of Assam, probably having accomplished its objective of humiliating Nehru. But it was that dagger thrust from across those hidden frontiers that shook New Delhi out of its complacency about its eastern borders.

Nothing was sacred any longer, the Chinese attack proved. And certainly not boundaries drawn by the British fifty years earlier that the Chinese had never accepted in the first place.

Over the next years, there was a frenzy of road-building and development work in NEFA to bring the remotest of places onto the road map. A heavier form of authority was established, new administrative norms were laid down and the earlier concept of letting the 'tribals develop at their own pace' was virtually abandoned.

The new, zealous Deputy Commissioners and their courts drew litigants, where earlier there had been none. 'Nowadays, everything goes to court, from property disputes to family fights,' one Deputy Commissioner told me on a visit to Khonsa, near Myanmar. In the process, customary courts have died. In these, an offender was tried before a group of elders, his view sought and those of the contending party. Reconciliation and punishment were seen as an inseparable part of these older ways. Both sentences were to be accompanied by gifts from the accused or the guilty to the victim: if it was a poor man, it would be an admonition or working in the fields of the sufferer. The richer the offender, the higher the degree of punishment: he or she would have to part with draft animals, poultry and money too.

'It does not make sense: how can a man expect justice if he confesses to his crime? There is no chance of a proper defence, which he is entitled to,' said one Bengali official in Arunachal.

But clearly such details of Anglo-Saxon jurisprudence did not bother the tribes: they decided on the basis of what was fair and just and the offender and his foe got equal opportunity before the wise men.

The people of Arunachal, who speak as many as fifty languages alone and are subdivided into fifty-three major tribes, now have embraced the new system with religious zeal and the courts are overloaded with cases ranging from the mundane to murder. The process has benefited the lawyers the most, with attorneys from different parts of Assam taking on cases in areas closest to them.

One of the starkest reminders of change, in Arunachal Pradesh is in the communication system across the area, that is home to less than half a million people but sprawls over 78,000 square kilometres.

Where once existed only bridle paths for pony and arduous treks for officials, such as Nari Rustomji, now roads and highways connect some of the remotest places to Itanagar, the capital.

The strategic importance of Arunachal is seen in that it does not have a single civilian airport. Yet, the state is linked to India by regular military flights that travel between Assam and different districts. One estimate of the daily bill for the Indian Air Force, which roars out of Bagdogra near

Siliguri and Dibrugarh for its daily runs of food drops, transporting officials, politicians and soldiers, runs into at least two or three crore rupees (about 600,000 to one million dollars) every day. Where forty years ago, mules and ponies would clatter up hill paths, helicopters these days transport doctors and officials, over mountain and plain, through rain and mist.

These are the lands of tribes with exotic names: the Noctes, the Khamptis, the Adis, the Mishings and the Apa-Tanis, communities that have travelled from the Stone Age to the present in a lifetime.

The man who shaped India's policies to these, the most distant of their frontier communities, was the anthropologist and historian of tribal India: Verrier Elwin. Elwin, an affectionate bear of a man, drew flak from leaders in the plains for what they regarded as his overprotective attitude to the tribes. The anthropologist defended his thoughts for the tribes gently and lucidly:

He did not want them kept as passive museum pieces, he said, and totally protected from the outside world. Change had to be brought about gradually, without damaging the community's self-respect and its sense of values, its relationship with the soil and the environment in which it lived, with the spirits of its ancestors and the freedom of its traditions.

The rest of India, not just Assam, had to be made aware, says Nari Rustomji, a close friend of Elwin and who helped implement his policy for NEFA, 'that the tribes had a culture and identity of their own'; without this awareness, the Indian public would see 'no justification for troubling about their survival as tribes—and the tribes would become soon engulfed in the vast ocean of India, to be lost and forgotten for all time[*]'

Essentially, Elwin and Rustomji battled against the bureaucratic mind-set in Delhi and Shillong that all people had to be moulded in the Hindu, cow belt tradition: they had to be 'modernized.' There was a wonkiness in the mainstream view of the definition of modernism: this included abandoning the tribal hut of bamboo and thatch, built of stilt to protect families against wild animals and allow scavengers such as pigs to clean their excreta. This was a sound, environmentally safe concept that made the best use of abundant natural resources.

Instead the babu mentality insisted that modernism also meant a

---

[*] See, Nari Rustomji, op. cit., p. 96.

change in lifestyle: live instead in cement bunkers that passed for homes, drawing concrete and other alien materials at expensive rates from places hundreds of kilometres away. It made no sense at all—but alas, this is what is taking over parts of Arunachal and other areas of the Northeast. These buildings required frequent repairs, which could be expensive and delayed by the lack of an engineer, a qualified mason and other technical personnel. A bamboo and thatch house, on the other hand, even if it was washed away in the rains could be rebuilt in a few days with the rest of the community pitching in, using local expertise, materials and labour.

The use of cement, of bricks, of iron rods benefited industries in the valley, owned by middle and large entrepreneurs who were often in league with local politicians and bureaucrats, sharing the profits and secure in the certainty that they would get projects to supply their goods.

Invariably, these manufacturers were not indigenous people. Elwin and Rustomji also attacked the concept that tribals must be developed at a rapid pace. In education, they insisted that the local tribal languages and culture be involved in the development of their area: those critical decisions, taken early on in the administration of Arunachal, spared it the horrors of Mizoram and Nagaland.

The Hindu nun smiled as she remembered. 'We came to this place twenty years ago, and at the time there were only a few hundred people living here.' But what shocked her was not the remoteness of the place or its smallness—it was the presence of a welcoming party which included one naked tribesman, who wore a necklace of shrunken heads.

'We didn't know where to look or what to say, it was so embarrassing,' she said as she looked over the low valley of Khonsa town. In the distance, loud Hindi music blared from a shop and people called to each other through the stillness of the day. On a clear day, you can hear a call from a mile away.

Though head-hunting had been banned in the parts for many years, the practice was still reported occasionally, even in the 1970s.

Khonsa, now the capital of Tirap district, has a population of about 5,000. It has a museum, a library, a large Circuit House and a workshop where artisans carve rough-hewn statues of Nocte men and women. But it is still normal to see men wearing little more than a loincloth and carrying a *dao* or machete walking through the narrow main street, without attracting any attention, on a weekly visit to buy provisions for their village home.

The drive to Khonsa is just over two hours over a narrow bumpy road from Dibrugarh, the largest nearby town in Assam. We were warned about the dangers of running into herds of wild elephants. But on that drive, my driver and I encountered no elephants on our sturdy Maruti Gypsy nor did we pass more than two vehicles going in the opposite direction. Not a single car or truck overtook us en route to Khonsa, making it the only place on the subcontinent where I have come across such light traffic.

Khonsa is also the constituency of T.L. Rajkumar, a former Speaker of the Arunachal Pradesh assembly and now a cabinet minister in the state government. Rajkumar's home is an incongruous, sprawling cement structure behind the Circuit House; at any point of time, there were at least three cars parked in his driveway, which was also of cement.

Rajkumar's brother, a contractor who dabbled in the town's politics—and was shot dead apparently in a dispute—built a house for a wife on another hill nearby. But he selected the land poorly: the hill slope was young and vulnerable to erosion. Within months, the bungalow had become unusable and lies empty and decaying by the side of the road. That his marriage also collapsed is quite another matter. The poor selection of the site and the obsession with grand construction, of mansions of glass, cement, brick and iron rods, which cling to the mountains like so many offensive, cancerous growths, totally out of place, is a barometer of the changes of taste and appetite for the loud and vulgar that has grown with the injection of easy money.

But Rajkumar's father, a hereditary chief of the Noctes, lives at Thankip village in a magnificent home of bamboo and thatch, high and vaulted, the floor moving spongily and easily under one's feet as one walks on it. The staircase is a ladder hewn out of a single log of wood. And the breezes cool the cavernous rooms inside where the only concessions to modernity are electricity and a radio.

For more than thirty years, the old man was a P.I. or Political Interpreter for the British and Indian rulers. He translated for men like Rustomji—in whose honour a gate stands at the entrance to Khonsa, marking the inauguration of a new township—and he watched the transformation overtaking his peoples and their lands.

He mourned the passing of honour and dignity and contemptuously referred to the leaders—without naming his sons—who flitted in and out of power, building edifices to themselves and doing nothing for their people. 'Not all the old ways were bad, there is something good in our traditions that have to be retained, otherwise these changes that are coming so fast, we will be unable to stand in their way, we will be overwhelmed, we will lose ourselves, we will be the nowhere people,' said the old man in his lungi and vest.

His eyes misted over behind a pair of ancient spectacles as he looked out at paddy fields across from his house on stilts. Outside, the rain poured, turning the hillsides into a slush of slippery red mud.

For decades, the tribes of the Northeast frontier were lightly administered—if at all—by the British. The Indians inherited this situation upon independence. Rustomji says that the British restricted their presence to waving the flag on annual excursions and that for the most part the tribes were left to themselves.

Some of these groups were closer to the Tibetans and even spoke a form of Tibetan. The Tawang Monastery, one of the great Buddhist monasteries in the world, resembles Tibetan structures and the people in its neighbourhood even paid taxes to Tibetan tax collectors who came every year until an Indian official put an end to this practice in 1948 and established India's hold.

The Chinese invasion and consequent disruption of the indigenous communities, which, despite the setbacks, decided to stay loyal to India and more so to men like Rustomji, accelerated the perception of the area as a key strategic and military zone. India saw the need to develop it adequately in infrastructural terms: roads, bridges, telecommunications, so that it was not caught napping again.

A three-tier system of governance, based on the panchayat system, was developed in the 1960s. It led to the creation of a Pradesh Advisory Council, then a territorial legislature (for it was a Union Territory until 1987) and then to the state legislature. One-time village leaders are now cabinet ministers at Delhi, able to stand up to grilling from more erudite Members of Parliament there, and ministers and high officials in New Itanagar, the state capital.

In thirty years, Arunachal Pradesh had stepped out of the mist but at high cost to its old ways and the fabric of society. New skills were learned, such as corruption and malfeasance, and administrative and political abilities honed, during the collision of the new and the old. Not all the changes were bad. But they created a lethargic, corrupt upper class that is not very different to its counterparts in other areas of the Northeast.

Arunachal's remoteness, its forbidding yet unsuspecting ways, made it a natural route, especially the thickly forested valleys by Khonsa, for insurgents travelling to Myanmar and China.

The Nagas have long used this corridor; so did some Manipuri and Mizo groups. And later, the Assamese from the United Liberation Front of Asom (ULFA). It is also a listening post for Indian intelligence agencies, enabling them to look into Myanmar and Tibet and glean details of what is taking place there.

In recent years, the number of paramilitary troops has been increased around Khonsa to curb the outflow of rebels. This has been fairly effective, officials say.

And although local groups like the Arunachal Peoples Liberation Army (APLA) exist and has connections with the National Socialist Council of Nagaland, there are many of these groups who have surrendered. What is unclear is whether Elwin's influence, the paternalism of Rustomji and the solid common sense of the tribes will enable Arunachal Pradesh to resist violent change in the next decades.

Yet, what is absolutely sure is that their vision, and the gentle pace of change that laid the foundation for Arunachal and its people, has saved the area from the bloodshed that even states such as Meghalaya suffered, not to speak of Nagaland and Mizoram.

SECTION TWO

The New Rebellions

The Boys In Business

In 1985, the Asom Gana Parishad (AGP) came to power in Assam, ending forty-nine years of rule by the Congress and briefly the Janata Party. The AGP was the child of an alliance between the All Assam Students Union (AASU) and the Asom Gana Sangram Parishad (AGSP), an umbrella organization of political rejects and right-wing subnationalists seeking a ticket to power.

That ticket was the foreign nationals issue which first sprang to the forefront of the Indian political consciousness in 1979 and with which AASU has since been identified. It became in the 1980s, a one-point programme that drew support from villagers, townsfolk, farmers and industrial workers, government officers and even politicians.

But what made it so powerful? What are the origins of its mass appeal? To understand this, it is important to step back to the death of one man, which perhaps more than any other single factor, was the catalyst for the anti-alien movement that propelled regionalists to power.

In 1979, Hiralal Patwari, a Member of Parliament from the new-born Janata Party, died. He had represented the Mangaldoi constituency in Assam in the Lok Sabha since the 1977 elections that had for the first time ousted Congress from office in Delhi in thirty years. There was a new Prime Minister, Morarji Desai, who had promised a new beginning after the nightmare of Indira Gandhi's nineteen-month state of internal Emergency.

Ultimately, as in the National Front (NF) case ten years later when individual animosities and differences proved too wide to span, Desai was undercut by a revolt led by Charan Singh, his one-time Deputy Prime Minister, and the bearded, buffoonish Raj Narain, who was nobody's fool although he had made a joke of the family planning programme and set back the population control drive by at least one decade.

The Janata Party collapsed under the weight of its disparities, the government fell and Indira Gandhi, played the Gopinath Bardoloi style-role, by promising support to Charan Singh and then withdrawing it on the eve of a crucial vote of confidence. Charan Singh resigned without facing Parliament and President Neelam Sanjiva Reddy recommended fresh general elections.

While all this was going on, the Assam cauldron was beginning to simmer and bubble. Delhi paid little heed to it, for it had little time apart from the brutal politicking that bruised politicians and administrators alike.

Yet, in the middle of this political haemorrhage, one man kept his balance and fulfilled his constitutional role. This was the country's Chief Election Commissioner at the time, a slight Kashmiri Pandit named Sham Lal Shakdher, a constitutional expert and former secretary general of the Lok Sabha, who paid attention to the election necessitated by Patwari's death. The Election Commission ordered a fresh poll to fill the vacancy and the revision of the voters' lists.

In April 1979, the Commission's local representatives began updating the voters lists in Mangaldoi. The operation continued through May. Revision of rolls involves a door to door check of eligible voters, deleting the names of those who have died or shifted residence, adding those who had become eligible to vote in India (the minimum voting age is eighteen) and new arrivals.

A trickle of complaints came to the electoral officers, some of whom encouraged the complaints, alleging that many Bangladeshis were on the rolls. In several weeks, as many as 70,000 complaints were registered against illegal immigrants. A tribunal was set up by the state government to investigate the complaints. It upheld 45,000 complaints or sixty-four per cent of the cases out of a total electorate of 6,00,000.

The decision stunned public opinion in the state and galvanized opposition groups, always chary of the immigrant Mymensinghia who had come from East Bengal and Pakistan over the years, into action. Two Muslim ministers, Zahirul Islam and A.F. Golam Osmani, strongly protested the deletion of the names provoking reactions from AASU.

AASU was the first to jump into the fray with a call for a bandh or strike throughout Assam in June 1979 to demand the deportation of foreign nationals. It had decided to move step by step on the issue, first of all by legitimizing its demand by winning support from all parties, barring the Congress.

Other powerful organizations, including the tea garden workers, teachers' associations, the state government employees and even the local unit of the All India Sikh Students Federation (AISSF) announced their backing to the agitation. The main literary organization, the Asom Sahitya Sabha (ASS), and small and until then inconsequential regional parties, also threw their weight behind AASU.

These parties were not regarded as politically significant because for decades, the Congress had stood like a banyan tree in the political life of Assam, allowing nothing to grow under its shadow.

The first opportunity to break free of the thrall of the Congress Party came in 1977 after the fall of Indira Gandhi's government and the defeat of Congress at the state hustings later that year by the Janata Party led by the veteran, portly Socialist, Golap Borbora.

The basis for the anti-immigrant bias had been set by Shakdher himself who told a conference of election commissioners from across India in 1978 that he was alarmed by reports especially from the Northeast that foreigners were being included on the electoral lists.

'In one state [Assam], the population in 1971 recorded an increase as high as 34.98 per cent over the 1961 figures and this increase was attributed to the influx of a very large number of persons from the neighbouring countries. The influx has become a regular feature. I think it may not be a wrong assessment to make, on the basis of the increase of 34.98 per cent between the two censuses, the increase that is likely to be recorded in the 1991 census would be more than 100 per cent over the 1961 census. In other words, a stage would be reached when the state would have to reckon with the foreign nationals who may probably constitute a sizeable percentage, if not the majority of the population, of the state.

'Another disturbing factor in this regard is the demand made by the political parties for the inclusion in the electoral rolls of the names of such migrants who are not Indian citizens without even questioning and properly determining the citizenship status.'

Shakdher was not far wrong in his Nostradamus-like predictions.

Even with a drop in the population growth rate, the population of

Assam in 1991 was 22.3 million or about 120 per cent over the 1961 figure. Of course, one must bear in mind that after 1961, Assam was reduced to one third of its then size because political compulsions meant the formation of new states and Union Territories such as Nagaland, Mizoram, Manipur and Meghalaya.

Under pressure from all sides, Golap Borbora decided to act. He dismissed Osmani and Islam for opposing the demand to oust foreigners and set up several tribunals to investigate more complaints against the presence of aliens. But the Muslim MLAs from his party supported by the former Chief Minister, Sarat Chandra Sinha faction of the Congress Party as well as the Indira Congress [Congress (I)] aligned with the Communists and toppled Borbora in 1978. These groups were basically opposed to the revision of the voters lists for this would mean the deletion of tens of thousands of their supporters who had been installed illegally over the years to establish solid vote banks.

In the process, the migrants too became a vocal minority, although to ingratiate themselves with the local Assamese, they accepted Assamese as the language of instruction for their schools. This attitude contrasted sharply with the Bengali Hindus who demanded Bengali language schools for their community across the state, but most vociferously and naturally in the Barak Valley, seat of Bengali Hindu dominance.

Soon after Borbora's fall, Jogendranath Hazarika formed a government, which included the dismissed Muslim ministers. But he too found himself unable to cope with popular resistance: hundreds of thousands of people poured into the streets of Guwahati to express their opposition to the government and to the settlement of aliens. Hazarika was finally forced to reactivate tribunals to detect illegal migrants creating another political crisis for the government. The same block of Muslim MLAs withdrew support and as pickets swamped government offices across the state, and students boycotted classes with government employees joining the agitation, Hazarika resigned.

His ministry had lasted a bare three months.

Governor Lalan Prasad Singh, the former Home Secretary and a shrewd administrator, saw that no party had a realistic chance of forming a stable government. At his recommendation, the Centre proclaimed President's Rule and kept the legislature under suspended animation.

The situation was developing into a full-fledged confrontation between the agitators led by two men barely in their twenties—AASU President, Prafulla Kumar Mahanta, bearded, already balding and mild-mannered, and his general secretary, Brighu Kumar Phukan, precise and incisive as a negotiator—and the Government of India. The government of Assam was a helpless spectator here, as it remained during the United Liberation Front of Asom (ULFA) days until military muscle helped to stiffen its spine. The critical decisions were being taken by senior officials working closely with Governor L. P. Singh and the Home Ministry in New Delhi.

The fall of the Charan Singh government in August 1979 worsened the situation. For, as was to happen eleven years later, Delhi had little time to watch developments in the turbulent east. The country was caught up in the whole exercise of coming elections and speculating whether Indira Gandhi would return to power.

The elections in Assam gave the agitators the right platform to display their new-found strength. Without a revision of the electoral rolls and the deletion of foreigner's names, they said, they would physically block the election process.

Matters were not helped when Election Commissioner Shakdher, in obvious submission to the Indian Government's demand, said that no voters would be eliminated from the rolls 'on the grounds of citizenship as the process of establishing citizenship is time consuming.' The Commission advised 'scrutiny of electoral rolls after the election is over.'

This gave the students the handle they were looking for and brought together all parties opposed to the Congress on a single issue. In one week alone, 3,20,000 complaints were filed against alleged aliens on the rolls. The wave of popular resentment against decades of neglect of the region by Delhi, its exploitation of the oil and gas reserves while doing little to plough back large enough investments into the area, had acquired an unstoppable momentum.

No revision, said the agitators. No elections.

Two days of strikes were held on 3 and 4 December that year, the very days that candidates were to begin filing their nomination papers to contest the polls to Parliament. Crowds swarmed the gates and streets in front of the homes of powerful ministers and politicians refusing to let them pass. Police lathi charges cleared the groups in some areas; where this failed, police fired bullets into the protestors and lobbed tear gas shells. The picketing continued in front of the offices of the district magistrates who were to scrutinize and accept or reject the nomination forms.

Dev Kanta Borooah, the former Congress President, told me at the time that the tactics were 'sheer intimidation' and accused local authorities of collaborating with the agitators. When the elections were finally held, only two parliamentary districts voted: both in the Barak Valley. Santosh Mohan Deb, a football enthusiast from Silchar, and Nihar Lashkar won easily from Cachar district. Both were members of the Congress (I) and Lashkar briefly became Minister of State for Home at the Centre as a sop for his victory. Deb's turn as a minister was to come later.

As Indira Gandhi swept to a landslide victory over her scattered and humiliated foes, the agitators decided that they could not be ignored. In secret meetings, they picked on a new weapon that would hurt the Government of India and the economy far more than a prolonged agitation over foreign nationals with pickets before government offices.

The new weapon was oil, used so brilliantly as a pressure tactic in the 1970s by the Arab world and the oil-rich nations of Indonesia and Iran to extract their price from the West.

The agitators in Assam knew that if they cut off or curbed the production of oil in the state and forced the closure of the pipeline that fed the black gold to the major refinery in Barauni, Bihar, they would be striking at the heart of the Indian economy and challenging the very basis of Central governance in the Northeast. At the time, Assam produced nearly half of the country's crude oil production of about twelve million tons.

On 27 December 1979, AASU supporters—men, women and children—organized pickets before oil production facilities and offices throughout the state, blocking the transport of petroleum products and closing the two small refineries at Guwahati and Digboi.

The struggle had begun.

It was a confrontation that would linger for six years, the fruit of policies implemented fifty years earlier by Syed Mohammad Saadulla and the Muslim League.

Assam, long industrially backward with little foreign investment or direct investment from other parts of India because of its great distance from major ports, had tolerated the migrants as long as they were labourers and peasants. Tensions began to rise when they began to prosper.

The anti-alien agitation underlined the fact that the Assamese, especially the middle and upper caste Hindus, were as concerned about the potential loss of political power as they were about their cultural identity. Their concerns were voiced by an Assamese legislator at the time who spoke of the immigrants as 'an absolute majority in seven of (a district's) nineteen constituencies . . . . In five more constituencies they are numerous enough to be crucial for an electorate victory.'

These days, as many as forty of 126 assembly constituencies, Bengali migrants—largely Muslim—make the difference between winning and losing for candidates.

AASU leaders estimated the number of such foreigners, or Bangladeshis as they described them, at four million. 'We demand our constitutional rights and that foreigners be deported and detected to save Assam and the Assamese,' said Prafulla Kumar Mahanta, the AASU President.

Pickets, strikes, bandhs, and curfews and new satyagrahi strategies such as switching off all lights in homes and offices in the evening began to take their toll of the agitators and the administration. As a result, Indira Gandhi, who returned to power in the 1980 December elections, called the students to Delhi for talks.

The students refused to budge from their demand of deporting the Bangladeshis after their detection by law enforcement agencies. 'All parties are involved in creating this crisis, especially the Congress,' said Mahanta.

The negotiations and the violence stuttered on but the students refused to accept Indira Gandhi's appeal to call off their agitation. The government, she said, would detect and deport aliens who had come after 1971. As the talks failed, Indira Gandhi decided to force the issue through an election. She could not have made a worse mistake.

RESISTANCE, VIOLENCE

Indira Gandhi's election meetings that February of 1983 were lightly attended. The Assamese in the towns largely stayed away from the campaign.

And the AASU made its position clear: no detection and no revision—no election. They called on people to resist and oppose the voting and declared people's curfews outside polling centres.

Bridges were burned, villages were attacked, roads were dug up and teachers and other junior government officials who usually do polling duty refused to do so.

Balloting officials were flown in from Delhi and transported to the voting centres under armed escort. Most voting places were deserted, excepting in Bengali Hindu and Muslim majority areas—and among some indigenous communities.

Frightened polling officials manned their posts, doodling on paper with nothing to do, no voters to guide, no ballot papers to arrange and surrounded by hostile yet sullenly quiet crowds of villagers who stayed—as instructed by the AASU—fifty metres away from the voting booths.

There were few candidates and few voters.

The whole exercise was bizarre and farcical: it would have been funny had it not been for the brutality and the killings.

On the flat fields of a sleepy village called Nellie, barely forty kilometres from my grandparental home, occurred perhaps the worst pogrom on a single day in independent India.

The tribes in those areas were dominated by the Lalung group, which had lost many of its farms to immigrants from East Pakistan and Bangladesh who had come in and settled over the years, buying land from the illiterate tribal. The aliens bought the rich paddy fields from the tribals, getting their thumb impressions, a mark of acquiescence, on documents they did not understand but which signed over their properties to the immigrants.

At the time of the elections, there was talk that tribal women had been molested by Muslims.

The anger of the Lalungs, contained for many years, brewed over. And when the Muslims announced that they planned to vote and defy the boycott call from the AASU, the tribes went into secret conclaves.

They attacked early one February morning from three fronts: each comprising about 2,000 men, armed with muskets, spears, machetes or *daos*, bows and arrows. The Bengalis fled across a shallow channel into the fields, thinking they would be safe there. But the attackers were relentless and kept on coming.

For five hours, the killings continued: of men, women and children. The worst sufferers were children, older men and women for they could not outrun their pursuers. The survivors fled several kilometres to an Indian Air Force base before they felt safe. The police and paramilitary forces arrived well after the killings and the attackers had dispersed.

Bodies were scattered across acre after acre, field after field. In some cases, entire families were wiped out. I remember visiting the massacre site and seeing a family of seven laid out neatly near the bank of a canal: father, mother and five children. The youngest was an infant not more than a few months old; he had been beheaded.

The groans of the wounded and the stunned disbelief on the faces of those who had been attacked—in some cases, they said by their own neighbours—was painful as one walked through a hastily-arranged refugee camp, housed in a local school.

The toll was more than 1,700.

Indira Gandhi flew to Nellie to comfort the wounded and assure victims of her support. But she was not in the least remorseful for calling the elections. I got to speak to her briefly after other journalists had been barred from meeting her by overzealous policemen. She blamed the students for the tragedy, saying they had created a climate of violence.

Across the state, incidents of violence were repeated.

In most cases, the victims were Bengali Muslims or Bengali Hindus. In some, Muslims attacked Assamese villages, torching homes, seizing cattle and destroying grain. In one, Assamese Hindus and members of the Bodo tribe clashed with each other in an old dispute over land and forests that saw the Bodos driven nearly 100 kilometres away into Arunachal Pradesh.

The final toll was between 3,000 to 4,000. And weeks after the first clashes, bodies were still turning up in places like Sawolkhuwa Sapori, an immigrant village that had been devastated by the riots.

The election results were predictable: Congress won a landslide victory. But the cost was frightening not just in terms of bodycounts but also since it irrevocably damaged Indira Gandhi's political integrity and hurt the sinews of administration.

There had been a massive failure all along the line: of the police, of the administration, of local leaders in curbing violence; and the students too had failed to rein in their stormtroopers.

Over the next months, the confrontation between the agitators and the state government continued with the students' arrests, crackdowns, curfews and pickets. But clearly, the enthusiasm was waning, the credibility was cracking.

The students met secretly with Indira Gandhi and agreed to continue off-the-record meetings with a series of intermediaries. They too wanted a way out of the mess that was costing the state exchequer heavily and devastating local commerce. For agitations end by initially hurting those in whose name they seek benefits, especially since communications and sales are disrupted, so are schools, colleges and responsible behaviour.

The moves for a settlement through intermediaries, including a businessman from Chandigarh, intelligence officials and even Congress leaders, followed the scale of the violence as well as its rapid spread that had stunned the agitators. That they had been in jail while it took place was little comfort to them.

As the contacts between the students and the Centre continued, both sides also maintained a sense of 'normalcy' in their conduct toward one another.

Calls to boycott and oppose the new Congress Party government led by Hiteswar Saikia were met with varying responses. But he had a striking inauguration: minutes after Saikia was sworn into office at Raj Bhavan, on a hill above the Brahmaputra at Guwahati, anti-Congress engineers switched off power lines, plunging the city into darkness and announcing their defiance of their new boss.

The movement ebbed and flowed, occasionally lurching forward. It remained consistent on one main demand during the negotiations with the mediators: it would not deal with the 'illegal' Saikia government, which had captured power on the minority of the vote in the most unrepresentative of elections in India.

Saikia was unperturbed. He tried whipping the bureaucracy into shape. He changed officials in senior positions, bringing his own trusted aides into sensitive posts. He dispensed favours liberally and spoke of how members of the students union met him secretly to seek favours or contracts for their relatives and friends. And he was quite aware that he would last as long as the Centre would support him in his stand against the agitators. He knew too that if it ever struck a deal with Prafulla Kumar Mahanta and Brighu Phukan, his government would be the first victim.

Stories of corruption abound of that period: of contracts struck between senior officials, politicians, ministers and businessmen. In one, there was an official investigation later that Saikia had used his position to benefit personally from a logging and forestry scandal that involved about twenty million rupees (the equivalent of about 600,000 dollars). As with most of such investigations, nothing was ever conclusively proved and Saikia shrugged off the accusations as so much hearsay. He blamed the natural prejudice of the media and his detractors for distorting issues.

After Indira Gandhi's assassination on 31 October 1984, the reconciliation process took a back seat as Rajiv Gandhi, her son and successor, called elections to take advantage of the huge sympathy wave that swept India. He then consolidated his gains within the Congress Party.

For all of India, the sudden ascent of Rajiv to the centre of the political stage symbolized a new hope. Or so it seemed. He spoke of conciliation and modernism, of shedding old unprincipled alliances based on caste and creed, of bringing India into the twenty-first century, of encouraging modern industry and technology, of professionalizing government services, of rooting out corruption and of bringing in a new age. He seemed genuine and sincere, this young man of forty with the good looks and clear, fair complexion of a film star.

For many of us, it was a time when Camelot was in touching distance. When there was a Prince Charming on a white charger, who wouldn't drive all the dragons and evil spirits away but who could understand us, who related to us and to whom we could relate.

'This man speaks our language,' I thought as I watched him sprinting up the steps to address a meeting from a platform near the Prime Minister's official residence at the time, 1, Safdarjung Road. Rajiv spoke of his dreams for a new India not far from the site where his mother was brutally murdered.

'He looks like a schoolboy who's topped his class,' I added to fellow scribe and friend, Tarun Basu. Tarun is as much a cynic as I am but he too was moved by the moment.

Over the next months, Rajiv could seemingly do no wrong. The press was in love with this intensely telegenic man. Not quite the Teflon political executive of Ronald Reagan, Rajiv was very open and a good communicator, despite stumbling at Hindi—which we chuckled at and sympathized with.

But as the years went by, he lost his early verve and style. Yet, he retained a strong personal charm.

Rajiv took advantage of his early popularity to strike deals with seemingly intractable groups. He came to an understanding with the leader of the mainstream Akali Dal in Punjab, Sant Harcharan Singh Longowal, in July 1985 promising a political and economic package for the state that has yet to be implemented. Longowal was assassinated within a month of the accord by extremists opposed to a deal with Delhi.

Punjab's brief respite from its nightmare, one that began in 1982, had ended and it was not until nearly eight years later that it would see a return to peace.

But the mood appeared more upbeat for the Assam agitators.

Here, months of negotiations with Home Ministry officials and unofficial mediators had yielded much give and take on both sides.

The AASU gave up its obduracy on immediately deporting foreigners and toned down its opposition to the disenfranchisement of those who came to Assam illegally between 1966 and 1971 (clearly aimed at Bengali Hindu migrants who fled riots in East Pakistan), no longer insisting on their dispersal. There was talk of cases against the AASU and other agitation leaders being dropped, the preventive detention and anti-terrorism laws that gave such sweeping powers to officials and troops—even to kill without being questioned in a court of law—were to be lifted and elections to the state assembly and fourteen Lok Sabha seats were to be held in December 1985.

In response, the Centre accepted the AASU demand for Saikia's removal, pledged to deport immigrants who had settled in the state after 1971 and promised to set up a third oil refinery, reopen a nationalized paper mill that closed after losing money heavily, establish an Indian Institute of Technology (IIT) and a central university. The announcement of the university touched off another controversy with the Barak Valley demanding that it be given to the Bengali-speaking districts since these areas were discriminated against by Dispur and lacked a university. There were already two universities in the Brahmaputra Valley, the pro-Barak platform declared, as well as the agricultural and veterinary colleges, not to speak of two major medical institutes.

But the Assamese agitators also made a crucial compromise: they agreed that they would contest the elections on the basis of electoral lists prepared in 1984 for the general election (Assam did not participate in that year's poll either because the Election Commission had ruled against it, given the experience of 1983). Those lists were prepared on the very rolls that the agitators had opposed all along: the 1971 lists.

Their condition that the 1966-1971 migrants would be disenfranchised was immaterial, for the accord allowed these very people to vote in the ensuing election. The disenfranchisement for ten years (until 1995) was to take place after the December 1985 poll. During this period, their properties, educational status, trade and businesses would remain untouched.

In short, the accord turned logic on its head as far as the main demands of the agitators were concerned. Despite reservations among factions of the AASU, the accord was signed by Home Secretary, Ram Pradhan and the AASU President, Prafulla Kumar Mahanta on 15 August 1985 at the Prime Minister's house. Details of responsibilities of the state government was signed by the acting state Chief Secretary, Mrs H.P. Trivedi. Saikia and his colleagues were nowhere in the picture.

The second rung of the movement's leadership had been flown by a Border Security Force (BSF) aircraft to Delhi after the parameters of the accord had been accepted by the top rung. Mahanta and Phukan, among others, were kept at the secluded BSF camp at Tigri, on the southern edge of Delhi. The press was barred from meeting them. After long consultations among themselves, there was general agreement on the conditions of the accord.

The overriding consideration was that the agitators wanted to get off the streets and, encashing the goodwill and support that their movement had generated in Assam, come legitimately to office and power at Dispur.

A few hours after the accord was made public, I visited the Tigri camp to meet with Mahanta and Phukan. They seemed as relieved as they were elated. But when pressed on the compromise on the disenfranchisement of the 1966-1971 batch of voters, they were defensive. 'How long could we have gone on with the movement,' said Phukan. 'There are limits to everything and people were suffering in Assam.' He added, 'We had to make compromises otherwise it would have gone on without any result.'

Within a few weeks of the accord, the leadership of AASU banded with the regional parties to form the Asom Gana Parishad. It picked the elephant as its election symbol and trundled to a smooth victory in the December elections, winning a clear majority of its own and then drawing several independents into its fold to boost its tally.

The Congress finished a poor second with a bare twenty-five seats. The other national parties got a mere look in, picking up a handful of seats between them. The mandate was clear and unambiguous.

Riding the trend of regional party victories as with the Telugu Desam (TD) in Andhra Pradesh in 1983 and 1984 and the Dravida Munnetra Kazhagam (DMK) and the All India Dravida Munnetra Kazhagam (AIADMK) in Tamil Nadu and anti-Congress votes in Karnataka, West Bengal and Kerala, the Assam voter had chosen a regional party to govern the state for the first time in its history.

The mood was buoyant and sharply anti-Congress.

At a public ceremony in the large and dusty Nehru Stadium in Guwahati, most of the city turned out in their holiday best to watch 'the boys' take the oath of office and savour the heady drink of power.

It was a time of change, it seemed, when the old guard stepped aside to make way for the young. But as with Rajiv Gandhi, it was only a matter of time before disenchantment set in. The first off-screen problems began with new ministers tussling over which rooms to occupy in the government complex at Dispur. It extended to which of them would have what numbers on their white Ambassador cars.

Relatives and friends and supporters began to demand their pound of flesh, seeking contracts, cash and comfort.

From spartan lifestyles gained from living in university hostels where food was cheap and not particularly tasty, the bachelors developed a taste for the high life. Many of them got married quickly. Their wedding receptions were lavish and talked about because of the large number of expensive gifts that were bestowed on the couples. One minister received as many as a dozen refrigerators and an equal number of television sets from businessmen at his marriage reception. Needless to say, he neither had the grace or the common sense to return any of these gifts which can be construed as bribes to a public servant under existing laws.

Even AGP supporters developed a disdain for the party leaders. A small contractor in Delhi told me a few years after its installation that the ministers were 'petty corrupt.' When I asked for a definition of 'petty' corruption, he said that they *took* commissions worth *lakhs* on deals where they could have made '*crores*'. 'Even their *dalals* [middlemen] are smarter, these chaps can't govern, they can't think straight, they can't even make money properly,' said the contractor.

The goodwill from the Assamese middle-class was ebbing, although by a mix of pressure and patronage, they ensured that part of this remained. Assamese contractors and businessmen were given precedence over non-Assamese in contracts and licences. Pro-AGP businessmen, even if they were non-Assamese like the Marwaris, also were helped out.

On the political front, things were falling into disarray.

The Plains Tribal Council of Assam (PTCA), till then the mouthpiece of the Bodo/Kachari community, the largest single indigenous group in Assam, spoke angrily at the time of the Assam Accord against the manner in which traditional parties like theirs had not been consulted or included in the decisions that were to shape their lives.

'Once again it has been proved beyond doubt that the movement leaders are concerned with the security of the Assamese linguistic minority only, and they are neither concerned about nor do they represent the indigenous linguistic and ethnic groups of Assam,' the PTCA said.

The Assam Accord placated, at least for the time being, the basic grievance of the caste Hindu Assamese: to hold and wield political power with a freedom that had rarely been given to any party since the days of Gopinath Bardoloi. But it did little for the many other strands of the ethnic and religious-cultural mosaic that made up the social fabric of Assam.

To the Bodos and to communities such as the Karbis in the autonomous district of Karbi Anglong and North Cachar Hills that formed a triangular wedge with the borders of Mizoram and Nagaland, the Assam agitators were essentially colonialists, a powerful community that had settled in the Brahmaputra Valley several centuries ago by ousting their forefathers. To them, the Assamese caste Hindu or Assamese Muslim was as much an interloper as a Bangladeshi, a Marwari or a Hindu Bengali.

The Bodo-Kachari community is a large and complex one which once ruled a kingdom in the Middle Ages stretching from Cooch Behar in Bengal to the Naga Hills with Dimapur as its capital. Its leaders described its current strength at about four million but the 1991 census, an exercise the Bodo leaders have rejected, puts their numbers at much lower: 1.1 million. Its size causes concern among smaller plains indigenous groups which fear domination by the more numerous and politically powerful Bodos.

In a twist to the Assamese-Bengali, Bodo-Assamese tale of exploitation and superiority, these smaller groups—and there are more than twenty in Assam's plains alone—are worried by the prospects of Bodo suzerainty over their tiny communities.

What had fuelled Bodo resentment over the years was the supercilious and arrogant attitude of the Assamese bureaucrats and politicians, most of whom had a 'we know better than you attitude', who talked of the plains' tribals—the true indigenous people of Assam—with disdain and even contempt and who had done little over several decades for these disadvantaged groups. The Bodos and other plains' tribe groups were essentially subsistence farmers; most of them barely eked out an existence.

Few of the funds that were allotted to them ever reached these groups. Like other communities, they strongly opposed and resented attempts to impose Assamese on them as their lingua franca. The Bodos, with a rich oral and literary history of their own, formed their own Sahitya Sabha. They campaigned and won agreement from Assamese leaders and New Delhi that Hindi and the Devanagari script would be the main language of instruction in their schools, such was the hatred of Assamese. They were to learn Bodo through Hindi, a painful process. This, their leaders now feel, was a mistake. They should have then insisted on Bodo as the language for primary and secondary school instruction.

The use of Hindi meant that the Bodos were unable to progress either in their own language or in Assamese, for Hindi was useful only up to a point. After all, communications with officials, politicians, newspapers and businesses was largely in the lingua franca of the region: Assamese or its variations such as Nagamese, an amusing pidgin of Naga words and phrases with a strong Assamese base. They were left behind in the race for jobs.

'We had primary education and higher education in one language and college education in a second,' said Sugwai Bwasumatari, then President of the All Bodo Students Union (ABSU). 'This meant that we were deprived of jobs within Assam itself because of the language problem.'

Some of the difficulties were caused as much by Bodo obdurance as Assamese recalcitrance.

That there was deliberate and callous neglect of Bodo grievances is unquestioned. For this, Congress regimes as well as the AGP were to blame. In 1974, the government of Chief Minister Sarat Chandra Sinha sanctioned 5,000 posts for teachers in the Bodo areas. Ashok Saikia, a boyish-looking bureaucrat from Guwahati whose balanced work as Education Commissioner in AGP-rule won him much praise, said that the difficulties were aggravated by a cumbersome three-language formula which included English as the medium of instruction at colleges. Assamese was being taught in the rest of the state while in the Bodo areas, students struggled to learn their own tongue in an alien language: Hindi. 'Even these days there are only six or seven who can teach and translate Bodo into Devanagari,' says Saikia.

There were few Hindi typewriters and only a handful of teachers. Most of them were Assamese. The situation developed to a point where the Assamese teachers, few of whom lived in the Bodo villages, would come to the schools to collect their month's salary and then vanish for the rest of the period before salary time came again.

For years, the posts of teachers remained unfilled. During the AGP days, Saikia managed to get 700 posts filled, virtually without official sanction. But the rest of the posts continue to be untouched, waiting for takers. And in the meanwhile, Bodo children languish, untaught and illiterate.

The seeds of division between the Bodos and the Assamese were sown in the 1930s and 1940s when Bodo delegations met with the Simon Commission and other British Parliamentary and Constitutional groups to press for recognition as a separate entity, different from the Assamese mainstream. They were not politically inactive either: Rupkumar Brahma joined the Saadulla ministry at first and then Gopinath Bardoloi's government.

'They kept joining and leaving the ministries,' said Sugwai Bwasumatari, as we talked in the bare visitor's room of a Bodo Member of Parliament, Satyen Brahmachowdhury.

ABSU was the most vocal advocate of Bodoland in the 1980s, after the AGP failed to negotiate terms for autonomy and economic assistance of the Bodo-dominated areas of Kokrajhar and Darrang districts. Kokrajhar and parts of Goalpara are Bodo strongholds running along the strategic and narrow Chicken's Neck, the tiny land corridor that is a bare twenty kilometres wide in parts between Bhutan and Bangladesh, and which the Bodos could shut down at a moment's notice. Through this slip of land runs the only train and road lines that connect the Northeast to the rest of India.

ABSU was formally launched in 1967 but it was not till twenty years later that it flung aside the mask of moderation and began speaking the language of militancy.

The sense of hurt and deprivation was deeper in the 1980s for it was nourished by the failure of the AGP government to do anything for the Bodos, despite the fact that ABSU had thrown its full support to the anti-alien agitation.

According to the Bodos, it was Gopinath Bardoloi, who, despite his statesmanship, erred against them during his chairmanship of a special constitutional subcommittee that developed policies toward the tribes of the Northeast. In that subcommittee, which was mandated by the Constituent Assembly in 1948, Bardoloi and his colleagues described the plains' tribals as part of the overall Assamese stream and said that with time these groups would be assimilated into the dominant community. Such decisions rankled with the Bodos for they found themselves without any special rights or privileges or even protection of their culture and identity. Unlike the Nagas and other hill tribes, said the Bardoloi committee, groups like the Bodos did not need special protection because they were part of the larger Assamese identity. In this, Bardoloi was badly mistaken.

In the 1960s, the Bodos supported hill tribes in the Khasi, Jaintia and Garo Hills as well as Naga and the Mizo Hills when they opposed the imposition of Assamese as the state's official language.

From the 1970s, the Bodo leadership under the PTCA demanded Udayachal, a separate autonomous region within Assam. Then the demand changed to a Union Territory and finally a separate state.

The separate state of the Bodoland of their dreams was to encompass the whole of the northern bank of the Brahmaputra, dissecting Assam neatly into half, using the river as a natural boundary. This was illogical for the Bodos were not even a simple majority in a single district of this area. Many of their villages and lands were not contiguous, making the marking of a state a very difficult task and, of course, there are large numbers of Bodos on the other side of the Brahmaputra—in Nagaon and Kamrup districts.

The response from the Assamese was predictable and natural: a fierce refusal to part with any more land, having seen their state shrink to less than one third of its size from the 1970s to the 1990s. The reorganization of Assam in 1971 took away Mizoram as a Union Territory, created a new state of Meghalaya out of the Khasi, Jaintia and Garo Hills and carved a Union Territory out of the former North East Frontier Agency (NEFA) now designated as Arunachal Pradesh.

Twenty years later, the Bodos echoed the language of the Khasis and the Mizos. 'We cannot live with the Assamese any longer, their attitudes are intolerable,' said Bwasumatari, as we talked in the stifling heat of summer at the flat of his friend, S. Brahma Chowdhury.

In the demands of the Bodos, as well as those of the smaller subnationalities such as the Karbis and the Mishings, there runs a common theme of fear of domination: not of Bangladeshis or foreigners but of the irredentist Assamese.

The bitterness over the Bodo-Assamese clashes of 1983 was sharpened when the Bodos found many families were being ousted from forest lands under the terms of the Assam Accord. And to add insult to injury, Upendra Brahma, the young firebrand leader of ABSU, found himself cold-shouldered by the AGP leadership when he went to Guwahati for talks on the Bodo issue.

'On one occasion he had been invited to talks with the Chief Minister by the Home Minister,' said one Assamese official who knows the Bodo tangle well. 'Mahanta refused to meet Brahma—he felt that he was being undercut by Brighu Phukan, his Home Minister, and that Phukan would then get the credit for arranging the talks.'

This petulance and immaturity was at the root of many of the AGP's domestic problems: a failure to see the state's problems in a larger perspective that embraced the communities of the valley and their special concerns. There was no grand vision of where the AGP wanted to take Assam and the Northeast and how its leaders could develop the region. Internal differences reached the stage where Prafulla Kumar Mahanta and Brighu Phukan traded charges and counter-charges in newspaper interviews. Mahanta even accused his deputy of failing to maintain law and order. Phukan ignored the obvious hint to quit and stayed on, retorting in similar language.

A few months before the 1991 elections, the AGP split and Phukan headed a breakaway faction that won just three seats that summer. The Mahanta group did better but could still scrape a miserable sixteen. Two years later, and chastened by time in the opposition, the two factions merged.

The divisions in the AGP so disgusted Upendra Brahma that he decided to stay away from talks with Dispur and instead go straight to his people. The result was increased militancy: bridges were blown up, trains were dislocated for days, prices of essential goods soared as commodities became scarce and attacks on police personnel, Assamese officials and government offices were stepped up.

Yet, over the months in 1987, the attacks became more precise, the violence and strategies better organized. It was at this time that whispers were circulating about the role of the Research and Analysis Wing (RAW) in training Bodo militants. The AGP denounced the Congress government of Rajiv Gandhi at the Centre, accusing it of trying to destabilize an opposition party government. Mahanta held news conferences describing the RAW assistance, saying it extended arms and explosives training. The Central Góvernment, true to form, denied it. But there is little doubt that the RAW did play a role in organizing the Bodos into a formidable opposition to the AGP.

The game was the old one: destabilize a non-Congress government by using a local grievance and using large funds that did not need to be accounted for. The hatchet man chosen for the job, Mahanta and AGP politicians say, was Santosh Mohan Deb, then Minister of State for Home and later Minister of State for Steel in Prime Minister P.V. Narasimha Rao's government. Deb was a tough-looking, cigar-smoking Bengali from Silchar who was a former football referee.

The Bodos deny the whole thing. But Cabinet ministers in the National Front (NF) government of V.P. Singh said that they came across evidence of RAW's involvement and that the operation was disbanded soon after V.P. Singh came to power.

As the political battle increased in speed and noise, Upendra Brahma was fighting another struggle, his loneliest and most painful. He was diagnosed as having cancer and was being treated, secretly at Bombay and at hospitals in southern India.

For months, Brahma, a cheerful young man of about twenty-eight with an infectious smile, had become a familiar face to newspersons in Delhi and the Northeast. He was swift in repartee, spoke flawless English and was quick to laughter. He made a refreshing change from the serious conservatives of the AGP and New Delhi's dhoti-clad bunch.

His leadership had mobilized the Bodos into a visible opposition force that used some of the very tactics that AASU had used against Hiteswar Saikia and the Centre in the 1980s. It was ironic, to say the least. And no one enjoyed the situation more than Upendra Brahma. 'We got good training from AASU,' he would say dead-pan. 'We must be very thankful to them.' And then would burst out laughing in great gusts.

The AGP, of course, did not find the situation at all funny. It used the very measures against the Bodos that it had accused the Indian Government of using against AASU at the height of the agitation: preventive detention, curfews, arrests, lathi charges and teargassing, occasional police firings. And for a change, non-Assamese were complaining of police atrocities—atrocities by Assamese police officials.

At no point did Upendra Brahma speak of the physical agony that he must have suffered during these months because of his illness.

But as his hair fell out and he wasted away, it was clear that the Bodos would have to find new leaders.

Brahma died in 1990 and was given a hero's farewell at his last rites by a huge crowd at Kokrajhar. Before his death, he had had the satisfaction of forcing the Bodo issue to the national level and getting the Assam government to participate with ABSU and the Centre in tripartite talks to resolve the mess. 'Guwahati gave the Bodos the treatment that it has always been complaining about from the Centre,' said one senior Assam official. 'It dealt with them insensitively, more interested in scoring political points than negotiating larger issues.'

One of my last meetings with Upendra Brahma took place at the Yatri Niwas Hotel in Delhi, the government's hotel for backpackers from the West which also functions as a pick up joint for foreign women and men. We spoke in Assamese and English of the Bodo issue and Assamese attitudes. At the end, I turned to him and said that I only wished I could have spoken with him in Bodo and that more Assamese should have learned his language. He was, I think, surprised and moved.

But what was clear then and is even clearer now is that the Bodos, like the Jharkhand groups of central India, are not prepared to be treated as second class citizens any longer. They want to control their own lives and take responsibility for their communities instead of depending on babus in Delhi, Patna or Dispur and Assamese or Bihari politicians.

The Bodos have had long experience in weaponry. Many of Assam's police and paramilitary personnel are raised from the Bodo community and a related group, the Rajbangshis who inhabit villages in Bengal's Cooch Behar area as well. Apart from their expertise with traditional weapons such as bows and arrows, the Bodos have also received training—as have many other groups in Assam, including the politically influential caste Hindus—in firing guns and explosives.

Their trainer: none other than the Government of India.

This strange story goes back to the aftermath of the 1962 military debacle with China when Chinese troops had sliced through NEFA and were at Tezpur's doorstep before withdrawing abruptly. Jawaharlal Nehru, distraught and bitter, decided that the people of the region should not be caught napping a second time and should be trained to resist enemy aggression as well as carry out raids into enemy territory.

A special force was created to impart this training: the Special Security Bureau (SSB).

Over the years, instructors trained men from the civil services, village leaders and even college students, after careful screening, in how to use weapons, dismantle and clean guns, make and set off explosives, gather intelligence and live underground as well as communicate with other groups. The training was carried out at Haflong in the North Cachar Hills of Assam, and at Chakrata in Uttar Pradesh, ninety-five kilometres north of Dehra Doon, and at Mahableshwar in Maharashtra. Chakrata was the centre of another major secret operation in the 1950s when the United

States' Central Intelligence Agency (CIA) tied up with Indian security officials to train Khampas fighting against Chinese rule in Tibet. Those efforts flopped.

Some of the SSB-trained groups were activated during the Bangladesh war when they went in ahead of Indian regular forces, wearing the East Bengali dress of green lungis and vests. They spoke Bengali and communicated with Indian forces and the free forces of Bangladesh, the Mukti Bahini, without the Pakistanis learning anything about it.

Men who had training with the SSB used that training to good profit in the 1983 elections when, working to a strategy, they did the first thing that any guerrilla movement would do in the case of an insurgency: isolate their targets by cutting off telecommunications, setting up road blocks and destroying bridges. Of course, the violence during that election was spontaneous as well as organized. But it was an important barometer for future events.

The AGP's failure to come to grips with the Bodo crisis and the growing intransigence of the Bodo hardliners served to fuel the confrontation.

With the death of Upendra Brahma, the leadership passed onto a handful of men: chief among them were Sugwai Bwasumatari and S. Brahma Chowdhury, the Member of Parliament. This group proved more easy to handle than Upendra Brahma, from the Centre's point of view. They breathed fire and brimstone but always pulled back from the edge. They were content to wait in Delhi for weeks for meetings with Prime Minister Narasimha Rao. They were increasingly aware that the movement was slipping out of their hands and into a far more militant group, the Bodo Security Force (BSF), that unlike ABSU demanded an independent state and had established military and personal links with the ULFA and the NSCN, first in Myanmar and then within Assam and Bangladesh.

With the Bodos, the Central Government found itself falling deeper in a quagmire.

By assisting them during the anti-AGP years, it was playing the same kind of extremist politics that it had tried in Punjab by setting up the militant preacher, Jarnail Singh Bhindranwale against the Akali Dal party. The results were disastrous all round.

But Delhi and its intelligence agencies have appeared to learn little from these experiences. The multiplicity of agencies leads to contradictory signals and strategies.

By early 1993, an accord on Bodo demands was thrashed out at meetings between Rajesh Pilot, the Union Minister for Internal Security, Hiteswar Saikia, the Chief Minister, Assam Home Commissioner, Tapan Lal Baruah, and the ABSU leadership. The Bodos were desperate for a settlement—they had an irate community to placate. Plus they wanted a face-saving device. Their dream of a state became more and more distant with each passing week as pressure mounted from within Assam and the unbending middle class that had seen the state carved up to less than one third of its original size.

The final accord said that there would be a Bodoland Autonomous Council with 2,200 villages on the northern bank of the Brahmaputra. These would cover three districts and the formula was simple: any village in the area with a majority of Bodo speakers would qualify as part of the Council. The Bodos were dropping their demands for 4,000 villages that sought to encompass some of the prosperous tea-producing regions, a view strongly rejected by both the tea labourers as well as the Assam administration. Later, Bwasumatari resigned over non-implementation of the accord and Prem Singh Brahma, a militant ABSU leader was appointed to his post. Brahma took the job when the government offered to drop a number of cases against him. Also in the deal was Brahma's agreement to accept Dispur's terms of territory.

The Council was to be armed with financial powers for its local development. But it would not have any control over law and order and security and ordinary revenue matters. Control over these important subjects would remain with the state government. The money would come directly from the Centre. However, there would be no division of the state, the Centre said, adding its voice to that of Dispur on the subject.

The mountain that the Bodos had demanded was turning into a molehill. Again, Hiteswar Saikia had struck, edging his opponents into a corner and forcing them to accept a face-saving truce.

But it was clear also that the Bodo Security Force would not brook such a peace. In one strike, the BSF walked into the headquarters of a Assam Police battalion which comprised almost entirely of Bodos. Helped by the directions provided by a Bodo constable who had defected

The Boys In Business

d gone on leave (which his officers suspected) and a sympathetic guard
the gate, the insurgents reached the armoury.

Here, the guard opened the cache of weapons and helped the rebels
ad it onto a truck. Token resistance came from a few other guards who
ere soon overwhelmed. The Commanding Officer, showing a rare
oncern for his own safety, stayed within the precincts of his house,
uarded by several policemen. He was watching a movie on television
d was not to be disturbed. But he did show some enterprise: he called
e Central Reserve Police Force (CRPF), the army officers in the area
d local officials to find out what was going on in his own camp.

He ventured out only after the rebels had roared away into the night
1 their truck, carrying dozens of machine-guns and rifles, and vast
mounts of ammunition.

The entire battalion was disbanded and the officer dismissed.

The agreement with the Bodos was farcical, although Rajesh Pilot,
e prime mover of the accord as the powerful Minister of State for Home
ffairs at Delhi, was a long-time trouble shooter for the Congress in the
ortheast who thought he knew the area well enough. What Pilot did not
derstand was how to strike a delicate balance between a clutch of
mmunities holding long-felt grievances against each other. He erred
ieviously in rushing through with the Bodo accord in the teeth of
oposition from Assam's ruling élite.

There was a major flaw in Pilot's scheme: villages which were
on-Bodo in character were placed in the Council area. The Assamese
d non-Bodo indigenous groups resented this, finding themselves
ddenly at a disadvantage. The areas were hardly contiguous: many
llages had mixed populations and neither language, religion or territory
ound them together. These very factors are bitterly divisive questions
roughout the Northeast.

As a Bodo élite emerges along with a middle class in urban and rural
eas, a class of growing tastes and ambitions, the larger
mmunity—excluded from this small minority of the privileged—will
come disillusioned with the failure of the system to provide them with
bs, money, hope. As this happens swiftly—for the same experience is
peated across India wherever élites among the underprivileged have
merged—there will be violence and greater violence, and insurgency
ill be seen as the only way of redressing the problem.

This is the story of democracies everywhere in the Third World—the

fatal flaw of aspirations never being met, of implementation of policie
always lagging behind hopes, of plans unfulfilled and of corruption. Th
sense of betrayal is deeper when leaders of a community, elected on th
strength of a nationalist appeal, fail to do right by their people.

Such a situation exists in the Bodo areas and this will legitimize th
Bodo Security Force (BSF), that has connections with ULFA and th
NSCN, as a political entity with popular support. This is alread
happening in addition to the BSF hogging the headlines with kidnapping
and extortions.

'I don't think they (the Council) will last long,' said an Assan
official. 'They have failed to set up the Council properly, all they want
power, money and prestige and a car with a siren and flag staff. They hav
no political or technical competence.'

Once the failure of the ABSU is evident to all, the BSF will surg
forward and cash in on the bitterness of lost hopes and broken promise
gathering support from jobless young people.

One of the starkest failures of the Bodo accord was the inability o
the Assam government and ABSU to force the surrender of any of th
major hard-core militants. Although government-controlled televisic
and media reports showed scores of young men in uniform surrenderin
to authorities, including handing over their weapons to Hiteswar Saik
and Rajesh Pilot, nothing of the sort actually happened.

These were not BSF surrenders but a faction of the armed wing o
ABSU led by Prem Singh Brahma. They had no connection with the BS
and, in fact, opposed them. Yet, for weeks after the accord, the newspape
of the Northeast were filled with photographs of surrendered Bodos. Th
events were sheer fiction.

The government at one point announced that the number o
'surrenderees'—a new word in the Anglo-Saxon lexicon—was more tha
2,000. The actual number of armed militants with the BSF then was rare
more than 200. And it was their knowledge of the lay of the land, the
extensive intelligence networks and their skill at ambushes that mac
them so feared.

The BSF, thus, was hardly touched by the drama enacted by ABS
and the government. Openly showing its contempt for ABSU,
audaciously kidnapped the son of Gopinath Bardoloi, the first Congre
Premier of Assam, from Guwahati in April 1993 and held him hostag

'ata Tea, Bolin Bardoloi's employers, received a ransom notice of five
nillion dollars to be paid in foreign currency.

The kidnappings were not merely aimed at announcing that the BSF
vas alive and well or at frightening the tea industry into fresh compliance
vith terror tactics. The signal that went out was that no one, no matter
ow distinguished their lineage, could regard themselves as free from
anger and that an accord signed by one faction had no power over a more
nilitant group.

Pressure mounted on the state government to act—Bardoloi's
nother resorted to a hunger strike—and a flood of news reports and angry
etters filled newspaper columns demanding his release. The company
lew hot and cold: angry at the family for publicizing the issue, saying it
vould harm the kidnapped man. As the public outcry grew, Tata entered
nto parleys with the BSF. It reiterated that it would not pay any ransom
ut would be prepared to invest the money in Bodo areas to develop the
egion. The talks went on without any end in sight.

It was at this point that the government responded in its own fashion,
n moves that were to recoil on it.

A few gunmen came for Jones Mahaliya at 11:30 p.m. in April 1993,
vaking him and his family with a sharp rapping on their front door.

Mahaliya's wife opened the door after one man identified himself as
rom the *sangathon* or resistance. 'We were just terrified, thinking they
vill start shooting,' said the woman at their small first-floor home at
Guwahati, recalling the horror of the time.

Two men entered the home and asked for her husband, a deputy
irector of the Films Division, a Government of India unit making
locumentaries, who was on leave from his job at Calcutta. Mahaliya tried
o escape stealthily, jumping a few feet from the open patio onto the
round below. But he was immediately seized by other men—the entire
ouse had been surrounded—and hustled off to a waiting car. His son too
vas pushed into the vehicle; the men were blindfolded and driven for
bout twenty minutes before they were taken out of the car and into a
uilding.

Only in the morning, when his blindfold was briefly removed, did
he heavily-built Mahaliya realize that they were at a police station in
orabat, on the trijunction that branches off with roads leading to Shillong

and Nagaon and further north in Assam. This little settlement of paa
shops, pokey roadside restaurants and wine stores (on the Meghalaya sta
side, since the Assam government does not permit liquor stores on i
highways) is constantly bustling with traffic, especially with the heav
Tata trucks carrying goods and people across the Brahmaputra Valley.

When the interrogation started, Mahaliya told his captors that he wa
simply an artist with no political connections or interests. They asked hi
about the Bodo Security Force and accused him of harbouring Boli
Bardoloi at his home. 'I know nothing about these groups or people, yo
can kill me if you like but that is all you will get from me,' he said. Afte
some time, he was joined by Subodh Daimuri, a brother of Ranja
Daimuri, the BSF chairman. And when he heard that Anjali Daimuri, th
BSF chief's sister, had also been picked up, the whole puzzle slid int
place.

Anjali had acted in a Bodo film that Mahaliya had made some yea
ago. He was questioned about why he had selected her and whether
meant he was a BSF supporter.

By this time, word had spread in Guwahati about Mahaliya
kidnapping and the government's plan had been exposed: it believed th
by kidnapping Mahaliya and the Daimuris, it could bargain through th
Tatas for Bardoloi's release. The people it had seized were expendab
bargaining chips. Dispur had tried to do what the Punjab police have don
successfully and repeatedly in their state: counter-kidnapping to force th
release of officials or businessmen. In that state, such a developmer
would have hardly caused a ripple despite the usual protests by huma
rights groups: society has become so brutalized over the years that peopl
accept such developments as normal.

Things had not quite degenerated to that level in the Assam valley

The government, stung by the newspaper reports, tried to ease ot
of a sticky situation by announcing that the Mahaliyas and Daimuris wer
being held under the Terrorist And Disruptive Activities (TADA) Act an
'confessions' were published as government's advertisements in the loca
press.

After much pleading with the Chief Minister, Mahaliya's wif
secured the release of her husband and son. At the time of their release
they were held in different jails. Neither of them complained of eithe
torture or verbal abuse.

Once again, the state had revealed its ugly and incompetent face.

'The script was good, the production was okay but the direction wa

ıd,' said Jones Mahaliya of his nightmare. The irony of the episode was
at when Chief Minister Saikia sent for him after his release, Mahaliya
ıas shown a file that contained a proposal for a film. Mahaliya had given
ıe outline a year ago: the film was to be about Saikia and his return to
ıe centre stage of politics. Mahaliya was not amused.

ıs noted earlier, the Bodos had received training in arms and tactics from
ı number of government agencies. But what is little known is ULFA's
ıle in their initial foray into organized violence.

In 1987 ABSU's star was on the ascendant under the charismatic
ıpendra Brahma. And the BSF, under Ranjan Daimuri, was struggling to
ınerge as a counter-force. The fledgling group drew a number of
ımmitted Bodos but the majority were with Upendra Brahma, a man
ıho so impressed a senior Home Ministry official from Delhi that he told
ıe that 'Brahma has the ability and vision to create a revolution for the
ıodos, unlike the AGP which is too soft and corrupt.'

At the time, ABSU was fiercely anti-Assamese. Assamese officials,
ılicemen and villagers were targeted for attacks. The BSF was also under
ıessure from the ABSU's militant wing, the Bodo Volunteer Force
ıVF) led by Prem Singh Brahma. In order to protect themselves, the BSF
ıught help from ULFA's Kamrup unit, at that time strongly influenced
ıy Sunil Nath (also known as Siddharth Phukan), ULFA's spokesman.

ULFA began by training Bodos in the use of gelatine sticks to set off
ıasts and simple weapons for self-defence. The training was given at a
ınall town near Guwahati called Goreswar, which was once the scene of
ıerce attacks on Bengali Hindus by indigenous groups such as the Rabhas
ıd Deoris. Those assaults took place in 1983 at the height of the
ıti-immigrant agitation and the Bengalis, in this case, were accused of
ıspossessing the local tribes of their lands.

From these beginnings, the BSF established contacts with other
ıilitant northeastern groups. These included the National Socialist
ıouncil of Nagaland (NSCN) and the United Peoples Manipur Liberation
ırmy (UPMLA) which even took a BSF proposal to the Kachins in
ıyanmar in 1987: they wanted to come over and train with the Burmese
ıbels.

The Kachins were direct in their response. While they were pleased
ı see growing interest in their work and capabilities in the Northeast, they

would accept such requests for assistance from Assam on one condition. Future Assamese groups would have to come through ULFA, they said, which they had identified as the pivotal insurgent group in the Brahmaputra Valley. Thus, ironically, the very ethnic group that asserted its differences with the Assamese had to go to Kachinland as an Assamese entity.

This was how Ranjan Daimuri and a small group of the BSF went to the Kachin training camps where they made contacts with ULFA and with both factions of the NSCN. When the KIA parted company with the NSCN, the BSF turned to the Thuengaling Muivah faction for arms and other help.

Thus, when the ABSU-Assam Government accord was signed in 1993, the BSF remained unaffected. It continued to maintain base camps in the thick forests of the southern Bhutanese plains and a network of supporters in the Kokrajhar and Udalguri areas.

'They are rising in power because the Bodos will be fed up with ABSU for selling them out for the sake of power, and ABSU is making the same mistakes that other political élites have made in other parts of the country after similar agitations,' said one former ULFA leader. That will give the BSF the political legitimacy that it needs.

ABSU's failure will not create a vacuum for there are rarely vacuums in politics: only pauses before one entity and one set of ideas are replaced by another group and a different set of values.

Since 1994, the Bodo Security Force has found a new arrow in its quiver, one that exposes the minority politics of the ruling élite in Assam. In mid-1994 and again in January 1995, militant Bodos slipped into Assam from hideouts in Bhutan and machine-gunned Bengali Muslim settlers. The immigrants are the most vulnerable of the communities—yet ironically, they have been a strong foundation for the ruling parties in the state. But the BSF, realizing that this is the weakest spot in Saikia' armoury and the devastation it could wreck on his public support, has hit repeatedly at them. The settlers have fled their villages time and again after attacks and turned against their one-time protector. This is a ominous portend of things to come.

The Rise And Fall Of ULFA

the 1980s, a new force was rising among younger Assamese.

ULFA was its acronym, pronounced by most Assamese as alpha, iving the organization a ring of mystery and secrecy. It was a word that ould strike terror through the state in a few years when ULFA leaders nd cadres virtually dismantled the administration and ran a parallel overnment.

The United Liberation Front of Asom or ULFA took shape in April 979 at the deserted Rang Ghar pavilion in Sibsagar, once the seat of the hom kingdom, and the sporting and cultural centre of that dynasty of nmigrants who 'assimilated', as did many others, with the people they onquered.

The young men who met there that day were to become household ames a decade later: Rajiv Konwar, better known as Arobindo ajkhowa; Golap Barua (also known as Arup Chetia), Samiran Gogoi and aresh Baruah. Rajkhowa's father was a veteran Congress member who ad been active in the freedom movement. He himself led the Asom atiyabad Chattra Yuva Parishad, a student wing of the Jatiyabadi Dal, at took an active role in the anti-migrant agitation.

Samiran Gogoi's real name was Pradip Gogoi and he too was a ember of the Chattra Parishad, studied science at Sibsagar and worked riefly at a government thermal power project before involving himself ıll-time in ULFA.

Paresh Baruah was one of the best footballers that Assam had roduced in years. Slim and strong, he was later to develop a military trategy that ran rings around the Assam police, paramilitary and even rmy troops for months without engaging them in direct combat. lthough he was the youngest of the original founders, Baruah was chosen s the head of the organization's armed wing.

Later, Baruah had two able deputies: Hirakjyoti Mahanta,

powerfully built and touched with a streak of cruelty and Chakra Gohai nicknamed Lambu for his height. Another influential figure was Gola Barua, later the organization's general secretary who studied at Chabu near Dibrugarh town, and who was the general secretary of the Chatt Parishad in that district. Gohain, too, is a native of the small town Chabua, located in tea garden country.

The key figures of ULFA had thus several things in common.

Some of them were also Motoks, dispossessed communities wit links to the Ahom rulers, and this factor bonded them to other disaffecte ethnic groups.

The Dibrugarh-Tinsukia sector is a broad corridor that covers the large and wealthiest tea and oil-producing areas of Assam. Tea gardens hem i either side of the highway, stretching for miles in either direction. Eac acre produces millions of rupees worth of tea every year.

These sprawling estates were among the first set up by the Britis and comprised fertile farming lands. In the days before the British, th Motoks ruled the area. Their capital was Bengmara which literall translates as 'Place where frogs are killed.' The Motoks held sway fo many generations but after the coming of the East India Company, the were thrown out of their lands and fields to make way for the great te gardens of Imperial India. There was little, if any, compensation.

'They found they had nowhere to go,' said an intelligence offici who has analysed the movement. 'ULFA began really as an expressio of opposition to more than 100 years of exploitation.' The Ahoms to flocked to ULFA to assert their dormant identity: these were rulers witho a kingdom, and a community, like many other indigenous grouf worldwide, which has found it difficult to cope with rapid social an economic changes.

In April 1979, at Sibsagar, the young men spoke of their belief th the All Assam Students Union's (AASU's) proposed agitation against th immigrants would not work, that a long-term solution was needed an that Delhi would not listen to mere satyagrahas but a more militant voic They talked of the need for a *swadhin* (free) Assam, where 'scientifi socialism' would be the way of life and where its natural resources woul be exploited for the benefit of its own people—all its people, includin the immigrants—and not to benefit unscrupulous power élites in Delhi.

Strangely, the first chairman of ULFA was not Arobindo Rajkhowa as is widely believed. It was a little-known figure: Bhadreshwar Gohain, who was active in the anti-alien movement, won the 1985 elections from the area and served as the Deputy Speaker of the Assam legislative assembly as an Asom Gana Parishad (AGP) nominee. Rajkhowa became chairman after Gohain drifted away in the early 1980s to more active, mainstream politics where the benefits were a bit more tangible.

ULFA was dormant for a long time after the April 1979 meeting. One of the reasons was the Chattra Parishad's involvement in the anti-alien movement and that of the initiators of the new ginger group. They explored their ideas further, discussing them at greater length.

After the chaos of the 1983 election, they began talking with another like-minded organization, the Assam People Liberation Army (APLA). The APLA was founded at the same time as ULFA by Arpan Bezboruah in the city of Tezpur, on the Brahmaputra. Among its key activists was Munim Nobis of Guwahati. The APLA had networks in the central belt of Mangaldoi and Barpeta as well as in Nagaon. ULFA, at the time, was building up its network and had little clout beyond its immediate circle. Rajkhowa and Paresh Baruah recognized the need to tap the APLA's channels as part of a long-term strategy aimed at liberating Assam.

After intermittent talks, Nobis and Hirakjyoti Mahanta signed a formal agreement in Nagaon in 1985 merging the two groups. But at that time, the APLA had disintegrated with the arrest or surrender of its leadership.

'Those who surrendered were finished and from then on there was only ULFA,' says Nobis, a powerfully-built, stocky man in his thirties, who is wary of visitors but talked at length when I put notebook and pen away. Outside the simple, small home in Guwahati, his father and sister sat on the veranda. It was early morning; Nobis was bleary-eyed and yawning after a late night.

The others placidly sipped tea and read the morning newspapers.

It could have been a perfectly normal moment in a perfectly normal middle class home in Assam, except that the man sitting before me was the one who had opened negotiations with the Afghan mujahideen in Peshawar, Bangladesh authorities in Dhaka and with Pakistani intelligence officials in Karachi and Islamabad on ways to help ULFA. He was credited with the assassination of Girdharilal Harlalkar, the burly president of the Kamrup Chamber of Commerce, at his home in 1988.

That was among the first of the killings that terrorized the state and turned it into a ULFA stronghold. There were other criminal charges against him, but he seemed unworried as he talked about his organization. Nobis refused to speak of the cases pending against him except that he was free on conditional bail nor would he talk about the Pakistan and Afghan connections. He did confirm the Bangladesh link although he would not be drawn out on it.

But if Nobis was not prepared to speak about these connections, there were others who were.

THE PAKISTAN CONNECTION

I met with one ULFA activist who was willing to talk on the issue on a muggy summer evening at the Bellevue Hotel in Guwahati. The humidity of May hung over the city like a thick, soggy blanket, leaving people irritable and perspiring. The well-known ULFA leader had agreed to come to the hotel late that evening, but left his personal bodyguard in his car.

I suggested a cold beer. His face lit up. 'Just the right weather,' he agreed and rapped out orders to the worried waiter in the room: salted peanuts with finely chopped onions and chillies as one dish and tandoori chicken as the other.

So, that evening over several bottles of beer and platefuls of hot peanuts and spicy chicken, one of the most fascinating and perhaps least-known aspects of the ULFA story opened up.

And this is how it was told:

In 1988, Munim Nobis made the organization's first effort to internationalize their campaign. That year, he travelled with a Bangladeshi businessman, who was well-connected to the political-military establishment in Dhaka as well as to the Pakistanis, to Karachi. He hoped that through the businessman, he would establish contacts with Pakistani intelligence agents, especially the Inter Services Intelligence (ISI), the Pakistani equivalent of the Central Intelligence Agency (CIA) and India's Research and Analysis Wing (RAW), charged with creating unrest and trouble in its larger neighbour.

Over the years, the ISI had stirred the Punjab insurrection, arming and training Sikh extremists, until a ruthless police official named Kanwar Pal Singh Gill crushed them with an iron hand. The ISI's most successful foray was with the Kashmiri militants; this was easier than the Punjab situation for here was a local Muslim population already alienated from India and ready to take to arms to fight a common enemy—the Indian State. Of course, widespread human rights abuses such as rape, torture, illegal detention, outright murder and intimidation by the Indian security forces also helped a great deal in creating these conditions.

Through the 1960s, until the creation of Bangladesh in 1971, Pakistan had put its money, intelligence personnel and arms behind the Nagas and later, the Mizos. Dhaka's hostility to Islamabad after the terror in East Pakistan that sent refugees into India and resulted in the birth of Bangladesh meant the severance of Pakistan's relations with the Nagas and Mizos. Several top Mizos were captured and the leader of the insurrection, Laldenga, barely managed to escape to Islamabad. Laldenga signed a peace accord with New Delhi in 1986 and led his Mizo National Front (MNF) to victory in state elections the following year. But his government did not last long and in a few years, the Congress was back in the saddle and the MNF, now a legitimate political party, was in the opposition.

Thus, it was after a long gap that a Northeastern insurgent group was seeking to make contact with Pakistan. Nobis apparently returned without meeting anyone from the Pakistan intelligence because his businessman friend was too cautious and unable to reach his contacts. Returning from Karachi, Nobis discussed the issue in detail with the ULFA leadership.

According to the ULFA source, the decision was taken to send Nobis back the following year—without the Bangladeshi businessman.

Nobis, according to this account, did not want to repeat the earlier fiasco. He did something that was daring and amusing. Having landed at Karachi, he marched into a local police station one night and demanded to be taken to the highest officer.

'I am from Assam and we have come for Pakistan's help,' he proclaimed. The policemen told him that he was drunk, asked him to calm down and return to his hotel. That he did—but he left the name of his hotel, his own name and that of his organization with the man in charge at the station.

The next morning, there was a knock at his hotel door.

The man at the door introduced himself as from the ISI. He was friendly but cautious: who did Nobis represent? What did ULFA want? He was sympathetic but noncommittal and said that a larger and more representative ULFA delegation would have to visit Pakistan for a fuller meeting.

Indian intelligence officials say that this account is partly true. But they believe that ULFA established contact with the Pakistanis in Dhaka first, which was obviously easier than taking a chance in a strange city in a new country.

Be that as it may, as the Indian Government prepared its crackdown against ULFA in 1990, the top political leadership and one senior army commander was in Pakistan, having flown there on a Bangladesh Biman flight. Met by ISI agents at the airport, the men were taken from Karachi to Islamabad and kept at a sprawling safe house. There were two days of sightseeing before the group was taken to Peshawar, headquarters of several Afghan mujahideen groups. The meetings at Peshawar included one with Gulbuddin Hekmatyr, the chief of the Hezb-i-Islami, which was patronized both by the Pakistanis and the Central Intelligence Agency and several Arab nations in the fight against the then Soviet-backed regime. Hekmatyr, now Prime Minister of his devastated country, which is still riven by inter-rebel and inter-clan fighting, expressed a moderate interest in his visitors but said that they were too far away for him to help.

The ULFA delegation included Arobindo Rajkhowa, Hirakjyoti Mahanta, the deputy commander of ULFA's military wing, Pradip Gogoi, the vice-president, Arup Chetia, the general secretary, and Manoj Hazarika.

All except Rajkhowa, ULFA's Chairman, took intensive training conducted by Pakistani operatives which lasted nearly a month in strategy, tactics, counter intelligence, disinformation and, of course, use of weapons.

But Islamabad was not yet going to give them arms. They needed one more round of talks to convince themselves of the commitment of this potential ally.

The next to travel to Pakistan was a two-man team. Paresh Baruah, the commander-in-chief, and Sunil Nath, his Boswell and ULFA's publicity secretary. In fact, of all its leaders, Phukan/Nath, who now uses his real name, was the most voluble, the most accessible to local and visiting journalists and the only authorized spokesman of the organization.

In September 1991, the two men landed in Islamabad. At home, Operation Rhino, that was to devastate ULFA's ranks, was about to begin.

'We were introduced to our handlers, who called themselves mujahid,' said Nath. They were put up at a large bungalow with high walls, another of the many safe houses that are located in Rawalpindi and Islamabad. But Paresh Baruah was soon restless, resentful and fretful at being cooped up indoors. An extrovert and sportsman, the ULFA army chief also disliked the domineering attitude of the Pakistanis, led by a man who identified himself only as Choudhury.

Baruah and Nath were becoming difficult guests: they refused the basic training that the others had taken. When one of the trainers tried to explain to Baruah how to pick out a tail—or a silent pursuer—the ULFA leader turned to Nath in anger. 'You do not train a man in the most elementary of tactics after he has been in the field for three years,' he snapped. 'Enough is enough! Let's go home.'

Nath calmed the furious military chieftain. 'How can you listen to their instructions? Their lectures?' Baruah exploded at his aide. But the junior rebel won the day, pointing out to his leader that they had come for a specific mission and walking out in a huff would only harm them.

After tempers had cooled, the Pakistanis took the ULFA men to Darrah, the hill town in the North West Frontier Province (NWFP) that is one of the world's biggest, open, illegal arms bazaars. Here, visitors can pick up Chinese—or Russian—Kalashnikov rifles, mortars, handguns (locally made or from the best European and American companies), grenades and anti-tank guns shoulder-fired. All for a price. (This bazaar at Darrah did flourishing business during the Afghan mujahideen war against the Soviet-backed regime of President Najibullah. Now it supplies arms to groups fighting each other in the chaos of post-Najibullah Afghanistan.)

The Pakistanis were keen for a large-scale operation in Assam that would use high-powered explosives and strategic attacks on top officials and politicians as well as strategic locations, such as oilfields and government buildings.

Baruah and Nath refused.

'This is not like Afghanistan, you cannot repeat that experience here,' they told the agents. The Pakistanis were surprised. 'We have run such big operations as in Afghanistan, your campaign is small compared to that,' the Assamese were told.

If ULFA was unyielding, so were the Pakistanis. But ISI wanted to know the logic behind Baruah's refusal to launch a high-level rebellion.

Paresh Baruah and Sunil Nath explained that in a resource-strapped state such as Assam, millions of people depended on the local government for jobs and economic security. 'Major attacks on government property will alienate us from the people and they will turn against us, not the government,' Nath told the Pakistanis.

Their hosts made two clear points: do not fight the Indian Army: it is too strong. Disrupt communications and economic targets, such as oil pipelines and gas fields, create chaos and pave the way for a general uprising against the government.

The ULFA men tried to explain that they were confident of taking on the army but reiterated their opposition to the major strikes advocated by the Pakistanis because their loyalty as Assamese came to the front. This added to the horror, as they saw it, of being instructed and to be seen by their own people as being instructed, by a foreign power to destroy institutions on which many in the region depended.

Later, several ULFA men confessed that thinking they could tackle the Indian Army was foolhardy. That realization set in after the army's onslaught with Operation Bajrang and Operation Rhino in 1990 and 1991.

'We told the Pakistanis, leave the strategy to us, give us weapons and arms,' Nath said. Weapons did not come easily from the Pakistanis although they continued to be in touch with ULFA through the Pakistani mission in Dhaka. These contacts remain strong for the Paresh Baruah group, that is exiled to Bangladesh and parts of Assam.

In a conversation with Baruah after his capture in December 1991 at Guwahati, Nath appealed to his commander-in-chief to join the peace process. First, he heard a furious attack on ULFA men consorting with the Indian Government and Hiteswar Saikia, the Chief Minister. But the conversation ended on a poignant note.

Referring to his decision to battle on and take the help of the Pakistanis, Baruah told his one-time aide: 'I'm riding a tiger and cannot dismount—either it will destroy me or I will survive it.'

At the time that ULFA was forging its Pakistani links, the Nagas of the Thuengaling Muivah faction were also active. The capture of a National Socialist Council of Nagaland (NSCN) leader, simply called German, gave intelligence officials in the Northeast a wealth of material. From German's diaries and interrogations, emerged more proof of ISI involvement. In this case, German and others simply walked to the Pakistani High Commission in Dhaka—in much the same way as Munim

Nobis had surprised a police station in Karachi—and asked to meet with people who could help their cause and renew old relationships. That took place in 1990. More meetings followed in Dhaka, Kathmandu and in Islamabad.

The ISI strategy was hardly surprising and needs to be seen in the light of RAW's involvement in assisting anti-Pakistan activities in Sindh. But more than that it falls into a pattern of Pakistani destabilization of India's border regions, making the people covertly and overtly hostile to New Delhi, such as Punjab and Kashmir, and rendering those areas more vulnerable to Islamabad's pressure.

'It is basically a war of attrition: you kick us, we kick you,' was how one intelligence official in the Northeast described the situation. These days, the Islamic connection has become a major factor in Kashmir with hundreds of fundamentalists from Afghanistan, battle-scarred veterans of the long fight against Russia and its puppets in Kabul, targeting army officials, ambushing and capturing paramilitary troops and using a range of weaponry and tactics that has shaken the Indian defence and intelligence establishment.

The advent of ULFA brought a new style to the plethora of guerrilla movements in the Northeast. The Assamese widened the description of guerrilla war in the region: from jungle camps and an uncertain income from villages—in the form of taxes levied by the Nagas and Mizos—the rebel movements soared to the five-star culture. As a result, with a few well-directed words and bullets, hundreds of thousands of rupees was offered to the militants to buy peace, protection and contribute to their 'war chest.' The rebels now travelled to Bombay, Delhi and Calcutta, staying at the best hotels and guest houses.

They combined this with a social message that reduced the obviousness of their lifestyle. That message was seen in their village reform and development programmes, where entire villages—at a spoken command from the local ULFA leader—turned out to build new roads, repair old ones, construct bunds (small earthen dams) to block floods. ULFA's power was such in 1990 that wives of police officials, and in one case, the Deputy Commissioner—or the head of the civilian administration in a district—turned up to participate in these projects. The legitimacy endowed by the presence of government officials undermined the authority of the government itself and strengthened ULFA's hold, while diverting attention from its other activities.

ULFA's ascent to power coincided with the years of the AGP regime at Guwahati. Whispers and rumours floated in of men and women arming themselves for a revolutionary struggle against the Indian State. Guwahati is a city with the dubious distinction of being one of the filthiest in India, where roads constantly either need repair or are being dug up. It also is the state's commercial capital. The talk was of young men playing judge and jury in people's courts—beating and sometimes killing individuals involved in drugs and prostitution; and banning liquor. And of extortions—gentle, persuasive requests for financial help in small, limited amounts that became demands for lakhs of rupees to be donated to the 'Emergency Fund of the Central Committee of the ULFA.'·

Fake ULFA gangs roamed the state seeking funds and extorting money at will, especially in 1989 and early 1990. Angered by the bad publicity, the ULFA leadership first issued threats to all impersonators to stop their work or face 'severe punishment.' When the threats failed to work, ULFA struck, killing extorters and their supporters in a series of incidents and summary executions.

The 'fake' ULFA began to fade although the slaying did not completely end the extortions. 'We made some mistakes in 1989 and 1990 when a lot of young people were recruited to ULFA in the various districts without proper screening,' said Sunil Nath, the one-time voice of the insurgent group.

I first met Sunil Nath in 1990 a few months before the dismissal of the AGP government and the ban on ULFA. It was an elaborate ritual.

Contact was first made through two local journalists who were known to be sympathetic to ULFA. I got a message one night at the Bellevue Hotel, located on top of a hill commanding a sweeping view of the Brahmaputra, asking me to be ready the next evening. The next day, I picked up my contact and we drove out of Guwahati to the Nalbari area without meeting a single security check.

We drove along bumpy village roads on a moonlit night to our rendezvous. Only to find that Nath had left a few minutes earlier. Later, he described life on the run as 'never spending more than one night at any one place.' Word was sent through a series of messengers as we waited and sipped tea at the local tea stall.

We were instructed, after half an hour, to drive to another village. A young man was waiting for us; the car was backed into a courtyard and our contact led us on a forty-minute walk through tiny lanes.

That walk was more out of a novel than real life. The moon flooded our path with light. It was already 11 p.m. and the villages were absolutely silent. We met no one on the lanes and most of the homes were dark. But the night was filled with the grunts and croaks of a million frogs and toads, shrill cicadas with their long cries: cheek! cheek! cheek! And fireflies flitted through the air, weaving glowing, undefined patterns of tiny, flickering lights.

We reached the new rendezvous and were fed fish curry and rice in a villager's home. We wolfed the food down by the glow of a kerosene lamp. And immediately afterward, I was escorted to meet Sunil Nath as he waited by a small pond nearby. With him were six or seven other men, one of whom was the local village teacher, simply addressed as Master.

The immediate impression was of a very cheerful man, quick to repartee, and striking in his youth. Bearded and wearing a shirt and trousers, Nath sat on a rush mat with a revolver and grenade beside him. Rather melodramatic, I thought.

Indeed, as a senior intelligence officer specializing in the Northeast said, 'The thing that strikes you most about them is their ordinariness. They do not look like the [Kachin Independence Army] KIA and the NSCN fighters, who look every inch the tough warrior.'

After initial pleasantries, the discussion on aims and means and ends really began. And throughout, Nath was prepared to take a sharpest of questions. At one point, I did ask him to remove the weapons, saying that I found their presence offensive since I was unarmed and could scarcely be a threat to him. And anyway, the presence of weapons was always not conducive to a free discussion. The gun and grenade were moved away.

'We will not make the mistake of the other insurgencies, we have learned from the Nagas and the Mizos and will not repeat their mistakes,' he said at one point, responding to a question about how his organization could confront the might of the Indian State and the Indian Army. The point that I was making to him was that the government would at one point surely use the army, which was far better equipped and tougher than the Assam Police. It would then use the crackdown to seek out and encourage divisions in the ULFA as it had so successfully done in the case of the Nagas.

'Everyone says they won't repeat the mistakes of earlier revolutions but they end up doing the same thing,' I remarked. He reaffirmed his position: they would not bow to the power of Delhi but instead would force the army to retreat from Assam.

Of course, eventually, it did not work that way at all.

That meeting and the conversations with Sunil Nath and his associates, some of whom had been trained in Myanmar with the Kachins and the NSCN, established one point beyond doubt: that the AGP and its surrogate organizations, such as the AASU, were closely associated with the ULFA. Not officially of course, but at the village and other local levels.

Thus, the Master was the local secretary of the AGP. Another young man was the village chief of the AASU unit. The networks that the ULFA used to spread its message and gain information included these channels as well as their own.

'We were in the andolan (agitation) together, many of us know each other,' said Nath of associations with the AGP leadership.

ULFA's power was not drawn solely from money and arms, although both were crucial factors. It lay in its understanding of the Northeastern mind, but especially that of the Assamese who were fed up with annual floods, failure of political promises, growing unemployment, unease that the anti-alien movement had not won them tangible gains despite the AGP's presence and the knowledge that New Delhi was still trying to bulldoze its diktat through.

ULFA also tapped a source that had been first touched by the Nagas: the Kachin connection.

ULFA'S first major contact with the Kachins came in 1986 when Paresh Baruah travelled to northwestern Myanmar through the eastern edge of Arunachal Pradesh, along the little-travelled road to Khonsa in Tirap District and then slipped across the forested terrain.

He also established contact with Thuengaling Muivah of the NSCN and met with Manipuri rebels and others in the Kachin camps.

In 1980, after breaking away from Angami Zapu Phizo, Muivah's group captured most of the weapons from his mentor's faction, the Federal Government of Nagaland, and drove them further into the wilderness.

S.S. Khaplang, who first supported Muivah, fell out with him over the latter's insistence on a tough moral code of conduct for his followers and a stop to opium use and liquor. The dispute between Khaplang and

Muivah over principles and aims simmered in the background as Baruah and others like the handsome, powerfully-built Jugal Kishore Mahanta, took groups of young Assamese men and a handful of women across from the Brahmaputra Valley to the NSCN camps and after 1988, to the Kachin Independence Army.

The Kachins agreed to give training to the ULFA men and women—but at a steep price. The relationship between the two groups was controlled as much by cash as by nationalist aims, though directed at different regimes. The moneyraising spree that ULFA embarked upon until late 1989 can be partly seen in this context: the need to pay their trainers and suppliers. In 1988, the Kachins demanded about one million rupees, then worth about 60,000 US dollars, for arms they proposed to sell to the ULFA fighters.

To meet the demand, the NSCN and ULFA planned and executed several daring bank robberies in Guwahati and elsewhere. They raised a total of 4.2 million rupees through robberies and extortion from local businessmen and sent their contribution amounting to one million rupees to the KIA. Since it was a joint operation, the NSCN helped itself to forty per cent of the booty from the banks.

The money for the proverbial 'war chest' had begun to flow. But the Kachin link was soon to suffer a blow. For in 1989, the Research and Analysis Wing, established contact with the Kachins. It was a time when Burmese pro-democracy students and politicians had taken shelter in India from a crackdown by the military regime, stung by popular support to the opposition led by Aung San Suu Kyi.

The Kachins were told bluntly that if they continued to back ULFA and the Nagas, the government would turn out the thousands of refugees in Manipur and other parts of the country. And since politicians from the mainstream groups of Myanmar also had taken shelter in Kachinland, this counsel prevailed.

That year, the Kachins let ULFA know that they could no longer sustain the armed support. The KIA wanted ULFA to look elsewhere for assistance. This came as a setback to ULFA but it was not before long that Munim Nobis, whose tough exterior camouflaged a street-smart negotiator, was picked to tap the Afghans, the Pakistanis and Bangladesh intelligence officials.

When the Kachin connection was finally snapped, the ULFA cadres turned to the Nagas. The Kachins were more expensive and gave training over a longer period because their camps were further away from the border. The NSCN camps were near the Indo-Myanmar frontier in areas controlled by different Burmese Naga tribes: the Konyaks across from Nagaland under Khaplang's command; then there were the Angamis and Tangkhuls who backed Muivah and Isak Swu. Swu was the other major leader of Muivah's faction and officially its chairman.

The NSCN camps were mobile ones: shacks of bamboo, thatch and tenting material. Muivah lived simply among his people, aware of the need for absolute vigilance although the camps were at heights of above 8,000 feet. In 1987, when Jugal Kishore Mahanta went, there were already small groups from the Manipuri Peoples Liberation Army (PLA) and the Peoples Revolutionary Party of Kangleipak (PREPAK), also from Manipur.

There was little interaction among these groups at the NSCN base camp, across the border from Ukhrul district in Manipur, Mahanta said. At one point, they were surprised by a Burmese army attack. (The Burmese are among the toughest and most brutal soldiers anywhere. They are also incredibly mobile in that mountainous, wet terrain covered by thick jungle.)

In that incident, the NSCN soldiers and the ULFA trainees fled through the thickets, firing defensively as they escaped. At least two Assamese were killed in that encounter. Apparently there was little on-the-spot training given to recruits in weapons or explosives. That was because the size of the armouries was limited. However, recruits were taught the elements of armed strategy for guerrillas: how to survive under difficult conditions, how to operate undercover and build up networks of informers.

After this spartan schedule that lasted six months, Mahanta taught children of different ages at a school. This was, he says, part of a 'service' that ULFA would do for its fraternal associates. Other cadres also went through such a training and teaching period.

Mahanta said that he was surprised by the ignorance among many Nagas. 'They would say that the earth was flat and I had to explain to them why it wasn't,' he said, speaking of the primitive knowledge of these communities. And when some Burmese Nagas came over to Assam with the Assamese insurgents, they were astonished by the size of the towns, the quality of the roads, the bright lights of the shops and homes and the relative affluence that was visible in the clothes which people wore as well as the vehicles they rode.

'But what are you fighting for,' some of them would ask Mahanta in bafflement. 'You have electricity, drinking water and cars—you are already free.' To Mahanta and others, this came as a surprise: that to other nationalist struggles, especially those which have long fought for independence under harsh conditions, the symbols of freedom were those which ULFA and others took for granted.

Some ULFA men and women also trained at the Khaplang headquarters further north. And it was the relationship with the Khaplang group that later separated ULFA from Muivah, albeit temporarily.

In a surprise attack in 1989, S.S. Khaplang's forces smashed one of Muivah's major bases at Tahabashti near the international border. Thirty-six men and women fled from the camp. Only six survived. They included Muivah and his wife. Angami Zapu Phizo's one-time top aide escaped by leaping down a rockfall, gashing his head badly in the process.

He sent word to his former trainees at Dibrugarh that he needed time to recoup and reassemble his scattered forces. Could they keep him safely for some time? The response was quick and positive.

Thuengaling Muviah, general secretary of the National Socialist Council of Nagaland, slipped into Assam through one of the many jungle routes and was escorted discreetly to safe houses in the Dibrugarh area.

For two months, under the nose of the Indian security forces—including its numerous intelligence agencies—Muivah lived in villages and towns, in Dibrugarh itself, in the township of Margherita (named either after a colonialist's lost love, perhaps, or the sparkling Spanish concoction that someone in the area was fond of) and in Sonari town. The most significant name in the insurgency lexicon of eastern India lived in this manner for two months until ULFA received a curt warning from the Khaplang group.

There were about 200 ULFA cadres at the Khaplang camp and they were being virtually held hostage. If ULFA wanted these men and women safe, then the Assamese would have to let Muivah go. The risk was too great. Reluctantly, for they respected the man's intense drive, his commitment as well as his ability to take a broader view of things, ULFA's leaders told Muivah of their problem.

He understood, he told them, and decided to return to take on his foes. The Assam rebels escorted him to Dimapur, the untidy plains town at the foot of the rise to the Kohima hills. From there, Thuengaling Muivah slipped into Kohima, the Naga capital, and then quietly moved back to his faction on the other side of the border. By this time, his forces had regrouped.

The Indian Government's intelligence department received word of his presence in Nagaland but no one moved to capture the rebel leader. This was surprising although it was not the first time that he was reported to be in Nagaland. He had come earlier over the years, to nurse wounds or to seek recruits. The answer to how he managed to evade detention is simple, according to one intelligence specialist from the area. 'We are not there to arrest the man, our job is to provide information to the Government about a person's location, to analyse events and set out possible scenarios,' he said. Often—as in the case of Muivah—the police, bureaucracy and political connections slowed the process of information filtering to the top. In such cases, the 'spotter' gives the details to a local police official of the state government; this is then sent on to district or state headquarters before it is conveyed to Delhi. By the time it reaches senior officials either at state or at the Centre, the subject of the report has long gone. Plus there are the strong connections between the underground and politicians, especially in Nagaland. This relationship cuts across party labels and includes both serving and former ministers of the Congress Party as well as the different opposition factions, members of which were once active underground figures and who maintain links with Muivah and his men.

Yet, for ULFA at least, the Muivah link had been snapped. For the next months, ULFA sent their groups to the Khaplang faction in Myanmar for further training.

All this time in Assam, word was fast spreading about the 'boys' going to Myanmar. During a visit to Dispur, I was talking with a senior official in the state capital when a former president of AASU dropped in. After some general talk, the bureaucrat asked, 'Where is your brother?' 'He's still abroad,' the former AASU leader responded. A little later, he left.

I turned to the official. What was that little aside all about, I wanted to know.

The bureaucrat grinned: 'His brother has gone to Burma for training

182

with ULFA. "Gone abroad" is the phrase that these days identifies people who have gone to Burma.'

In Assam many people were openly dismissive of ULFA's aims. The Assamese middle class was regarded as too soft, too set in its ways, incapable of sustained effort, too enamoured of the security of government jobs and unable to launch and organize a long-term, large-scale insurgency. It just would not work, they said. Violent struggle was not part of the Assamese ethos. Eventually, they were proved violently wrong.

The boys from Myanmar came back and set up a near-flawless organization that struck at the roots of government authority. Yet, the ministers in Assam were in the know. ULFA also capitalized on the differences in AGP as much as its own anti-Delhi views.

The dissensions within the AGP surfaced soon after it came to power. For a long time, despite accounts of corruption and abuse of office and nepotism, the public was prepared to look the other way. But by 1989, relations between the major leaders of AGP, Home Minister Brighu Kumar Phukan and Chief Minister Prafulla Kumar Mahanta had deteriorated to the extent that they were hurling charges at one another in public. 'I am not happy with Brighu Phukan's functioning as Home Minister,' said Mahanta to the *Illustrated Weekly of India*. 'He has not been able to do justice to the department.' Responding to this vote of no-confidence against him, Phukan replied in the same issue of the *Weekly*: 'Mahanta is not sincere about implementing the (Assam) accord on the basis of which we were elected to power.'

Mani Shankar Aiyer, the sharp-tongued Congress Member of Parliament from Tamil Nadu and long-winded but entertaining columnist, described them in the *Sunday* magazine as 'this quarrelsome Odd Couple.' Aiyer added that the two men 'hate each other with a venom they usually reserve for non-upper caste, non-Hindu, non-tribal, non-Assamese speaking settlers in the Brahmaputra Valley, i.e. themselves and their immediate kith and kin.' His graphic description was somewhat off the mark on facts: the AGP and especially Mahanta and Phukan were largely anti-tribal and pro-non-tribal, who largely comprised the caste Hindu Assamese.

Much had happened between 1985 and 1990 that caused a failure of public confidence in the AGP. Among them was a series of scandals, financial and moral, and sheer arrogance, that enveloped Mahanta and his colleagues.

In one, the associates of a minister attacked a passenger on an Indian Airlines flight for refusing to surrender his rightful seat to the pompous politician. In another, the Minister for Forests (who also happened to be the Chief Minister) was accused of acting improperly in the cutting of trees for railway sleepers. But the one that hit the headlines for a sustained period of time was what came to be known as the Statefed scandal.

In this, a group of contractors cornered twenty million rupees (about 600,000 dollars) worth of contracts for supplying foodgrains to the statewide network of ration shops, where the poor drew their rations at subsidized rates. The grain supplied was rotten and, as the scandal broke, the AGP politicians ran for shelter.

Ashok Saikia, an upright official who was then Education Commissioner, was asked to look into the charges. But when he began to nose around too much for the comfort of the party and complained about of the pace of the investigation at a state cabinet meeting, he was led aside by the Chief Minister and told gently, essentially, to keep quiet. 'The money is for the "boys,"' he was told.

One of Assam's leading writers, Homen Borgohain, said the following of the AGP, whose Home Minister described the ULFA as 'from among us':

They have introduced a different political culture, if you can call it a culture, which is totally devoid of refinement and respect for moral values . . . . I do not mean to say that all politicians before them were saints and only the AGP politicians are a bunch of rogues. But they frighten me by their arrogance, intolerance, bad manners and disrespect for our age-old values.

By the end of 1990, there were few who disagreed with Borgohain.

Thus, AGP's slide in popular support came at the same time as ULFA's ratings soared. The AGP did not understand that its shortsightedness was preparing its own political grave but also eventually readying the ground for an eventual Congress return to power. In the short-term, though, it appeared that ULFA would profit most and fill the political vacuum.

Not only did the AGP fail to control itself; it also allowed the law and order situation to deteriorate so widely and rapidly that it was virtually asking to be dismissed by the Centre.

In the interregnum, ULFA was everywhere: it gained an almost invincible halo. Its informants infiltrated the police to the extent that when the state's Director General of Police watched a video film seized from an ULFA camp in 1990, the policemen on duty outside the room passed on the news to militant activists. 'They were inside all day, the D-G and at least two other senior police officials,' said an ULFA functionary, gloating over the knowledge that the underground knew instantly what its opponents were doing.

Meanwhile, the money was flowing in. It was deposited with a range of officials, businessmen and others, apart from direct collections. In one case, money was left with a Deputy Commissioner. When ULFA cadres were courageously challenged by some who wanted to know their identity, they would respond contemptuously and demand that the money be left at a politician's home or even at an official's residence.

Yet, within ULFA's power structure too, there were cracks. Since the central command was spread out, these differences began to show. For one thing, not all the local military commanders turned in their dues. Some scorned threats of punishment and kept substantial amounts for their use and that of the local organization.

There was another problem: many young Assamese were seeing these large sums of money for the first time. It was only a matter of time before temptation overwhelmed the shaky.

That warning had been fired at ULFA leaders when they met Bijoy Hrangkhwal of the Tripura National Volunteer Force (TNVF) which fought against India—but more against the Bengali-dominated Left Front government in his state—for eight years before surrendering arms in 1988. Hrangkhwal told me that the ULFA men had gone to seek contacts and assistance from him.

'I told them, "You are too soft, you need to be much tougher to last in the jungle, you depend too much on jeeps, motorcycles and good shoes,"' he said of that encounter. The response of the boys is not known but Hrangkhwal's warning struck home when reports of luxurious lifestyles by ULFA leaders and their supporters began to circulate in Assam in 1990.

Yet, when the pickings came, even ULFA was surprised by the swiftness with which the state abdicated its responsibilities and businessmen succumbed to pressure. A simple telephoned threat, the display of weapons by tough-looking militants, 'friendly advice' or even an occasional roughing up was enough to help local traders part with millions of rupees. In Assam, apart from the public sector which was built around oil, gas and jute, and a few private industries, as well as tea, there was little in terms of an industrial base. Most of the business activity was confined to trading, which required little capital investment or market strategies.

By firing the least number of bullets, by capitalizing on the Assamese caste Hindu distaste for physical violence, by drawing the tacit support of the AGP (which never criticized ULFA attacks even on its own law enforcers) and gaining the political middle ground, ULFA had become more than a parallel government. It had gained legitimacy and was virtually ruling several parts of the state. The de jure regime at Dispur found that its writ ran only inside the warren of tacky sheds doubling as the capital of a state and in a few places outside.

As ULFA grew bolder, it also grew harder in its demands and harsher in spirit. The days of bargaining for contributions, when businessmen could discuss and plead with militants for a reduction in the demands made on them, had gone. 'It was easily the most efficient money gathering extremist machine in India,' said one intelligence analyst. 'This is likely to be the way that future insurgencies function: disrupt the economy and the authority of government by simply controlling the flow of funds and diverting hard cash. It would reduce the need for sustained armed struggle and also achieve the aim of fuelling local resentments.'

Non-compliance with demands for money, given on ULFA letterheads with the symbol of a rising sun, were met with warnings of 'punishments'. Clearly, such a stand would be bad for the health of anyone who challenged the legitimacy of the demand.

Girdharilal Harlalkar, the head of the Kamrup Chamber of Commerce and Industry, was an early victim. He was mowed down by a hail of bullets in his home at Guwahati in 1988. There had been differences between him and the militants on payments, although the Marwari businessman had been a long-time funder and supporter of both the AASU and the AGP.

Other businessmen were targeted in Guwahati. The leader of the United Minorities Front (UMF), a grouping of non-Assamese communities, including Muslims and Bengalis, was shot dead. As the graph of violence grew, Congressmen too bore the brunt of the attacks.

A sense of fear ruled the Brahmaputra Valley. Parties were discreetly thrown; marriage receptions were low-key. Politics and ULFA were not discussed openly and noisily as in other parts of the country where a conversation on politics usually drew much heat and little light.

By 1990, there were few businessmen who had not been touched.

'It was amazing, we asked for a little and they were prepared to go well beyond what we wanted,' said one ULFA leader. 'That was when we realized how soft the state was, how weak the businessmen were, how much black money they had, that they could pay up and still have enough for themselves.'

The tea gardens too succumbed. Most groups paid 1.5 to two million rupees for each garden. Others paid more. Some, which were doing poorly, paid less. But few gave less than 5,00,000 rupees. All this time, ULFA's treasury, or what some referred to as its 'war chest', grew. Militants also sought and politely took away licensed weapons from their holders. No one informed the police.

Young men would 'request' also the use of vehicles and promise to return them by a given date. The cars would be used for ULFA operations—largely ferrying people from one part of the state to another—and then returned on the appointed date to their legal owners. There was fear—but respect too. Needless to add, requests for such assistance were rarely denied.

ULFA also selected several businessmen to keep their money. On its list of money and ULFA harbourers were medium and junior level government officials, including policemen and contractors. In some cases, there was willing co-operation. In other cases, people were warned that if they did not hold the funds, their corruption would be exposed publicly and they would be 'severely dealt with.' 'It was a classic dilemma for many of these businessmen,' said a contractor at the business centre of Tinsukia. 'They chose the easy way out.'

It ultimately turned out be a good business deal for many who guarded the money. They had a large, assured source of credit on tap. And when ULFA called in its debts, the businessman or agent would pay up the money with a five per cent interest. The arrangement suited both parties. In the case of one prominent Guwahati businessman, who was arrested for assisting ULFA and later released, the militants 'found him convenient and he found them an easy source of money,' said a police official.

Those who were not cowed by threats did exist. But they were miniscule in number. In one case, a young Assamese tea plantation manager rolled up a letter from ULFA and flung it into the waste paper basket saying that he had neither the authority to negotiate with them or even to accept such a demand.

Yet despite these pressures, ULFA's popularity was not merely mandated by fear. There was genuine backing from villagers and the middle class as well as academics and students.

Many said they were pleased that ULFA had stopped money from flowing out of Assam: they wanted funds and profits generated there to be used for local development. Another sentiment was that corrupt officials, politicians and businessmen had been taught a lesson.

ULFA's supporters and cadres fanned out in the countryside and organized camps and programmes that emphasized self-help. But unlike other organizations, they were far more effective. An entire village would participate in the construction of a dirt road or an embankment against floods at the call of local organizers.

Farmers were helped to farm fallow lands and the excess production shared among the peasants. Officials in the Agriculture Department at Dispur acknowledged that in many parts of Assam, their extension projects had been virtually abandoned except in the ULFA-dominated areas. 'We do not even have to go there; the ULFA men and women support the programme because it helps the local people and thus strengthens their own political base,' one official said. Dry-season farming, multiple cropping, use of new seeds and hybrids were developed in some of these areas.

Thus, ULFA used the government's projects to secure its rural base. One official said that a commune concept for agriculture was tried in Assam in the 1960s but largely abandoned. Yet, in ULFA's rural strongholds, these pioneer multiple cropping systems actually worked. Only twenty per cent of the original projects had survived. Most of them were in the ULFA-dominated places, especially in north Lakhimpur district.

Even a prominent Member of Parliament, Bijoy Handique of Tezpur, remarked that there was 'genuine sympathy for them at one point.' 'When the people saw the Congress was weak and they could not get justice from the AGP either, they turned to ULFA,' Handique said. Alcoholics were beaten or ordered to do sit-ups holding their ears; several who ran prostitution and drug rings were warned and later kidnapped and shot when the threats did not work. Summary executions even had the support of an ultra-nationalistic middle class fringe that felt betrayed by the independence movement of the 1940s as well as successive governments and political parties in Delhi and in Assam.

This was Assam in November 1990, pulled in different directions by different forces, all of which claimed to speak in the name of the state or a community which had settled there. Few, if any, had the region's long-term interests in mind. Most were set on marginal, short-term political gains.

That year, ULFA was at the peak of its power.

Its writ ran unchallenged, watched by a cringing state administration and the ruling Asom Gana Parishad, whose members were hand-in-glove with it. In the words of Subodh Kant Sahay, who was then the Minister of State for Home Affairs between 1989 and 1991 under two Central Governments, it was 'in full command' of much of the Brahmaputra Valley. Not a leaf stirred without its approval, especially in the Assamese Hindu-dominated areas.

The Centre watched with a mixture of outrage and impotency, unable and unwilling to dispatch the military machine of the Indian Army against the extremists. It was handicapped by two considerations. One, it did not want to repeat what New Delhi had done in Kashmir—by divesting Farooq Abdullah of power and appointing his *bete noire* Jagmohan to the Governorship, it had destroyed the last remaining buffer, as the then Railways Minister and Minister for Kashmir Affairs, George Fernandes, described it, between a politically legitimate government and extremism.

Second, the AGP was a member of the coalition National Front (NF) that functioned under V.P. Singh. The then Law Minister, Dinesh Goswami, handsome, elegant and outspoken, was the AGP's saving grace at the national level. With grace and political sophistication, he made amends for the inefficiency, corruption and incapability of the AGP otherwise unable to either articulate a coherent programme or stand up to militant pressure or that exerted by hardliners within its organization. AGP hardliners sought to bulldoze the political hopes of smaller indigenous groups, insensitive to the swift destruction of the state's fragile social fabric.

Ministers in the National Front argued that getting rid of the AGP, imposing President's Rule and a military crackdown on ULFA would destabilize the Central Government, giving an opportunity to the Congress to get on with its party-breaking programme, both in Delhi and Dispur, and alienate the Assam valley from 'mainstream' India. Assam was regarded as the only state in the Northeast which was essentially mainstream—because it was basically Hindu, had a strong tradition of involvement in the freedom movement, had largely been free of communal trouble (which means free from the Hindu-Muslim strife that characterized much of northern India) and was a stronghold, despite AGP's accession to power, of a nationalist party: Congress.

Delhi dilly-dallied and took the easy way out. It called in Chief Minister Prafulla Kumar Mahanta and his rival for power, Home Minister Brighu Phukan, who was even believed to have harboured ULFA militants, and told them to toughen up their act. Mahanta responded with monosyllabic acknowledgements of the problem but did nothing.

One of the cabinet ministers in Mahanta's government was regarded as an ULFA nominee. The Centre made several demands that Mahanta drop him but the Chief Minister held off until circumstances totally unconnected with New Delhi forced his hand. The minister turned up drunk for a Cabinet meeting, made a pass at a Bodo woman minister, Renukarani Brahma, called her a prostitute and then vomited in front of a stunned group of colleagues before collapsing. He was carried out of the meeting in a stretcher. Later that day, Mahanta dismissed him.

'The whole machinery was with the ULFA,' said Subodh Kant Sahay of the state government at the time.

The failure of the AGP became evident within hours of the enthusiastic swearing in of Assam's youngest Chief Minister—and India's for that matter—and his victorious colleagues at the sprawling, dusty Nehru Stadium in Guwahati in December 1985. The squabbles were over trifles: which cabinet minister would get a particular car with a particular number.

There were clashes over wanting specific rooms in the untidy Dispur Secretariat, a warren of corridors and rooms smelling of betel nut, tobacco and tea. The sprawl was once a dilapidated bunch of tea warehouses that were converted into Assam's temporary capital in 1972 when the state government moved its headquarters from the bracing climes of Shillong where a new state of Meghalaya had been created.

The police were outgunned and leaderless, a helpless organization cowed by the political clout of their opponents and too frightened in many places to even venture out of their police stations to investigate a complaint or reports of an attack. 'We had .303s, they had automatic weapons, they would threaten our families, what could we do?' one constable told me in 1991 in helpless anger.

One of the results of this overwhelming demoralization was that large numbers of police personnel, at the lower ranks, began associating with ULFA. They began with passing on information of potential raids and security plans and went on to give details of the travel routes of senior officers on the hit-list of the militants. In turn, they were paid handsomely.

By the end of 1990, not just the police administration but the intelligence gathering activities of several agencies in the area: the Special Branch (SB), the State Security Bureau (SSB), the Intelligence Bureau (IB), the Subsidiary Intelligence Bureau (SIB), the Central Intelligence Department (CID), not to speak of the Research and Analysis Wing and Military Intelligence (MI), had virtually ground to a halt. Source of information dried up. Informants were threatened or beaten. Some were killed. Agents were reluctant to work in the areas. It was a nightmare for operatives, says one intelligence official.

The climate of fear was all-pervasive.

People were reluctant to talk with visitors about the political situation. No one quite knew who would inform either the militants or the government about an anti-militant view. Conversation would dry up at parties when ULFA came up for discussion.

'No one but no one was prepared to talk to us,' an IB official said. The businessman who paid out whopping sums as protection money was not prepared to complain out of fear. The government officer who was threatened with exposure and ridicule and forced to pass on large amounts of illicit black money, sourced to years of corruption and bribery, was silent. The tea plantation executives were afraid to call in the government, because it was seen as an extension of ULFA, and lose their managers to bullets. They paid quietly out of their large profit chests.

The swiftness with which the tea industry, especially, capitulated with contributions for ULFA's 'war chest' took even the militants by surprise. 'If we asked for something—in terms of lakhs or crores—it would be paid within days, before the deadline that we had set,' said one senior ULFA leader.

Ultimately, one company did take courage in both hands to defy the diktat of the militants. And that marked the beginning of the turning point for ULFA and its campaign. That refusal from a company in the town with the unlikely name of Doom Dooma had everything out of a Jack Higgins thriller: intelligence operatives, diplomats and business executives in London and Delhi, a secret midnight flight to evacuate frightened men, women and children and high-level Cabinet meetings that ultimately led to a crackdown.

The only thing missing was a good dose of romance and sex.

When Chandra Shekhar took office as Prime Minister in November 1990, having ousted V.P. Singh by a mix of money power, political sleight and sheer audacity, the first briefing that he received from the Director of the Intelligence Bureau was on Assam and the crisis created by ULFA and the failure of the AGP.

India's ninth Prime Minister was appalled by the total collapse of the intelligence, administrative and political setup in the state.

Chandra Shekhar set his government two priorities in Assam: one, the ouster of the AGP government and two, the destruction of ULFA's military and social-political base by the military by declaring President's Rule. From being the darlings of the Assamese middle class and installed with such high hopes in December 1985, the AGP had degenerated into a bunch of squabbling, impotent factions led by spineless politicians. It had become a cloak for ULFA's activities.

But Chandra Shekhar, canny and clear, needed a reason to swing the executioner's axe to decapitate the state government.

It came in the form of a request for assistance from London and from Unilever Brothers, the multinational with worldwide interests in detergents, cosmetics and tea, and their tea garden in Doom Dooma.

The story began in May 1990, when several companies in Calcutta received a summons from the ULFA leadership to visit them and hold talks on the 'economic development of Assam.'

Several executives, including representatives of Tata Tea, Macleod Russel and MacNeil Magor, executives from Unilever and the state's foremost Assamese planter, Hemen Borooah, flew into Dibrugarh on 28 June 1990. That evening, a young man turned up on a scooter to meet them. No drivers were allowed and the executives were to drive the cars on their own. The ULFA contact man left his scooter and sat in the front car, directing the small motorcade as it bumped over the town's small lanes and then to a small tea garden in the neighbourhood. As they approached the plantation, young men in military uniform armed with automatic weapons stood at attention on either side of the path. Dusk was gathering and the pressure of intimidation was working as the executives, unaccustomed to such tactics, began to worry about their safety.

The cavalcade drove into the estate manager's home and the visitors were ushered into the bungalow and made to wait in a room.

The lifestyle of India's tea planters conveyed a sense of British gentility and an old-world tranquillity. Pretty tea sets of bone china and the *Daily Telegraph* from London specially flown in for weekly reading, conjured up a life of ease and luxury that was out of step with the turbulence in the valley. There were the nightly rubbers and chota pegs downed with cheerfulness at the decaying planter's clubs and servants to attend to every bidding.

But the manager's home that the executives were visiting looked different to their familiar pleasant world: it had been converted into a military base and was swarming with men and weapons.

They were taken to the ULFA negotiators in batches representing individual corporations. The first to go were Ravi Rikhye, a Vice-President of Macleod Russel and Goutam Baruah, another company Vice-President. Baruah had, before leaving, spoken to his wife in Calcutta about the mission and the dangers it posed. They talked till late about the future and the assurance that the company would take care of her and their daughter should anything happen to him.

Tapan Dutta, the lean, young commander-in-chief of the Dibrugarh unit of ULFA led the questioning. Armed guards kept fiddling with their weapons behind the executives, clearly aimed at unsettling them.

'Aren't you ashamed of exploiting Assam all these years?' snapped Dutta, starting on an aggressive note. Rikhye replied that his company had ploughed back its profits into the state, with welfare projects such as hospitals and schools and hostels for its workers and their children. When they were questioned further, Goutam Baruah pointed out that the company's hospital was the most modern in the Northeast with imported equipment and specialized medical staff.

Since they had been invited to discuss the economic development of the state, Baruah said he wanted to give some practical ideas to improve things. He offered, on behalf of the company, to donate 100 tractors to different villages to help local farmers set up sunflower seed farms. The climate and soil conditions, he said, were just right for the crop in Assam. The Indian Tobacco Company (ITC), one of India's biggest conglomerates, would set up small oilseed pressing plants to extract the oil. The oil could be marketed across the country and the villages would benefit financially.

Dutta responded, says Baruah, with a sharp retort: 'Save us your lectures. We want one crore rupees [about 300,000 dollars] from you.'

The executives said they needed time to consult their directors and could not give a decision on the spot. Baruah remarked that the demand for cash had not been mentioned in the letter at all. The militants were unrelenting. If the money was not paid out, the local managers and garden executives were at risk, they said. After a while they said the interview was over and signalled for the others to be let in separately.

By midnight, the discussions had been completed and the executives were prepared to drive back to Dibrugarh. But ULFA was not quite finished with them yet.

Earlier that month, when they received the ULFA letter, members of the tea industry's apex body, the Indian Planters Association, went to Dispur where they met Chief Minister Prafulla Kumar Mahanta, Chief Secretary Haren Das and Director-General of Police, S. Subramanium. The Chief Minister told them, in no uncertain terms, that they were on their own and the government could do little to bail them out.

In the muggy night, as the executives waited, the ULFA leaders sounded another warning: 'We know you have complained about us to the Chief Minister. We know everything that happens in Assam and if you go and spread the word about this meeting, the consequences will be very severe.'

With this ominous farewell, the party trundled its way back to the town, leaving the next day for Calcutta to consult with their bosses.

At Calcutta, they made their presentations to their respective boards. Several of the key players paid up, but few of the negotiators ever came to know of it. One man resisted: Hemen Barooah. As a result, the short, cherubic Barooah, the only true industrialist that the 'natives' had produced in decades, was forced to take the protection of security guards. During the years that ULFA reigned supreme, he lived most of the time outside his home state, spending much of the time at his corporate headquarters of Calcutta, elsewhere in India and abroad.

Another organization also balked at the idea of paying: Unilever. Although the company had a policy of not yielding to pressure internationally it could not risk its managers and executives in Assam. ULFA had demanded 3.5 million rupees (about 1,10,000 dollars at the time) from Doom Dooma's seven estates to fund its 'war chest'. Half a million was to come from each estate. Unilever's Indian subsidiary, Hindustan Lever Limited (HLL), sent an urgent message to the head office in London, asking for directions. London got in touch with the then Indian High Commissioner to Britain, Kuldip Nayar. Nayar, one of India's best-known newspaper commentators, especially on India's relations with its neighbours, in turn urgently messaged his friends in the National Front government urging them to take tough measures against ULFA.

In the beginning, the Indian Home Ministry was reluctant to act against ULFA. It did not want to needle a constituent of the Central Government or give the volatile student movement in Assam a chance to cry foul. But as the days passed, Mahanta's government agreed to Central pressure to enforce the Disturbed Areas Act in the state's ULFA-dominated districts: Dibrugarh, Sibsagar, Jorhat, Nagaon and Kamrup which would give local officials sweeping powers to arrest and search suspects.

Yet, the Assam government dragged its feet; at one point, a senior official said that the government could not act if the planters did not file an official complaint—a First Information Report or FIR—about the threats at the local police station. That, the dismayed planters felt, would be tantamount to announcing their intentions in a full page colour advertisement in a local paper and inviting the wrath of ULFA. As a result, they turned to the then Commerce Minister Arun Nehru, the Machiavellian former Internal Security Minister under Rajiv Gandhi. Nehru was portly, powerful and arrogant. But even his intervention did not go far enough.

Time was slipping by. In Assam and at Calcutta, the sense of desperation in Unilever was increasing. Frustration grew as the Central Government teetered and tottered with factionalism wrenching it apart. Devi Lal, the then Deputy Prime Minister and old Haryana war horse, switched sides and put his weight behind the ageing Young Turk from Ballia, Chandra Shekhar. The political manoeuvring went on through September and quickened in October. Prime Minister V.P. Singh in his martyrish style virtually invited defeat on the floor of the Lok Sabha and paved the way for Chandra Shekhar, who had lived in a perpetual sulk since November 1989 after the opposition defeated Rajiv Gandhi's bid for a second term.

At that time, in Parliament's sprawling and high-domed Central Hall, Devi Lal and V.P. Singh pulled off a coup of sorts: they persuaded Chandra Shekhar not to run for office, indicating that Devi Lal would be given the job. Secretly, the two had planned it in such a way that Devi Lal spurned Professor Madhu Dandavate's request that he take the top job. Devi Lal suggested that Singh be picked instead.

Livid with rage but silent in his anger, Chandra Shekhar commended V.P. Singh but never got over the betrayal. He was to refer sneeringly to this when in his blistering attack on V.P. Singh, he let his real feelings out in the open: 'Stop lecturing us about morality,' he snarled. 'We know how principled you were when you came to office.'

In 1990, V.P. Singh was destined to defeat, having lost the support of the right-wing Bharatiya Janata Party (BJP). V.P. Singh had alienated the BJP by arresting its President, Lal Krishna Advani in Uttar Pradesh as the latter travelled on his infamous Rath Yatra. The Yatra was supposed to express BJP's determination to build a temple at the birthplace of the god Rama at Ayodhya in that state, a view opposed bitterly by Muslim groups and centrist parties, on the site where a non-functional Muslim mosque stood prior to 6 December 1992.

As the infighting in Delhi continued, the Research and Analysis Wing, the Intelligence Bureau and Military Intelligence decided to take a hand. Under the tacit supervision of Minister of State for Home, Subodh Kant Sahay, they began drawing up plans that would involve first the evacuation of Unilever staff from the plantations at Doom Dooma and then the dismissal of the AGP government.

Without fuss and publicity, a control room began functioning in Delhi co-ordinating this operation with London and Calcutta and, of course, the Assam sector. Unilever officials kept in touch from Calcutta, where they had set up their own operations room. But to maintain absolute secrecy, none of the middle and junior management officials were told about it, especially in Doom Dooma.

An initial plan to fly out the staff and their families from Guwahati on scheduled Indian Airlines flights was dropped when the company made a demand for 100 tickets. The airlines suggested that a special plane be chartered instead. To make the escape smoother, the intelligence authorities located a little-used RAW airfield a few kilometres from the plantation. A Boeing 737 would land here, it was decided. And a date was fixed: 8 November.

All this time, tension was rising in the Doom Dooma fields, especially since ULFA had increased its demands and incorporated Brooke Bond and Lipton to their list of companies which needed to pay up. Brooke Bond and Lipton are Unilever companies, although they have separate corporate entities and managements, and have traditionally bought nearly sixty per cent of all tea auctioned at the auction centre in Guwahati.

The price for Doom Dooma was now nearly fourteen million rupees (about 7,00,000 dollars), fixed at the rate of two rupees per kilogram of tea produced on its gardens. Brooke Bond and Lipton were told to cough up five per cent of their net profits.

The trading companies simply closed shop in Guwahati and bolted. The tea market suffered a free fall on the stock markets as prices slumped.

On 3 November, ULFA presented its latest demands to Doom Dooma: two million rupees within one week and 2.2 million rupees as investment in a local sports stadium. The noose was tightening and Delhi decided to move quickly.

On 7 November, the Boeing 737 flew into Calcutta and then went the next morning to the airstrip near Doom Dooma. After midnight on 7 November and in the early hours of 8 November, senior executives from different tea gardens of the Doom Dooma group wakened their deputies and families. They were given two hours' notice to pack their belongings, especially valuable goods, and bundle their families together. Waiting cars and vans sped them to the airfield. But they had to move without drawing the attention of ULFA's intelligence system. So, the vehicles moved at intervals, taking different routes and timings to get to the airfield. Many families were terror-stricken, and did their best to keep children quiet and out of sight.

The tension increased and became palpable when plane technicians realized there was a hitch which would slow the departure. 'We just sat and hoped and prayed that the ULFA boys would not notice any unusual activity,' said one of the senior managers who stayed on after the airlift. By the time the engine snag was fixed, it was too late to carry out the second part of the plan: to pick up company officials from Guwahati and take them on to Calcutta. Instead, the Boeing lumbered over the runway and took off, heading straight to Calcutta and safety.

More than a 1,000 kilometres away, in distant Delhi, another drama was being played out.

The Raja of Manda, Vishwanath Pratap Singh, had just lost his throne in Delhi, unseated by the calculating Thakur from Ballia, Chandra Shekhar.

For Assam, but especially for ULFA, the countdown had finally begun. For Chandra Shekhar was clear from the outset that there was no alternative to a military crackdown and the ouster of the AGP regime. It was a difficult decision for a man who swore by democratic socialism and was one of the most prominent followers of the late Jayaprakash Narayan and his anti-authoritarian struggle of the 1970s. Chandra Shekhar had himself been imprisoned for opposing Indira Gandhi's authoritarian state of Emergency between 1975–1977, although he was a prominent leader of her Congress Party at the time.

But, in the words of one of his closest advisers, there was no choice. Operation Doom Dooma effectively closed all options. It provided the security agencies and the anti-AGP forces within Assam, which meant the Congress and the Home Ministry in Delhi, a solid reason to press for a strike against the Assam extremists.

Chandra Shekhar and his team gave Prafulla Kumar Mahanta a few more days of respite. But the abrupt manner in which he dealt with the AGP leadership in the two weeks after he came to power gave Dispur no illusions about what he had in mind and his concern over Assam's anarchic descent into chaos.

THE EMPIRE STRIKES BACK

In September 1990, Lieutenant General Ajai Singh, a burly officer from the armoured corps, the tank arm of India's war machine, was summoned to Delhi by the then Chief of Army Staff, Alfred Rodrigues. Ajai Singh, then on the western front with Pakistan, was told he was being made Corps Commander in Eastern India. He was to be based at Tezpur, one of the forward bases of the Indian Air Force. Lieutenant General Singh is a jolly man who peppers his conversations with 'Roger!' and wears a pukka accent as well as a silk scarf. Troops of the Eastern Corps manned the hostile, mountainous northern frontiers with China and also kept a watch on the Bangladesh and Myanmar borders, which were hilly and densely forested. Both frontiers were difficult terrain.

Ajai Singh was told that he should be prepared eventually to 'deal with a law and order situation.' It was his first assignment in the Northeast but within days of his arrival, the tension in the area was obvious. His wife would go to the local bazaar, under tight security, and return with what Ajai Singh called 'strange tales' of people doing situps, obviously as punishment for some wrongdoing, of shopkeepers being threatened, of extortion, beatings and street fights.

As the situation deteriorated in Assam and ULFA's power grew, the Indian Government, under Chandra Shekhar, decided to act.

On 18 November, General Singh was called to Calcutta by the officer commanding all the eastern units of the army, General K.S. Brar. The latter was a tough officer who had taken part in Operation Bluestar at the Golden Temple in Amritsar against the Sikh militants in 1984 and also led the campaign against the Liberation Tigers of Tamil Eelam (LTTE) by the Indian Peace Keeping Force (IPKF) in Sri Lanka. Both operations were bloody; they scarred fighters and peoples on either side.

General Brar was precise: the army was likely to be called out soon in Assam to deal with ULFA and, Ajay Singh should begin preparing, he suggested. Fine, said Singh, but what about local intelligence to home in on ULFA, its camps, network and leaders. Forget it, he was told. The Intelligence Bureau, the state Central Intelligence Department, the Special Branch and the Subsidiary Intelligence Bureau had been scattered and ineffective, their operatives were targets of ULFA and too frightened to volunteer information. In fact, decisions made at Dispur often reached ULFA before it could reach local officials. Intelligence, Ajay Singh was told, had been compromised. He would have to set up his own sources.

'You have to start with nothing,' Brar remarked.

Ajay Singh returned to Tezpur to organize one of the largest peacetime military operations in India. Over 30,000 soldiers had to be transported from different parts of India, but particularly from parts of the Northeast, to other areas where they would see action. All this was to be done without attracting the attention of ULFA.

The process took nearly ten days. By the evening of 26 November, the soldiers were in place, Ajai Singh was ready and New Delhi was prepared. The official Presidential proclamation ousting the AGP from office was signed by President Ramaswami Venkataraman just before midnight.

At 4 a.m. on 28 November, a few hours after the AGP government had been dismissed—heavily-armed troops in jungle combat uniform and camouflaged gear swept out of barracks in trucks, jeeps and light armoured personnel carriers. Helicopters took off from army and Indian Air Force bases to drop paratroopers and were prepared to give covering fire should ULFA resist.

Operation Bajrang had begun. The army would stay, General Brar told reporters, till confidence was restored. He did not identify a time frame.

ULFA was declared a terrorist and secessionist organization and banned: this meant that association with or membership of the rebel group was a criminal offense, amounting to a treasonable act and punishable with life imprisonment or the death penalty.

When Assam woke up that morning, the jungle green of the army was everywhere, stunning village populations who were roused from their beds in house-to-house searches.

Naturally, the mild-mannered Assamese villager was offended at this intrusion of his privacy. It was a face of the army that Assam had never seen although other parts of the Northeast were familiar with it: the harsh, demanding, accusatory questions; the pushes and shoves that accompanied initial interrogations; and the rounding up of suspects, many of them frightened and uninvolved, pulled out of their homes before tearful children and family members, pushed into trucks and taken to army camps for further questioning.

The first ULFA camp that was struck was at Lakhipathar, in the heart of a thick jungle of teak and bamboo thickets, a short distance from both Digboi and Dibrugarh, the tea capital. The troops encircled the camps, banking on information supplied by police and other informants. The army's distrust of the police and local officials was demonstrated through the operation: during the Lakhipathar operation, the Deputy Commissioner and the district Superintendent of Police of the area were restricted to the local police station with clear orders not to move out. They, too, were clearly regarded as suspect. It set the pace for a strained, mutually suspicious relationship which meant that neither side co-operated with the other. The army kept blundering into situations that it could have avoided if it had taken the district administration into confidence. It did not want to do that because of concern that word of its plans would be leaked to ULFA.

When the soldiers attacked Lakhipathar, they found a deserted camp. ULFA had been tipped off more than a week earlier of the possibility of an army assault.

ULFA'S preparedness was visible from the fact that as far back as 17 November, Paresh Baruah ordered ULFA cadres to vacate the headquarters at Lakhipathar. The intelligence leak was at a high level for the information about the army assault was known only to a handful of officials in the Home Ministry and the army command.

ULFA was ready—but the army was not.

More than 30,000 soldiers from different divisions were assembled and put together to fight in a totally unfamiliar terrain. 'Assembling troops from different formations transgresses the command and communication structure, which is the basis for success of any army operation,' said Pravin Sawhney, a columnist who specializes in security matters.

There was no resistance because there were no rebels to confront the army. It was the first meeting with the elusive enemy and the encounters took a toll on the soldiers as they became increasingly frustrated with the lack of progress.

The Lakhipathar camp was empty but ULFA leaders had left behind a batch of books, weapon training manuals and documents which confirmed the existence of women insurgents. But there was little in terms of people or details of the organization and how it worked. The element of surprise was totally missing, the frustrated officers realized. And they also realized that Lakhipathar was not the only camp for men like Paresh Baruah, the commander-in-chief. There were as many as seven satellite camps from which the militants operated and which kept a vigil on comings and goings, and gave warnings of troop movements. The rebels planted what the army called Improvised Explosive Devices (IEDs), or booby traps at the entry to the camps, to delay entry and cause confusion among the attackers.

Lakhipathar and its neighbouring camps had been chosen well: not only were they secluded but they were also close enough to the Burmese border—about three hours via Khonsa in the hills of Arunachal or a few hours to Dimapur in Nagaland and then across hill roads to Myanmar—for a quick getaway. Further, the camps were surrounded by a ready source of funds: the tea estates.

Its very inaccessibility made Lakhipathar easy to defend and difficult to attack directly.

Apart from the books, there was other evidence of the extremist presence that shattered the Robin Hood image that ULFA had cultivated so assiduously.

On 4 December, a large grave was found with fifteen decomposed bodies. Many of the victims had been dumped in the graves after being shot and their hands and feet bound with rope. The discovery of the graves was described by P.P. Srivastava, one of the advisers to the Assam Governor appointed by Delhi after President's Rule, as 'concrete evidence of the brutalities of the militants on innocent people'. P.P. Srivastava, who handled the Northeastern desk in the Home Ministry in Delhi, said that the corpses could be those of people kidnapped by ULFA over the months and who had simply vanished thereafter.

Essentially, Lakhipathar, according to a ULFA leader, was a torture and picnic spot. It was a place where the senior officers of the rebel outfit relaxed and planned their future in the silence and seclusion of the forest. It was also a place where hapless detainees, captured for various 'crimes' such as selling goods on the black market, running gambling and prostitution rackets as well as not paying up to ULFA, were kept, tortured and then killed. There were reports that several missing police informants were among those kidnapped.

At Saraipung, not far from Lakhipathar, ULFA had set up a camp with twenty bamboo thatch huts with separate living quarters for men and women. This was more of a training centre, for it had a large lecture hall, a reasonably well-equipped six-bed hospital and a kitchen. In the centre of the camp was an open field for daily drills and marches with a flag staff in the middle. The cadres kept fit with these daily drills as well as exercising with games such as volleyball.

Saraipung, also in the dense forest near Digboi, was one of the few camps where the army faced resistance. But it was not a prolonged firefight. Three bodies of ULFA men were picked up from here while five wounded cadres were captured. Also seized were a few television sets, cars and motorcycles and some bed rolls.

The scale of the seizures were dishearteningly poor.

A majority of the weapons that the army showed to reporters who were driven and then guided on foot to the forest camps were duds: wooden rifles used for training and thus little better than toys.

Yet the Saraipung camp was a clear indication of the capacity of ULFA to move silently and swiftly from its bases as well as its ability to organize large training camps. One estimate said that the Saraipung camp was capable of training about 200 recruits and cadres. It had large amounts of rations, including eighty large bags of rice—which is the main staple of the Northeast—and other food.

Most people asked how it was possible for such a network of camps to be set up and sustained with visitors, permanent residents and food supplies without the local police and villagers coming to know of it.

The fact is that villagers knew that large amounts of food were going into the forest. They knew too of total strangers, who did not belong to their villages or neighbouring ones. Yet, they kept their peace. The reason was simple: 'They had not interfered with us, they did not harm us and we saw no reason to harm them,' said one villager from the Lakhipathar area. 'We did not ask them their identities, these were tough-looking men, and we would simply greet them and go on our way.'

The police knew of some 'activities' in the forests. At one point, they even held two ULFA men briefly before Operation Bajrang in the Tinsukia area. But the men were released swiftly, apparently on orders from senior AGP members.

The most celebrated story of the ULFA presence in Lakhipathar was about a handsome and brilliant footballer who organized inter-village football tournaments or matches between village teams and ULFA. He was the fastest man on the field, who would set up the maximum number of goals or score the highest himself.

On one occasion, the young man led a village team in a local match against the local police eleven.

Later, the police discovered that the fleet-footed young man was none other than Paresh Baruah and several of his teammates were ULFA cadres.

Yet another insurgent legend of the Northeast had been born.

In fact, the guerrillas watched the army floundering in the jungle with a mixture of apprehension and amusement. For when the troops struck Lakhipathar, Arobindo Rajkhowa the Chairman of the militants, as well as Paresh Baruah and Sunil Nath were several miles away at Saraipung.

At Saraipung, the ULFA leadership held two days of discussions on how to respond to the security crackdown. 'We held the General Council and then the next day fled on the different routes that we had already chosen,' said Nath.

Baruah told Nath to take the young women recruits in the camp away to safety. They were concerned that the troops would rape and torture the women if they were captured. And that they would break quicker under pressure from their captors and interrogators.

All that Nath had for a weapon was a .38 revolver. As the stillness of the night of 28 November was broken by distant shots, he escorted the group of frightened women out of Saraipung through friendly villages before establishing contact with other ULFA supporters. The group then dispersed.

It was not for a few days that the official reaction came from the militants. Chairman Arobindo Rajkhowa called on the people to resist the army and said that the action reflected New Delhi's colonial and imperialist presence and interests in Assam.

Throughout Operation Bajrang, Sunil Nath and Paresh Baruah spent most of their time criss-crossing Assam and avoiding arrest. Arobindo Rajkhowa and General Secretary Golap Baruah, also known as Arup Chetia, fled first to Meghalaya and then across the border into Bangladesh.

But there were differences in ULFA on how to tackle the military intrusion. Men like the Dibrugarh unit's Tapan Dutta and the feared marksman, Jugal Kishore Mahanta advised against precipitating a full-scale confrontation with the army. 'We told Paresh Baruah that we cannot fight the army,' they said later. ULFA would not find it possible without heavy weaponry or the backing of a strong neighbour that was unfriendly to India, to fight an effective, sustained guerrilla struggle.

But there was little positive response to these views from the ULFA leaders. In one meeting called after the military operation was closed in April 1991, the Dibrugarh unit's organizers sought to raise the issue of inner-party democracy at the General Council, which comprises all political and military commanders from the districts. This was the second highest group in the hierarchy of the organization. The top was the Standing Council, comprising the Chairman, the commander-in-chief and general secretary Arup Chetia.

According to one newspaper account, the Dibrugarh commander was 'not allowed to proceed with the subject. After this, when he tried to raise it again, he was once not given the opportunity to express his point of view.' Later, said the *Times of India*, the Standing Council 'vetoed the move toward inner-party democracy.' The ULFA constitution gives sweeping powers to the Standing Council.

The scale of the crackdown in Operation Bajrang frightened the Assamese in the rural areas. 'They did not know what to expect and panicked,' one of the former insurgents said. In the process, people who had been open and welcoming turned into sullen, cautious supporters, unwilling to go beyond simple assistance, worried about raids, arrests, torture at the hands of the security forces and long periods of detention.

The opponents to the plans of resisting the army were brushed aside by Paresh Baruah and the others. The struggle would continue, they said, on their terms and with the help of the local population.

That turned out to be far more difficult than they thought.

In Madras on 28 November, Jugal Kishore Mahanta was preparing to travel to Sri Lanka to reestablish contacts with the most powerful insurgent group in Sri Lanka: the Liberation Tigers of Tamil Eelam. The Tigers were one of the best-organized, fanatical (even suicidal as the later attacks on Sri Lankan military officials and especially on Rajiv Gandhi showed) who brooked no opposition, even from fellow Tamils seeking to fight for a Tamil homeland against the authority of Sinhala-dominated Sri Lanka. They were brilliant tacticians and guerrilla fighters. They had fought the Indian Army—the Indian Peace Keeping Force—to an exasperated, frustrated standstill, resulting in angry attacks on civilian populations as well as on the Tamil militants, and were continuing their unending struggle against the Sri Lankan military.

In October 1990, ULFA had played host to an LTTE operative, Dinesh Kumar. He had visited Lakhipathar for one night and had stayed in Assam for a total of three or four days before returning to his country via Madras. The ULFA/LTTE link never progressed much beyond this but Mahanta's mission was meant to be the major step forward: to set up channels for training and arms supply for ULFA.

The news of Operation Bajrang changed all that.

The ULFA man flew back to Guwahati instead, via Calcutta. He landed at Dibrugarh Airport and, as in earlier, untroubled times, walked straight past the security guards—including army troops kept there just to nab men like him—without being frisked, checked or even studied with suspicion.

Once inside Dibrugarh, he was able to activate his network of supporters and friends and slipped out of the town into the villages and forests of the district. But his luck was running out.

In December that year, Mahanta was fleeing from an encounter with the army when he fell into a village pond. Several jawans hurled themselves on him, wrestling him into submission. In the process, he suffered a broken leg. They carried him away, without knowing they had stumbled onto a prize catch. It was only when he was identified by local police a few days later that he was medically treated and his leg wound properly strapped and plastered.

In June 1991, just about the time that Assam was preparing for elections and the army had been ordered back to barracks to allow politicians to move about in an arena cleared by security forces, Mahanta scaled the high walls of Dibrugarh prison and fled in waiting vehicles kept positioned by ULFA cadres.

He was not caught again but finally opted to surrender to the government of Hiteswar Saikia, who became Chief Minister after the 1991 elections that returned the Congress to power. But even these days, he has to turn up in court to face charges of murder and extortion as do other ULFA leaders. But they are free, under the terms of a general amnesty, to move around Guwahati and the other towns and villages of Assam.

For their personal security—which is under threat from their former comrades-in-arms, who remain based in Bangladesh and across Assam and who refuse to negotiate with the Central Government or Saikia, as well from vengeful relatives of those they have allegedly shot—they still carry automatic weapons, especially pistols that can be whipped out quickly from a coat pocket or a belt holster.

Yet, as Operation Bajrang continued to struggle forward, reports began surfacing of ULFA surrenders. Most of these were stage-managed and comprised informants, not the hard-core fighters, whom the troops had managed to crack. The leadership of ULFA remained largely intact and elusive. The first fourteen days had resulted in the capture of 500 informants and a handful of low-ranking cadres, who passed on little information for they knew little.

The structure of the militant organization was such that those at the village level would know only what they were told. Their next level of command was at the district level. Even the district-level commander was assigned specific tasks by the central command, which basically functioned as the General Council. Fund raising was delegated to the district committees which were then to hand over the money to representatives of the Council or specific couriers of the top-ranking leaders of the Standing Council.

It was clear that the army intended to stay. But within a few days of Operation Bajrang, it also became clear that its task was changing: it was no longer assigned to merely capture ULFA members—a job that was proving difficult because the enemy was so elusive—but of marginalizing the organization. This meant that the troops were to ensure that ULFA stopped functioning as a smooth network of extremists, able to move and strike at will.

The task was made more difficult by the swampy terrain, the lack of co-operation of the Assamese—who can be as stubborn as they come—and the incessant monsoon rains that flooded the land, creating a body of water as far as the eye could see.

The army strategy of 'marginalizing' ULFA was three-fold: first, to maintain such pressure on the activists that they would have to scurry for cover constantly and to also make their safe houses vulnerable; second, to ensure that their sources of communication, by wireless, telephone and by physical movement, were curtailed by tapping telephones and intercepting wireless messages, setting up hundreds of road blocks and checkposts along major and small roads, within and outside towns and villages, to stop vehicles and frisk their occupants; third, to cut off their sources of funding.

'It was a psychological struggle against ULFA as much as an armed one,' said a top security official. 'We had to maintain relentless pressure.'

Efforts to increase the pressure were getting stymied in several ways. For one thing, army searches were failing to turn up the millions of rupees that ULFA was supposed to have extorted from the tea industry, businessmen, contractors and professionals such as engineers and doctors.

Where was ULFA's proverbial 'war chest?' A few breakthroughs led to the capture of businessmen conduits in Tinsukia and also to the seizure of funds amounting to about twenty million rupees in different parts of the state. In one case, a police sub-inspector was found with about 2,00,000 rupees for ULFA. Other homes where weapons and funds were found were more vulnerable. A government official who opened a bag which had been left behind by his younger brother, who was ostensibly travelling on construction projects, found that the bag contained pistols and bundles of hundred-rupee notes. Stunned by what he regarded as his brother's betrayal, the man kept silent on the issue until army soldiers crashed into the house one evening and pulled out the cache. He was about to be taken away for questioning when the younger man broke down, owned up the responsibility and was swept away for interrogation.

Despite these occasional successes, the security searches yielded little in terms of hard-core activists, weapons and cash. There were reports of army men extorting money from villagers, much in the manner of the police in Punjab—taking away a young man for questioning and then demanding money for his release. Intelligence reports confirmed a series of these cases. There were also strange stories about ULFA men on elephant-back carrying great bundles of cash out of Assam into Myanmar.

In Dibrugarh of February 1991, an army colonel (who did not drink for a change), the owner of the Mona Lisa Hotel, a hearty Assamese, and I talked for more than an hour at the hotel bar about the army's operations and the ULFA 'war chest'.

'Where the hell is the money?' said the colonel in exasperation. 'We have looked everywhere and we can't find it.'

He waited for an answer. When none was forthcoming, for we were far more interested in what he had to say than in responding to his statement, he went on: 'The trouble here is that nobody tells us anything. The police don't want us here, they are secretly supporting these fellows, the villagers don't like us, they are too scared or too committed to give clear information.'

In his confession lay the roots of Operation Bajrang's stalemate. It had failed to win the confidence of the local population as well as the administration and its sinews—especially the local police. The declaration of President's Rule meant that the political process had come to an abrupt halt. The Governor, Lokenath Mishra, and his advisers were the power players in Dispur but they were not really in touch with development in the state. At senior levels of the bureaucracy, as well as the police, there was deep dissatisfaction with the way advisers like N.K. Prasad, a former policeman and, a friend of Chandra Shekhar threw their weight around.

Yet, the pressure was sufficient for ULFA to indicate through news statements that it was prepared for discussions on the substantive issues of sovereignty but only after the government withdrew the 'black laws' such as preventive detention and the Disturbed Areas Act that empowered soldiers to shoot and kill at will without their authority challenged even in court.

Some of its sympathizers in the press spoke of a growing feeling that the organization had perhaps jumped the gun: that it should have begun with negotiations in the late 1980s before openly confronting and revolting against the authority of the State.

'There is that feeling, I think, among them,' said Parag Das, the editor of *Budhbar*, one of Assam's most influential and anti-establishment magazines. 'They may have gone too quickly in one direction.'

Das, who also is the secretary of the Guwahati Stock Exchange, was later arrested and accused of propagating and helping the ULFA cause. In March 1992, he was picked up by the army along with another editor of a pro-ULFA magazine, *Saatdin*, and a prominent lawyer and civil rights activist. They were later released. They had apparently committed the crime of exposing army atrocities through their newly-formed human rights group, Manav Adhikar Sangram Samiti, better known as MASS. Several months earlier, MASS had published a report that had recorded thirteen cases of death in army custody, seven rapes, 120 cases of torture,

139 cases of illegal detention and sixty-three cases of 'indiscriminate' army raids on villages and neighbourhoods.

Their detentions followed the arrest a few months earlier of two young journalists who were accused of acting as low-level couriers for the banned organization and helping to transmit some of its statements. The press created a furore over the detentions and eventually, all of them were freed. Parag Das says that he was kept at one point in a bare room with no toilet or washing facilities, barring a bucket and a mug.

As summer began, India prepared for elections to Parliament. And T.N. Seshan, the blunt and abrasive Chief Election Commissioner outlined a schedule of polls for the country. Assam was to go to the polls in June after Punjab. This, the Election Commission and the Centre believed, would enable the movement of security personnel to protect voters in the two states and reduce threats from militants.

Clearly, with the elections in hand, Operation Bajrang had to be wound down. As bureaucrats and politicians from different parties threw themselves into the turmoil of campaigning, the army was ordered to return to barracks in April 1991. The move angered senior military commanders in Assam who said their job was still far from over.

'I knew that we would be called back,' said one senior army officer later.

All political parties had agreed to the army's withdrawal before the election. The AGP took special pride in declaring that the Centre had to bow to its demand on the withdrawal of the army.

The withdrawal of the army, cleared by the advisers to the Assam Governor, Lokenath Mishra, gave ULFA the breathing space that it needed so badly. It would not intervene during the elections but concentrated in the preceding weeks to reestablish links with its cadres, boost the morale of its supporters and forge a new strategy to battle Dispur and Delhi.

This was precisely what Ajai Singh had feared. It was also what any simple observer of the Assam situation could have told Delhi. Overruling the army, the Central Government announced it would stop military operations during the run-up and during the balloting.

But the army did take a few elementary precautions.

According to Brigadier Deepak Bhanot of the 73rd Mountain Brigade, 'The ULFA made our job easy.' After the suspension of army operations, 'They came out and started revamping their organization, collecting funds, recruiting youths and hitting their targets. Our intelligence operatives tailed them, got details of their hideouts and their party structure, all very discreetly, so that now when we have been asked to crack down, we know whom and where to hit.'

Bhanot made these remarks in October 1991, nearly one year after Operation Bajrang and a month after it had been renewed in the form of Operation Rhino.

During the elections, ULFA said that it neither supported nor opposed any group or political party because it did not believe in the Indian form of democracy which was 'exploitative' of Assam, its people and resources. It said it would scrupulously stay out of the elections, but added that it supported candidates who backed its aim of an independent nation. The intelligence agencies feared that if the AGP returned to power, then ULFA would simply stage a mini-coup and assert its authority over the government.

However, nothing like that happened.

In the meantime the AGP had split. The differences between Brighu Kumar Phukan and Prafulla Kumar Mahanta, who squabbled like bad neighbours, erupted finally in a bitter division. Dinesh Goswami, Steel and Law Minister in the National Front government, sided with Brighu Phukan.

In the campaigning that followed, Goswami—simply known as Dinesh Da—was killed in a car accident. The loss was felt across Assam for he represented a more dignified representation of its political life. In 1990, he had quit as minister—and later withdrew his resignation—after members of the All Assam Students Union resumed an oil blockade to protest the slow progress on the 1985 Assam Accord. He was recording, he said, his anguish and helplessness at the open defiance of his own government by AASU.

The split in the AGP provided the Congress an opportunity for which it had been long waiting. Tarun Gogoi, one of the prominent Congress leaders in Assam, said, 'Quite frankly, if we do not win this election on the basis of the division in AGP, then we do not deserve to win any election.'

211

The AGP split confused the Assamese, dividing their vote. The Congress, whose basic support had changed little during the years, with backing from Bengalis and Muslims and some tribes, took full advantage of the situation. It cruised to a convincing win with an easy majority of 126 seats. Hiteswar Saikia, reviled for years, cold-shouldered and distrusted, having lost several relatives to ULFA's bullets, was picked leader of the Congress legislature party. Saikia was anointed as Chief Minister again after a gap of six years.

Prafulla Mahanta's AGP won nineteen seats. Phukan trailed with a bare three.

And as Saikia, savouring the taste of victory and the stunning defeat of his foes, took office, ULFA struck.

On 1 July 1991, a few hours after Hiteswar Saikia was sworn in as Chief Minister, ULFA kidnapped fourteen junior and senior officials from Assam's oilfields as well as the Additional Secretary in the General Administration Department, A.S. Srivastava, from outside his home in Guwahati.

It was a well co-ordinated, daring strike that planted ULFA back in the public eye. Some of the oil engineers and executives were picked up from their homes. One of them was a Soviet national and engineer at Digboi, Sergei Gritchenko. Sergei was actually not the man who was to be seized: the actual target was a Soviet couple who were away from their home at the time of the raid. And it was the burly Sergei's misfortune that he happened to be in the house when the ULFA men arrived.

Sergei did not give up without a fight. He fought his captors as they hustled him to a waiting car, ignoring warnings that they would shoot him if he did not stop struggling. The car held one other hostage and as it sped away from Duliajan town to an ULFA hideout, it was flagged down by T.S. Raju, another engineer with the Oil and Natural Gas Commission (ONGC).

That was another fatal mistake. Raju's car had broken down and he wanted a ride to the nearest drilling site. He found himself dragged into the car, another unwilling hostage.

Saikia found himself in the middle of a first class crisis and he searched for ways to tackle it.

There was little good news those days. ULFA declared first that it would release the hostages if twenty-four of its men were freed from prisons.

Then on 9 July, Sergei was reported killed after ULFA said he attacked his guards, tried to overpower them and escape. But actually, he was killed within a day or two after his kidnapping, because according to one ULFA source, he simply could not be subdued by threats or physical intimidation.

Three days later, the state government released eleven of the 'wanted' militants as part of a general amnesty that freed a total of nearly 400 ULFA suspects from prison. The army was aghast and furious.

Director-General of Police, Prakash Singh, a veteran policeman from Uttar Pradesh who had taken over from another state-mate, B.G. Kharkhowal, was upset. He had met the Chief Minister and had urged strongly against giving in to the demands of the militants. The Chief Minister, he felt, had agreed with him.

When the announcement came through, Prakash Singh did the only honourable thing: he asked for a transfer to his home state where he was appointed Director-General of Police. There he was to tangle with another ugly problem: communal divisions and violence promoted by fanatics among Hindus and Muslims.

But Hiteswar Saikia went on with his policy of freeing the prisoners. At the same time, he moved quickly to consolidate his political position by talking to all shades of opinion: artists, writers, editors, opposition politicians, businessmen, tea barons, professionals and bureaucrats. He would visit even the homes of his foes, surprising them, seeking their counsel and advice.

As opinion veered around against ULFA for its kidnappings and the killing of Sergei Gritchenko, as well as the long incarceration of people seen as innocent pawns, engineers in Assam's oilfields went on strike, refusing to work until they were assured of safety and demanding the release of their kidnapped comrades. It was one of the first major acts of defiance of ULFA and it gave Saikia an added political strength.

By late August, public patience had worn down and Saikia laid the ground for his next move.

At Jorhat, to the surprise of the audience that included the then Deputy Commissioner Papa Rao, Saikia declared that he was the 'Chief minister of 2.2 crore [22 million] Assamese not merely of the hostages.'

He was coming to the end of his patience.

On 8 September, T.S. Raju, the engineer who had been kidnapped, was to be released. Instead, he was let go by ULFA militants near a railroad track and shot dead. The killing sent shock waves through Assam for it showed a rarely seen ruthlessness.

Saikia had had enough. He also now had an excuse to confront ULFA. The Chief Minister sent word to Delhi that there was no option but an army crackdown to bring the rebels to heel. He had exhausted his political options and had released twenty-one of twenty-four militants sought by ULFA. ULFA had responded by releasing three hostages. He could not, he told ULFA, release the remaining three because they had been arrested by police in Meghalaya and Nagaland. Their cases were not in his jurisdiction.

All along, the hostages were being shifted from place to place and ULFA issued threats one after another that any effort to save them would end with their executions. In one incident, a hostage was killed when troops and police stormed an ULFA safe house.

Throughout the hostage crisis, ULFA and the Chief Minister were in touch with each other. First through intermediaries which included journalists, then police officials and government functionaries. 'They wanted some absurd demands: like releasing all those held on heinous crimes,' said Histeswar Saikia. He refused to yield but the messages kept coming. Then ULFA told Saikia that if they released two hostages, they wanted nine of their men out. Arup Chetia, the general secretary of ULFA, called Saikia several times to press for the release. He gave the same answer: that he could release all not charged for murder but that he could do nothing about the three ULFA figures held in jails in Meghalaya and Nagaland. A message came through the mediator on 15 September saying that Paresh Baruah would call Saikia.

'At 5 p.m., he called and spoke to me,' said Saikia. 'He demanded the release of the ULFA men, but I told him it was not possible. I could not do that.' The conversation ended. Afterward, the Chief Minister was pensive. He had been elected to administer the state. But ULFA was making that impossible. He had lost several close relatives in their attacks, including two nephews and a brother and remained at the top of their hit list. But from the point of statecraft, Saikia realized that it was not viable to have talks with them and allow them to go ahead with their campaign. As a result, that night, the army assault on ULFA targets began.

THE CHARGE OF THE RHINO

But the preparations began much earlier. On 4 September 1991, Ajai Singh received a fresh summons from his headquarters at Calcutta. He was told that the army was required for a new anti-insurgent operation because the kidnappings and other attacks by ULFA, which were rocking the state, were also eroding the authority of the Central Government and jeopardizing national security.

Ajai Singh decided to base at Guwahati and not at the traditional headquarters of Tezpur. The reason was simple: this time around, there was a power centre in Assam in the shape of Hiteswar Saikia who had gained a popular mandate to rule—however limited it may have been in the eyes of his opponents. The advisers to the Governor, who ran the state during President's Rule, had been men of little vision or ability and completely out of touch with popular sentiment.

It had been clear to the military authorities even in Operation Bajrang that ULFA had a popular base and that it was not merely feared but also respected.

The question was how to erode this influence.

To Ajai Singh, there was clearly a political as well as a military battle to be fought and won. And he knew that the political game had to be played by a master of manoeuvre, Hiteswar Saikia. According to the General, there were three 'spaces' in society. 'One is the political space for governments and parties, a second is the public space for people to function normally and the third is the military space that enables these other spaces to function.'

ULFA had occupied the military space by rendering the police ineffective, destroying sources of intelligence; it had seized the political initiative by weapon power that terrorized the political parties. Its larger than life image permeated every sphere of life: professional, business, farming and social interactions.

One of Ajai Singh's first calls was to Haren Das, the Chief Secretary of the state. He wanted a meeting with the Chief Minister. It was set for 10 September.

At the Chief Minister's office in Dispur, the two strangers sized each other up. To Ajai Singh, here was a man who played his cards close to his chest but who knew the system as no one else, who was both shrewd and capable of strong action. Hiteswar Saikia smiled at the General and said: 'So, General sahib, we have had to call out the army again within a few months.' He asked Ajai Singh if he would get the army's full co-operation. Ajai Singh responded: 'Mr. Chief Minister, we have been asked to aid the civil government and we will do anything that you ask of us.'

The statement buoyed Saikia.

'Then, General,' he declared, 'we shall smash these fellows.'

Ajai Singh also made a promise to himself: that he would try and complete the military operations by 31 December 1991.

Within hours of that initial meeting, the government and the army set up a Central Command Coordination Council, comprising the Chief Secretary and Home Secretary as well as senior representatives of the paramilitary force, the Assam Police and state and Central intelligence agencies. Saikia sent orders to his Deputy Commissioners in the districts to hold daily meetings with local military commanders and police chiefs on operations planned and strategies finalized. Saikia said, he wanted a report every evening on the action in each district.

Ajai Singh ended up by dominating the Council as the officials turned to him for advise on tackling the rebellion. Politically, it was very different to the situation that the army faced in Operation Bajrang when the people, the media, the officials and even the police were hostile. This time around, for a change, even the press was not bitterly opposed to the Operation.

As the Operation began in the early hours of 15 September, Ajai Singh was ready with the political, intelligence and administrative backing that he had lacked the last time. As Brigadier Bhanot of the 73rd Mountain Brigade remarked to a reporter later, the army intelligence agents had quietly tracked several ULFA operatives who took the opportunity of the elections to move about freely. As in Operation Bajrang, more than 50,000 men were moved into positions over a period of several days. And when the strike came, it was unexpected, scattering ULFA and forcing its members underground again for the second time in less than a year.

The first strike was in Arunachal Pradesh, where ULFA camps had been set up in the Namsai forests of Lohit district. The area was ideal for hiding:

thickly forested and lightly-populated but with few proper roads or telecommunications.

Soldiers from the Mountain Division and the 13th Punjab Regiment, rolled into the area. Since the marshy land made quick movement difficult helicopters dropped three columns of commandos at night and others, in jeeps and trucks, positioned themselves at all possible entry and exit points to catch fleeing rebels.

Three bases, little more than clusters of huts, were destroyed but no ULFA cadre were located. Documents disclosed the names of a number of militants. But the army was not disheartened.

'We forced ULFA to return to the home base where it will be possible to zero in on them,' said one army commander. The game plan was to flush them out into the open countryside of Assam where the army was prepared and waiting.

And that is precisely what happened.

The initial foray was called Operation Cloudburst. Rhino was to continue as a natural sequel.

To carry the battle to ULFA, the army leadership also drew up a secret list of insurgents who were not to be taken alive. It was clear to the army brass that the troops could not hope to break ULFA without physically liquidating these men.

Heading that list was Hirakjyoti Mahanta, the deputy commander-in-chief of the rebels, who was operating in the Guwahati region. Mahanta was dreaded for his power and brutality; he also was known to be close to Paresh Baruah. There were at least five others on that list. 'Mahanta,' said a military official who developed the overall anti-ULFA strategy, 'had become too powerful and he had to be eliminated.'

Within a few weeks of the second assault on ULFA, the results were showing: 4,300 suspects had been captured by the army. After initial interrogation, 1,770 were released. The remainder were handed over to the police for further questioning. In addition to the capture of weapons, the army said it had seized the equivalent of seven million rupees (about 230,000 dollars).

In November, a major catch in Calcutta helped the Operation. That month Arup Chetia was captured at a guest house along with three others, including a Guwahati businessman and his wife who were later released.

Chetia's movements had been watched for some time. He once even travelled to Sanawar, an exclusive school near Kasauli (Himachal Pradesh), to attend an annual function there, so confident was he of not being caught.

Chetia was unco-operative to start with but one of his interrogators later said that he broke without any physical pressure. The man from RAW said that intelligence officials were discussing leaks to the Calcutta press on the detained suspects when he spoke of the possibility that such publicity could harm Chetia's family. The harm, would come from ULFA, which could be quite ruthless.

At this point, Chetia called the agent across and said he wanted to speak with him privately. 'He broke down and said that the ULFA boys could get his wife and son and could we protect them?' The RAW man said they could arrange for protection and to take the family to a safe place. But Chetia must co-operate. He agreed, disclosing information that intelligence officials said helped them track down operatives, networks and also provided some leads to the inner workings of the organization. Chetia was clever too; he passed on information that was completely false and mixed fact with fiction in his statement, leading the agencies astray.

In late December, working on a tip-off, soldiers tracked down Sunil Nath, the elusive spokesman of ULFA, as he rode a scooter in Guwahati. Next to fall in the army dragnet was Kalpajyoti Neog, another articulate thinker. But their arrest was planned, not accidental: in a series of secret messages to the state government, they had agreed to be picked up, to end their years in hiding and flight to establish a bridge between the insurgents and the government, to find a face-saving formula to get out of the crisis.

Within a few hours, the army nosed in on a top ULFA figure: Moon Ali, who was trapped in a hotel room.

Some days earlier, the remaining hostages from ONGC had been set free—unconditionally. Saikia was jubilant: his decision not to compromise was paying off.

The noose was tightening for the real target: Hirakjyoti Mahanta, the deputy commander-in-chief who also was operating in Guwahati. Mahanta was unable to get out of the security net and with the hostages gone, there were few cards to play with.

On 31 December, troops stormed the house in Guwahati where Mahanta was hiding. He was taken away for questioning. That very evening, according to the official version, Mahanta was shot while trying to escape after he promised to lead soldiers to ULFA hideouts.

That New Year Eve, the All Assam Students Union had called for a strike to protest army assaults on villagers and the general crackdown in the state, saying that the operation was leading to attacks on women and innocent villagers. So the news of Mahanta's death did not get out until the following day. Naturally the government sought to play it down.

There was much anger in Guwahati against his killing for no one believed the government's version of events. A large gathering turned out for his funeral procession and there was widespread condemnation of the death.

Ironically, at the time, no one spoke about those who had fallen to the bullets of ULFA. Those who wanted to speak out kept their silence. After all, for how long could the army be relied upon to keep the peace? And suppose the 'boys' returned after the crackdown to assert their power as they had done after Bajrang, who then would be safe? Therefore, wisdom prevailed and the anti-ULFA voices stayed muted.

But Mahanta's death was not an accidental killing. It had been ordained at the top levels of the government apparatus, including the military and the Central Government. According to intelligence accounts, he died bravely. As he was taken to his death, Mahanta was asked by his captors whether he had any last words. He is believed to have said, 'I know what is going to happen to me, I have no regrets, you can do whatever you want.'

The news spread through ULFA's ranks like wildfire, even as the security forces gloated in their triumph. This was no ordinary ULFA cadre; it was the organization's deputy commander-in-chief, a man who had the ear of Paresh Baruah. Baruah trusted Mahanta implicitly and had given much of the daily control of the armed network in Assam to him. His deputy's death was a stunning blow. There were dark rumours in the organization and outside that those who had been captured before Mahanta were responsible for leaking out his whereabouts and thus signing his death warrant.

Manash Ghosh explained Mahanta's significance to the insurgent movement in *The Statesman*. Describing the guerrilla leader as an 'unwavering hardliner who opposed any solution within the framework of the Indian Constitution,' Ghosh said 'the strapping 27-year-old youth, a science graduate of Gauhati University,' a week before his death, had become 'the rallying point for the ULFA's cadres and supporters.' These cadres had 'projected him as their future leader who, unlike other "opportunist" leaders, would not compromise on ULFA's principles and objectives.'

To them, he was hero and fighter. To the security forces, he was an unmitigated thorn in the flesh who had to be plucked out.

But even before his death, by mid-December, it was clear that ULFA could not hold out any longer against the army. Searching for a way out, it had modified its stand. In a startling announcement on 18 December, Sunil Nath declared that 'We had been forced to take to the path of arms as the only alternative because the democratic approach did not work.' He also said that ULFA had always maintained that it was not opposed to 'seeking a solution to the problems of Assam through discussions and dialogue.'

In the most important part of that statement, Nath said: 'In the absence of specific and acceptable initiatives by the Indian State machinery to honour the self rights [*swadhikar*] of the people of Assam, we will not abandon the path of struggle.'

ULFA was appealing to the Indian Government and to Saikia to come forward with a face-saving device.

To its supporters in the state, the 18 December announcement and those that were to follow came as a series of unexpected stunning blows and struck at the image of a relentless fighting machine that ULFA had carefully developed for itself over the years.

ULFA was abandoning its quest for an independent Assam and instead insisting on the vague right for self-determination. As M.S. Prabhakara of *The Hindu*, one of the most perceptive commentators on the Northeast, put it: 'In plain English, greater autonomy for the State.'

The ground was being set for a compromise and what men like Hirakjyoti Mahanta would have described as a sellout. ULFA was in the process of capitulation, a process that would lead to a sharp and bitter split and create further confusion in the political situation in Assam.

Some had sensed the shape of things to come. Nikhil Chakravartty, the veteran political commentator and editor of the leftist magazine *Mainstream*, said in December 1991 that 'Assam is on the mend.'

Chakravartty said after a visit that while ULFA had a 'measure of popularity . . . which is difficult to understand or appreciate by people outside Assam,' it had also long cultivated the image of a Robin Hood cult 'of robbing the rich to help the poor.' He said that the huge accumulation of funds by ULFA 'has smudged its image of upholding revolutionary purity.' He added that 'the image of Robin Hood was changing to that of the cruel bandit' and ULFA had to move quickly to take corrective action.

He rapped the security forces for violating human rights in the state and praised AASU for looking at a new issue: the reshaping of the Indian Constitution to ensure true federalism. Old themes of foreign nationals and voters lists alone were not catchy enough, it had realized.

The pressure and the losses were becoming too painful for ULFA. After Hirakjyoti Mahanta's death, Arobindo Rajkhowa, the ULFA Chairman, wrote a letter to Prime Minister P.V. Narasimha Rao declaring his willingness for a cessation of hostilities. It was a follow-up of a secret missive sent to Rao the earlier month by Rajkhowa where the ULFA chief spoke of the Indian Government's wish for a 'written commitment from the ULFA about its having agreed (a) to accept the Constitution of India for the resolution of the Assam problem and (b) to give up arms and abjure violence.'

But he also sought 'Government facilities for secret negotiations for thrashing out the above points and a central committee meeting for ratification.' He wanted the consideration of a swift end to the ban on ULFA as well as army operations and the use of sweeping powers to arrest, detain and shoot, conferred by the Armed Disturbed Areas Act and the Armed Forces (Special Powers) Act.

The New Year letter set out the details of ULFA's capitulation:

'We, hereby, confirm our resolve i) to accept a solution of the Assam problem within the Constitution of India, (ii) to abjure violence, (iii) to deposit arms at an appropriate time mutually decided upon.'

A follow-up letter sought the Prime Minister's intervention for meetings of the banned organization's various top councils and, as he had urged in the first missive, an end to the army crackdown.

Sunil Nath, in a series of meetings with Hiteswar Saikia and intelligence officials along with Arup Chetia, the general secretary, Pradip Gogoi, the vice-chairman, Kalpajyoti Neog and others agreed to talks with the Central Government.

Gogoi had actually been picked up in mid-December by troops and the army, delighted with another catch, had announced his capture to the press. Within a day, Gogoi had been handed over to the police and then, to the astonishment of the army, quietly set free. Military officials learned later that Gogoi was among those who had been secretly talking with the Chief Minister.

'Who would we negotiate with if we detain everyone?' asked Saikia.

General Ajai Singh had been able to keep his promise of virtually ending operations by the end of December. He had overstepped by a few days but one of his aims had been completed: ULFA's humiliation and the blunting of its military presence.

He had recaptured the military space.

Now it was up to the master-manipulator, Hiteswar Saikia, to strike the political blows.

After intense talks with the Chief Minister and top officials, including the then Assam Home Secretary, Tapan Lal Baruah and senior bureaucrats in the Home Ministry in Delhi, a team from ULFA flew to the Indian capital by a special Border Security Force (BSF) aircraft for meetings with the leadership in New Delhi.

The talks in New Delhi in January 1992 began with officials in the Home Ministry and Cabinet Secretariat, including members of the intelligence services. Later, there were meetings with Home Minister S.B. Chavan. The ground had been well-prepared not by intelligence officials but by Saikia's sleight-of-hand.

After the meeting with Chavan, the ULFA leaders were taken to P.V. Narasimha Rao's sprawling Race Course Road house, home to three prime ministers before its latest occupant. They were kept waiting briefly before they were ushered into Rao's presence.

It was a brief meeting and Sunil Nath said he got the distinct impression that the Prime Minister was talking down to them as if they were errant schoolchildren. 'He was aloof, a bit cool toward us,' he said. But the rebels had little choice.

The Prime Minister received assurances that they would formally declare an end to violence and pledge their support for a solution within the framework of the Indian Constitution. In return, he said, as Home Minister S.B. Chavan and Hiteswar Saikia listened, he was prepared to put the army operations on hold. But it would be a limited stop to the operations. ULFA, he made it absolutely plain in his reticent, scholarly style, would have to deposit arms, get clearance from its higher councils for the accord and then move ahead with the surrender of its cadres.

The cease-fire and suspension of operations were to be used by ULFA to meet these conditions.

The five-member team listened and agreed unhesitatingly.

The next day, Chavan made a brief, formal press statement announcing the terms of agreement between the two sides and described the move as 'a measure of our goodwill.' He also asked the Assam government to 'create an atmosphere conducive to facilitating the process of future negotiations.' In other words, the officers and the police chiefs in the districts were being told to allow ULFA meetings to discuss the debacle.

As the ULFA team made its way back to the Brahmaputra Valley, murmurings about betrayal were circulating. In Bangladesh, Paresh Baruah was furious and isolated. He denounced the compromise as an unacceptable sellout to India's colonial masters in Delhi. The message to his colleagues in Assam was loud and clear: men like Hirakjyoti Mahanta had not died in order to facilitate a surrender.

There was hostility from the men and women who had supported ULFA's rebellion in a manner that their far-flung, resource-rich but politically feeble state could force Delhi to sit up and take notice of their demands. The AGP was seen as being totally compromised and the Congress as a weak servant of Delhi's diktat.

The fiercely nationalistic intellectuals, for whom ULFA could do no wrong for they were responding to forty years of colonial control, denounced the accord as a craven backing down. 'Only opportunists compromise,' one leading Assamese was quoted as telling *The Statesman*; the newspaper noted that he spoke 'quite abrasively.'

Many in Assam were quite prepared to overlook ULFA's record of 'excesses', said *The Statesman*, because they justified these actions as 'inspired by the nationalist urge of a true patriot.'

Added to this overt hostility was the total confusion and bitterness among hard-core supporters and activists of the organization who just could not believe that everything they had battled for, all the power they had enjoyed without challenge for three years, was just vanishing. There was an acute sense of betrayal, of being let down, of not being consulted. It was to this group, to this feeling that Paresh Baruah appealed directly.

Yet, the cessation of hostilities came as a breath of fresh air to the entire state. The end of violence meant that, for some time at least, the Assamese and other communities of the area could sleep in peace, work without being harassed, walk on the streets without being submitted to the indignity of humiliating body searches or sudden questioning.

It was as if an ominous shadow had been removed and a weight taken off the shoulders.

To meet Delhi's demands and their own deadlines, ULFA decided that their top men would be deployed for the most difficult task of persuading the cadres to the Delhi agreement.

Arobindo Rajkhowa, Arup Chetia, Sunil Nath and Pradip Gogoi led teams to speak with their followers. The meetings were held in an atmosphere of tension and ill-concealed hostility to the pro-accord group. It was the same everywhere and Rajkhowa and his aides found themselves facing the same questions and fumbling for answers.

Long accustomed to their unquestioned leadership, the Chairman and his functionaries tried to explain their difficulties in waging war against the state. Yes, came one retort, 'If that was the case, then why didn't we do all this three years ago.' The critic was asking whether the struggle should have continued all this time, with such loss of life and economic hardship for many ordinary people.

The cadres were divided, though. While many wanted the struggle to continue, they were also keenly aware that the old aura no longer surrounded them. It would be much tougher and a return to 'normal life' would not, perhaps, be out of place. A strong but vocal group, albeit smaller than the pro-talk faction and the neutrals, was meanwhile rallying around the unbending figure of Paresh Baruah.

Baruah held firm for he believed that his way would finally win the day. He would telephone his supporters in Assam from bases in Bangladesh, urging them to hold out against the talks, to continue the armed fight and to denounce those favouring negotiations.

Once, he spoke to Hiteswar Saikia who urged him to tone down his opposition. He argued that in peace lay the progress for Assam. Baruah ejected the thought, his main ire being directed against Rajkhowa and Chetia. 'Why did they bypass me, I cannot agree to talks,' Saikia quoted him as saying.

After that there were no more contacts between Saikia and the ULFA army chief, who had emerged as the rallying point to those opposed to the dominance of the political faction, represented by Rajkhowa, Chetia and Nath.

The suspension of army operations was to end on 1 February and the campaign by Rajkhowa to sell the accord was getting bogged down. The Research and Analysis Wing was getting alarmed; so were the Intelligence Bureau and other power centres in the Home Ministry in Delhi. Saikia was under pressure but superficially maintained good cheer and confidence.

A stalemate was the last thing that either Delhi or Dispur wanted at this stage.

Meanwhile, Arobindo Rajkhowa began slowing his campaign of persuasion. On the other hand, pressure from Paresh Baruah was building up. RAW still believes that Bangla intelligence operatives were putting pressure on Baruah but this is unconfirmed. In fact, Delhi also believes that Pakistani operatives from the Inter Services Intelligence met with Baruah several times in Bangladesh as well as at Bangkok in 1991 and 1992. They say that the ULFA chief travelled to Pakistan on a Bangladeshi passport in March 1992 and that he also has a Pakistani passport that is used occasionally. The control of either Bangladesh or Pakistan over Baruah and his group is unclear. Baruah functions largely on his own and in co-operation, especially since 1992, with the Muivah-Isak Swu faction of the National Socialist Council of Nagaland. As Rajkhowa's meetings with the cadres slowed, the government continued its pressure for a meeting of the organization's General Council to approve of the Delhi talks. ULFA held out for more time saying it could not rush the process.

One deadline after another passed without result.

To ease the pressure from its cadres, ULFA issued a statement saying that talk about divisions were imaginary and that it had not signed any accord with 'the Indian state machinery' not had it held any formal talks with the Indian government. It insisted that contacts had been informal and continued to be so. 'We reiterate that we will not abandon the path of struggle, and we will not surrender. We will decide our tactics adapting to the existing reality.'

Four days after that statement, ULFA's Central General Council me at a little town near Nagaon. One account of that meeting at Morigao described it as stormy and that Paresh Baruah called from Bangladesh t speak to the members opposing any moves for reconciliation with Delh and surrender of weapons.

Within a few days of the meeting, which generally approved forma and substantive talks with the government, a team led by Pradip Gogo the vice-chairman of ULFA, was in Delhi.

This time, the group kept a very low profile. It refused all meeting with the press. Its talks with officials in the Home Ministry were intens but few. And it submitted a letter to the Prime Minister outlining ten-stage 'Programme of Action' which provided for 'depositing o weapons by ULFA' to be begun and completed at specific places betwee 22 March and 10 April.

But all along, Rajkhowa and Chetia as well as Gogoi develope growing doubts about their ability to implement a peace plan and to disar their followers. They told the Home Ministry and its various intelligenc arms that they needed to talk with Paresh Baruah and his band of follower in Bangladesh to persuade them to join the peace process.

They demanded and got a safe conduct from Delhi.

By end-March, the main rebel leaders had slipped out of Assam. But the were not going to Bangladesh to persuade anyone. They were travellin there because they had no intention of returning to Assam. They neede to meet Baruah and assure him that they had not sold out, as he was saying It was essentially a move to ensure their political survival within th organization and their own physical well-being.

According to one account, they were met at the Bangladesh borde by an old friend and comrade, Thuengaling Muivah.

When it was clear that the Trinity of Rajkhowa, Chetia and Gogo were not going to turn up like good boys, as Dispur and Delhi ha hoped—against logic and experience—another group within the outfi was persuaded to attend a meeting in the Assam capital with Hiteswa Saikia.

On 31 March 1991, sixteen ULFA activists including Munim Nobis the man who set up the Pakistan and Bangladesh connections, Sunil Nat and Kalpajyoti Neog arrived at the State Secretariat in two Maruti Gypsy jeeps. They signed a statement opposing the use of arms and denounced the top leaders of the Standing Council, now in Bangladesh, for failing to give a specific direction to the movement.

This leadership had 'distanced themselves from the people' and said that the new group, led by Nobis, would hold talks directly with the state and Central Government openly and freely. By this time, seven district units had opted for the path of negotiations. More were to follow in the days to come.

The 31 March meeting was crucial for that was the deadline for ULFA to meet the terms set by the Centre for talks.

The same day, Rajkhowa, Chetia and Gogoi issued a statement rejecting the precondition of arms surrender, called for a renewal of the armed struggle and announced their determination to fulfil the aspirations of the people of Assam. They accused New Delhi of deceit and forcing a settlement on ULFA.

'ULFA was born with the aim of carving out an independent, sovereign Assam. We are still firm in this goal. We condemn the Indian state machinery for conspiring to isolate the ULFA from the people and weaken it by creating rift within its ranks,' said the declaration from Bangladesh.

The split had come less than six weeks after ULFA had proclaimed its unity and warned against 'imagined' divisions.

Although he was irked by what he regarded as a betrayal of their word by Chetia and Rajkhowa, Hiteswar Saikia was not going to quibble. A man who believed in taking risks, the Assam Chief Minister prepared to make the best of the situation.

Yet, even he could derive some satisfaction from the fluid situation: the master manipulator had nudged along the divisions within the organization, forcing ULFA to bend at every point of the way. When he found that a few of his cards had fallen out of the pack, he used the remaining jacks to ace them.

It was no mean achievement. Hiteswar Saikia had regained for Assam and India what the AGP, through its bungling, deceit and shortsightedness had lost: the political middle ground.

Ajai Singh had recaptured the military space. Saikia had won back the political space to enable the people to breathe again. He had paid a high personal cost though.

Two of his nephews and a brother had fallen to the bullets of ULFA
for no reason save that they were related to him. It was a personal pain
that he bore stoically. 'I know who killed my brother and nephews but
have overcome these feelings, I have to think not just of my family but of
the whole of Assam,' he said when I asked him one evening how he
managed to emotionally deal with people known to be involved in these
killings.

'People want peace at all costs and I have to accept that these things
have happened, I cannot forget that I am Chief Minister of the whole state,'
he said in a two-hour interview in the summer of 1993.

Several of his close friends, all Congressmen, had fallen to ULFA
bullets too. High in that list was the respected trade union leader
Manabendra Sharma, who was shot as he returned from a morning's
shopping for groceries and vegetables in Guwahati. His body lay on the
road outside his home for more than an hour before the police arrived.
The neighbours at the time had been too frightened to help carry the body
home. Manabendra Sharma's widow is said to have told Saikia that by
releasing the men who had gunned down her husband, he was not doing
anything particularly patriotic or honest. 'You have rewarded killers,' she
told him, saying that her children would neither forget nor forgive either
the killers or him. To assuage her, the Congress leadership in Delhi
nominated her to the Rajya Sabha.

Hiteswar Saikia is a compulsive worker. He works almost twenty
hours a day, calling senior officials like the then Home Secretary, Tapan
Lal Baruah at their homes at one or two in the morning to check a point
and bounce an idea off them. Baruah, a tall, strapping man, with a
reputation for competence and proximity to the Chief Minister, handled
the ULFA and Bodo issues on a day-to-day basis, meeting with key figures
over the past years. Needless to say, his wife had seen little of him during
these years and was looking forward, not with a little exasperation, to his
retirement, when the Chief Minister's early morning calls would cease.

The flight of Arobindo Rajkhowa and Arup Chetia was taken by Hiteswar
Saikia as a personal affront. He had known Rajkhowa's father, a fellow
Ahom, and also an old-time Congressman. 'I've stayed at their home
when I was a younger man, when we were both working with the
Congress,' said Saikia, describing the father as a man of dignity and

conviction in the Congress ideals of socialism and equality.

But beyond the slight that he had suffered, Saikia knew that his foes in the state Congress would do their best to hurt him politically. So he moved swiftly to secure his flanks, pushing the breakaway rebel group as the real representatives of ULFA. He launched a furious public relations campaign against the ULFA insurgents in Bangladesh, accusing them of betrayal of the Assamese cause by going back on the very principles that the Assam agitation of the 1980s had enunciated and of seeking help from Bangladesh, identified by most Assamese, emotionally if not logically, as the main factor behind the ills of their homeland. The Bangladesh factor, as we have seen, is marked in the presence of the outmigrants who have flooded the towns and countryside of Assam and other parts of eastern India, disrupting the demographic process and cultural and social interactions. Economic and political calculations have been upset as the migrants put pressure on scarce resources and services such as housing, power, drinking water, sewage and sanitation.

Hiteswar Saikia also floated stories that the local and national media lapped up about Paresh Baruah being under house arrest in Dhaka and that ULFA's funds being frozen by the Bangladesh Government. Nothing of the sort happened. The only funds of ULFA that were stuck were when the Bank of Credit, Commerce and Industry (BCCI), launched by a Pakistani banker, collapsed worldwide in 1991. ULFA had about half a million rupees in that.

However, Baruah was able to travel to Bangkok and Singapore to buy weapons and ammunition and also to hold meetings with Pakistani agents in Bangladesh and with Thuengaling Muivah in Southeast Asia.

New Delhi too was not pleased with Hiteswar Saikia's handling of the situation now that it was clear that the top ULFA men had fled, with the full knowledge of the state government. It was as much as a slight to the Prime Minister as to the head of the state's elected government. The Intelligence Bureau was angry because it felt that Saikia had bypassed it in his desire to rehabilitate himself as a true Assamese among his own people and to show his legitimacy. Saikia had not forgotten—nor had he been allowed to forget—the years in the wilderness after the Centre dealt directly with AASU in the 1980s, keeping him out in the cold all through the talks. Nor could he ignore the fact that for years, he had been an object of hate and derision for many Assamese.

Saikia knew he was in a corner and had to show some tangible results

beyond the political gains of dividing ULFA. Once again, there wa
confusion in Assam about the emerging political scenario.

As a result, in efforts to divert public attention and also to offer a
economic carrot to the pro-talk group, Saikia got the support o
intelligence groups and the Home Ministry to offer 1.10 billion rupee
(about thirty-four million dollars) to rehabilitate the ULFA men an
women who had returned to seek a new life.

Of this figure, half would go in the raising of two police battalion
to battle future insurgencies. These would be specifically anti-terroris
organizations. The other half would be paid to ULFA followers, wh
wanted to resume normal lives, in the form of grants. The money was t
help them with projects that would generate employment and capital
These included motels, hotels, restaurants and fisheries.

Assam, despite its ideal climate and soil and water conditions, is
fish-importing state with a pathetically poor record of fisheries. On
senior official said that even ULFA cadres, who were trained to believ
in a classless society, were reluctant to go into fisheries because it is a
occupation that is associated with a low Hindu caste.

'Jorhat town gets two truckloads of fish from Kakinada in Andhr
Pradesh every day,' said Papa Rao, a calm Indian Administrative Office
who was running Jorhat District in 1992. He said that he ran into the cast
problem when he tried to speak to surrendered ULFA cadres abou
fisheries. 'If the trucks don't come, the price of fish shoots up,' h
remarked with a grin.

As he talked, two young men strolled into his office. In th
background, his security man, armed with an automatic rifle, hovere
discreetly. The young men were from ULFA and they wanted to know
what they should do with bank loans and grants that were being arranged
They were thinking of starting a restaurant.

'Have two types of restaurants,' said Rao. 'One that serves rice an
curries for truck drivers and ordinary people who like quick, cheap foo
and another which serves Mughlai cuisine—like tandoori chicken anc
naan. And you can even build one floor on top of the better restaurant sc
that it can double as a motel.'

The men seemed to like the idea and left soon afterward, promising
to return after they had surveyed the area and thought things over.

But many, officials say, chose easier ways of money-making. The
most popular was working as a contractor at building sites or simply

getting a contract to supply cars and other vehicles to government departments. The investment as well as the payments were taken care of by the government itself—either state or Central.

As the weeks and months rolled by, it was clear that ULFA was vanishing from the Central Government's agenda, if not from that of the state government. The 'new' ULFA men would stroll into Dispur, meet with Hiteswar Saikia and other ministers, discuss their problems and plans and also meet senior bureaucrats like the Home Secretary. But there was little happening in terms of political consolidation, at least on the surface.

The differences between groups in ULFA also burst into the open. Munim Nobis and Sunil Nath, who began a weekly news magazine, fell out with each other. A new leader emerged among the pro-talks faction who seemed to have Saikia's support—Chakra Gohain. Although he was identified by the state government as a deputy commander-in-chief of ULFA, a post that the late Hirakjyoti Mahanta had held, Paresh Baruah clarified that he was no deputy chief. Chakra Gohain, also known as Lambu, had come overground in mid-1992 after the talks with Rajkhowa and Chetia broke down. But Gohain's actual standing in the undivided ULFA has been questioned and others see him as a means for Saikia to keep men like Nobis and Nath in check.

Because of these personal differences and frictions, the pro-negotiation group was unable to present a joint front until the end of 1992 when, Chakra Gohain, Munim Nobis, Sunil Nath and others joined the Chief Minister in sending a message to Prime Minister Rao, seeking a resumption of the peace process so that Assam could once again be renewed.

That process, continued desultorily, with more and more former ULFA activists turning up at offices such as Papa Rao's in Jorhat to discuss what they can and should do.

At a higher level, the question of means and ends is not quite resolved, although there is a show of unity.

According to Munim Nobis, no one has the right to take up arms again and put ordinary people through the trauma of the early 1990s. 'We did all that without asking local people for their opinion and they were the

ones who suffered the most, we didn't,' he said. But Sunil Nath, heavie
now than during his days of hiding, minus his beard but retaining his chee
said that despite his current comfortable lifestyle—he runs *Deoba*
(Sunday), an Assamese language magazine that gets generous advertisin
from the government and local businessmen—he will be prepared t
respond to a call from Paresh Baruah. But only on condition that Arobind
Rajkhowa and Arup Chetia, whom he describes as 'pseudo', are remove
from authority.

Nobis is more diplomatic about the future: no one, he say
philosophically, can predict it with any degree of accuracy. But he wa
vehement about one issue: no one had the right to force an insurgency o
an area that was ill-prepared for it. 'It just shouldn't happen,' he said a
we stood outside his father's small home off a lane in Guwahati. H
reiterated that ordinary people, especially the villagers, suffered for th
acts of others.

There are those who believe that this ULFA group will eventuall
taking a leaf from the experience of a large chunk of the Naga undergroun
movement, enter the flow of the political stream. They may do so in th
form of a new regional party or by joining a national party.

There is no question, however, that the opponents to the peac
process will continue to operate boldly, even if they have lost their origina
power. New strategies are being devised, new partnerships forged, nev
sources of funds located.

One of the reasons for the drop in public support to ULFA was its chang
on what Assamese regard as the Bangladeshi or *bideshi* (foreigner) issue
Any Bengali-speaking migrant is adduced to have come from Banglades
and is hence seen as a threat, especially since most settlers are far mor
hard-working and innovative in their farming techniques than loca
farmers. The attitude on this issue borders paranoia.

In a fifteen-page booklet issued in July 1992, ULFA declared tha
people from East Bengal had become 'an inseparable part of the toiling
people of Assam.' In confused, semi-Marxian jargon, it declared that the
'erstwhile residents of East Bengal,' who had been encouraged to migrate
to Assam by governments in the 1930s and 1940s, 'are part and parcel o
the national life of Assam.'

Although it opposed illegal immigration, ULFA said that the

migrants now produced as much as eighty-five per cent of the state's agricultural produce and were a key factor in the state's economy. It even criticized the All Assam Students Union as saying that it had been too emotional on the issue and had not given political direction to the anti-alien agitation.

AASU struck back quickly, denouncing ULFA as anti-Assam. It pointed out that ULFA activists were based in Bangladesh and that was probably the reason for this new attitude to migrants. AASU said that ULFA's 'misguided movement consisting of extortion and murders . . . had destabilized the situation in Assam.' It was a strong and unequivocal position, rare for an Assamese organization. In ULFA's declaration, said AASU, lay the basis of a plan to reduce the Assamese into a minority.

This was not the first time that the two organizations had clashed. The previous year, AASU had criticized ULFA for kidnapping and torturing several students in Nagaon district. The students warned ULFA that they would not 'tolerate threats or attacks from any quarter.'

AASU was not the only mass-based movement to speak out. Ronesh Pegu, the chief of the United Reservations Minority Communities of Assam (URMCA), a conglomeration of associations of indigenous peoples and tribes that opposed ULFA, has organized rallies and marches against the militants. Pegu described them as the 'military arm of the AGP.' 'They are simply chauvinist Assamese middle-class people masquerading as leftists and seeking to portray a pan-Assamese identity,' said Pegu, who himself is a leftist.

Why did the talks between the recognized leaders of the undivided ULFA fail?

M.S. Prabhakara of *The Hindu* analysed it succinctly. Prabhakara, who speaks, writes and reads Assamese—he once even taught at Guwahati University—says that the negotiations were flawed from the start. He compared them to those conducted by the leaders of the Mizo insurgency.

In Mizoram, Laldenga, the undisputed leader of the insurgent Mizo National Front, was associated 'actively and directly at every stage of the negotiations.' But in ULFA's case, he said, it was unclear whether Arobindo Rajkhowa enjoyed 'a corresponding authority. Further, his physical absence from every stage of these preliminary negotiations has

robbed these of popular legitimacy.' The commentator pointed out that
ULFA's ambiguity could have been the result of a deliberate policy
'which saw the advantages in speaking in several voices simultaneously.'

Continuing the comparison with Mizoram, where rebels laid downs
their arms in 1986, Prabhakara said that while ULFA was forced to agree
to a constitutional settlement, end violence and surrender weapons at a
specific time, the MNF was asked to abide by the first two conditions. It
did so, setting the ground for detailed talks that led to the surrender of the
weapons over a period of time and consequently to the capture of political
power as it had become a legitimate political party by then. Laldenga
became Chief Minister, perhaps the first insurgent leader to be thus elected
in the history of South Asia or any part of the continent. And he kept his
word by respecting the Constitution. His followers continue to be
members of the legislature, although they are now in the opposition and
the MNF is distant from power.

It is a different story that hard-core insurgents were corrupted by a
comfortable lifestyle and easy money, especially among ministers in the
MNF government, which became the talk of Aizawl.

The pro-talk group in ULFA had not, until the middle of 1993,
decided to join politics. But it had used the months after the split to
reorganize its district units. A significant aspect of the reorganization was
that the military wing took second place in the hierarchy to the civil
authority. Earlier, the military commanders were the top figures and their
authority was unchallenged. This changed dramatically after ULFA was
divided.

Conventional insurgency places greater value on the political wing
and ideological purity and ranks the armed group second. In ULFA, it
appears that, apart from a brief time at the beginning, the military wing
has always held sway—as it continues to do in the group that remains out
of the talks.

There also is a new face to ULFA. It goes beyond the flood relief
work that it has resumed. Or the fact that many former activists have
turned their attention—along with many well-known figures in the media,
law, and education—to issues such as illiteracy and land management.

One of the most visible features was seen in December 1992, when
Assam was sucked into the nationwide rioting that followed the
destruction of the Babri Masjid in Ayodhya. More than 100 persons were
killed in the state, most of them inhabitants of the Nagaon and Goreshwar

areas not far from Guwahati. In both cases, Bengali-speaking Muslims attacked Bengali Hindus. But these were not simple communal riots.

Again, as in earlier events of violence and ethnic conflict, the issue involved migrants and land. The Muslims were latecomers from Bangladesh and East Pakistan. The Bengali Hindus were earlier settlers from pre-partition East Bengal and East Pakistan. The anger over the Ayodhya incident provided an opportunity for the Muslims to try and evict the older settlers from prime agricultural land.

At one point in this mayhem, Muslim settlers threatened to attack Hindu-dominated areas of Nagaon town. Nagaon is set in the middle of a ring of Muslim settlements, many of which are more than sixty years old. When word of the threat got around, the local ULFA leadership reached the site in vehicles with automatic weapons. They sent word to the Muslims that they would not hesitate to fire and kill. The mob melted away.

In Assam, that incident was seen by many as part of the pro-Hindu bias that is inherent in any Assamese organization—political, cultural or otherwise. The ULFA was hailed as a saviour in its new guise although critics suggested that it was functioning as Hiteswar Saikia's unofficial sword arm.

ULFA has a significant stake in the future of the Northeast. Its development of this role does not depend on merely the pro-talk group but also on how active the pro-war group, based in Bangladesh, continues to be. The latter group appears to be scattered and weakened by large-scale surrenders and arrests.

The Paresh Baruah faction has training camps in which 200-to-300 men and women can live, work and train. These are in Mymensingh district and are usually reached through Meghalaya—although that route is under tight Indian surveillance now—or through Cachar.

One favoured route takes a traveller through Maulvi Bazaar in Mymensingh district and on to Soborgram. This is about a three-hour bus ride from Maulvi Bazaar. There are other training camps at Bhemugach, Nilfarman and Dhamai, all located in the Maulvi Bazaar area.

Prime Minister Narasimha Rao handed over pictures and documents about these camps to Prime Minister Begum Khaleda Zia when she visited Delhi in 1992. The response was cool: Bangladesh, she said, did not support or have such camps.

There are many in Bangladesh who think that India is making a big fuss for no reason. To them—these include editors and politicians as well as officials—the ULFA groups are like brigands who come in and out at will. But senior officials privately acknowledge that there may be covert operations about which the Foreign Office as well as Begum Khaleda Zia would keep quiet : the reason is the military's power. The army remains an undeniable factor in Bangladesh's destiny—now in barracks but still an overwhelming presence with its firepower and relative discipline.

Public support for ULFA in Assam has dwindled. Editors and other public figures speak out openly against it and some even suggest that top Congress politicians are associated with the militants who have surrendered.

The Sentinel newspaper commented caustically in January 1995 on the spurt of crimes by 'surrendered ULFA activists (or the SULFA) and of the kidnapping, vandalism and looting indulged in by them . . .' It attacked them as a 'public menace' and criticized the State Government for 'rewarding' acts of violence by promoting monetary awards for those who surrendered after a spell of criminal activity. It added that it appeared to the public that the 'design' appeared to be the creation of 'a private army . . . which can be used in elections.'

Barely a decade after launching its insurgency, ULFA appears to be fading away although the core issues behind its growth remain unresolved. Since these factors remain untouched, a revival of the cycle of militancy cannot be ruled out, drawing upon the frustration and alienation of people from political parties.

The NSCN Takes Wings

The political conditions in Assam—as well as in other parts of the country—are steadily getting worse. They show no improvement at all.

The Bodos fluctuate between agitations, threatened agitations and limited insurgencies and extortions. The Assamese are cautiously watching the drama involving the United Liberation Front of Asom (ULFA) unfold. Other indigenous groups are similarly studying the situation and their future role.

Militants opposed to talks are still active in the sporadic attacks and ambushes on security troops, including the blasting of army vehicles by remote control devices.

The most prominent among them is Thuengaling Muivah's National Socialist Council of Nagaland (NSCN) but even that has some lesser known aspects.

The NSCN marks its presence in the colleges and schools of Shillong.

Across this hill town, far from the war-torn jungles of Myanmar and the insecurity and dangers of flight and fear, young boys and girls are enrolled into its many schools. Their addresses are given as towns and villages in Nagaland and Manipur and they do have relatives in these places. These are the children of the NSCN warriors of Myanmar.

They study and grow under the watchful but distant eye of intelligence agents. In a way, these children are virtually hostage should the government wish to strike against their parents. But here is an arrangement that suits both sides, without too much of a fuss being made by either. To the parents, their children are safe and in a place where a decent education is assured: and what is more, they are giving them a choice of making their future within India, no matter what their hearts tell them about their own sense of identity. For the government, it is a useful arrangement which enables them to keep an eye on a large number of associates and relatives of insurgents and suspects, without risking confrontations.

In a strange and silent way, the NSCN as well as the Federal Government of Nagaland, the pro-Phizo faction, has compromised with the system. For where they live in Myanmar and Bangladesh, there are no schools beyond an elementary level. Clearly, their children seek a better deal. And a parent, whether guerrilla or otherwise, seeks the best for its offspring.

It is at this intimate, emotional level that there is a chink in the rebel armour, a certain, even if limited, vulnerability.

The NSCN has spread its influence across the southern belt of Assam too. Here, it has established camps and training and joint co-operation programmes with ULFA (Paresh Baruah group) and with a little-known outfit called the Hmar Peoples Convention (HPC).

The Hmars are a tiny community of less than a 1,00,000 in Assam, although there are more in Mizoram and Tripura. In Assam, they are largely concentrated in its North Cachar district. They had long sought a separate status in the form of a mere autonomous district council, with special funds for their development, but were denied it over the years.

It was their representative that B.K. Nehru, the then Governor of Assam and Nagaland, had snubbed in the 1960s, saying that their number did not even warrant a separate district.

The HPC was active especially in the North Cachar Hills. Although its army was not more than a few hundred strong, they had a nose for laying ambushes and a well-oiled network of informers that enabled them to escape the security net time and again.

In 1992, the army was called out in North Cachar to deal with the problems caused by the NSCN, collaborating with ULFA and the Hmars.

The number of clashes with security forces were limited but that was not important. What was significant was that a new militant front had opened up for the country's security forces, which were already stretched to the limit.

If the Hmars had been handled a little more tactfully some years ago, they would not have been pushed to the road of armed revolt. But there is a dissatisfaction with life in the jungle and negotiations have been on for some time on accommodating the HPC in the legislature and the politics of Mizoram especially, where their numbers are largest.

The focus of the NSCN in the Cachar belt is to milk the prosperous tea gardens. The modus operandi is the same as that employed by ULFA: kidnap vulnerable tea executives and managers, demand a ransom from their wealthy employers and threaten to shoot them if the money is not paid.

In one case, involving MacNeil and Magor, the prosperous tea company, the Nagas picked up a plantation manager and held him for several weeks. Their demand: a whopping ten million rupees. The company quietly paid and the manager was released.

S.K. Bhasin, the then President of the Indian Tea Association, the apex body of all national tea associations, told a reporter that the situation was 'very, very bad. The entire plantation community is living in terror.'

In fact, to combat terrorism, the tea lobby drew up plans to set up a large security force to police the plantations. The effectiveness of such a force has been seriously doubted for it will not have the manpower to protect all estates, large and small, and its recruits will be drawn from former military and police personnel. It will be controlled and armed by the local police. The funds to equip the force and establish its housing and transport will come partly from the tea industry.

Extortion is not new to the Naga rebel ethos. Taxes have been levied on border villages in Nagaland and Manipur over the decades to raise money for the cause. In some places, the taxes took the form of farm produce: grain, a pig, poultry, vegetables as well as cash. This caused much hardship among the villagers but few complained during the early years of the struggle when the nationalist fervour was still fierce and passionate. As the years went by, resentment and deprivation sharpened among the farmers and they openly voiced their opposition to paying more taxes. This caused conflicts and even led to troops being summoned to deal with the rebels.

In Myanmar in the mid-1980s, resentment against the NSCN flared with a group of Nagas enticing the rebels into their villages and then setting upon them with axes and *daos*. Scores were beheaded and many more died in retaliations by the guerrillas.

Funds for the rebels also came from sympathizers in different political parties, including regional groups and even the Congress Party.

The police speak of members of the Nagaland cabinet who have secretly harboured militants in their homes and villages.

The Naga rebellion was undergoing an unmistakable metamorphosis. From a well-oiled fighting machine, it was turning into a group of antagonistic factions which were used against each other by local politicians. Of course, there was a price to be paid. The terms; strictly cash.

In order to settle rivalries, armed factions have been set upon specific targets.

The Shaiza brothers, Yangmasho and Lungshim, are examples of this. The Shaizas are Tangkhul Nagas of the same tribe as Thuengaling Muivah and the younger, Lungshim, was married to Rano, Angami Zapu Phizo's niece. He also played an important role in bringing the underground to Shillong for the 1975 peace accord. Yangmasho was briefly Chief Minister of Manipur and was gunned down at his home. The killer was never traced although relatives say a senior politician in Manipur was responsible.

A few years later, Lungshim was campaigning for elections in Manipur's Ukhrul district; he too was shot dead.

The changes overcoming the Naga insurgents reflected a larger transformation in Naga society.

It was to be seen in the 'get-rich quick' mentality that had swamped the towns of the state and reached out across the Northeast. The entire region has lost this battle against the corruption of traditional values.

Corruption exists on a staggering scale: there are commissions and cuts on every major contract, whether it is for the construction of a government office, a hospital or a road. The kickbacks flow from the contractor or the businessman to a network of officials and to politicians and ministers.

In one case, a Nagaland government official told me of how the Public Health Department had placed an order for thousands of bedside tables and lamps for local hospitals with a company in New Delhi. At that time, the number of beds in government hospitals in the state was not more than a few hundred. The tables were priced at about five times their actual cost, giving the ministers involved as well as the bureaucrats and the firm concerned a handsome profit.

The looting of public money goes on unchecked, not just in Nagaland but across the states of the Northeast. In Nagaland—and in Mizoram too—the logic is very simple. It was explained to me by a former Chief Minister of Nagaland.

'You see, all this is Indian money, we don't pay taxes here,' he remarked. 'So whatever is being done with the money is only benefiting some Nagas, it is not taking money away from them. It is only Indian money that is being used.'

This logic continues to be echoed across the hills and plains. There are no compunctions on this point at all and corruption is accepted and relished.

By the 1970s, India had fully developed its strategy against the Nagas and the other recalcitrant hill groups: one prong of the strategy was to pour in huge amounts of money to 'soften up' the Nagas so that, as one Home Ministry official at Delhi said, 'they will become too comfortable to fight in the jungle again.'

The other element was to keep the pressure on, politically and with the armed troops, so that the options of continuing the fight or joining the political process became starker.

The results of the vast amounts of funds coming into the small hill states was staggering: it led to the breakup of the fabric of society, especially in the towns. Drug and alcohol abuse has become rampant. Acquired Immune Deficiency Syndrome (AIDS) is growing as a menace not merely because of sexual promiscuity but because infected needles are used for injecting heroin.

Easy money also has meant easy weapons.

The new élite comprises politicians and their relatives, contractors (and their relatives) and senior bureaucrats and police officials. Over the years, the dream of independence has faded for many, only to be replaced by a *nouveau riche* culture of sex and violence, drugs and music, bribery and corruption.

Those who speak up are intimidated or even murdered.

One such prominent victim was Chalie Kevichusa, son of one of Nagaland's most prominent leaders, who criticized corruption both in the Naga Congress and the opposition. Kevichusa had fought and lost as many as four electoral battles to the state assembly and few expected his new

Labour Party to win elections to the assembly. But the party gave him a platform to articulate Naga grievances and political demands sharply, much too sharply for his opponents.

Kevichusa spoke of the need to resolve the Naga-India question, or basically the issue of independence that had become relegated to the background. He also talked of the need to release political prisoners, a question that most Naga politicians preferred to avoid.

One day, as he drove his daughter to a tuition class, armed men in a jeep opened fire after having tracked his movements over several days. Kevichusa was killed and his daughter was wounded. The assailants were captured but escaped in a daring break as they were being brought to court.

In Dimapur and Kohima, large protest processions against his killing as well as the turnout at his funeral were sufficient indication that he had touched a chord in the Naga heart although only one of his Labour Party candidates won the election to the state assembly. That resonance is almost everywhere in the state, although it still remains unspoken, unpublicized.

It was visible though when Vamuzo, the chief minister who was ousted by Delhi in 1992 for alleged corruption, once sidled up to me at the state guest house in the national capital. He looked around to make sure that no one was listening. Then he hissed conspiratorially: 'No Naga believes in India: if you really ask them they believe in freedom and Delhi doesn't understand that yet. The movements in other parts of the world for freedom have encouraged them. And if you have a referendum today on the issue of independence, you will see that the Nagas still believe in it.'

But the bitter truth remains that the many tribes and rebels of Nagaland, despite the yearning that Vamuzo articulated, are fiercely divided on ethnic lines. This has been most visible in recent years in the growing killings in Manipur, along the border with Myanmar, between the Kukis on one side and the NSCN on the other, represented by Tangkhuls and a tiny tribe known as the Anals, whose number is a bare 10,000 or so.

For long, these have been hidden wars, camouflaged by the violence of the times, giving those unfamiliar with the area or its multi-ethnic problems, whose knowledge is limited to headlines broadcast on television and radio or reports in newspapers, an impression that this is another insurgency. However, it is nothing of the kind.

The Kukis have settled in Myanmar, Manipur and Nagaland. In Myanmar, they are known as the Kuki-Chins, inhabitants of the Chin hills, a terrain made famous by Allied and Japanese fighting in the Second World War. However, they are disliked by the regime at Rangoon—they too seek independence of the military regime.

The Kukis in Manipur and Nagaland migrated hundreds of years ago from their homelands and have been regarded with suspicion for long by the ethnic Nagas, who see them as landgrabbers and outsiders. In some ways, it is a microscopic view of the Bangladesh Syndrome, played out among tiny communities. 'We permitted them to stay in our land but that does not mean they can part with it. Would you permit strangers to take over your house?' asked a Tangkhul leader.

That resentment erupted more than fifty years ago openly when a Naga leader, Jadugang, and his main follower, Rani Guidaleu, asked Nagas to attack Kukis—blaming them as the root of all their troubles. The British crushed the revolt but left the suspicion and enmity untouched.

In a belt between the channel in the south of Manipur and Ukhrul and Senapati towns to its north, the clashes between the Kukis and their rivals have been played out across scores of villages decades later, leaving hamlets torched, smouldering and deserted, more than a 100 dead in 1993 alone and giving security forces another problem to grapple with.

The trouble erupted first in 1987 with a new outfit, the Kuki National Organization (KNO), demanding an autonomous state in Myanmar. This group is based in Myanmar. But the Nagas were troubled and suspicious and even more so when another new group, the Kuki National Front (KNF) demanded a Kukiland comprising parts of Manipur and Myanmar. In turn, the NSCN of Thuengaling Muivah called for a Greater Nagaland comprising 'eastern Nagaland' in Myanmar as well as parts of Manipur and the present state of Nagaland.

And the KNF developed a striking arm: the Kuki National Army (KNA), comprising guerrillas—men and women, some of them stunningly attractive—which decided to take on the NSCN. The NSCN said that the Kukis were in league with the state and Central governments and planned to drive Nagas out of their native lands.

According to intelligence accounts, the KNA is backed by Kukis in the Manipur bureaucracy and by Congress leaders from the state. They see it as a way of undermining the growing Naga influence in the state's politics and also of hitting at Thuengaling Muivah. The Burmese Government, which is inimical to the Kukis because of their demand for a separate state, is apparently prepared to go easy on Muivah's bases, indirectly helping the NSCN. This has enabled the NSCN to reorganize movement of its forces between Bangladesh and Myanmar, after years of pressure that followed its break with the Kachin Independence Army (KIA).

The NSCN too has its supporters in the Congress in this bloody conflict and both sides have freely used Chinese-made automatic weapons as well as American guns, AK-47s, G-3 carbines, hand grenades and M-16 rifles. The NSCN accuses the Kukis of assisting Indian troops, especially members of the paramilitary Assam Rifles, with information about their movements and bases.

As in any conflict, the worst sufferers are ordinary Nagas and Kukis, their homes destroyed, fleeing into the jungle for safety under the protection of one armed band or the other, and always on the edge of survival with fear and hunger as constant companions. Villagers have surrounded themselves with bamboo fences to ward off possible attacks and guards check inmates leaving the camp or visitors for identity cards.

The honour and dignity shown by earlier rebels—of not picking innocent targets—has been discarded and guerrillas have turned their weapons on one another and on unarmed men, women and children. Rape is common, torture and slaughter routine.

The farewell that the earlier Naga insurgents gave each other as they set off on dangerous journeys—*Kuknalim* which can be translated freely as Good Journey or May the Lord be with You—has never been more relevant.

A result of this fighting is that entire tracts of the state are neither controlled wholly by the state governments, Indian troops or insurgents. Ethnic rivalries and military power dictates control of the roads, villages, ricefields and jungle. In some parts, the writ of the Indian Army runs—especially along some stretches of the highway between Imphal and Moreh, the main trading town with Myanmar. The remaining areas are a no man's land, with rival groups claiming and battling for supremacy.

In the process, the Indian Army's work has been made a little easier, as Delhi sees it, with the internecine fighting taking up much of the time of the rebels.

There are not less than 25,000 army and paramilitary troops in Manipur, assisted by thousands of state police personnel. They are opposed by rebels who do not number more than 2,000 in the state and who are organized only in some areas. Superficially, Manipur is a classic example of jungle wars being fought between unequal foes.

What makes the situation ironic is that despite occasional ambushes by security forces, the guns of the insurgents are trained on one another and that too with the tacit support of governments in Imphal, Delhi and Rangoon, trapping them in a spider's web of ethnic hate.

The killings underline the fact that for these areas, the cycle of violence continues and peace is never more than illusory.

In October 1992, police in Meghalaya, neighbouring Assam and Bangladesh on different sides, stormed a guerrilla camp in the jungles, about fifty kilometres from the capital of Shillong.

The training camp was being conducted by the National Socialist Council of Nagaland—the Muivah faction—and two Nagas were seized and two automatic weapons were captured. Diaries found at the site showed that the organizers of the camp had raised large sums of money and that they were training young Khasi men.

The proximity of the camp—which was set up in March 1992—to a major state capital shows how easy it is to conduct such training undetected in the relatively thinly populated hills where patches of dense forest remain. It also is a clear pointer to the way violence is likely to dominate places which were hitherto largely free of it.

Although Shillong is no Shangri-La—as the recurring anti-Bengali and anti-outsider riots testify—it was far more peaceful than any other state of the region, barring Arunachal Pradesh.

But in Assam, the situation has become more complex over the years. For example, the Karbis, the other major indigenous community which has made common cause with the Bodos and also seeks a separate state, have hardened their attitude. This followed the dismissal of their elected District Council and the arrests of their leaders in 1992. The Karbis wanted more powers within the state of Assam.

Similar demands for more power and facilities are coming from smaller indigenous groups such as the Lalungs, who were involved in the Nellie massacre of 1983, the Rabhas, and the Mishings.

The Autonomous Implementation Demand Committee (AIDC) of the Karbis, led by the leftist, Jayanta Rongpi, suffered a setback with the dismissal of the District Council. Investigations showed that the AIDC paid several workers regularly in villages in the district out of development funds meant for the area's uplift. The job of these political workers was to organize bandhs, strikes, picket offices and rallies.

When the largesse of the AIDC was abruptly stopped, these workers did what other political groups do elsewhere in the country when the going is tough: they joined the winning side and walked across to the Congress.

A significant factor in the NSCN-Hmar-Bodo-ULFA network is that there are now linkages between each and all of these groups. The only one left out of that circuit are the Karbis but it is surely only a matter of time before they too are swallowed by the insurgent maw. The Bodo Security Force (BSF), which has had some training with the NSCN in the Myanmar hills, worked closely with ULFA. Ranjan Daimuri, the commander-in-chief of the BSF met with ULFA commanders and organizers to forge common strategies although these were disrupted by the army operations.

Yet, as ULFA's history too has shown, such periods of militant ascendancy are followed by divisions in the face of an armed onslaught by the State, frustrated and concerned about its inability to control a rebellion. 'This is the history of all accords,' said Sunil Nath, ULFA's one time publicity secretary, referring to those relevant to the Northeast and other parts of India.

It took less than ten years for ULFA to soar to power before collapsing in disunity and being scattered by the Indian Army. The Sikh uprising in Punjab lasted eleven years before it was suppressed, to a large extent by K.P.S. Gill, the state's police chief, and his fierce police force. K.P.S. Gill, the Sikh IPS officer with twenty-two years of service in Assam, led from the front in that relentless assault on some of the most hardened extremist groups that South Asia has seen. But Gill, a well-read man with an infinite capacity for liquor and absolutely unflappable even under fire (I can vouch for that: I was once interviewing him at his command post in Amritsar in 1988 when the place was being strafed by

Sikh militants from the Golden Temple a short distance away), knows that insurgencies can never be completely wiped out. They leave behind what he describes as 'a residual criminality.'

That is hardly how militants in the Northeast or the Northwest of India would like to be described. And Gill's analysis is correct—to a point. Insurgencies can never be erased : they disappear for some years only to reappear in a different incarnation, not perhaps in a militaristic mould but with a new face, a new rebel, a new batch of ideas to revive old grievances.

Residual criminality is the basis for many recruits to take to rebellions across the world: causeless, aimless, thoughtless thugs in search of pleasure, easy money and easy power.

And over the years, the wheel of insurgency in the northeastern theatre, has moved away from the hills and jungles to the towns and cities, to easy prey, to looting and extorting funds from officials, businessmen and even banks, by people with and without a cause.

The state of rebellions in the region indicates increasing co-operation among the militants, falling short of a united guerrilla army, under a central command. The ethnic, social and cultural differences of the place are just too great to permit this. The insurgents too are now clear that they will not be able to win independence from India in the foreseeable future.

Indeed, they have found that the pickings are easier when one operates with force within the system. The use of insurgent gangs to settle political scores has become common place, especially in Nagaland and Manipur. In the process, the aura of heroism that was associated with the earlier rebellions of the 1960s and 1970s has fast disappeared. In its place has come a cynical balance of power in which politicians set up guerrilla groups, and drug smugglers and couriers make their peace with members of the state administrations as well as the armed forces, extending their web of evil and deceit.

Meanwhile, the divisions in ULFA has created complications that were unpredicted and remain unpredictable. Some believe that of the pro-negotiation group, there are a number who may return to the jungle.

There is an ULFA faction known as the United Peoples Forum of Assam (UPFA), led by Mridul Nath, a former assistant organizing secretary. Revelations by supporters of this group—made in public forums and not behind closed doors—also have damaged ULFA's image irretrievably. Apu Goswami of the Barpeta district told a seminar in a college after the split that 'We were told to kill a certain number of people within a specific time-frame. But since our cadres were not equipped to take on the security forces, they had to kill innocent people.'

UPFA on the other hand says that neither a dialogue with the government nor a struggle for an independent state will meet the crisis. It says that a 'mass revolution' is the only answer.

But the defenders of the original dream are unrepentant. And like Banquo's ghost in Shakespeare's *Macbeth*, the figure of Hirakjyoti Mahanta returns time and again to torment Assam. In early 1993, for example, Parag Das, the editor of the influential *Budhbar*, and his publisher and printer were arrested under the National Security Act (NSA) for bringing out an issue on Mahanta, his death and his beliefs. The ban was not so much against the three men as against the exposure of the manner of the rebel's death.

One thing is certain: Assam and the Northeast have presented India with a difficult case of resolving the sense of grievance felt by a partner in a nearly fifty-year-old experiment. They have raised serious doubts about whether numerically small people can secure political, social and economic justice from New Delhi.

The answer to that question is likely to change the shape of India, for it is a question and a demand that is being voiced by an increasing number of indigenous peoples, beginning from Kashmir and Punjab to Tamil Nadu in the South.

A failure to answer these questions will, inevitably, spawn more insurgencies.

Assam has seen a return to both low-level, low-casualty insurgency as well as to the extortions that followed kidnappings. This time, businessmen and contractors as well as tea garden managers are prime targets.

As Holiram Tarang of the Karbi movement, the Autonomous Implementation Demand Committee, said after ULFA's sudden collapse in early 1992, there could be no meaning of a settlement with that group unless there was a 'package for the whole of Assam.'

Extortions will grow. Pressure on land will burgeon. Populations will soar. And the wheel of violence will continue to turn inexorably.

A Stepmother In Delhi

The intractability of the problems of the Northeast and Delhi's piecemeal, ad hoc policies toward its people have complicated an already difficult situation. Policies toward the Nagas and other pro-independence groups seemed to revolve around three factors: brute force to crush the physical capacity to resist, a flood of funds to soften the resolve of indigenous groups and a fierce campaign to portray them as renegades, 'misguided' elements who would see sense if only they were given a chance.

But Delhi's 'We know best' attitude, the superciliousness of its bureaucracy and the overwhelming ignorance of its politicians from the cow-chappati-dust belt to understand the compulsions and beliefs of proud but small nationalities, sees it blundering into one insurgency after another. Adding to the emotional turbulence was, of course, the superior attitude of the Assamese to the indigenous groups such as the Bodo-Cacharis and the Karbis. They were, at best, looked down upon, especially in the chief ministership of Bishnuram Medhi who sought to force the Assamese language down each non-Assamese throat.

Over the years, it became clear to the Northeast that Delhi would not budge on any major issue without a battle. Thus, Gopinath Bardoloi unfurled the flag of revolt against the Congress leadership in 1946 for trying to sell out Assam's interests.

Bishnuram Medhi's demand for an oil refinery in the state was rejected by various technical committees. Jawaharlal Nehru, who had the last word on such matters, did award a tiny refinery near Guwahati. The issue triggered much resentment and led to agitations on the street that shook Medhi's government. In a 13 June 1957 letter to Medhi, Nehru expressed impatience with the Assamese and added that he was especially irritated with the Congress Legislature Party's opposition to the main refinery being awarded to Bihar. In addition, he said, the Defence Ministry had told him that it was safer, in terms of national security, to locate the refinery in Bihar.

Medhi replied tersely: 'If Defense cannot undertake to protect the refinery located in Assam, how will they protect the oil fields and the transport system in the Eastern Region. We feel that the proper course is not to think of the protection of the refinery separately from the oil fields and the transport system, but to treat the refinery, oil fields and the lines of transport as parts of an integrated defence system in national interest...

'In that case we do not understand, how the Defense will be able to protect the pipeline to Barauni, 140 miles of which will necessarily have to pass along the Pakistan border. We also do not understand how the pipeline would be more defendable than the Railway system as a good bit of it will have to pass at a distance of only 20 miles from the border.'

Overruling Medhi, Nehru announced the toy refinery and urged the people of the state to stop pursuing 'negative and wasteful policies that would only hinder their development.'

That feeling of being let down swamps visitors to the Northeast when they speak to local people. It is sharpest perhaps when Assamese talk of the 1962 war with China when Indian troops, routed and hopeless, were fleeing from a swift Chinese advance in the North Eastern Frontier Agency (NEFA). The Chinese were in striking distance of the Brahmaputra Valley, creating a massive panic in the government and the general population. At this point, Nehru broadcast to the nation saying that his heart 'went out to the people of Assam.'

Instead of a stirring, evocative oration in Churchillian style, urging people to fight on and assuring them of his full support—as only he could—Nehru was seen as bidding farewell to the Northeast. Many years after his death, those words evoke bitterness—Nehru has not been forgiven for abandoning his people.

Meanwhile, as the Naga and Mizo rebellions flared, seeking their separate places away from the power of Delhi, and the anti-foreigner movement in Assam gained momentum, followed by the United Liberation Front of Asom's (ULFA's) ascent, it became more than evident that only sharp pressure would rouse the political and bureaucratic mandarins in the Indian capital.

This attitude was again witnessed when the Congress Party in Assam took up the touchy issue of illegal immigration, one that it had shied away from all these years.

Although Indira Gandhi and Rajiv Gandhi reluctantly acknowledged the presence of these migrants, the local Congress Party, especially its Muslim and Bengali Hindu factions, remained hostile to the concept of "foreigners".

'There are no foreigners in Assam,' said Abdul Muhim Majumdar, the leader of the Muslim Front, which was started as a dissident force to confront Hiteswar Saikia's growing clout among the religious minorities in the state. Majumdar has been the state's Advocate General and has consistently maintained that those in Assam are all Indians and there should not be any deportations or detections of 'so-called aliens.'

Majumdar was especially dismayed in July 1992, one year after Saikia came to power, when Prime Minister P.V. Narasimha Rao made a stunning declaration at Guwahati. It was Rao's first visit to the state after assuming office. At a public meeting there, that coincided with the convention of the North Eastern Congress Coordination Committee (NECCC) in the city, Rao dropped his bombshell. As reported in *The Sentinel*, Rao said that,

> the demand made by the students of the State on the issue of illegal immigration of foreigners into the State was justified . . . such illegal migration of foreign nationals into Assam and their permanent residence here has created a serious problem in the State. In order to check further infiltration . . . work on putting up barbed wire fencing along the border has already started.

> [Mr Rao said that] he understood the deep-seated feeling of alienation and anger of the youths of Assam which he identified as having been born out of the influx of foreigners to the state.

The Prime Minister also declared that the Centre was prepared to consider amending a law that is aimed at detecting foreign nationals and their deportation. This particular legislation, the Illegal Migrants (Determination by Tribunals) Act of Assam (IMDTA) has drawn much flak. Among other things, it says that any complaint against a suspected alien must be accompanied by a payment of a fee by the complainant. In addition, the accuser must live within four kilometres of the person he is seeking to oust.

Most villagers are reluctant to put money down for such causes. The migrants and settlers live in thickly-populated villages and communities. Their large numbers is part reason why villagers are loath to go before a tribunal or a police officer to complain.

Prime Minister Rao and Home Minister S.B. Chavan raised the issue with Bangladesh Prime Minister Begum Khaleda Zia when she visited Delhi in 1992. Her response was bland and predictable: there was no migration from Bangladesh into India, said the Begum. Efforts to raise the question of ULFA sanctuaries were dismissed with a general statement: the government knew nothing of them and would look into the matter.

For Dhaka, migrations and ULFA were not real problems.

What was important was the release of enough Ganga waters during the dry weeks to irrigate the fields in the north without which, thousands of villages face acute shortage. In 1992, the year of Begum Khaleda's visit, about thirty million people were affected by the dry spell and their crops and hopes destroyed. India says it needs the water, from the Farakka Barrage, to flush the silt from the Hooghly and keep Calcutta port operational.

The Bangladeshis reject this argument, saying that India is behaving unilaterally and without either sensitivity or logic. India, on the other hand, says that it cannot assure Bangladesh of a specific amount of water from Farakka. It says that with the increase in population upstream and the growth of industries, agriculture and irrigation, there is far less water in the Ganges these days than at any other time.

'No government is going to sacrifice the interests of its farmers or tell them to draw less water to benefit Bangladesh, it just isn't feasible politically,' said an official at the Foreign Ministry who has handled the issue for several years.

'It is like a tap in the hands of the Indians, they can turn it off and on at any time they want,' said Farooq Sobhan, the Bangladesh High Commissioner to India.

In Assam, meanwhile, the Prime Minister's remarks on the student agitation embarrassed the Congress, especially Hiteswar Saikia.

Yet, there was no holding back the anti-immigrant sentiment within the Congress. It came out, during Rao's visit, in the form of a glossy, ninety-four-page report, smartly decked out in the Congress tricolour of orange, white and green. The statement was innocuously titled "Report of The General Secretaries (1st March 1989 to 2nd July 1992)" and was a report to the seventh general conference of the North Eastern Congress Coordination Committee.

The reports were signed by B.B. Dutta, the general secretary of the NECCC, but its overall craftsman was Purno Sangma, a bright, gregarious Garo, who speaks fluent Assamese and swiftly rose to political power in the Garo Hills and in Delhi under the benign eye of Indira Gandhi and her son, Rajiv. He was India's longest serving Minister of State for Labour, with independent charge of that portfolio under both Gandhis. P. Sangma assumed charge of Labour and Coal under Prime Minister Rao in 1991. Although he was competent, aggressive and respected by his colleagues in Delhi, he did not quite carry that same clout in Meghalaya.

The report analysed in great detail the growth of fundamentalism in East Pakistan and the curbs placed on it by Sheikh Mujibur Rahman after the 1971 liberation. Four major fundamentalist parties were banned after 1971 which included: Jamaat-e-Islami, Nisan-e-Islami, Pakistan Democratic Party and the Muslim League. The ban was lifted by President Ziaur Rahman who came to power after the 1975 coup against Mujib.

The ban's end led to a boom in the number of madrasas or Muslim theological colleges teaching the Islamic way of life to young Bangladeshis. In 1972–73, there were 7,792 secondary schools and 1,351 madrasas. In 1989–90, there were 9,822 secondary schools and 5,766 madrasas.

Under President H.M. Ershad, Islam was declared the state religion, shutting the doors to liberal ways and, according to the report, given the fundamentalists an opportunity to virtually drive religious minorities in the country—namely, the Hindus—out. The report said: ' . . . migration of minorities continues unabated . . . Minorities today find that they are seldom able to protect their faith, property and women. Reports of forced marriages and conversions have been pouring in . . . there is a rising pressure on land and minority properties are the obvious targets. Even temple lands are not being spared.'

The Congress document also traced the problems in the Chittagong Hill Tracts (CHT) and the fact that the Jammat-e-Islami sought the settlement there of the Rohingya Muslims, who have fled Burmese oppression in the Arakan hills.

In its findings, the report went against traditional Congress wisdom in the Northeast. 'Between 1971 and 1981, Bangladesh census records show a reduction of 39 lakhs [3.9 million] in the minority population.

'Between 1981-89, 36 lakh [3.6 million] religious minorities were missing from that country.

'In 1972, there were 7.5 lakh [7,50,000] Bihari Muslims in the camps in Dhaka. As a result of mediation by Saudi Arabia only 33,000 of them were accepted by Pakistan. At present, there are less than two lakh [2,00,000] in the camps. Where have the rest gone?'

In simple figures, that added up to more than eight million missing people in Bangladesh, although not all these figures can be taken at their face value. The Bihari Muslims are those who seek to be repatriated to Pakistan and have spoken of their loyalty to their country. Since the report, Pakistan has agreed to take back the remaining refugees and settle them.

The document said in absolute terms, however, that the number of Muslims crossing into India was higher than those of non-Muslims. Fundamentalists too seek to promote the vision of a larger Islamic nation, merging Bangladesh and the Northeast, it said. The natural hostility to Islamic forces in the Northeast has been strengthened by the growth of the Bharatiya Janata Party (BJP), the right-wing platform of Hindu views, which won as many as nine assembly seats in Bengali Hindu-dominated areas in Assam. Earlier, these were Congress strongholds. The two Lok Sabha seats from Cachar also went to the BJP.

'There is a direct correlation between the rise of fundamentalism and increase in influx,' says the Congress paper.

The report went on to say that Bangladeshi journalists met families from their country in Delhi 'took their pictures and wrote about their lifestyle . . . . According to them, there are about 1.5 lakh (150,000) Bangladeshi Muslims) in Delhi.' In 1990, Muslims of Bangladeshi origin formed a group in West Bengal called the Bangladesh Mojahir Sangstha. The following year, a spokesman for this organization told reporters that there were 1,00,000 Bangladeshi nationals in the state and another half a million across Delhi, Bombay and Ahmedabad. The then Minister of State for Home Affairs, M.M. Jacob, in the Government of India said that 'there were one lakh (100,000) Bangladeshi nationals in Delhi and 5.87 lakh [587,000] in West Bengal.'

The Congress document further said that Bangladesh's poor economic conditions had compelled many Muslims, as well as Hindus, to come to earn their keep in India. It described a 'floating population' which comes and goes with whatever it earns and that many were being settled 'with no questions asked as we require cheap and scarce labour in construction and in farm and household work.'

While the Congress document carefully criticized the student-led anti-alien agitation as 'misconceived and misdirected,' it also sought to assure Muslims in the Northeast that they would not be harassed.

'But the emerging trends in Bangladesh today and the increasing infiltration have thrown a challenge to the minorities living in the region to take a wise and farsighted stand. To turn a blind eye or to oppose any such talk, using a forum in the name of a particular community, in a tone and temper that strengthen only the fundamentalist forces, will be the height of folly.'

Its conclusions also were stinging, especially those involving the Centre and West Bengal.

'Unfortunately the Government of India appears to be suffering from a half-hearted approach or no approach to this challenging problem,' it declared. 'The External Affairs Ministry has not done the job it should have done. The concerned desk has virtually been a non-functioning one. For years, the practice has been: if anything appears to be wrong there, ask Mr. so and so of West Bengal who is in the limelight at that time.'

The tone and content of the Guwahati papers were such that they could have been prepared even by the Bharatiya Janata Party, which is campaigning on the Hindutva platform.

Yet, beyond these cautions, the Congress Party was unable to map out a plan of action. The recommendations remained on paper, and the Congress failed to followup its revelations.

The situation called for a leader of vision like Gopinath Bardoloi or B.P. Chaliha who could stand up to the Centre and press for the legitimate rights of the state.

Fifty years after Bardoloi's famous confrontation with Nehru, Vallabhbhai Patel and M.A. Jinnah, Assam was led by Hiteswar Saikia who was far more fascinated by the game of manoeuvre and power politics and lacked far-sightedness.

Saikia was also not free of allegations of corruption and

maladministration. His former colleagues, officials and editors and businessfolk in Assam speak bitterly of his allegedly crooked deals, of buying out inconvenient writers and officials. There was a large forest scam during his first administration between 1983 and 1985 in which he was allegedly involved, along with several senior officials: the contracts were supposed to have been fixed by the Chief Minister and his cohorts in advance of the bids. One of these officials was later Saikia's mediator in the crucial talks with the ULFA leadership. Despite the unending list of charges, Saikia tended to land on his feet at all times, like a cat. The charges of corruption and malfeasance multiplied over the years but nothing seemed to stick or even bother him in his singleminded pursuit of power, undercutting his foes and rewarding those who did well by him.

In the process, allegations began to be increasingly heard against his close relatives, including his sons, one of whom was nicknamed Chota Nawab. This young man, with a printing press, became one of the most sought-after persons in Assam; and, of course, many government printing jobs went to him.

As the months went by, Saikia's intolerance of opposition grew as did his own view of himself as virtually indispensable to Delhi in its grand design for the Northeast.

That intolerance of dissent—within his party and outside of it—was manifest in his second crackdown on the press. In this case, the enemy of the state was an old foe and relentless critic: the pro-ULFA editor, Parag Das, for publishing a special issue on Hirakjyoti Mahanta, one of the casualties of Operation Rhino and the then deputy commander-in-chief of the insurgents. In early 1993, the government seized Das, and the printer and publisher of his weekly magazine, *Budhbar*, which had been fiercely critical of the pro-talks group in ULFA and booked them under anti-terrorist laws. The press reacted by courting arrest, publishing blank editorials and demanding the release of their colleagues.

Journalists and editors who protested the jailings were attacked at the Press Club by Guwahati Police with lathis and abuse.

The Press Club was a shambles and so was Saikia's relations with the media. He appeared unconcerned for that very morning his government had signed a tripartite agreement with the Bodos giving them an Autonomous Council with judicial and economic powers.

Yet, despite his cockiness, the conditions are too complicated, the

nmities too deep, the resentments too fierce, the economic realities too
aarsh and the lack of statesmanship too obvious to bear repetition.

This discordant picture has roots in hard economic facts.

ECONOMIC REALITIES

The economic problems of the Northeast, while rooted in a series of
inter-related factors, can also be traced to the days of independence when
a British-drawn line divided the subcontinent into two nations.

That artificial division spelt catastrophe for several areas which
suddenly found themselves on the frontier. And as we shall see, the
economic cost to the region proved the very idiocy of Partition. A loose
common market would have made much more sense.

For centuries, the peoples of the hills such as the Garos and the
Khasis, for example, had traded with the Muslims of East Bengal, in
Mymensingh and Sylhet districts. The trade involved a fair amount of
barter. From the Garos and Khasis would go ginger, potatoes and cattle
in exchange for beef and local handicrafts while Marwari traders would
also add oil, spices and grains, especially rice and lentils, to the Bengali
diet down in the plains. From East Bengal, came jute products such as
sacking material, rope and twine, fish—the best hilsa and rahu as well as
prawns—chillies and salt. A large consumer of the Bengali fish was the
Assamese community in the hills, since many lived in and around
Shillong, the capital of undivided Assam.

For either side, it was not just a traditional way of doing things and
thus acceptable to generation after generation. But it made sound common
sense and thus good economic sense as well. For groups like the Garos,
Khasis and Jaintias, the plains of East Bengal were a short trek away. To
the East Bengalis, the hills were as much part of the hinterland as any
other area. Neither the hill tribes of the plainsfolk needed a convoy of
trucks or a large network of roads and railway lines to get their economic
systems functional. It made more sense to deal with each other than to lug
their wares and products hundreds of kilometres more to the Assam plains.
It was cheaper, took less time and energy.

It was do-able—without reliance on extraneous factors and
government and the dalals or middlemen. The communities preferred this
way because they made the profits, not a middleman on either side of the
border.

The Radcliffe Award changed all that. It bred a new creature: the smuggler.

Partition devastated the well-developed river transport system that sustained village economies down the great rivers that flowed through Bengal, Assam, merging, splitting and merging again before emptying their silt and loads of water into the Bay of Bengal. Of course, the barges and steamers and ferries that chugged along the Brahmaputra, Meghna, Padma and Ganga essentially helped the tea industry, the coal and the grain and wholesale traders and industrialists, who had large investments in these regions. To them, as to the ordinary ferry passenger travelling from Dibrugarh to Guwahati, it was cheaper although time-consuming to send goods by ship.

The shipping industry never recovered from the aftermath of the Partition. The owners did not have enough business within Assam or Bangladesh to generate profits or even make ends meet. Many of them went out of business, hurting many other families that depended on the ships for their livelihood.

In turn, the governments on either side began emphasizing the importance of roads and railways to passenger and goods movement. This strategy was effective up to a point. But it meant that India had to develop the Chicken's Neck, the thin land corridor that connects the Northeast to India, on both fronts and provide tight security, during the days of its confrontations with China and Pakistan, to the oil pipelines and the communication systems running through this sliver of land.

Yet, it took the Government of India as much as forty-five years to ensure that the broad gauge track went beyond Guwahati. In fact, it reached Guwahati only in the 1980s, giving the people of the region another grievance against the Centre: that while much of the small gauge railways elsewhere in India had been converted to broad gauge in this period, a region that remains battered by insurgency, potential international threats and supplies most of the country's tea exports and a large chunk of its oil was not important enough for the Centre to upgrade its railway network.

Originally, the British had developed the railway system to feed and not replace the natural waterways tradition, which was cost-effective, time-tested and an economic support to local fishing, trading, boat-building and other local communities, creating jobs in all these sectors and in the ancillary professions: carpenters and sailors, fish netmakers and coolies for loading and unloading operations.

Partition changed this completely, as it had done with the trade between the hills of what is now Meghalaya and the plains of East Bengal.

The new strategy also led to heavy investments in the oil, gas and timber sectors, tying up precious resources. As a result, funds for developing other economic fronts were just not available.

In the process, the umbilical cord that tied the eastern regions and its lush waterways to Calcutta, the main port of the East, was slashed. Calcutta found itself without the vast funds generated by shipping and transport. A natural hinterland had vanished overnight.

The economic idiocy of Partition, apart from its political stupidity, is never better seen than in the following fact:

From Agartala, capital of Tripura, to Calcutta is 2,200 kilometres by road or train. That is the nearest Indian port. It will cost, at the least, a few hundred rupees for a second class fare by train via the Siliguri neck. But it is hardly six kilometres to the nearest rail and road head in Bangladesh: Akhaura. From Akhaura, it is another 150 kilometres to the main port of Chittagong. A few hours by road is all it takes to reach a port that is recognized as one of the finest natural harbours in Asia and one that does not entail weeks of waiting to load and unload which is the bane of shippers at Calcutta.

The other reason why this has not worked is the short-sightedness of Indian and Bangladeshi-Pakistani policymakers who have failed to overcome suspicions and political and economic obstacles to generate co-operation and common sense.

After the 1965 India-Pakistan war, the river route between the two countries was blocked. Only in recent years has it been revived a little and that too only in relation to transit traffic or ships that are moving from one part of India to another, using the Bangla rivers as their route. No loaded steamers and barges head for each other's towns and cities. As a consequence, one of the most environmentally-sound, cost-effective and community-beneficial ways of developing the region has been neglected and virtually destroyed.

Instead, roads and bridges and railway lines are being constructed to overcome the barrier of an international frontier. The cost is enormous to poor states that can ill-afford to spend such funds. The environmental cost too is high, especially in Bangladesh and other low-lying countries. Here, the construction of roads and railways means that artificial belts of high land are created, criss-crossing the country which, during floods, trap the flood waters, ensuring that the soil damage is higher than it would have been otherwise and that the recurring cost of repairing the annual damage by floods to these very roads, railway tracks and bridges will be several times what it cost to build them in the first place.

Nearly fifty years after independence, the economic shackles that bind the Northeast, and especially Assam, which is the mother state and the gateway to the region, to New Delhi remain firmly in place.

Faulty planning and distorted development has meant, for one thing, that the state government, despite its vast natural resources, depends totally on the Centre. In recent years, this crutch of support has grown longer and heavier. The 1990–91 Annual Economic Plan for the state, presented by the Central Planning Commission, placed borrowings from the Central Government at sixty-eight per cent of the outlay.

A study by the Laxmi Chand Jain Committee looking at Assam's economic and developmental problems showed that, by any economic yardstick, it lagged behind the rest of the country. This was fairly pathetic for a state that was, at the time of independence, regarded as among the top five in terms of income and agricultural self-sufficiency.

In the 1990s, Assam's managerial base is weak; its skilled manpower strength low and the infrastructure extremely shoddy with power supplies interrupted for days, and sometimes weeks, in the baking heat of places such as Nagaon in the flatlands of the Brahmaputra Valley where temperatures could rise above 105 degrees Fahrenheit. The sticky humidity of the place make conditions unbearable.

Literacy stood at thirty-five per cent against 36.2 per cent of the national average; female literacy especially was down to 18.6 per cent, below the national figure of 24.8 per cent. Installed power capacity for every 1,000 persons was 17.5 kilowatts compared to 57.3 kilowatts nationally. This too, despite the fact, that the Northeast has the potential—if mega, medium and small dams on the Brahmaputra and its tributaries are built—of tapping most of the 45,000 megawatts of power from the swift-flowing rivers that cause floods downstream before emptying themselves in the Bay of Bengal. Such a vast capacity would not only meet the needs of the entire eastern region for several decades but would also prove profitable to India for it could sell power to its neighbours in Bangladesh, Nepal and Myanmar.

The Jain Committee said that the manufacturing sector generated per capita income worth only seventy rupees while for India the corresponding figure was exactly twice that of Assam: Rs 140. Fertilizer consumption was a low 5.4 kilograms compared to forty-five kilos for India. And each engineering college reached out to 7.1 million people. For India that figure was 4.6 million people to an engineering college.

Yet the primary school condition was somewhat better with each such school enrolling 823 children while the overall figure was one for 1,405 children.

These figures indicated the broad trend of government inputs: these went into the major infrastructural sectors in successive Five Year Plans. In the Fifth, Sixth and Seventh Five Year Plans, power, flood control, communications and transport usually took a share of more than half of all plan funds for the Northeast, not merely for Assam. Social services such as health, education and water took about twenty-seven per cent to thirty per cent while agricultural production, animal husbandry, dairy products and fisheries came a poor third with twenty-three to twenty-eight per cent of the total Central investment. Yet, these investments have done little in terms of making the region, and particularly Assam, self-sufficient. Instead, dependence on the Centre for doles has grown.

It has been estimated, that despite its rich soil and wealth of water resources—both ground water, riverine as well as from precipitation—Assam purchases foodgrains and oilseeds among other agricultural commodities worth an estimated seven billion rupees (about 230 million dollars) from other states and Central Government corporations every year. This heavy drain on its resources and shaky infrastructure services—such as the small railways network and the bumpy, narrow roads is the result of faulty planning and lack of perspective.

For decades, most Assamese farmers stayed with the single crop pattern or monoculture, essentially rice. They rarely experimented with new breeds or sought to change their cropping patterns. The results were singularly poor: the summer crops were invariably damaged by recurring waves of floods and there were only sporadic efforts to exploit the moisture in the soil during the winter months to grow crops intensively as has been done both in Punjab and in Bangladesh.

As a result, summer rice production rarely went beyond 2.8 million tons although at times it dropped to 2.4 million tons.

Farmers tried the new fast-growing varieties, which had been used successfully in northern India, in what is known as Assam's rice bowl, Nagaon. And here the pioneers were not Assamese Hindu peasants but the settlers from East Bengal and their descendants who were hard-working, prepared to experiment and take calculated risks.

The Assamese farmer was, in contrast to his industrious neighbour, content with a lifestyle that earned him enough and rarely grew more than one or two crops, with small vegetable patches and groves of banana trees. In addition, most Assamese homes even with middling incomes, especially in the villages, have tiny *pukhuris* or fish ponds where householders can net a few small fish every week to supplement a diet of rice and lentils, with milk products such as sweetened curds and cottage cheese.

One other factor inhibiting high agricultural growth in Assam was the low use of chemical fertilizers. Traditionally, farmers have used fertilizers for one crop but rarely bothered to use them for the next season and the next crop. As a result, the network of fertilizer stores is inadequate and packets of chemical fertilizers are often unavailable.

Agriculture experts believe that the state's farm production can be doubled by 'increasing the use of chemical fertilizers along with some irrigation and drainage facilities.' Then there is the lack of simple skills at the village level. While most medium- and large-sized villages in western and northern India these days have some people with mechanical skills and access to repair and maintenance of equipment such as diesel pump sets and tractors, farmers in some Assam districts say they need to travel as much as twenty or twenty-five kilometres to get such repairs done. In addition, the size of the holdings is a significant factor in the lack of progress. The *Agricultural Atlas of Assam* places the highest number of holdings at those with a farm size of less than half a hectare. They did not, when the *Atlas* was published in 1985, comprise the largest area under farming. That went to those with an average holding of between one and two hectares.

It is difficult with such small holdings to develop a modern strategy revolving around multiple cropping. One factor is the risk, should one crop fail. Such failure could wipe out the savings of a family, force it to turn away from planting new crops, seek help from the local moneylender and fall back to the old single crop pattern.

The room for manoeuvre is far less in the small holdings of Assam than in the large farms of Punjab and Haryana.

Pressure on cultivable land is also caused by the large tea plantations, which take up more than 2,20,000 hectares of prime land. Tea is and will remain for many generations to come the main cash crop in Assam. More than half of the national production of tea as well as at least sixty per cent of the foreign exchange that India earns through exports of packed tea comes from Assam's gardens.

The lifestyles of affluent planters can be the envy of the rich and famous anywhere in the world.

Some of them, like the Jalans of Dibrugarh, have tea estates in the heart of the city. The bungalows look out on manicured lawns and an army of loyal servants, drivers and helpers is always at hand to respond to orders and requests. The drive from Dibrugarh airport to the *bagan ghar* or literally, 'garden house' of the Jalans, involves a brief trip on the highway to the fringes of the city before turning off onto a road of packed earth over which vehicles bump at a stately pace, flanked on either side by green tea shrubs shaded by mulberry trees. Labourers—the women with cane baskets for carrying the freshly-cut leaves, and the men with spades and riding atop pickup trucks—can be seen at work in the fields. The noise of the bus-stand nearby, the shouts of hawkers and of the medical college abutting the tea fields are muted by distance and the vegetation.

It is a short drive to the Brahmaputra, with its sandy banks in winter, when the flow is at its lowest; and across the river, are the hills of Arunachal Pradesh, swathed by strips of cloud and mist. Warnings about venturing out too far onto the bunds or flood prevention zones, strips of boulders piled on top of each other and reinforced by sand, concrete and iron mesh, proliferate.

During the months of high water, the Brahmaputra reaches out over the bunds, slicing away more land from the city's edges and flooding its markets, neighbourhoods and even the tea gardens.

Economists say that the area under tea plantations take away a major chunk of good cultivable land that could have been used to develop greater self-sufficiency in foodgrains and oilseeds. But the counter argument to that is, of course, that there is no other industry or crop that would give the per hectare returns on investment that tea yields. Plus, it employs more than one million people and sustains four to five times that figure in terms of those who depend on the employment of the workers. It provides opportunities for those in ancillary services such as dhobis, accountants, carpenters, mechanics, cooks, maids and gardeners.

It can be argued that most tea companies have exploited Assam by not ploughing their profits back into the place where they have made their money. It took the fear of ULFA and of the Bodo Security Force (BSF) to force a change in this attitude. These days, large and small companies vie with each other in the setting up of schools for their workers and neighbouring villages, good roads, medical facilities and special training centres for promising athletes, especially footballers. But much of this has been forced out of most companies at the point of a gun or a veiled written or telephoned threat. It has been accompanied by large 'donations' either to ULFA or the BSF and even this has not prevented the kidnapping of plantation managers and executives in exchange for ransoms.

Had the tea companies shown some foresight, as a few have done, they could have saved themselves a lot of tension, insecurity and money. Their failure to understand that it was as important to tend their roots as to look to profits has cost them heavily. While planning does not always reduce vulnerability to extortion, it does reduce the price that people pay to do what they like doing the most: in the case of industrialists and businessmen, that is business.

There are some areas where simple planning and individual initiative could have paid dividends for entire communities.

Nowhere is this more obvious than in the case of fish.

Assam, which is abundant in its water resources, is criss-crossed by tens of thousands of *beels* or lakes. These come in all shapes and sizes. Most of them are natural formations in the wetlands of the plains, renewed every year by floods and heavy rain.

For centuries, fish has been the main source of protein for the plain-dwellers, whether caste Hindu, Muslim or any of the many tribes. Most middle-income village households have *pukhuris* where fish are bred and caught whenever needed.

Yet, despite the ideal conditions for pisciculture, Assam is a net importer of fish. As Papa Rao, the District Magistrate at Jorhat pointed out, fish is shipped from his home state of Andhra Pradesh.

One of the reasons why ponds and *beels* are not being used to their full is the ecological degradation of these wetlands and the growing pressure of village populations. Most of the *beels* are swamped with hyacinths, a mass of bobbing, shining green that invades the water body and sits like a gigantic parasite, a blob, sucking the oxygen from the water. The fish stocks have become depleted because of the failure to clear the mess of hyacinths. Villages near the wetlands have encroached upon the *beels*, seeking to increase the area under farming.

And if private initiative is lacking in this area, then the state government's inability to encourage fisheries and devise a meaningful way of using the state's abundant wetlands to feed its people is also flawed. Successive governments have abandoned their basic mandate—to ensure that people get a better standard of living by looking at practical, village-level strategies—and instead focused only on gigantic projects. In the process, neither the development of the rural areas by alternative strategies, such as traditional and modern methods of fish culture, or by large projects such as big hydro-electric projects has taken place.

Water-deficient Haryana produced about 2,600 kilograms of fish per hectare in its fisheries. Assam produced about one fourth of that per hectare: 650 kilograms.

'Quite frankly,' said one top state official, 'it has everything to do with the Assamese attitude to work. It may sound clichéd and most Assamese may not accept it, but why should Andhra Pradesh and Haryana, which have large areas of dryland, be able to produce more fish or foodgrains?'

The fact was, he remarked, that the Assamese still took life too lightly and were not prepared to work hard and use existing opportunities—or create new ones. 'It's the easiest thing in the world to blame someone else for your problems,' he said, referring to long-time Assamese grievances of neglect by the Centre.

Yet, there is justification for one of Assam's major gripes against New Delhi. This relates to the exploitation of its oil and gas reserves by the Centre and the failure to get a fair royalty for the use of these resources.

Assam produces more than one quarter of India's total oil production, or about ten million tons. In percentage terms this represents a drop in its overall contribution to the national oil pool over the past years.

This is not merely because of shrinking production from the oilfields but because other parts of the country are finding exploitable oil and gas deposits elsewhere, such as in Gujarat, the off-shore finds in the Arabian Sea and other oilfields located in the Bay of Bengal and the western coast.

Most of the crude produced is sent for processing outside the state. Another refinery at Bongaigaon processes oil into a series of downstream products such as wax, used for candles and lamps and DMT. At Namrup is a small methanol plant but plans have been finalized for the Numaligarh oil refinery which is to have a manufacturing capacity of three million tons.

For many years, Assam's revenue from the black gold was pegged at a miserly forty-two rupees or about three dollars per ton at the then rupee-dollar exchange rate. That was grudgingly raised to 315 rupees per ton in the 1980s. It took some political dexterity on the part of the chief ministers of the two major oil- and gas-producing states, Gujarat and Assam, in 1992 before they won another raise.

Assam's financial collapse, despite its generous natural endowments, is seen in the near monthly crisis that the state administration faces in paying its salary bill. In fact, according to L.C. Jain, the development economist, a large chunk of the state's annual budget and plan outlay goes to the payment of salaries to its employees. 'The government must reduce the number of jobs it generates every year,' says Jain. 'If it spends so much on salaries, how on earth will it have any funds for development?'

In 1992, the state government was bailed out at least once by the Centre with a one billion rupee (thirty million dollars) payment. At one point, the police department had many of its telephones disconnected for failing to pay its bills.

The desperate straits that the state government found itself in through the late 1980s into the 1990s can be traced to the few failures that Gopinath Bardoloi suffered fifty years earlier. He had not been able, despite his best efforts, to ensure a substantial return to those states whose natural resources were being developed by Central agencies.

A Parliamentary report in the 1970s also reinforced what Bardoloi and his successors had sought the location of a large refinery in Assam 'The Committee feels that in retrospect it was an entirely wrong decision to have located the refinery at the present site [Barauni in Bihar] in spite of the strong objections on technical grounds both from Indian and

Russian experts. That facts proved experts to be right and decision makers wrong is too obvious.' The report went on to give the figures on comparative costs of oil refining in Guwahati, Barauni and Gujarat. The per ton cost worked out respectively at twenty-one rupees, 37.93 rupees and 37.48 rupees.

R. Gopalakrishnan in his book* estimated the reserves of oil in Assam at 89.32 million tons and natural gas reserves at 64.91 billion cubic metres. This means that at the current rate of exploitation, Assam's oil reserves will dry up in about twenty years although its vaster oceans of underground gas will keep going for much longer.

Earlier, the state watched the appalling waste of about 100 million cubic feet of gas flared daily in the upper Assam oilfields, lighting up the night skies. In energy terms, one million cubic feet of gas is equal to about twenty-five tons of oil. And although every Assam government and agitation—whether it was AASU or ULFA—made the flaring an emotive issue, explaining it as part of the exploitative nature of Delhi's Durbar, they did not bother to assess the cost to the environment and to the population where the flaring took place.

One night in the winter of 1992, when I was driving from the hills of Arunachal Pradesh to Dibrugarh, I stopped to watch the great gushing fires soaring into the night air, turning night into day.

The grumbling roar of the hot gases interrupted the silence of the darkness. That evening, it had rained and gloomy clouds hung low above he ricefields and villages.

The whole scene looked like something out of Kuwait during the Gulf War, kindling memories of the fires of those hundreds of oil wells hat retreating Iraqi forces had lit in 1990. The remembrance of Kuwait prompted me to have a closer look at the night sky. That closer view explained the blackness of the clouds: the fires were sweeping into the air a thick swathe of smoke that billowed across the underbelly of the clouds and then slowly settled on the sleeping villages.

To me, the starkness of the view revealed the hollowness of the hypocrites who had claimed, for decades, to speak for Assam but had done

See, R. Gopalakrishnan, *Northeast India: Land, Economy and People*, Delhi: Har Anand Publications, 1991.

nothing about the hazards from such unadulterated pollution.

'We were worried about the environmental and human cost of the Kuwait oil fires—but these fires have been burning for decades and no one has even bothered to think, let alone hazard a guess at the cost to our own villages,' I remember telling friends at Dibrugarh and elsewhere in Assam. To them, as well as to former ULFA leaders I met at Guwahati, this was a completely new thought.

Apart from the hypocrisy of politicians, the issue also exposes the failure of the environmental-scientific lobby, which focuses largely on 'mainstream India' or non-eastern India, except to consider the question of floods and soil erosion or perhaps the endangered one-horned rhinoceros in the Kaziranga National Sanctuary.

There has not been a whimper about fixing responsibility for the oil and gas emissions.

One would have thought that the Bhopal disaster of 1984 that killed more than 4,000 persons was enough reason to tackle errant chemical and polluting industries. All the State Pollution Board needs to do is to test the soil, water and the health of the local inhabitants in a reasonable radius of the flared gas and announce the results of these tests. If the results are indeed bad for health and soil fertility, as I believe they will be, then the villages have every right to prosecute the responsible agencies: the Oil and Natural Gas Commission (ONGC), the district authorities, the Indian Oil Corporation (IOC), the Assam Oil Company (AOC), the Gas Authority of India (GAI), and the governments of India and Assam.

Assam's underground wealth has been exploited but its fruits have not been evenly distributed. Amiya Kumar Das, a civil engineer who lives in the United States, pointed out in his book, *Assam's Agony* *, that the Indian Government's treatment of the Northeast reflected 'colonial characteristics' such as 'taking out raw materials from the Northeast and developing industries outside the region . . . employment of the own people of the colonizer as much as possible . . . neglect in overall development . . . marketing the products of the colonizer in the colony (and) taking the lion's share of the revenue created by the colony.'

The Centre's failure to develop the state and open it to the entrepreneurial skills of the region and other parts of India, is seen in the

---

* See, Amiya Kumar Das, *Assam's Agony*, Delhi: Lancer Publishers, 1982.

amount of private investment related to the oil sector. In nearly fifty years of independence, there has been just one major private investor who has sought to tie his fortunes to the petroleum industry in Assam.

That man came from Bombay, the home of India's commerce, and had honed his skills at the corporate giant Reliance and its petrochemical complexes in Maharashtra. Yet even Hemant Vyas, a portly, short man, fond of drinking tea from stainless steel *batis* (cups) as in the style of his native Gujarat, did not go to the state until 1990. 'I tell you, the Government of India is blind and our industry people are stupid, they do not see the potential in Assam,' Vyas said at a meeting in his office in Parel, one of the textile mill centres in Bombay. His office was located at one of his factories, the Bombay Silk Mills (BSM). The shining glass door leading to his chamber bore the name, Prag Bosimi.

During several visits to Assam over the years, Vyas had seen the richness of the state and the vast potential from existing hundreds of thousands of handlooms. He planned to produce yarn and fabrics used in high-quality fashion garments as well as polyester byproducts used for a wide range of other goods, such as polyester film.

It was, he realized, a potential gold mine.

Using contacts he had built up over the years with the state's top bureaucrats and politicians, especially Hiteswar Saikia, Vyas plugged away at his vision of a modern synthetic factory that would do several things in one go: make profits, naturally; meet growing demands for polyester yarn—the polyester industry is one of the fastest growing industries in Asia; sell its products at home and in foreign markets. Vyas realized that because of its proximity to the Bongaigaon refinery which could supply the basic DMT for its conversion processes, Prag Bosimi could outbid its huge competitors such as Reliance by cutting freight and transport costs.

In addition, there was the support from the state government: more than forty-five million rupees came in assistance from Assam to set up a dedicated power line and develop the plant site.

Vyas' technical experts picked Sipajhar, an hour's run from Guwahati, as the best site for the project. Tacitly, the government also agreed to give Prag Bosimi other major projects such as a gas cracker plant to manufacture ethylene.

Vyas' friends and foes in equal measure, thought him, quite mad.

'They said, "Hemant bhai, you are crazy; it is unsafe there, there are no facilities, no infrastructure, it's just jungle. You are doomed",' said Vyas, as he sipped his tea and held forth as I listened.

Vyas said he had responded simply: 'Wait for a few years: people said that Jamset Tata was crazy for prospecting for iron in Bihar and then building a town there in the heat and jungle. Wait, and Assam can be like Southeast Asia.'

He did his sums himself, not relying on the expertise of his financial department. During visits to Guwahati, he would drop into a store selling Bombay Silk Mill material. He would chat up the unsuspecting shopkeeper, who did not know that he was talking to the company's boss, ask about prices. This is what he found in one case: the fabric would leave the BSM factory for its retailer in Bombay at about thirty-five rupees a metre. The retailer would sell it to another agency handling the east at about forty rupees a metre. It would then go through at least one other middleman before reaching the store in Guwahati. At this point, the cost of the cloth would be about sixty rupees. The shopkeeper, Vyas found, was pricing his material at seventy-five rupees per metre or more and people were coming in to buy it. 'They were buying because the choice was limited,' he said.

That incident convinced Vyas of the size of the local market and the capacity of people in the Northeast to pay for good, locally-produced textiles. 'They were paying two times and more of what the material actually cost but they had the money to do it. Why should I sell my goods to retailers who make profits down the line when I could do it myself if I had the factory and network of outlets here.'

On top of it, Assam had a quiet work force, plenty of water and land available for industrial needs; there were reasonable air, railway and road communications.

Vyas saw a series of good deals working out for him and Prag Bosimi. For all this, he would rely on India's largest handloom industry: there were 1.4 million handlooms in the state. Most traditional homes had one.

In the old days, a bride's entire trousseau or a good part of it was woven by her mother and other women relatives on the loom at home. I remember one of my great-aunts using a loom when she was well past seventy at Nagaon. To the gentle tug of thread and the crack of wood as the loom moved, Assam's wondrous silk garments of rich *muga* and *endi* were created. Golden in colour, the *muga* silk was especially prized for its feel and graciousness. But the demand for traditional *muga mekhela sadors*—the two piece saris—has fallen because of high making costs and the price tag on the end product. Many weavers now use new patterns and mix polyester to reduce the manufacturing costs and ensure that there are enough buyers.

For decades, the focus of India's economic planners has been on the combination of oil-tea-plywood and jute as a way of developing Assam. In the process, the opportunities in the handloom industry, which is the state's single biggest employer, barring agriculture and tea, have been completely neglected.

Assam's 1.4 million handlooms account for more than one-third of the total number of handlooms in India. Yet, most of these looms are used for domestic production and consumption. Tens of thousands of other workers are involved in the preparatory processes, such as mulberry cultivation, silk farms, transporting and selling the raw silk.

The weavers, who are largely women, produce yarn and cloth for personal use. In the past years, as a wealthy, large middle class has grown in the towns and cities of the Northeast, small organized groups have begun producing and marketing the *muga* and *eri* silk as expensive saris and kurta material, apart from the traditional use as the *mekhela sador*.

Jaya Jaitly, one of India's prominent handloom experts, says that the country's handloom weavers continue to be among its most neglected economic groups. Many have given up their traditional skills and turned to physical labour and other work to make ends meet—they simply do not earn enough from producing yarn or cloth and are exploited by business groups and dalals. Yet the cloth they make is invariably cheaper than the synthetic stuff produced by the giant factories of Bombay, Baroda, Ahmedabad and the south. Because it is cheap it has been preferred by those who cannot afford the polyester-cotton shirts and trousers of the big corporations.

While the government at Delhi continues to subsidize fertilizers (used largely by middle and large peasants), support the import of silver, gold and chemicals used in polyester and textile manufacture, it has neglected the lot of the loom-user. Jaitly, a tall, elegant woman who wears handlooms and propagates her concern for weavers at every opportunity and from every platform, says she is not opposed to better quality, wider looms. 'But what is lacking is the vision to see the capacity for employment and sustainable development that exists in the handloom sector,' she said during a conversation in her office on Delhi's Tughlaq Road.

The government's priorities were all wrong, Jaitly said. She pointed out that the annual budget of the Institute of Fashion Technology (IFT) was usually at least two times that of the Institute of Handloom Technology (IHT). Both institutes are funded by the Central Government but the fashion centre turns out slick designers who quickly set up their own design and manufacturing places. The handloom centre, on the other hand, plods painfully on. Jaitly once compared the two groups in a typically terse remark: 'Little wonder that short skirts and sequinned gowns take over our culture while weavers are trapped in a frozen time warp.'

She said that a problem that the handloom weavers face is their inability to cope with rapid fashion changes. 'They've been making the same stuff for hundreds of years and it is difficult to get them to change their styles, their product while maintaining quality,' Jaitly said, as she sat on the floor of her office. Light bamboo mats covered the floor while rush curtains closed out the harsh sunlight of the afternoon. The room was remarkably cool for the Delhi summer.

'Traditional designs should be changed to suit needs here: shawls can be converted into nice, light winter blankets,' she said. 'You have to make these goods saleable and you need the assurance of a market.'

Improved looms, adequate funding from state and Central governments, would enable the weavers to experiment with new products, styles and designs. It was only through change that the handloom industry would be able to be self-supportive instead of dying a slow, lingering death, she said. And improved products would strengthen their bargaining power with buyers, especially those who wanted to use yarn in manufacturing synthetic fabrics and material such as the Prag Bosimi group.

The Prag Bosimi factory at Sipajhar is struggling, despite the initial fanfare of its inauguration. The units do not have enough electric power, the buildings have not yet been completed and ULFA kidnapped a senior executive and held him for three months in 1992 before releasing him. The insurgents had sought a ransom of fifty million rupees (about 1.6 million dollars) and eventually released the executive at Bombay upon payment.

Hemant Vyas has had to quit as the company's managing director after he was named as one of those involved in the forty billion rupee stock market-bank scam that stunned stockholders and high-flying financial consultants in 1992–93. Vyas denies the charge, although he was briefly detained in connection with the scandal.

The Prag Bosimi example shows that while big projects are important, they are not the most effective way of developing the tiny producer and protecting his interests. One way of helping this group to develop its full potential is by arranging loans for the weavers. This would help them improve the quality of their product; sensitive designers and planners by their side would make their products better finished and more competitive. Quality controllers should also monitor their work.

That people are thinking along these lines was obvious during a visit to Assam in late 1992 when I talked with Papa Rao, the Deputy Commissioner of Jorhat District. An old Miri walked into the room as we talked. Rao, an affable fellow fond of horse riding and known for his hard work and efficiency, chatted with him briefly in his broken Assamese.

The visitor was a member of the Miri or Mishing tribe and lived on Majuli, the world's largest river island. Majuli, a short distance from Jorhat, is the centre of one of Assam's great Vaishnavite monasteries. It is also being eroded by the Brahmaputra at a ferocious pace every year.

The Miri wanted Rao to visit Majuli and see some of their woven fabrics. One of their special products is known as the *mirizin*, a smooth, dappled blanket of wool, cotton and silk with the lustrous texture of satin and the warmth of angora wool. The *mirizin's* traditional use is that of a shawl. But over the years, its place has been taken by cheaper, mill-made, mass-produced material—cotton, wool and synthetics from Punjab and Haryana.

Rao believes that with better quality and designs, the *mirizen* can hold its own and even be exported to other markets in India and abroad.

Both he and Jaitly look at the problem from the aspect of what benefits the producer and the society in which he or she works and lives. Better quality goods can be marketed to government institutions, guest houses and hotels which need no longer buy poor quality goods at exorbitant prices (an arrangement that benefits middlemen, outside entrepreneurs, politicians and corrupt officials).

There are formidable hurdles in doing business in the Northeast for example, the lack of skilled managers and technical manpower; building materials cost thirty to forty per cent over prices in other parts of India; floods disrupt communications, supplies and often shut down plants.

But there are substantial attractions too. One of them being the availability of three billion tons of limestone which is used for cement production. Yet, the entire region has just three cement factories.

The estimated deposits of coal are about one billion tons. Oil shale, which can be converted into petroleum products, is plentiful. Estimates of goods that can be shipped by boat into and out of the region are pegged at more than 1.3 million tons of foodgrains, tea, cement, coal and jute.

Nowhere is the need for co-operation among the states and nations of the area more evident than on the question of water resources and flood control.

A series of medium-sized dams in Arunachal Pradesh, on the Dibang and the Subansiri rivers, could reduce the flood plain at peak times in the Brahmaputra Valley. Areas that are flood-prone would be liberated for cultivation: this is estimated at 2,50,000 hectares of land or nine per cent of the total flood-prone area in the valley.

The benefits downstream would be equally if not more substantial.

Others counsel restraint saying that big dams have never solved any problems but only have created new ones. They point to the high seismicity of the Himalayan ranges and to the swiftness and big silt loads that rivers like the tributaries of the Brahmaputra carry in Arunachal. These, experts say, will halve the life span of a dam in these areas from the normal life of about 100 years.

The disputes between pro- and anti-dam lobbies will continue indefinitely. So will the arguments between those who speak of sustainable development and others who talk of the price of progress—meaning that it is necessary to inflict a little pain, a little (or even a lot) of pollution on a small and preferably powerless community, to benefit a larger group of people. The larger group usually comprise powerful urban or rural élites.

B.G. Verghese, the journalist, speaks of a 'powerful development trigger waiting to be pulled.' He talks of the issues of flood control, of energy, of tapping the power of the rivers, of the potential for agro-industries given the moist, semi-tropical climate where anything can (and does) grow, as well as of the need for co-operation in the region and to improve communications: of road, rail and water.

Then he comes to one of the most essential issues: the future of the Northeast, says Verghese, a former editor of the *Hindustan Times* and the *Indian Express*, 'lies essentially with its own people.' 'They have to want, to will and to do with the aid and support of the rest of the country. The region cannot continue to exist on élite rentals siphoned from huge central subventions.'

B.G. Verghese is being diplomatic. For the truth lies in the people of the Northeast working hard and with dedication to fulfil a vision which statesmen can place before them. There is little use blaming New Delhi, or Dhaka, or the gods of the rivers, or communities and institutions for the mess that exists.

All these factors may indeed have a part in creating the difficult conditions that exist these days. But the essential responsibility for getting out of the quagmire is up to the people of the region and their leaders. For too long have the eastern lands been hoodwinked by leaders who speak of reviving the lost glory of the states but blame a specific group or community for the crisis. Or they have been misled by other groups which seek to take the units of the Northeast out of the national fold, saying Delhi does not care and that it is an imperialist government.

A practical vision that forces co-operation among the states and nations that are by nature bound, is the only way forward. That way lies some chance of saving the situation before it becomes unmanageable. In confrontation lies further chaos and economic misery—and more opportunity for the mandarins of Delhi to alternatively crack the whip and dole out bowlfuls of pittances to the bad boys of the east: whether they are from Assam, Nagaland or Bangladesh.

Neighbours, Secret Affairs

Early in the morning of 15 August 1975, tanks and military trucks rumbled through Dhaka, capital of the four-year-old republic of Bangladesh, and headed for the presidential palace, Banga Bhawan, where President Mujibur Rahman and his large family lived, inured in its sprawling isolation from the poverty, inequity, corruption and nepotism that ravaged their nation. The ruling family of Bangladesh, but especially Mujib, was regarded as increasingly despotic, intolerant of dissent even within the ruling Awami League, and obsessed with power and money.

That morning, soldiers and officers stormed Banga Bhawan brushing aside feeble resistance from startled guards in a precise and well-co-ordinated assault. Surprised by the crackle of gunfire, Sheikh Mujib walked toward the soldiers who had rushed in. Fearless till the end, he demanded: 'What do you want? Go back to your barracks.'

For one tingling moment, the mesmeric power of the man held the assaulters in thrall. Sensing that the situation could easily swing toward Mujib, the major who led the coup raised his gun desperately and fired. The first bullet broke the spell. And a hail of gunfire smashed Mujib against the wall and to the carpeted floor of his mansion, his blood soaking the thick rug.

As the founder of Bangladesh lay dead, other killers scoured the rooms of the house, tracking down and shooting other members of the terrified family. When the massacre was over, Mujib's wife, three sons, two daughters-in-law and a grandson lay in bloody heaps in different parts of the presidential palace. The place smelt of blood, death and gunpowder.

One survivor was Sheikh Hasina Wajed, Mujib's bespectacled, quiet daughter who was visiting Calcutta with her husband and children. She was to play a significant political role in Bangladesh later. But for the next years, she stayed in exile, sustained by the Indian Government.

News of the coup reached Delhi within minutes. It was India's Independence Day and Prime Minister Indira Gandhi was preparing to address the nation from the sturdy ramparts of the 300-year-old Red Fort as she had done on earlier occasions and as had other prime ministers before her—Lal Bahadur Shastri and her father, Pandit Jawaharlal Nehru.

It was a special Independence Day for India. Two months earlier, the country's vibrant democracy had been silenced by a dictatorial internal state of Emergency proclaimed by Indira Gandhi to stave off a popular revolt led by Jayaprakash Narayan. Narayan, known across India as JP, was among the last respected leaders of the Gandhian legacy. He and tens of thousands of others were imprisoned, including Chandra Shekhar, who was a prominent rebel in the ruling Congress Party.

Fear prevailed, the press was censored, and men like Sanjay Gandhi, the prime minister's belligerent younger son and his set of cronies, ran affairs of state. Opposition leaders such as George Fernandes went underground and clandestine literature with news of sporadic acts of defiance against the State flourished.

Indira Gandhi's thoughts of her address that day were interrupted by a flustered aide who brought the news of the assassinations in Dhaka. Later, she was to claim that the Indian opposition—without bothering to name specific individuals or groups or providing evidence—too had planned to eliminate her but that the Emergency had forestalled such designs.

The news grieved and angered her. For despite his megalomaniac ways and arrogance, Mujib represented a strong bond between India and Bangladesh. He was strongly pro-India and indebted to Indira Gandhi. Without India's military destruction of the Pakistani Army in the 1971 'war of liberation,' Bangladesh would have continued to be a much-abused, raped colony of West Pakistan. And Mujib would have been either rotting away in a remote prison or been executed by firing squad for treason and fomenting rebellion.

Mujib's death, Indira Gandhi knew, signalled cool relations with the military men who would guide the destiny of Bangladesh. They did not like to be beholden to India. She watched the situation unravel for a few weeks: an Indian-inspired counter-coup backing a rival of General Ziaur Rahman was quickly crushed. Ziaur asserted his authority although first Khondakar Ahmed and then Justice S.M. Sayem were named President. They were figureheads without clout. Real power rested with Ziaur.

Then came the jail massacre: former Prime Minister Tajuddin Ahmed and several other members of Mujib's cabinet were gunned down in prison. That was the proverbial last straw for the Indian Government, especially Indira Gandhi. The men who had harmed Bangladesh and her friends had to be punished.

It was time to play the Chakma card.

In 1972, after Mujib and the Awami League had swept to power in countrywide general elections, representatives of hill people from the Chittagong Hill Tracts(CHT), on the edge of Bangladesh bordering Myanmar, called on Mujib. They came with a memorandum to discuss the possibility of greater autonomy for the tribes and an end to the official policy of settling Muslims in the forested tracks. The organized migration of Bengali Muslims alienated and angered the Chakmas, who were predominantly Buddhist and Christian.

The Banga Bandhu or friend of Bengalis as Mujib was known, was in no mood to listen. 'Come back and see me when you have all become Bengali,' he thundered at the group, which included Members of Parliament and the Chakma leader, Manobendra Larma. 'We are all Bengalis, we cannot have two systems of government,' shouted Mujib at his dazed audience.

The meeting lasted all of three minutes. As for the memorandum, Mujib picked it up and hurled it at Larma.

A few days after the meeting, military forces, using jet aircraft, the police and army, attacked villages in the tribal areas. The free Government of Bangladesh was doing to its own people what it had accused Pakistan of doing to the Bengalis: unleashing a reign of terror.

Amnesty International said at the time that 'several thousands of men, women and children were killed according to sources close to the tribes people.'

From that time onward, for the handsome, quiet-spoken Manobendra and his restless younger brother, Shanto, there was no looking back. They knew that they were to be treated as second class citizens in a country they had not chosen, a nation that was Islamic and hostile to its religious minorities as had been proved by successive anti-Hindu riots in the 1960s.

They wanted to fight back. The question was how.

In 1972, Manobendra launched the Jana Sanghati Samiti(JSS),

278

which sought to unite and promote the interests of the indigenous people of the region, giving it a pan-tribal, nationalistic flavour.

In 1974, the Chakmas established their first contact with Indian intelligence in Dhaka and then across in nearby Agartala, capital of Tripura state. The Larmas sent word that they wanted to launch an uprising against the Bangladeshi presence in the Chittagong Hill Tracts. Could India help?

The requests went through the usual Intelligence Bureau (IB) channels before it landed in New Delhi at the Cabinet Secretariat, which supervizes all intelligence and covert operations, and specifically at the Research and Analysis Wing (RAW), the external arm of Indian intelligence. It later went on to the Prime Minister's Office (PMO).

At the time, Indira Gandhi was not interested in doing anything that could hurt Mujib and his pro-Indian stance. The breakup of Pakistan meant that India needed no longer to position thousands of troops on its eastern front. Instead, New Delhi could concentrate its military power on its border with China and Pakistan and disperse troops to battle insurgents in Nagaland and Manipur along the Myanmar frontier. The appeals from Larma and the Chakmas therefore, went unheeded.

Mujib's death and the installation of an anti-India government (although Ziaur had led the military operations against Pakistan from the Bangla insurgent side in alliance with Indian troops) changed all that.

RAW was instructed in 1975 to assist the rebels with arms, supplies, bases and training. The closest bases to targets in the CHT were along the border with Tripura. Training was conducted in these camps but specialized training in the use of explosives and ambushes were given at the centre at Chakrata, about ninety-five kilometres north of Dehra Doon. Members of Shanto Larma's fledgling military wing, the Shanti Bahini, were flown to Chakrata and then sent back to Tripura to exfiltrate into the CHT.

According to Priti Chakma, a colourful former commander of the Shanti Bahini, as many as 200 were trained at Chakrata. A RAW office and operatives at Agartala monitored the progress of the trainees, as well as who was doing well and who could be entrusted with responsibilities of leadership.

In 1976, the Shanti Bahini launched its first attack on Bangladeshi forces. A new insurgency had been born. And India's secret war in the hills of Bangladesh, fought by the tribes of that land, had begun.

The rebellion resulted in a natural crackdown against the tribes of the area by the Bangladesh security forces. Tens of thousands have fled India time and again over the past twenty years to escape Bangladeshi brutality.

The Chittagong Hill Tracts cover an area of 5,093 square miles or sixteen per cent of Bangladesh. The hills are home to great flowing forests of teak, swift streams and *jhum* or slash and burn agriculture, where farmers set fire to grasslands and hillsides to fertilize the upper soil, preparing it for crops in the following weeks.

It is located between Assam in the north, Tripura and upper Myanmar to the east, the Arakan of Myanmar to the south, and Chittagong district on its west. There are twelve tribes and the largest groups are the Chakmas and the Marmas, who are predominantly Buddhist, and the Tripuris, who are both Hindu and Christian as their counterparts across the border. There are Mizos too, Pankhuas and Bawms. Barring the Tripuris, the hill peoples of the belt belong to the Tibeto-Myanmar language family.

The Chakmas lived further south before entering the basin of the Karnaphuli river in the seventeenth century. They suffered reverses at the hands of the Bengalis and moved back to the hills, where they have since lived.

The Marmas came from Myanmar after that country conquered the Arakan at the end of the eighteenth century. The Tripuris came into the Hill Tracts from the north and settled in the northern river valleys.

These groups are linked by bonds of kinship and once followed a pattern of accepting powerful chieftains as their leaders. When the British captured the area in 1860, they divided the Hill Tracts into three subdivisions corresponding roughly to the three chieftainships of the main tribes. As in other parts of colonial India, the pattern of administration revolved around a Deputy Commissioner with three Subdivisional Officers or SDOs in the subdivisions.

In 1900, the British announced the final administrative setup in the CHT by ordering the Regulation of 1900. This banned the settlement of outsiders in the district and the transfer of land to non-indigenous people. In 1935, the Government of India Act defined it as a 'Totally Excluded

Area,' meaning that the administration of the plains and politicians from Bengal could not control its destiny.

This 1900 regulation forms the core of the dispute between the hill peoples and the Bengali politicians in Dhaka.

Since independence, that edict was violated with impunity, first under East Pakistan and then under successive Bangladesh governments: Mujib's civilian rule and Ziaur Rahman's military autocracy that was later converted into a benevolent dictatorship. It was only President H.M. Ershad in 1983 who ordered curbs on the migration of Bengali Muslims to "Bengalize" the tribes. But the situation is starkly similar, in demographic terms, to the crisis next door in Tripura.

Bangladeshi officials told human rights investigators as recently as 1991 of their frustration with the British regulation for it directly contravened their Constitution. The Bangladesh Constitution enunciates the principle that any Bangladeshi national is free to settle anywhere within its borders.

The Partition of the subcontinent in 1947 also played an important role in determining Bangladeshi attitudes to the CHT issue. As Pakistan and India were largely carved up on the basis of contiguous Hindu and Muslim-majority areas respectively, the Chittagong Hill Tracts perhaps logically assumed that it would go to India since its population was ninety-seven per cent non-Muslim.

Delegations went to Delhi to meet Pandit Nehru, the interim Prime Minister and Sardar Vallabhbhai Patel, the Home Minister. They received assurances that the CHT would indeed form part of India when independence came.

The Chakmas were perhaps not being naïve when they believed that this would actually happen. After all, the district of Sylhet, which was Muslim-majority, voted in a referendum in 1947 to go to Pakistan instead of staying in Assam (much to Assam's relief).

But the Radcliffe Boundary Commission that worked out the frontier award dealt the Chakmas a severe and unjust blow.

On 15 August 1947, the Indian tricolour was raised at Rangamati, one of the largest towns of the Hill Tracts. The Burmese flag was hoisted at Bandarban. But according to the Radcliffe Award, the CHT went to Pakistan. As a result, on 21 August, Pakistani troops pulled the Indian and Burmese flags down.

The raising of the flags has remained in the Bangla psyche as an expression of betrayal. The loyalty of the hill people was always suspect, even after the birth of Bangladesh.

The reasons for the CHT's sudden inclusion in East Pakistan are not far to seek. Radcliffe had awarded Calcutta to India, despite it being a major port for the Bengal hinterland—all of it. Of course, Calcutta was a Hindu-majority city and India's claim to it was clearly greater than that of Pakistan. The alternative port was Chittagong and the CHT was its hinterland.

A poor compensation for Calcutta perhaps but compensation nonetheless.

The changes that the new order sought to impose on the CHT were clear from the start: for one, the tribal police force was disbanded. The special status of the region was first amended and then repealed. Further seeds of revolt were sown in 1964 when the Pakistan government built the Kaptai hydroelectric project displacing more than 1,00,000 persons. The huge lake that the dam created in the heart of the Hill Tracts flooded about forty per cent of all arable land in the region, forcing an estimated 40,000 tribespeople to flee to Tripura.

These wretched refugees were transported to Arunachal Pradesh, then known as the North East Frontier Agency (NEFA) that sprawls across the north of Assam, facing Tibet and straddling the Himalayas. They are still displaced people—without a voice, citizenship and living on the whims of an alien government.

Another 20,000 of the dam displacees moved to Myanmar while about 40,000 were dispersed elsewhere in the hills of the CHT. However, one thing is clear: the failure of Pakistan and later of Bangladesh to adequately compensate the dispossessed led to the birth of the Shanti Bahini and the revolt against Dhaka.

Leaders of the JSS told me in 1989 at the Korbook refugee camp in Tripura that the compensation issue was primarily responsible for the alienation of the tribespeople. They realized that the Bengali-dominated administration, Parliament and government were not interested in dealing with their problems. 'Government officials freely acknowledge today that there was little compensation or rehabilitation though it had been promised. They also freely acknowledge that the project triggered the modern troubles in the CHT. It left a deep legacy of bitterness and distrust,' said the report of an international commission, the Chittagong

Hill Tracts Commission set up to probe human rights abuses in the area, in 1991. The report was released at London that year and updated in 1992.

Yet, insurgency in the 1970s when it came, was not really new to the CHT. In the 1960s, Pakistani intelligence and army specialists helped train and arm Mizo rebels to fight against India. The Pakistanis cleared Chakma and other hill groups to make space for training centres for the Mizo National Front (MNF).

In the 1980s, Bangladesh tacitly supported Bijoy Hrangkhawl's Tripura National Volunteer Force (TNVF). Bangladesh saw this, as also its covert support to the United Liberation Front of Asom (ULFA) much later, as a way of getting even with its giant neighbour. It could not meet India head on but could hurt with a series of pinpricks.

The dominant theme of all these insurgencies is land : commitment to it, refusal to part with it or let others seize even parts of it. *Maati* or land is the biggest identifying factor for many peasant communities worldwide. It represents security, power, potential wealth. It is a factor that is often underestimated.

In the Chittagong Hill Tracts, according to Gautam Dewan, the chairman of the Rangamati District Council which is popularly elected, 'The land problem is the main problem.' And the CHT Commission quoted an unnamed Bengali political commentator as saying that 'Religion is not the issue in the CHT but land. The Bengalis want land and so the result is a "class struggle" but without the philosophy. Bengali Muslims want land and cheat the tribals.'

Estimates given to the Chittagong Hill Tracts Commission, placed the total population at about 9,00,000 including Bengali settlers and CHT peoples on a 50:50 ratio.

In the initial stages, Bangladesh tried its own way of dealing with the problem. It imitated other countries—including India's response to similar crises—with makeshift solutions. One was the reorganization of the entire village structure for the tribes: groups were resettled in new areas or several villages were compressed into one large unit. The aim: to make patrolling for the security forces easier and control of the rebellion better. As in Mizoram, generations of kinship, oral history and village life were devastated, for the gentle culture of the hills was very different to the rough and disruptionist ways of the plains.

These new villages or communities were known by a variety of names: model villages, cluster villages, even co-operative farms. A senior Bangladesh official told a reporter at the time that the government planned to use funds of the Asian Development Bank (ADB) to resettle many indigenous people 'who are now leading a nomadic life' because 'it would help the government establish the rule of law in the hill tracts.'

Bengali communities which migrated into the CHT were also grouped together for their own protection. Settlers would farm under guard. They would not venture out of their homes at night to tend their fields or straying cattle. The Shanti Bahini, despite the protection that the Bengalis received, found them easier targets than the military. Time and again, they would swoop on settlers working in the fields or those returning home and shoot, kill and kidnap.

The anger in the hills against the settlers and the military was fuelled by the daily assaults on villagefolk, especially women, and destruction and damage to Buddhist and Hindu shrines. Monks and villagers have spoken extensively of how soldiers would march into Buddhist temples with their boots on and beat the clergy as well as the faithful, kicking and knocking idols over and throwing food and milk offerings to the deities on the floor.

Traditional culture is sought to be scorned and debased by the administrators and security officials in the CHT. Although there is financial support to tribal culture institutes and weaving projects by the government at Dhaka, there are few that reflect the integrated approach of a truely indigenous society.

It was not until 1983, a year after General Ershad came to power in a bloodless coup, that the resettlement policy was stalled. It was one of the few pledges that Ershad was to keep in his turbulent years in office. Although no formal orders were issued, officials in the CHT stopped allotting land to non-indigenous people. This had an effect of removing the magnet that lured migrants to the lightly-populated region.

Ershad followed up by announcing a new policy that was to be the cornerstone of peace moves in the CHT. He and other leaders would parrot the elements of this policy as the way out of the mess. These included a general amnesty, with promises of money, rations and rehabilitation; a special economic zone in the CHT with tax and interest benefits for investors; and a five-year economic development plan.

As Ershad made his peace moves, internal divisions in the Shanti Bahini boiled over, weakening the movement and forcing many to return to their homes, weary of war and a life of hardship and tension.

Priti Chakma, the tall, strongly-built guerrilla commander, stumbled across correspondence and literature that showed that Manobendra Larma, the undisputed chief of the rebellion, was a deep believer in Communism with close links to the Burmese Communist Party. The correspondence revealed, Chakma told me in a long secret meeting in Tripura, that Manobendra had long concealed his duplicity from his closest colleagues, thus raising doubts about his commitment to the long-term goals of separation.

Priti Chakma deprecated his own lack of political sophistication but said that he knew that, to a believer, Communism prevailed over true nationalism. The class struggle was paramount and any kind of compromise could be explained away under its flag.

My meeting with Chakma was set up by a local journalist in 1989. We waited quietly in a car near the neighbourhood where the former guerrilla lived with his family. An intelligence agent was positioned near his house every day but as luck would have it, he had moved away for a short while. Chakma was able to come out and join us in the car as we drove to a government guest house, a short distance from the local RAW office. It was amusing and a little exciting, for we strolled out of the car one by one, with short intervals between each departure, as we walked to the guest house.

It was, quite frankly, like something out of a bad spy movie or book.

We arrived at my room, drew the curtains, ordered crisp fried pieces of fish with chicken cutlets. And then I just listened to Chakma, occasionally interrupting to ask a question.

'We were surprised by the letters and documents and we challenged them to choose an all-out fight against the Bangladeshis,' said Chakma, who was known as the best commander that the Shanti Bahini had had. Larma's response was equivocal, cast in the grey idiom of Marxist monologue. He viewed India, Manobendra said, as an 'expansionist bourgeois state' and preferred 'a long protracted form of armed struggle to achieve autonomy within Bangladesh, not to secede from it.' He described the Shanti Bahini campaign as 'part of the struggle of the toiling masses of Bangladesh.'

This Marxian gobbledy-goop and double-talk was unacceptable to

Chakma and his supporters. Meanwhile, RAW sought to reconcile the factions. Its efforts yielded few results as both groups remained unyielding.

The nationalists, who commanded a majority of the 1,000-strong Bahini army were further enraged when Manobendra ordered a halt to attacks on Bengali peasants who had occupied land in the Hill Tracts. The nationalists met secretly to discuss future strategies. Their decision was unambiguous: the Larma brothers must be eliminated because they had become a stumbling block. How could Manobendra Larma, who had sought an end to the settlements in the CHT, now turn around and tell his people that the colonizers were acceptable? The Chakma group, therefore, suspected betrayal.

On 10 November 1983, a small group of nationalist fighters scaled the sheer rock face at the Panchari hills in the CHT where Larma and his men had set up base. Slipping past the guards at night, they stormed into Larma's tent—he was writing by the light of a lamp at a table at the time. The surprise was complete. Manobendra Larma did not have a chance. Within seconds, he was sprawled dead on the floor of the tent, the first victim of the internecine fight.

Internal squabbles have plagued guerrilla movements around the world. Strategies, ideology and personalities constitute the pivots around which differences emerge and then, when unhealed, turn into wounds that bleed incessantly.

Shanto Larma, the military commander and Manobendra's brother, escaped by jumping out of a window in a nearby hut and fleeing in the darkness. The Marxist faction was routed, its members were taken captive.

When RAW heard of the operation, its operatives and managers were livid. They called in Priti Chakma and demanded an explanation as well as a ceasefire.

'They told us that we were weakening ourselves and strengthening the enemy by our divisions,' said Chakma. But his response was cool and calculated.

First, he told the Indians that they should go in with their army—as in 1971 with the liberation war—rout the Bangladesh Army and give the CHT its separate status.

Second, he offered RAW a choice: either back the Communists, now represented by Shanto Larma, who also had a reputation for brutality and eccentricity, or the nationalists. His group believed in strong relations with New Delhi and had no extra-territorial or ideological loyalties except to their own people.

After some dithering—during which the Bahini campaign slowed and almost stopped for two years (it was also influenced by the 1984 assassination of Indira Gandhi)—came the message from Delhi. Back the Larma group. There were no explanations.

Priti Chakma was disarmed with many of his followers inside Tripura. Others preferred to accept the Ershad offer and surrender. Although Bangladesh claimed that nearly 3,000 Shanti Bahini members surrendered, Chakma and others say that not more than 400 armed followers went back.

When I last met him in Tripura, Priti Chakma still hoped to return one day to his homeland, with honour and dignity. But right now, one of the fighting legends of the CHT struggle is a man without a country, without arms—but not without followers. And he is convinced that his time will come too. In the meanwhile, he lives under the careful eye of Indian intelligence operatives, who take care of his needs and those of his family. His children go to school in Agartala. But his heart remains in the forests and fields where his people live under the weight of an oppressive military regime.

The Chittagong Hill Tracts remain, even after Begum Khaleda Zia and her Bangladesh National Party (BNP) won the 1991 general election, the only part of the country which is still controlled by the Bangladesh Army. Estimates of the number of army, paramilitary and police personnel deployed there range from 1,20,000 to about 1,30,000. About 80,000 of them are army soldiers.

Despite intermittent efforts for talks between the rebels and the government, the Shanti Bahini remains active and so do its opponents, the security forces. Attacks and counter-attacks remain the name of the game. Independent investigations show widespread human rights abuse, including gang rape of tribeswomen by settlers and Bangladesh troops, extortion, torture, illegal detention and illicit appropriation of property.

Until the end of 1993, more than 50,000 CHT residents still lived in Tripura's refugee camps, too afraid to go back despite visits by Bangla

officials and politicians who assured them of safety on return. Of 15,000
who had returned, hundreds have since come back to Tripura despite
difficult living conditions at the camps where food and money is tightly
rationed. But a prominent Chakma leader, Upendra Chakma, and
Bangladeshi diplomats said in early 1994 that an accord had been reached
that would enable the safe return of some refugees.

The latest batch to return went on 15 February 1994, a pitiful band
of 282 men, women and children who trudged home as local, Indian and
Bangladeshi politicians showered praise and promises on them. But those
going back were under no illusions: 'New Delhi and Dhaka are keen on
improving relations and we are the victims,' said Arnab Jyoti Chakma, a
teacher, as he led his family of three across the border. The miserable
condition of the Chakmas was reflected in the manner of their leaving
children without shirts, men in tattered clothes, women in soiled sarongs
carrying their hopes and few material possessions in bundles on their
backs and heads, in bags and in tin cans. However, human rights activists
say that extensive assaults on the Chakmas continue.

The Shanti Bahini camps are located near Indian paramilitary centres
on the Tripura-Bangladesh border. They live in homes of thatch and
bamboo when they are not at these camps. The huts are set a little distance
back in Indian territory.

One of the homes that I visited was a pleasant little cottage with a
wicker gate. The man of the house was not around but his wife, clasping
a little infant, told us in Bengali that he was 'away in an action.' He was
to return in a few days, she said. On the wall of the spartan drawing-room,
a small picture with fresh garlands around it was hanging. A close look
showed it to be not of her husband but of Manobendra Larma, the
assassinated Chakma leader.

A dialogue is stuttering along between Bangladesh officials and
Shanto Larma. But few issues have been finalized and given the attitudes
on both sides, the CHT is likely to remain another region of unrest in south
and Southeast Asia. After a 1992 truce, RAW is reducing its support to
the Chakmas as part of the Indian strategy to force the refugees back.

A new problem now faces the CHT indigenous people: the influx of
an estimated 2,00,000 Rohingya Muslims from neighbouring Myanmar,
who are fleeing religious persecution and military oppression by
Myanmar's troops. While Bangladesh has set up refugee camps for these
groups, and the United Nations High Commission for Refugees

UNHCR) is seeking to ensure their repatriation, only a few thousand have
returned.

Bangladesh is also playing a new role with the Rohingyas: according
to a British Broadcasting Corporation (BBC) reporter, who visited the
site, Bangla officers are training Rohingyas in armed struggle. What
long-term impact this will have on an already unstable region is not clear
but it is certain that Bangladesh, despite its size, wants to play an
increasing role in the militarization of the subcontinent.

The exploitation of the Chittagong Hill Tracts did not stop with its land
or its forests. Its womenfolk, attractive and unburdened by the purdah and
restrictions of Islamic Bangladesh, were especially vulnerable to the
military forces. Members of the international commission on the CHT
were told time and again by military officers during their 1991 visit that
the tribeswomen were very pretty and 'they are freer.' There have been
innumerable cases of rape. Women who are still refugees in the Tripura
camps have complained of gang-rape, sexual assault, molestation, abuse
and torture by security forces as well as Muslim settlers. In many cases,
refugees said, the settlers, supported by troops, attack the villages of the
indigenous people.

Forced intermarriage is another way in which the hill women are
'integrated' into Bengali society.

Women in the hills also speak of how Muslim settlers have
kidnapped them, fathered their children and forced them to convert to
Islam. Many have escaped at the first opportunity. But clearly, the act of
seizing land and its women is part of a process of colonization and
subjugation.

This can be compared to conditions in Tibet, where women are
forced to marry Chinese Han settlers and military personnel. The aim: to
wipe out the Tibetans as a separate race and merge their identity with that
of China, thus obliterating history, ethnicity and demography. What has
happened in the CHT is little different to the Tibetan experience, although
it is taking place on a smaller scale.

Calculated sexual and military violence can only be seen in a pattern
that is repeated across the world, and is particularly relevant to South and
Southeast Asia where nations and communities have fought for decades
to free themselves of a foreign power or a repressive domestic regime.

The cases of Vietnam, Laos, Cambodia, Myanmar, Pakistan and Indi require scarce repetition.

But it appears that in their campaign to crush the hill tribes of th CHT, Bangladesh officials have forgotten their own sufferings at th hands of an occupying military force: the brutal West Pakistani army.

A woman from Dighinala told the Commission that in June 198(several groups of soldiers surrounded her village and entered some home; 'My husband had his teeth beaten out of him, all blood. My son ran to hi father and he was thrown to one side. The army ordered me to go into m hut and pointed guns at me . . . . I was raped by three soldiers in the roon After this I didn't want to live anymore . . . . I am still like ma(disturbed*.'

The Commission remarked that rape 'is used systematically as weapon against women in the CHT . . . Some young women told th Commission that they are no longer able to wear their traditional dres (long skirts and short blouses, which mark them out as indigenous people` If they do, they run the risk of being raped. For their own safety, they ar forced to hide their identity as much as possible. It is also too dangerou to leave their homes at night.'

NGOLOPS IN DRUK YUL

Dal Bahadur, a wizened, wiry, fifty-year-old farmer was woken by angry raised voices near the hut for storing wood where he and his wife wer(sleeping. They had taken to sleeping there, away from the larger home o1 the crest of a hill near the southwestern Bhutanese town of Chengmari after assailants had attacked and looted neighbours. Fears of other assault had spread after reports of hit and run attacks by anti-Bhutan rebels, o looting, extortion, as well as rape, by gangs of thugs. The gangs operatec from across the unpatrolled border between India and Bhutan, which wa: a bare kilometre away.

Dal Bahadur thought, as he woke, that a quarrel had erupted betwee1 his newly-married son and his bride. The couple were sleeping on th(veranda of the kitchen a few feet down the slope. Inside the kitchen wer(the older farmer's sister and her three young daughters.

---

* See, *Life is not Ours: Land and Human Rights in the Chittagong Hill Tracts*, London The Chittagong Hills Tracts Commission, 1992.

In the mist and darkness of the pre-dawn hours, the farmer rushed to
ell what he thought was a noisy domestic quarrel. A figure waited on
e path before him and Dal Bahadur slowed down, thinking it was his
n. And as he came closer, the figure swung a three-foot-long stick and
ashed it down on his head, splitting it like an egg.

The blood streamed across his face, blinding him, but Dal Bahadur
appled with the intruder before other assailants battered him with more
ows, breaking an arm and knocking him senseless. The men fled as the
mily raised an alarm and members of the village volunteer force, which
d been set up to ward off such attacks—for Bhutan only has 4,000
olicemen and is quite incapable of providing the kind of security that
ese inhabitants of remote settlements need—rushed to the site.

When he came to, the tough peasant insisted that he was not seriously
ounded and did not need hospitalization. His son had taken two minor
kri blows to a hand and on the back but was otherwise unharmed. But
al Bahadur's neighbours were more sensible; they bundled the injured
rmer into a blanket, carried him down the steep hillside and across dry,
rraced rice fields to the main road. An ambulance drove him to the
amtse hospital, the nearest large clinic, about half an hour away.

The Indian doctor at Samtse, a Dr Mohanty, a dark and smiling
urgeon, said that the deep cut was three-and-a-half inches long and had
equired many stitches. Had medical attention been delayed, Dal Bahadur
ould have died.

'It was the antis,' said Dal Bahadur as he lay in the emergency ward
f the hospital late one March night in 1993. The anti-government bands,
ho live in India and Nepal, are known as 'antis'. These rebels, all of
Jepali origin, are part of some 1,20,000 Nepalis, who have left Bhutan
ince 1990 and settled in India and in refugee camps, run by the United
Jations High Commission for Refugees (UNHCR), in Nepal.

A core group—about 35,000 of them—were driven out by a
overnment campaign against illegal settlers, all Nepalis, in the seven
outhern districts of Bhutan. The rest have left, with little pressure from
he government. Many that I spoke with said they were leaving because
t was impossible to cope with wild animals and the bare necessities of
ife in depopulated villages.

Coherent but still in pain, Dal Bahadur said that he blamed the rebels
ecause he had resisted demands over the past three years to support them.
A former headman of his tiny settlement, he said that he had received

several threats to his life. That was why he had moved out of the main house.'

'Most people in the villages sleep like this, the young men keep watch at night because we cannot rely on the police to save us,' he said.

It is a seven-hour drive from Thimpu, capital of Druk Yul or the Dragon Kingdom, known simply to the rest of the world as Bhutan, to Samtse. There is no direct road across the winding mountain valley between the two towns, and visitors must travel through West Bengal to get there. On the slopes of Bhutan, they pass breathtaking views: of waterfalls cascading hundreds of feet down sheer slopes, thick coniferous and deciduous jungles and the vibrancy of spring on the trees—pear and cherry blossoms, giant magnolias and flashing red rhododendrons that would put a New England show of autumn colours to shame.

Bhutan still presents to a traveller the magical appearance of a fairy-tale with great castles, complete with turrets, stories of shamans and magic, of yetis. It is peopled by a handsome community of Mongolian stock, the skin on their cheeks stained by the brightest hue of scarlet that I have seen anywhere, a result of the cold, altitude, wind and sun.

It is a land of exotic names: gewogs and dzongdas, chortens and ngolops.

After a series of unrelenting, dizzying climbs and descents, our Toyota Land Cruiser thundered into Phuntsoling, the main trading post in southern Bhutan and for long the only town connected to Thimpu by road and consequently to the outside world, and then cross into Indian territory.

A two-hour drive through tea gardens, pleasant plains and a handful of noisy, crowded villages, takes one from Phuntsoling, the clean, lightly populated hamlet on Bhutanese soil (which degenerates into the dirty town of Jaigaon on the Indian side) to a ceremonial gate which welcomes visitors to Samtse, Bhutan.

This is part of a 700-kilometre-long border that is one of the easiest to cross in the world because it is virtually unpatrolled on either side. Indians and Bhutanese need neither travel documents or visas to cross into each other's territories. All that is required is a simple identification card, such as a driving licence, establishing the identity of the traveller. In many cases, bands of marauders cross over illegally from Assam's Bodo-dominated regions into the thick forests opposite Kokrajhar in

hutan, waiting for Indian security forces to ease their pressure on Bodo
ilitants before moving back.

The belt is of strategic importance to India: the narrow corridor
nking India to its Northeast lies near here. Through this corridor flows
ll the oil, tea, jute and other commercial products as well as all
ansport—road and train—between the two regions of India. It also is
ndwiched between Bangladesh and China. Bhutan's importance to
dia lies not just in the 'historical ties, centuries-old, and shared
erceptions' that Indian politicians and diplomats parrot but because it
rovides India with the ability to look directly at its traditional enemy
cross the Bhutanese heights into the Tibetan plateau. Military
telligence is regularly shared between India and Bhutan. Indian
telligence agents have access to crucial areas, information and people
sensitive posts. The Bhutan Himalayas are an integral part of the long
order that India has with China. Bhutan too has a border dispute with
China over the demarcation of its territory although this is not as serious
s the Sino-Indian frontier dispute.

The Indian Ambassador in Thimpu, a pretty town of 30,000 people
at nestles in the Wang Chuu river valley flanked by snow-capped peaks,
s a powerful figure in the kingdom.

India bankrolls Bhutan's economic plans—as much as eighty-five
er cent of all plan expenditure for roads, power projects and
dministrative facilities comes from India; it trains Bhutanese technicians,
iplomats and administrators at staff training colleges and institutions;
ndian consumer goods, magazines, films, videos, music, vehicles,
etergent soap, cigarettes and even fruits and vegetables make their way
p to the kingdom.

India buys power from Bhutan and monitors the country's domestic
nd foreign policies through a 1949 treaty that gives it advisory status.
Some say it is far more than that. The narrow Bhutanese roads have been
uilt at the cost of life and limb by pioneers from the Indian Army and
ivil engineers; for decades, they have been maintained by the Indian
Border Roads Organization, whose blue colours are seen every few
ilometres along these lifelines of the kingdom. The roads carry Toyota
Land Cruisers, Tata trucks, Maruti Suzukis and Mercedes Benzs with
equal ease.

In turn, Bhutan controls the number of foreign tourists and visitors
hat its limited infrastructure can handle. The number of foreign—usually

European and American tourists—visitors is about 2,500 every yea
Although international aid agencies such as the Danish aid agency, th
Food and Agriculture Organization (FAO) and the United Natior
Development Programme (UNDP) have increased their presence over th
past years, access to many areas remains restricted and their organizatior
are small, tightly-run units.

Bhutan says that these controls are aimed at stemming any influence
on its people that could irreparably damage its traditions, as happened i
Nepal. The Nepalese example of destruction of forests, smuggling c
antiques and national treasures, the corruption of a venal bureaucracy an
political class, sexual promiscuity and total subjugation to foreign donor
and funds is cited as a mantra by Bhutanese officials as something the
do not want.

Photography of the shrines in monasteries is now banned. Th
reason: these inner temples hold priceless, gold-plated and painted idol
of the Buddha and Guru Rimpoche, who brought Buddhism to th
country. These are to be found in the centuries-old great *dzongs* c
fortress-monasteries that dot the high valleys and are strategically place
to control all movement through the areas.

Also off-bounds for most visitors is the joint Military Academy a
the town of Ha, four hours drive from Thimpu. Here Bhutanese and India
officers are put through a swift course in mountain warfare, intelligenc
gathering and leading men through difficult conditions, by a group o
highly-trained Indian military specialists. Ha is off the tourist track an
few foreign visitors, barring those cleared by the Indians and th
Bhutanese army, are allowed. The Ha programme prepares officers for
longer course at the Indian Military Academies (IMAs) at Dehra Door
and Pune.

There is just one newspaper in Bhutan, the government-owned *Kuensel*
This is little better than a publicity sheet for the administration, althougl
• it did focus at one time on the efforts put in by the government to stop
Nepalis from leaving the country. There is still no television althougl
video parlours are full of kung-fu and Hindi movies. Although Bhutanes
officials speak with disdain about the 'contaminating influence' o
Western television, the children of the élite and the upcoming
professionals, especially in the civil services, dance to the latest hits or

Music Television (MTV) at private parties in their homes. Discarded are the *ghos*, the short robe that male officials must wear, and the *kira*, the gown preferred by women, although some would say that the shorter gown would look better on the women. Rocking to Madonna, the Beatles or Bruce Springstein, these young Bhutanese in their jeans and jackets would be as much at home in a Western discotheque as in Thimpu.

Bhutan's houses and offices are pagoda-like buildings, made of wood, mud, stones and, increasingly of concrete and mortar, with a paganish sign of fertility hanging from the front veranda: a crude representation of the human penis, painted black and red, swinging gently in the breeze. Everywhere—in the restaurants and hotels, homes and guest houses, buses and the tail of the handsome Ba-141 jetliners that ferry passengers between Delhi, Kathmandu, Bangkok and Dhaka—are flowing, colourful patterns and portrayals of animals, dragons and gods.

Most popular are gentle pastel panels of the Buddha and his incarnations, especially the revered Guru Rimpoche. Also seen often is the *Shabdrung*, Ngawang Namgyal, a Tibetan prince driven from his homeland by jealous rivals and who found himself in a land of incredible beauty and ruggedness. Namgyal set about unifying the country and built the great *dzongs*—that perch on spurs of sheer cliffs— that were to control the destiny of his adopted nation.

His successor *Shabdrungs* were unable to consolidate their power and lost out to the growing clout of the warrior chieftains and governors. In the latter part of the nineteenth century, Jigme Wangchuk established himself as the strongman of much of Bhutan—he was then Governor or Penlop of Tongsa, a *dzong* commanding central Bhutan and perched high on a hillside. His son, Ugyen Wangchuk, was accepted by other chieftains as the country's first king this century in 1907, starting the line of Wangchuk dynasty which is still remarkably popular and respected.

The later *Shabdrungs* found themselves poisoned, exiled or falling off cliffs and the current incarnation of Namgyal lives under Indian police protection in Himachal Pradesh state: apparently, he is enough of a threat to the regime in Thimpu to warrant such Indian courtesy.

These days in Bhutan, the main power élite is a tiny group in the kingdom: it comprises almost entirely of the Drukpas, the Bhutanese of Tibetan origin. The number of this élite is miniscule: it is hardly more than 2,000. These are the people controlling the politics, development and the finances of this beautiful nation, which is still referred to as the last Shangri-La.

Adding to this image of mystique is the fact that Thimpu, the capit
which takes little more than a bare twenty minutes to walk briskly throug!
boasts of just one cinema. The whole country has just one college, locate
in the east, reachable after an arduous journey across mountain road
which are often hit by landslides and sleet. Many government officia
now in their forties are high school graduates and only the younge
generation have studied at colleges and universities, for the most part i
India while a handful have graduated from American and Britis
universities. School education is free and the number of junior and hig
level schools are going up. Indians are here too, working as teachers an
instructors in distant, inaccessible places, high in the mountains and in th
lowlands.

They provide the workers too, tired-looking road labourers from
Bihar and West Bengal as well as Orissa, who live in squalid settlement
on the edge of roads that they are constantly rebuilding or repairing, s
fickle and soft is the soil of the hillsides—these are especially vulnerabl
to landslips and rockslides in the monsoon downpours.

'Without them, I don't think we could have progressed even thi
much,' said one senior official referring to the Indian workers.

Radio Bhutan broadcasts for three hours a day in Dzongha, the mai
northern language, English, Nepali and the language of the Sarchops o
the east.

The overall impression is of a happy people who are neithe
impoverished nor too affluent—one sees no sign of beggary or th
miserable indignity of poverty that is so visible in India, Pakistan
Bangladesh and Nepal; they are ruled by a charming king with fou
beautiful wives, as out of a fairy-tale. And, as in a fairy-tale, there are
misty mountains, magical, green valleys, snow-capped peaks, gentle
flowing brooks, sheer, dizzying climbs and precipices falling thousand:
of feet in a straight drop off the roads. There are Himalayan postcard-like
scenes with cottages on hillsides and great stone and mud fortresse:
soaring fiercely into the sky, flanked by tall prayer banners fluttering
furiously in the high winds, and glittering in the sunlight, thei
yellow-painted tin roofs shining for miles to see.

Into this majestic Himalayan kingdom, Buddhism was brought, it is
believed, by Guru Rimpoche in the ninth century, flying from India or

he back of a great tiger and landing in Taktsang, the Tiger's Nest in the
Paro Valley.

Magical myth and mist, mountains and princes, a nation unspoiled
by the winds of change overwhelming the rest of the world, where trees
are still preserved and people take pride in their monasteries and faith and
retain a flawless courtesy and gentleness.

Of such stuff are legends created.

Of course, the pristine image was rocked a little when its handsome
monarch, who had touched many a maiden's heart in different parts of the
world, took not one but four wives. But even this could be explained away
in the magical setting. King Jigme Singye Wangchuck created quite a stir
a few years ago by marrying four sisters of a prominent family—he had
had affairs with all of them over many years. The reality of the
relationships is seen in the cherubic, smiling presence of the Crown
Prince, a boy of thirteen in 1993 and the fact that he was born of the third
sister, who is regarded as the King's favourite.

Bhutan is tailor-made to help us believe in a Shangri-La, for all of
us long to believe that there is actually such a place on earth, without the
miseries of commonplace life, where life is unspoiled by the crassness of
modernism. It is something that wordsmiths and adventurers have
succeeded in creating—if not maintaining.

Trouble has finally come to this Shangri-La and it has come in the
shape of the Ngolops.

These are not strange creatures out of an evil empire threatening our
Shangri-La. But hardy Nepali settlers, both long-time migrants and new
illegal aliens, who believe that they have been discriminated against and
feel the need to strike back.

The story of Nepali settlement in Bhutan is scarcely more than 100
years old. It was encouraged by none other than the chief of the King's
household, who also was the Governor of western Bhutan at the time. His
name was Kazi Ugen Dorji and he was the grandfather of the first and
only Prime Minister that Bhutan has ever had: Jigme Dorji.

The Dorjis were an influential family of Kalingpong in the
Darjeeling hills; they were liberal, forward-looking, rich and educated.
The Dorjis were encouraged in their efforts to allow Nepali immigrants
by the British rulers of India, who employed many Nepalis in the tea
estates in the Himalayan foothills. The British never exercised direct
control over Bhutan but through a war in 1865 forced a treaty on Bhutan

that made it lease, in return for annual payments, the contiguous plains or Duars (doors) that had long been its territory. This was how Bhutan lost its richest forest and agricultural lands and as Kanak Mani Dixit, the editor of *Himal* magazine in Kathmandu points out, 'Today the country begins where plains meet hills.'

But the settling of the Nepalis in the Bhutan plains led to a situation not dissimilar to what existed in Assam in the 1930s and 1940s, with unbridled Bengali Muslim migration blessed by the British and the Muslim League governments in that state.

'In no time, the land-hungry Nepali cleared the thick vegetation and organized themselves as cultivators in the southern Duars,' says A.C. Sinha, the bespectacled academic who is head of the Department of Sociology in the North Eastern University at Shillong. Sinha has a formidable reputation as a researcher and expert on the Himalayan regions, their peoples, structures of government as well as traditions and lifestyles. His authoritative book, *Bhutan: Ethnic Identity and National Dilemma**, is one of the best-researched on this issue. In a succinct article for *Himal,* a magazine published out of Kathmandu that surveys issues of interest to the Himalayan frontiers, Sinha laid out the growth of the crisis that has stunned Bhutan today.

Although there are many comparisons with the influx from East Bengal and Bangladesh into Assam, the Bhutanese see closer comparisons with next-door Sikkim. Here the native Bhutia-Lepchas, also Buddhists, were swamped by a Nepalese tide that forced an independent entity to be absorbed into the Indian mainstream in 1974. Devious politicians, Congress Party-organized demonstrations against the Chogyal, the tactless ruler of Sikkim, and Indian military muscle converted that tiny principality into an Indian state.

The Nepali immigration to Bhutan continued well into the present century, says Sinha, even though there was a shortage of arable land. The government at Thimpu eventually banned further Nepali immigration in 1959. In addition, the Nepalis were banned from settling beyond an imaginary east-west boundary drawn north of the Himalayan foothills. According to Sinha:

---

* See, A. C. Sinha, *Bhutan: Ethnic Identity and National Dilemma*, Delhi: Reliance Publishing House, 1991.

The bamboo and thatch houses of the Nepalis are less substantial than the multi-storeyed stone houses of the highlanders. The Nepali areas are predominantly agricultural, producing rice, maize, wheat, pulses, oranges, cardamom . . . . [As a result of] migration across from Nepal, Darjeeling and Sikkim over the past 125 years, the Nepalis turned this "negative land" into a productive breadbasket.

Speaking of their frugal lifestyle and readiness to do all types of physical labour, Sinha says that the development of several southern Bhutanese towns as commercial towns in the region owes much to the Nepali. 'Food, dress, the kukri, perseverance, industriousness and "mercenary character" make the Nepali-speakers one on an alien soil. They look to Nepal and India as the founts of their civilization, their historical achievement and where their places of pilgrimage are.'

Politicized over the years by education and training in India, many Nepalese, according to Sinha, sought a rightful democratic role but this was denied by the ruling dynasty.

The first stirrings of Nepali revolt came in 1952 when Girija Prasad Koirala, who became Prime Minister of Nepal forty years later, then flushed with the success of Congress victory over British imperialism in the Indian subcontinent—the Nepali Congress (later the Nepali Congress Party) and its leaders had taken part in that movement—came to Chirang, in the Bhutan plains, and launched the Bhutan Congress Party. Originally, the party was based in Assam but when it sought to follow up the Koirala visit with a satyagraha of 100 volunteers, it was sent packing by an onrush of enraged Bhutanese militia. That, for all purposes, ended the first Bhutanese skirmish with Nepali-run democratic concepts.

Until its dissolution in the late 1960s, the Bhutan Congress remained an all-Nepalese party with no support or roots in the highlands.

The involvement of the Nepalese in that aborted attempt as well as the absorption of Sikkim by India and the displacement of the ruling élite there—the Namgyals—by the Sikkim Congress which merged with the Indian National Congress kept Drukpa suspicions high. Matters were not helped by the unrest in the hills of Darjeeling fanned by the Gurkha National Liberation Front (GNLF), led by an untutored pulp novelist named Subhas Ghising.

The GNLF upsurge that traumatized the tea gardens and pleasant, rain-swept hills of Darjeeling for more than three years in part owed its spark to a migratory problem: refugees driven out of Assam and especially Meghalaya, during anti-Nepali riots of the 1980s. Scores were butchered, others were harassed and tormented until they left the land of their birth for safer refuges in the Darjeeling-Duar belt where they settled with friends and relatives.

Ghising saw in the influx an opportunity to let loose his brand of nationalism: the Nepalese, whom he liked to call Gurkhas, were unsafe in India and needed a homeland where they could run their own destinies. He sought that homeland in the Darjeeling hills, triggering an onslaught on Communist Party cadres as well as Bengalis, who were accused, not illogically, of dominating and pauperizing the hills. The Bengali politician and bureaucrat had long controlled the purse-strings and political power in the region, operating out of distant Calcutta. They looked upon the Nepalis as a rather slow-witted community that was good enough for physical labour, an image that stung the Nepalis.

During the Gurkha movement, attempts were also made by its leaders to involve the Nepalis settled in Bhutan in the demand for a greater Gorkhaland. The Nepalis of Bhutan, known as the Lhotshampa, stayed aloof, knowing that they were already regarded with much suspicion by Thimpu. But they were approached for funds by the GNLF and its breakaway faction, the Gurkha Liberation Organization (GLO), which is seeking to spread its support base among those Nepali-Bhutanese now living in the West Bengal hills and plains.

But for Bhutan's southerners, and its northerners, the problem began—as in Assam—with a simple headcount. In Assam, the death of a Member of Parliament from Mangaldoi led to the detection of aliens listed in electoral rolls and the surge of the anti-foreigner movement, leading eventually to an unending spiral of violence and insurgency.

In Bhutan, the 1988 census started the problems for the Nepalis. That census was part of what Thimpu enunciated as Ta-Wa Sum—the King, the Kingdom and the Country—or part of its effort to weld the mountainous country into a whole with a common dress code and a common language. *Ghos* and *kiras*, the traditional gowns of cotton and wool (the cloth is largely imported from factories in Punjab), were ordered as compulsory wear for all Bhutanese, irrespective of religion and origin.

The teaching of Nepali was stopped in 1989, creating much bitterness among the southerners who felt increasingly alienated by official decrees.

In the process, many Bhutanese officials used their powers to harass and drive out Nepali settlers. Those found without the *ghos* and *kiras* were either sentenced to labour for a week or charged ngultrun 150, the equivalent of 150 Indian rupees or about five US dollars. Much of the money was pocketed by corrupt policemen and petty officials, according to Nepali refugees.

The fear and anger in the south was escalated by the 1988 census which turned up, according to officials in Thimpu, tens of thousands of illegal immigrants—all of Nepali origin. The census based its evaluation of citizens on the basis of special categories devised by the government, ranging from F-1 to F-7, the one that identified aliens. The F-1 group had land tax receipts for 1958 and were regarded as genuine. The others, barring F-7, were allowed to reside in Bhutan but denied citizenship although they were eligible to apply for it, depending on when they had settled and the kind of land records and other details they possessed. This created a peculiar situation where husbands were described as 'F-1s' and the wives were 'F-7s' and the children were of different categories.

F-7 was the feared category: it meant that the person had no rights in Bhutan for he was an illegal immigrant who had come over in the 1960s and afterward and stayed on without acquiring proper citizenship. These individuals were asked to leave forthwith.

'The illegals were very clever, they used to marry across the border and then move here,' said a Bhutanese official at Samtse. 'The border is so easy to cross.' Jigme Tsultrun, the short and stout *Dzongda* or chief administrator of Samtse and a former managing director of Bhutan Tourism, pointed out the open border during a drive from his office to a temporary refugee camp set up for a group of forty-five Nepalis who planned to leave for Jhapa, Nepal, where the UNHCR refugee camps are located.

'There are people here who have married in Samtse, in a village here, and in Kalingpong or Kurseong, they have relatives in Nepal as well,' said Tsultrun who wears a Stetson hat over a round, smooth face and his official *gho* and walking shoes when he travels in the countryside.

'In most Hindu marriages, the women go to the men's home after the wedding but here in Bhutan, it's the other way around!' he remarked. Tsultrun, whose infectious grin hides a concern that he could be a target for anti-government militants, was referring to the way in which Nepali males from India or Nepal marry into homes in Bhutan and settle there.

'In the 1960s and 1970s, a lot of people came to work as labourers on the building sites, the roads and the dams,' said Tsultrun. These were, naturally, virtually all Nepalis from India and the other Himalayan kingdoms, although Bhutanese dissidents living in exile say that there were large movements of Nepalis, encouraged by Thimpu, between the southern districts in those years.

'My family and other families travelled from one district to another in the 1960s to work on these projects, we've been in Bhutan for decades, you can't call us foreigners,' said Bhim Subba, the former Director-General of Bhutan's Power Department, who fled to Nepal in 1991, a day after he was promoted to that post by the King's administration.

But Tsultrun and others who have worked in the southern districts say that the unpatrolled border and the easy-going ways of the northern Bhutanese have helped in the influx.

The 1988 census stirred alarm among the northerners, fuelled by the hardine Buddhist clergy. The King says that later counts have turned up as many as 1,13,000 illegal settlers and an overall population of over 6,00,000. Clearly, Bhutan cannot and does not wish to sustain this extra population. One of the questions before Bhutan, which wraps even its statistics regarding demography with secrecy, is the exact breakup of the population.

The anti-monarchists, who are Nepali, on the other hand say that their population is as much as forty-three per cent of the whole. The King dismisses the fact and insists that there are twenty-eight per cent Nepalis. The others, according to the King, are northerners and easterners of Drukpa/Tibetan traditions.

The accounts of the census led to a crackdown by Bhutanese security forces and militia against the Nepalis. Descriptions provided by those who have fled Bhutan as well as detainees and Bhutanese officials indicate that the Bhutan Government turned a blind eye for several months to overzealous officials who turned up with lists of people to be ousted, including genuine citizens. Houses were burned, women terrorized—in some cases rapes and molestations were reported—and people were forced to flee.

Matters were exacerbated when Nepalis attacked Bhutanese officials—largely Nepalis—and conducted raids on schools, teachers and government buildings in September 1990 across the south. The incidents forced Thimpu into believing that a mob of marauding Nepalis brandishing kukris and muskets was marching up the hills to take charge of the kingdom.

In a series of co-ordinated raids, dozens of schools were burned in the southern districts, including at Chengmari, marking the beginning of a full-scale confrontation with the north.

The Bhutanese blamed the violence on activists of the newly set up Bhutan Peoples Party (BPP) and later the Bhutan National Democratic Party (BNDP) and human rights groups. But more specifically, in Samtse, it was clear that Indian Nepali workers from neighbouring tea gardens had participated in the riots that set fire to school houses and resulted in several ugly confrontations with the vastly-outnumbered police.

In one case, on the approach bridge to Samtse, a mob of 6,000 men, women and children shouted slogans, hurled rocks and demanded access to the town as police watched tensely. The police were ordered to fire. Two were shot and later died.

The BPP went wild with charges that more than 300 had been slaughtered in the incident. It fed the news to Western news agencies which jumped at the bait. When the truth became known, several reporters were transferred out of Kathmandu because of the embarrassment. As a result, the BPP's credibility crashed to zero.

The mob that marched on Chengmari originated across the border and included, according to witnesses and police, many tribals, such as the Oraons as well as Indian Nepalis and even some Bodos, known in the south of Bhutan as the Mechs, a Bodo sub-clan.

The violence that began then and continued with bombings of security jeeps and patrols, the assassination of a deputy district administrator or *Dungpa* in 1992, has ebbed considerably in terms of anti-government strikes. Fear of the attackers has grown because of their brutality: in many cases, victims were decapitated and their heads left on roads, in full public view.

To a country and a people whose experience of violence had been limited to drunken brawls in Thimpu and villages, and whose small police force has hardly been used to tackle mob trouble, the beheaded bodies were a nasty reminder of the potential for violence that existed within their society.

These days the pro-government figures who are attacked include village elders. The aim of the marauders seems as much to spread fear as it is to loot and extort.

The Nepali Government has sent clear instructions down the line, says Prime Minister Koirala, that no political activities will be allowed out of Nepal. This is taken to mean that a bar now exists on armed violence being organized out of the camps at Jhapa. Yet, exiles continue to operate openly in Kathmandu, publishing newspapers, issuing reports, meeting journalists and visiting researchers and even holding meetings.

The violence thus is now limited to armed gangs who are far more interested in loot and banditry—as well as the occasional rape—than in overthrowing a monarchy. To that extent, the violence has been marginalized for the time being.

However, in the process, Bhutan has lost more than one-seventh of its total population. All of those who have left are Nepali Hindus. It has been a high price to pay for national stability and the gains are questionable, both in the short-term and in the long-term.

A 700-kilometre journey across Bhutan took me across high mountain passes into valleys where yaks grazed peacefully and into the southern lowlands where I met Nepalis preparing to leave and testy authorities trying to persuade them to stay. The trip underlined two things: by March 1993, the northern Bhutanese attitude, barring perhaps the King who felt the failure of his efforts to unite the country under a nationalist slogan more keenly than his minions, was that the problem was resolving itself by the migration.

'We do not want to be another Sikkim and look at your problems in Assam,' said one official. 'We are a very small nation and we have to protect ourselves in the best way that we can.'

Although the first 35,000 refugees into Nepal were regarded by the UNHCR as genuine cases of people who had fled either repression or a potential conflict situation, the rest are now regarded as freeloaders, who are going there not because of any pressure from Bhutan but because they were attracted by the UN dole of three dollars a day for every inmate, free rations and building material.

A total of 1,20,000-to-1,30,000 are believed to have fled or left Bhutan over the past three years. Of this figure an estimated 20,000-to-30,000 are in northern Bengal, creating problems for tea plantations and for relatives and friends with whom they have moved in. Groups of these migrants take part in the attacks on villages across the border.

People were still leaving in March 1993 when I visited Samtse. But what I saw must surely be one of the strangest migrations in recent times: there was neither fear nor panic, grief or perceptible anger. Nor was there even remorse at leaving the lands that their grandparents had cleared and tilled.

It was quite extraordinary. The migrants had got compensation from the government and signed over their citizenship. And now, stateless but free, they were preparing to move with their wives (many of the migrants were polygamous) and children to India and Nepal.

The first refugees had left in fear and disarray in the winter of 1990 and UN officials who saw them at the time said that they were reminiscent of the pathetic pictures of Somali famine victims: skeletal, famished, dehydrated and very sick.

Conditions improved over the months when food and fuel as well as other facilities reached the camps. But Nepali officials who used the issue early on to criticize the Bhutanese are finding that the refugees are a double-edged sword. 'There are many prostitutes there, the people have chopped down all the trees in the area and there is a lot of tension between the local people and the migrants; the locals ask why these people should get special food and favours, they say that the natives of the area are entitled to it more than outsiders,' said an aide to Prime Minister Girija Prasad Koirala in Kathmandu. 'It's difficult to reason with them.'

Clearly, the sheen of supporting the underdog is wearing off, giving way to much more practical politics. Nepalese Communist groups have been active in the camps, seeking recruits and trying to create political problems for Koirala, a quick-talking, chain-smoking leader.

The cause of Koirala's problems are as much in Bhutan as in the camps at Jhapa, which is one day's journey from Samtse.

In the courtyard of the Samtse *Dzongda's* headquarters, a whitewashed building of brick and cement, painted with the vibrant red, blue and green that makes even a concrete structure surge to life, a group of men sat sullenly. They were wearing *ghos* or robes that the King had decreed should be worn on visits to government offices.

They had just sold their lands, processed their applications to renounce their citizenship and emigrate from the lands of their forefathers—or at least two forebearers: their fathers and grandfathers. Now they were waiting impatiently for the local administration to let them go. Each of them had a similar complaint and it had nothing to do with the alleged pressure from the government. As they spoke, they looked around them with wary eyes, watching for officials spying on their conversations and somewhat suspicious even of the local member of the National Assembly, a fellow Nepali called O.P. Sharma.

'Many of our neighbours have left, close relatives have gone and now it is difficult to cope with all the farming work especially with the harvest coming up,' said Purna Bahadur Gurung, a village headman from Pungta, three days' walk through leech-infested jungles from Samtse.

Asked repeatedly in Hindi and Nepali if there were any threats that were forcing their migration, Gurung and others replied in the negative. They were going, they said, because their remote hamlets and homes were so far from each other that it was tough to protect their crops and livestock from wild animals.

'The bears spoil the fruit trees, the elephants and wild bears destroy the wheat and graincrops and there are leopards and tigers also, how can we protect our cattle if there are not enough of us?' Gurung asked. His fellow travellers nodded in agreement.

The villages in these remote areas bear little resemblance to the common perception of a village in the subcontinental plains, which conjures up images of clusters of houses, the noise and bustle of children and villagers, the humming of water pumps and the daily gatherings of women at the village wells and water taps, carrying pots and pitchers of water on their heads, walking sensuously, their hips swinging and silver anklets jingling to an ageless tune.

Life in the villages of southern Bhutan and parts of the neighbouring regions of Nepal, Sikkim and Arunachal Pradesh is very different to this comfortable vision. Here homes are scattered over several hills, making communication difficult except by direct meetings or long distance hailing. The main roads are far away. There are no wells and hardly any piped water. Water is harvested during the monsoons and gathered from the many streams and rivulets that flow through the valleys. There are no maidens with magically jingling anklets. There is the grime of work and dust on unwashed but beautiful faces.

Later, in the evening, after a bone-jarring, eight kilometre drive from the stifling atmosphere of the district headquarters, I reached the pitiful camp of bamboo and tarpaulin where Gurung and his fellow migrants had made their homes for the past four days. The Bhutanese officials were giving them twenty rupees per person per day, in an effort to extend their stay and dissuade them eventually from leaving.

The *Dzongda*, Tsultrun of the ten-gallon Texan hat, had made three attempts to persuade them. Each time, a sullen audience turned down his appeal.

The evening I visited, he made one last try. But before he arrived there, I had talked to one or two local council officials who had joined the exodus, and had the distinct impression that this was no panicked reaction. It was a well-planned trip that had villagers from several hamlets joining in.

'Our relatives have gone and we do not want to stay here alone,' said Mangal Lomba, a local councillor. 'No one is forcing us to go, no one has called us and we are sad that we have to disobey the King who wants us to stay. But if you lived up there, you would understand our condition: the wild animals are a real threat.'

As he spoke, the children from the camp leaned against stacks of firewood and freshly cut stalks of sturdy bamboo that they were allowed to take in their move to a new nation and a new home.

Although officials said that the emigrants had told them that they were eventually going to return and that camp leaders had promised them much more land and power when this happened, I did not meet a single Nepali migrant who spoke of such things.

All of them were travelling light, with the barest of clothes and cooking utensils. But a few had large bundles of cash stashed inside their *ghos* and bags. One of them, a shifty-eyed man with three wives and several children, had collected 1.6 lakh rupees in compensation for the sale of land to the government.

But not all that money is taken to Nepal or the camps. Worried by reports that entrants were being fleeced of cash and ornaments as they travelled into Nepal and even inside the camps, many farmers were taking the precaution of unloading some of that money with trusted Indian middlemen or relatives before they crossed the final lap of the journey.

As the adults and children gathered near the stone-covered track that passed for a road, the lights of another vehicle drew up. It was the *Dzongda*, indefatigable till the end. He had come to say goodbye but not before making his final pitch.

'What are you going to get out of this?' he asked the Nepalis. 'You are leaving the lands of your fathers, grandfathers for the life of a refugee? Here you are a citizen of a country; there you're just a piece of paper and people will exploit you, take your money, harm you. We want you to stay.'

But the émigrés maintained a sullen silence, looking in that peculiarly irritating hang dog attitude at their feet, and the earth between their feet, into the distance but never into the eyes of the speaker. Their silence was clear and precise: they had made up their minds and they were not going to be persuaded by a last minute appeal.

'Will we meet again?' the *Dzongda* asked Gurung as the Nepalis gathered to listen. 'I don't know,' said the expressionless leader of the homeless tribe.

That night, a truck came across the boulders and sand of the stream near where the Nepalis had camped. It loaded them and their belongings on and rumbled away through the night, heading for India and then Nepal, to the miserable shacks of plastic, cardboard, bamboo, tarpaulin and tin that were to be their future homes, far from the open spaces and lands that had sustained them for generations.

A short distance away, Dal Bahadur lay in the government hospital as he recovered from the sudden attack by brigands (or ngolops) who had split his head but spared his life.

In Kathmandu, the perception is different. So is the mood.

A few hundred kilometres across the majestic Himalayas, within sighting distance of Mount Everest, Kanchenjunga and Annapurna, and one meets a very different group of government leaders and views.

'I have told the King that it is better that he takes the refugees back before it becomes more of a problem for us,' said Girija Prasad Koirala, the Prime Minister, who is called "Girija babu" by colleagues and party workers.

Koirala had also told King Jigme Singye Wangchuk during a meeting at Colombo in 1992, when the South Asian Association for Regional Cooperation (SAARC) held a truncated summit, that he was concerned by the involvement of the Communists in the camps. 'It is their headache but if the migrants don't go back soon, it will be a worse headache for the King, especially if they are recruited by the Communists.'

That conversation had followed a meeting between the King and Koirala's predecessor in office, Krishna Prasad Bhattarai, the first Nepali politician to hold office as the prime minister of a democratic system in thirty years. Bhattarai took charge in April 1990 after the collapse of the 'partyless' system controlled by the monarchs of Nepal.

The two had met at Male, the sun-baked capital of the Maldives archipelago in the Indian Ocean later that year, at a SAARC summit.

'The King,' Bhattarai remembered over a mouthful of paan, 'was courteous to a fault.' Bhattarai, white-haired and with the avuncular air of a patriarch, is an inveterate paan-chewer.

As the young monarch and the veteran democrat—with long experience of imprisonment and exile from another royal clan—talked, Jigme Singye spoke of the need to change things in his kingdom.

'Do you think I am such a fool as not to know that democracy is the best system of government,' he told Bhattarai. But Bhutan needed time and when the time came, he said, he would personally ask for Bhattarai's help in establishing a more representative administration.

The changes in Nepal had shaken the King as had the Indian intervention in Sikkim in 1974 that saw the end of the line of Chogyals, the temporal and spiritual leaders of that little land.

The King was thinking in terms of a gradual easing of controls at the time; in addition, he was seeking to placate the Nepali Congress, then flushed with victory and making noises about democratic rule in Drukland and the need to overthrow despots.

Girija Prasad Koirala and his colleagues did not believe that the camp inmates are capable of running a full-fledged insurgency. Nor did they encourage such efforts, although statements by Koirala about the need for changes in Bhutan and his backing to democratic campaigns there soured the atmosphere between the two countries and encouraged the dissidents. The Nepal Government also turned a blind eye to the growing militancy in the camps and the raids across the borders, until things became too sticky for Kathmandu as attackers were traced to camps and villages in the Jhapa region.

As a result of a stiffening of political opinion in Nepal on the issue, and India's dislike of leftist elements destablizing the sensitive corridor linking the Northeast to the rest of the country, Girija Babu has told the exiles to stop their hostilities.

Bhim Subba, one of Bhutan's most prominent bureaucrats before he fled with his uncle-in-law, R.D. Basnet of the Bhutan State Trading Corporation—both are wanted in Thimpu for large scale corruption, a charge they flatly deny—says that while militants from the BPP were involved in the earlier clashes, divisions among the exile groups had badly affected unity.

Subba for one does not advocate violence or a violent overthrow of the monarchy. He says that most of the attacks across the border on Nepali-Bhutanese are conducted by criminal gangs. What is clear is that the anti-monarchists had committed a major error of judgement by making King Jigme Singye Wangchuck the main target of their attacks. The King, unfortunately for this group, is held in high regard by his countrymen, almost as a divinity. He is widely respected as strong and clean, capable of decisive action, magnamity and justice. And he is, unlike many elected rulers in the contemporary world, a truly popular figure, who is seen as a bulwark against corruption and the decay of the unique traditions of Drukpa and Bhutanese society.

For months, the talks between the two sides stalled on the identification of the refugees and whether Bhutan would take them back. Much of the future of these homeless, stateless people depends on India, which has absorbed not less than ten million people of Nepali origin in the past fifty years. The Indian role will not be merely in seeking to disperse the refugees but in forging an understanding between Bhutan and Nepal that will make it possible for all three sides to save face.

New Delhi wants the camps to be closed because it does not want leftist groups meddling with the refugees, instigating them and eventually creating a major problem for India as much as for Bhutan.

The camps, run by the UNHCR, contain several groups of people. These include genuine refugees as well as people holding Nepali identity cards. There are also Nepalis expelled from Northeast India; those who lived illegally in Bhutan and even Nepalis living elsewhere in southeastern Nepal. Some exiles are in Kathmandu, such as Subba and Basnet, who represent a major blow to hopes of integration for Bhutan's educated élite. Data available from Bhutan says that as many as 52(

Nepali officials resigned from the Bhutanese civil service between 1990 and 1992. As many as 475 absconded during this period.

The King's attitude of seeking to persuade dissidents from leaving has led to criticism from the national assembly, which is largely powerless. He and the cabinet have been under pressure for their exemption to the southern Bhutanese of payment of rural taxes as involuntary labour. Clearly, King Wangchuk is going as far as his wisdom and local politics will let him.

In the process, it is hardly surprising that there is concealed glee in Thimpu and other bastions of Drukpa power about the depopulation of southern Bhutan. The general accusations that flow against the Nepalis are that they cannot be trusted, that they are extremely fertile and reproduce at a rapid pace and they are disloyal to the land that gave them so much.

Bhutan Home Secretary, Jigme Thinley, told a conference on Bhutan at London in March 1993 that Bhutan could do little for those who had left the country, despite the government's best efforts to dissuade them. Thinley said that he could only hope that the migrants could live freely and securely in their adopted homeland.

He couched it in religious terms, pitching his view to an international audience. The issue, he warned, was deeper than the question of the thousands who had left Bhutan. 'The rich and splendorous culture of the Great Wheel of Buddhism [Mahayana] which once flourished in Sikkim, Tibet, Ladakh, Lahaul and Spiti is well on the path to extinction. Today, Bhutan, the last bastion of this rich cultural heritage is in a state of siege,' declared Thinley, adding that the Drukpas were 'faced with a real threat to their very survival as a distinct culture.'

Jigme Singye Wangchuk is a striking figure. At thirty-eight, he remains boyish and casual, putting visitors at ease and impressing them with a flow of statistics. But much more impressive than his command over facts and figures is his passionate commitment to his country. This is a working monarch who loves to meet people, discuss, travel—preferably in his own country and as little as possible in the countries of the region that he must, as part of his duties, visit.

One of his officials roguishly pointed out that taking care of four wives and eight children had taken a toll, and it showed on the receding hairline.

One of my favourite stories from him came during a marathon 150-minute meeting at his formal audience room in the schidzong, the great, silent centre of the government in Thimpu. This is a vast wooden monastery-administrative complex that is full of corridors and low, wood panelled rooms. But few more than a handful of people can be seen scurrying through its portals.

The story is from 1964 when a young boy of eight and an older sister came dashing out of their home, shrill with excitement about a special gift that had arrived for their father. The present? Bhutan's first motor car. The recipient: none other than the King of Bhutan. And the boy was young Jigme Singye.

In the space of thirty years, the young crown prince has travelled a thousand years, watching new horizons unfold, new opportunities arise and new threats as well.

In the 1990s, the major threat was from the unresolved Nepali question. Meetings with G. P. Koirala as well as six secret meetings between emissaries of either side made no headway. The Nepalese envoys, the young monarch realized, had no negotiating mandate and kept saying that they would need to refer back to the Prime Minister.

King Wangchuk believed that there was a compact between the Bhutanese dissidents and the Nepali government. And although he was stung by Kathmandu's remarks about him being despotic and his government feudal, he exuded confidence when he said that 'Our record of 30 years of development in Bhutan is far better than whatever development they've had in Nepal over the past 100 years.'

And on the demographic issue and the future of the Drukpas, the King said that he will ensure that the Bhutanese will not become a minority in their own country. And clearly, his patience is running out as is that of the local police and military, who are weary of not shooting at assailants and tackling the ngolops. The Bhutanese military is itching for action.

If the Bhutan government is to be believed then the chief of conspirators against the monarchy languishes in prison in Thimpu itself: an elderly Nepali, who was once an adviser to the King and wielded considerable influence in matters of state. His name is Tek Nath Rizal, whose erudition and commitment to his country saw him rise swiftly from what one official said was the lowly job of a bulldozer driver to that of adviser to the King.

'He created all the confusion,' said one Home Ministry official at

Thimpu. For years, the official said, Rizal misled the King, who believed his adviser implicitly on issues relating to Nepali settlers. Rizal would go to the south and say one thing, tell the commoners that the King had neither time nor patience to listen to their grievances; he would return to Thimpu and tell Jigme Singye Wangchuk that the Nepali settlers had full faith in his policies and were prepared to accept the royal order on a uniform dress code and lifestyle.

Attempts to interview Rizal at Thimpu were turned down by authorities who said that since he was being tried by a court, such a meeting with a journalist could prejudice the outcome of the trial.

Rizal was stripped of his powers and post after he submitted a petition in 1988 asking for the King's intervention in stopping harassment of the Nepalis during the census. In the space of one week, Rizal was barred from a cabinet meeting that met to consider his views; branded as treacherous and ousted from all positions; and finally, he sought forgiveness from the King, who pardoned him.

The former adviser then quietly fled Bhutan with two associates, set up the country's first human rights group in exile and lived in Biratmod in Nepal, near Jhapa. He refuelled the royal ire by publishing a booklet attacking the Bhutanese government and demanding basic democratic rights—freedom of expression, association, worship and movement which continue to be denied to Bhutanese citizens, whether they are Drukpa or southerners.

At the time, King Birendra was in absolute control of Nepal. A request went out from Thimpu for the extradition of Rizal and two others sought by the Bhutanese. The three men were picked up from Biratmod, rushed to Kathmandu airport and put on a Druk Air flight to Paro in the company of a high-level security force. Rizal has been charged with treason, for which the maximum punishment is death.

Although Tek Nath Rizal has been declared a prisoner of conscience by Amnesty International, the Bhutan government still refuses to release him after more than three years of imprisonment. Rizal is described as a man with the ability 'to bring unity among the refugees' and a figure of charisma and honesty. That is why it stands to reason that the Drukpa regime will not release him—although it has given a general amnesty to more than 1,500 persons, including the two men who were, with Rizal, virtually hijacked from Nepal to Bhutan in 1989, several months before the Nepali Congress and the anti-monarchist forces in that country surged to power.

Rizal remains both a thorn in the flesh of Thimpu as well as a trump card. Without him, the Nepalese dissidents continue to squabble with each other. They lack a man of his stature to unify them and bring Bhutan to the negotiating table. With him, Thimpu faces the constant glare of adverse international publicity, which is so sensitive in these times of upheaval and civil strife to violations of human rights.

Although the meeting with Rizal was not possible, I did interview two ngolops in custody at Thimpu. One of them is accused of shooting at the *Dungpa* of Geylegphug district, in the southeast. The official, Chimi Dorji, was shot as he drove in the jungle road winding along the Assam border, ambushed by ngolops, the government said.

The man charged with his assassination says that he and about twelve others were instigated by a *mandal* (leader) of their village who said that Dorji needed to be punished for his harsh drive against Nepalis. Those involved in the assault were all refugees from villages in the area and had taken shelter in Assam's Darrang and Kokrajhar districts. They were summoned by the *mandal*, given country-made pistols and told that Dorji was to travel on that route on a given date: the information clearly emanated from sympathizers in the administration or who knew of the official's programmes.

It would not be fair to identify this man by name but it should be known that his mother had been described as a F-7 by the administration and told to abandon her large family and go away. Naturally, her family did the right thing: all of them left Bhutan together, although her sons were identified as residents who qualified to apply for citizenship and her husband was a full-fledged Bhutanese.

Dorji is said to have been particularly hated: there were accounts of large-scale arson of Nepali homes and villages and intimidation of women and children.

Amnesty International as well as the International Red Cross have visited Bhutan to examine charges of human rights violations, torture, illegal detention and bad treatment of prisoners. Yet, Thimpu basks in the confident knowledge that despite their criticism on several counts, it has got off lightly. Senior government officials, including a district police chief, who were accused of troubling Nepali residents and forcing their flight, were transferred, suspended and even sacked from service. The King too relaxed the dress code, saying that the *gho* and *kira* were mandatory only during visits to *Dzongs*, government offices, educational institutions and at official functions. Pujaris or Hindu priests could conduct traditional rites without changing out of their dhotis.

A slow change was, therefore, evident.

The real breakthrough came in the summer of 1993 after Nepal's Home Minister, Sher Bahadur, Chakra Bastola, the Nepalese Ambassador to India, and other senior officials travelled to Thimpu for talks with the King.

This followed a failure of discussions between G. P. Koirala and King Jigme Singye Wangchuk at Dhaka during the SAARC summit, an annual gathering of seven heads of government from the nations of South Asia. The meetings had come close to a negotiated text when the Nepalese demanded major changes in the agreed statement. The Bhutanese refused, leading to a breakdown of talks.

For weeks afterward, there was virtually no contact between the two sides until Koirala and the King authorized the visit by Sher Bahadur, who directly handles the refugee situation.

Despite several days of blunt talk and a meeting with the King, where Chakra Bastola spoke sharply: 'One thing is sure—these are not our refugees, they are not our people and if you do not want them back then they can go anywhere out of Nepal—there is no reason for them to stay on our land at our cost,' the two sides came up with an agreed view: that there would be a joint committee to examine the nationality of those in the camps and then decide what should be done for them.

Whatever the settlement, there are bound to be unhappy voices and men like Bhim Subba are unlikely to be welcomed back to the Dragon Kingdom.

As both sides step cautiously toward a new relationship, their well-wishers can only hope that they avoid the failures and shortcuts that have caused such tragedy in neighbouring lands.

Only then will lasting peace return to this magical land, where time often seems to stand still or even step back, and where in the quiet of the hills, amid the birdsong and the rush of streams, one can still hear the rustle of a falling leaf.

SECTION THREE
A Search For Solutions

A Security Doctrine For The East

Over the past decades, India's policymakers have failed to develop an evolving, forward-looking security doctrine that covers the umbrella of national and international geo-political concerns.

It is this lack of a strategic doctrine, as much as other constraints such as a shortage of resources, if not of skills and people, that is at the root of the country's inability to deal with the confrontations that have arisen with its neighbours and the threats that it faces from new, unforeseen quarters.

Such a security doctrine would make no sense if it was viewed simply as a military campaign to subdue recalcitrant and smaller and thus, weaker, neighbours and impose pan-Indian solutions to multilateral problems. The fashioning of such a policy, especially for the east, must take into account the many factors that bear on a nation's security.

For instance, these include threats to security from environmental degradation, social and economic problems that cause population dislocation, migration, and reduce the quality of life. At the same time, such issues spur competition among subnational and national groups. 'And at the extreme,' says Peter Glieck, the Director of the Pacific Institute for Studies in Development, Environment and Security, these sharper competitions 'lead to actual violent conflict.'

The central question, Glieck says, is not whether environmental concerns can contribute to instability and conflict but when and where such conflicts are most likely to arise. He says that there are many places and scales of conflict, ranging from the village level to national boundary dispute. Research has turned up that 'Conflicts are more likely to occur on the local and regional level and in developing countries where common property resources may be both more critical to survival and less easily replaced or supplemented.'

Glieck is an environmental scientist whose work on water resources and conflicts is internationally respected. In 1991, he reported that with a rise in populations, international strains on limited water resources were bound to escalate. He predicted that while most disputes of this kind were resolved through negotiations, conflicts in some areas over water will grow more intense 'as growing development and population compete for limited supplies.'

Lack of water is not the problem in the eastern land mass of the Indian subcontinent which has seen unrest, insurgency, migration and violent social change over the past decades. If anything, it is the political inability of governments in the region—barring Bhutan—to harness the rivers flowing from the Himalayas that is creating some of the difficulties.

Thus, different factors, ranging from water-sharing to armed rebellions, make long-term planning difficult and complex. But that is all the more reason to enunciate a security doctrine that can be amended with time and developments. But the essence should not change: the enlightened self-interest of the biggest nation in South Asia/Southeast Asia.

One aspect that has hardly received any attention from policy planners in India is the rise of drug abuse and Acquired Immune Deficiency Syndrome (AIDS), the disease without a cure, that is spreading on the eastern borders. The source for this murderous package is found in the heroin factories across the India–Myanmar border, in the insurgencies that have held Rangoon's armies at bay for decades in the jungles of Myanmar and in the international drug and weapons cartels that operate through the rebels, heroin dealers and the military junta.

For decades, Myanmar has been an area of instability: racked by insurrections without number, far more brutal in their confrontations with government forces than anything that the Northeast has faced.

For more than fifty years, nationalist groups such as the Kachins, Karens, Shans and Chins have fought for their freedom from Rangoon's yoke. It has not mattered, for many, whether their opponents in the Burmese plains were democrats, autocrats or plain military dictators.

These wars in the hills for independence have ebbed and flowed over these past decades. Some have even made peace with Rangoon in return for pledges of non-interference: the latest group to have sought a truce is the Kachin Independence Army (KIA), that has conducted the longest running insurgency in this Asian military arena.

The move by the KIA has important implications for India as the Kachins and other anti-government fighters have also played host to the pro-democracy politicians and their followers after the generals in Rangoon crushed the student movement in 1989. These dissident groups are uncomfortable with the drug smuggling business of their hosts. But there is little either side can do to resolve the contradiction that it faces: the students and politicians need support and refuge; the militants need the legitimacy that supporting the democrats provides.

The drug cartels of Myanmar include insurgents, smugglers and military commanders who share a cosy relationship.

This relationship clearly makes life difficult for the pro-democracy students and politicians who also live and work among the rebels, for these are their only sanctuaries in Myanmar. The students in exile in India do not like to talk about these issues, seeking instead to focus on atrocities by the junta as well as drug-smuggling by the military.

India too has quietly opened the door to Myanmar's hated regime, with visits by its Foreign Secretary and businessmen. India's defence is that its border states need to trade with their large neighbour instead of depending on exporting everything or importing everything to and from India. Moreover, India feels that the Burmese market is easier to reach and cheaper to supply.

Such moves deflect from international pressure on Myanmar to clean up its domestic human rights record and control of the drug rings that smuggle heroin out to the world.

For many years, the Burmese government has been satisfied by the knowledge that its battles against separatist guerrillas are among the world's most forgotten wars, far from the international spotlight that South Africa and Bosnia have held. The rebellions too are far removed from the country's own populous plains and fertile deltas. There are a bewildering range of uprisings, ranging from the Communists to the ethnic militants, whose loyalties are based entirely on clan and tribe.

Rangoon's major military campaigns in the past years have been against the following recalcitrant insurgencies the Kachins, who trained and backed various Northeastern guerrilla groups; the Shans in the southeast on the Thai-Myanmar border, the Burmese Communist Party (BCP) and the Kachin rebels. Each group has separate military and political wings, a sophisticated command network and the capability of striking hard with the latest weaponry, including rocket launchers, mortars and heavy automatic weapons.

The BCP, once the most formidable of the anti-government forces, has been overwhelmed with a mix of diplomacy and military power. According to some experts, the BCP was also emasculated by the profits that it saw in the drug trade. It traded ideological purity for easy money. China, which backed the BCP for many years, has instead now thrown its support to the Burmese junta and is supplying millions of dollars worth of modern weaponry to its new ally. Beijing also was expressing its appreciation of an unpopular Burmese move: the support it received from Rangoon for the crushing of the 1989 Tiananmen Square uprising.

Despite India's slow overtures to Myanmar, there are many reasons to walk cautiously on the road to friendship with this neighbour.

For one thing, the lethal combination of drugs and AIDS that is flowing unstopped across the borders into the Northeast is harming societies in every part of the region. The Northeast has become a new smuggling route for Burmese heroin dealers, a conduit to Nepal and Calcutta and then to the West where the profits lie; but also it is a market where growing numbers of drug addicts seek refuge in one more fix.

The route for AIDS in the east is the same as the drug route: far more than sexual promiscuity, it is spreading from infected needles that heroin addicts use. Dozens of addicts share one needle, passing on their infections and diseases.

In Manipur, there is a camp for addicts, some distance from the capital of Imphal, where drug abusers are manacled with ropes to prevent them from harming themselves or one another.

Burmese exiles say that the drug rings have now moved closer to the Indian border. The All Burma Students Union (ABSU) says that at least thirteen heroin factories have been set up along the Nagaland-Myanmar and Mizoram-Myanmar borders. They say the roads have been built and the area cleared by Burmese government troops.

The problem is so acute in Manipur—where addicts are synonymous with AIDS infections—that one health official told me in desperation: 'Let us give them clean needles—we cannot stop their addiction but we can stop them from dying from AIDS and passing it on to others.'

To the trafficker in Southeast Asia, whether Thai, Burmese or Chinese, heroin is as much a commercial item as rubber or tin.

In such situations, a well-reasoned security doctrine will help.

It is here that India's military might should be used, instead of constantly being thrown against New Delhi's perceived enemies at home. Of course, China and Myanmar should be assured that no harm is meant to their interests.

New Delhi has stationed at least 2,00,000 soldiers and air force personnel in the Northeast sector, in an area stretching from the Darjeeling hills to Nagaland and Manipur to control insurgencies and keep a watchful eye on its foes and friends.

India must be prepared to strike at the heroin factories and Rangoon should be closely associated with such an operation. So, too, should powers interested in crushing the drug trade: the United States and Britain and other European countries that suffer directly the consequences of the illicit trade.

Myanmar's involvement in such a crackdown will be in its own interests: it will be perceived as serious in its endeavour to tackle a menace that jeopardizes the lives of millions of people across the world. It would give Rangoon some credit ratings that it badly needs in the Western world, where drug abuse is an epidemic and measures to control it—by fair means or foul—are widely supported by governments and communities.

Myanmar's druglords are at the heart of an evil empire that profits on man's venality and exploitation of others. India need not be chary about being branded an international bully and will be only doing a messy cleanup job that others want done but are unprepared to get their own hands soiled while doing it.

The time has come to strike at the soul of this empire. And since the West is so loud in its declarations of war against drug-traffickers, India must seek Western support for such a move, just as the United States has assisted the war on heroin in Columbia and other Latin American countries.

Should Myanmar decide not to co-operate in such a task, then an alliance of concerned nations must do the job anyway—risking Burmese armed opposition but also paving the way for a possible overthrow of the military regime and its replacement with a democratic and free government.

Myanmar has compounded its many problems on the ethnic front by launching brutal offensives against the Rohingya Muslims, some 2,00,000 of whom have taken refuge in the Chittagong area.

Bangladesh is a nation that can barely feed itself. How is it to take care of these extra mouths? The United Nations High Commissioner for Refugees (UNHCR) is, of course, helping with providing food and setting up camps. But efforts by the UN and Bangladesh to secure the return of the refugees have failed. Not because of Rangoon's stubbornness. A little known factor is that Western nations have put pressure on little Bangladesh to let the refugees stay on because it gives them another reason to blacken Myanmar's face.

The Rohingyas are not fleeing Burmese persecution for the first time either. A low-level insurgency that exists has the potential for flaring into a major rebellion with assistance from other groups.

The British Broadcasting Corporation (BBC) showed a news clip, after the refugees came over, portraying Bangladeshi officers training Rohingyas in military tactics in a relief camp.

Unless taken back, the Rohingyas will increasingly become a thorn in Myanmar's flesh, leading to the radicalization of the young men and women, either by Islamic fundamentalists or leftist nationalism. Refugee camps—in the Middle East, in Nepal and in India for the Chakmas—have been the breeding ground and recruiting areas for militants, fed up of moderation, weary of their wretched living conditions and prepared to die for their *maati*.

The plight of the Rohingyas underlines the need to examine refugee flows and migration in a new security doctrine. Planners must accept that migration will continue, whether it is from the Arakan hills of Myanmar, the Bangladeshi flood plains or the Bhutanese foothills. In fact, the 1991 Indian census turned up disturbing evidence of population growth in the Northeast of India. Here, only Assam had a growth rate commensurate with the national average of 23.85 per cent.

Nagaland recorded a 56.08 per cent growth over its 1981 population; Tripura spoke of a jump of 34.30 per cent; tiny Mizoram grew by 39.86 and Meghalayans increased their number by 32.86 per cent. Manipur recorded a 29.29 per cent growth rate and Arunachal Pradesh reported 36.83 per cent. This is not because these communities are more productive than other groups: the flow of people into their states from other parts of India, as well as Nepal and Bangladesh, continues unabated, despite government restrictions and threats.

There are several ways of dealing with this problem if tackled within a uniform and common forum.

One is to send firm messages to both Nepal and Bangladesh that further infiltration will not be accepted. It does not mean that India can throw out the fifteen million or more Bangladeshis living here. That would mark a violation of their human rights and trigger terrible communal riots. But added to heightened patrolling on the border—and the settlement along those borders of people hostile to migrants—India must work with the rest of the South Asian community and developed nations in improving the sustenance levels and lifestyles of Bangladesh and Nepal.

These questions are troubling other areas too. Illegal migrations are viewed by European governments as their biggest problem. In Europe, race is a major factor and non-whites face discrimination. Across that continent, once home to political and economic refugees, especially from the Communist nations, the walls are going up on the boundaries of Fortress Europe.

Attacks on refugees of a different colour and community are increasing, especially in Germany. And national governments are turning shriller and more right-wing in order to stop their supporters from turning to the new right.

Food production is another significant aspect of the security canvas. In the following years, India will need to produce another forty to forty-five million tons of foodgrains to feed its rapidly growing population. Failed harvests or monsoons could spell disaster for twenty per cent of the population which still teeters on the edge of survival. Currently, India's production has held steady at about 170-to-175 million tons of grains per year. The question to be faced is: where will the extra food come from?

Here again the answer lies in the fertile Gangetic-Brahmaputra-Barak Valley basins where intensive cultivation is a way of life. New agricultural techniques, fresh cropping patterns, control of flood waters and the increased use of quick growing rice, wheat and other grain varieties, with the tapping of gene banks, can spell prosperity. Again, co-operation among Nepal, India, Bhutan and Bangladesh is a must, if this is to happen.

The prospect of co-operation with Dhaka creates new fears in the Northeast about the floodgates to more illegal migration. This issue needs further open debates, not the polemics of Hindu chauvinists who see an Islamic invasion of India with every migrant that comes over, conveniently forgetting that millions of Hindus have illegally slipped into the region as well. For example, the Hindu Bengali migrants in Tripura have swept aside the indigenous people. What is truly surprising and frightening is the scale of disinformation and Goebbelsian double-speak that is emanating from the Bharatiya Janata Party (BJP) which raised the question of foreign nationals from Bangladesh time and again.

The BJP would have people believe that the Bangladeshis are coming with a secret mission to 'Bangladeshize' the Northeast and eventually do what Pakistan could not do: create a larger Islamic state comprising Assam, Meghalaya and Bangladesh. They differentiate between Hindu migrants who are 'refugees' in their dictionary and Muslims who are 'infiltrators.' This is nonsense for Hindu migration has converted Tripura in the space of less than fifty years into a Bengali-majority state. Surely, indigenous peoples too have rights.

Should illegal migrants, especially if they are Hindus, be rewarded with political power and economic leverage simply because the tribespeople are too small to matter to the BJP vote bank? Should detections and expulsions also not be the rule here as well as in other border areas? Clearly, the BJP has failed to give adequate thought to the issue and instead has taken the shortcut of blaming Muslim immigrants, a group that is both visible and easily targetable, for its short-term aim of consolidating the Hindu vote banks.

Attacks on Bangladeshi communities in India will be met with bloodletting of Hindus in Bangladesh. No one, not even the security forces, will come to the rescue of Hindus there. The BJP has to ponder this question before plunging into a storm that has the capacity of unleashing religious violence across the subcontinent on a scale that has rarely been witnessed since independence. The destruction of the mosque at Ayodhya on 6 December 1992 led to fierce attacks on Hindu homes, temples and settlements in Pakistan and Bangladesh. Thousands were wounded, many temples razed, women raped and kidnapped and homes and stores looted.

Jingoism is not going to answer such questions. It will make matters far worse. The subcontinent cannot afford more transfers of population—fifty years after the Partition killed hundreds of thousands and displaced millions more—without resolving the basic question of how Hindus and Muslims should coexist.

Yet, the 'Bangladeshization' of eastern India is an accomplished fact. But my definition of Bangladeshization is different to that of the BJP: it means that generations of Hindu and Muslim immigrants have made themselves an integral part of society in the region. They have voted with their feet and rejected Pakistan. It is an affirmation of their stake in the area. This means that they are unlikely to go much beyond occasional low-level conflicts with other local communities, for they will not want to jeopardize their stay.

To tackle migration, India must develop new immigration laws and take a fresh look at its citizenship rules. Identity cards for people along the borders must be made compulsory although it lends itself to fraud. The suggestions of 'sealing the border' are stupid for there is perhaps no border like this which zigzags through vale and dale, river, paddyfield and forest. Neither can it be clearly demarcated nor easily patrolled. Night crossings are easy, especially where the path is eased by bribery.

What would make more sense is to settle groups of people who are opposed to aliens along the border, invest them with some powers to make 'citizen's arrests'—seize suspicious persons and hand them over to the local police—and back them with firepower from the army, paramilitary and police. Some Bangladesh officials have even suggested that they are prepared to co-operate in joint operations against Naga and Assamese militants crossing the borders. But their message has a ring of desperation about it. In return they seek a greater share of Ganges waters than India is prepared to give.

No force has, however, succeeded anywhere in curbing migrants who are desperate enough to leave their own country. The experience of the United States is a pointer: despite the best of surveillance—night vision equipment, air patrolling, fences, security checks and mobile patrols as well as heavy weaponry—American border guards are unable to stop the influx of aliens from Mexico.

In the case of Bangladesh too, India must recognize that this frontier will continue to be porous.

One way of dealing with the illegals who are in India is to follow the example that was set by the United States some years ago by announcing a general amnesty to all illegal aliens. Otherwise, the task of identifying and ousting—or dispersing—millions of such aliens is a nightmare that no agency of the Government of India is prepared to or capable of tackling. A cutoff date could be a workable option and 1992 could be a possible year for such a measure. Those who came before this date and register with the police and local authorities should be accepted as citizens. A witch-hunt will make no sense and will instead raise the temperature of the country's simmering communal cauldron.

A key to slowing if not stemming the flow lies in helping Bangladesh improve its economic conditions. In this, clearly India must co-operate with the richer countries of the West as well as fellow nations in South Asia to make life more attractive for the average Bangladeshi. It makes far better sense than increasing defence spending and upgrading security levels on the border.

'The means to reduce migration pressures over the long term are to stimulate economic growth and job creation at home, and thus promote sustainable national development,' says the 1993 State of the World Report, published by the United Nations Population Fund.

Without this two-pronged approach, added to the long-term perspectives of regional assistance on specific projects in power generation and water sharing, good intentions and ideas will not work.

Soil conservation, better agricultural and irrigation planning and upstream reforestation can help reduce flooding. These steps will surely help slow the Brahmaputra and its tributaries in their dash for the plains. Water catchment areas in the lower- and medium-Himalayas should be organized on a massive scale to control run-off before the monsoons sweep through the Gangetic and Brahmaputra Valleys. Reforestation goes hand-in-hand with such a scheme and an obvious target for such a project is Nepal, which provides one of the best examples of a devastated forest system, ruined by unscientific and reckless felling.

The Centre for Science and Environment (CSE) reported as far back as 1986 that many hilly regions in India are ideal for setting up tiny hydroelectric power generators ranging from a few kilowatts to several megawatts to energize rural communities. Not only would this stop deforestation by people seeking fuel and construction material but it would reduce the long, arduous treks that women and even young children undertake every day in search of diminishing fuel supplies—twigs, boughs, branches and sometimes, whole trees. The CSE advocated small units that could be maintained by rural communities.

Much more ambitious is the dream of Masaki Nakajima, the founder of the Mitsubishi Research Institute of Japan, who has proposed a 500 billion dollar plan to stimulate the international economy though a series of projects. An initial study proposed eleven large dams along the Brahmaputra loop, where the river known in Tibet as the Tsang-po, rushes down the Himalayas into the flat Assam plains.

Indian river experts say that giant, multipurpose dams on large rivers in Arunachal Pradesh can store at least six million hectare-metres of water. This, they say, will reduce the level of floods in Assam and Bangladesh. Dams in Cachar would protect the Cachar plain and benefit the Meghna Basin and Sylhet in Bangladesh. According to B.G. Verghese, the journalist, the reduction of the Brahmaputra's flood flow could release as much as one-third of the normally flood-prone areas of Bangladesh for cultivation and settlement during the wet seasons and create opportunities for irrigation in the dry season.

The relevance of large dams is questioned by those advocating sustainable development. They say that India and other low income nations cannot afford such huge, expensive projects. There are doubts whether these dams will be able to withstand the high levels of seismicity of the Himalayas and problems of silting. According to them, such schemes will largely benefit urban areas, especially middle class groups and organized sectors, such as industries. Cities and industry are among the largest consumers of power. They also feel that the displacees as well as local villagers must be consulted on such projects when they are conceived, instead of being told to find new homes and occupations when the dams are built.

Across the world, there is a wave against gigantism, whether in the area of dams or canals. The region could perhaps be better served by a larger network of smaller dams that would not face the problem of silting, act as a restraint on the waters and generate power. Indian planners must also recognize that international funding agencies are no longer interested in backing huge projects, sensing the change both in public opinion and in the attitude of Western governments.

Despite the hurdles, there is little alternative for the countries of the region but to co-operate. They must pool resources and expertise and work for a marriage of dams, small projects and local conservation. This will help their people to avoid bitter conflicts arising from the destruction of the common, increased scarcity of cropland and diminishing jobs.

Time is of the essence.

India has wasted fifty years dealing with its rebellious minorities in the Northeast. It cannot afford to continue this piecemeal approach. Only a doctrine embracing regional, economic, environmental and security concerns can transform the jungles of unrest into communities of prosperity.

South Asia's eastern block has all the ingredients for success: hardworking people, rich land, thick forests, good agricultural climate and enormous natural resources of water, oil and gas, apart from coal and limestone. What is needed are men and women of vision and good sense who can inspire the changes and lead their communities in these challenging tasks.

The problem with Indian and other South Asian leaders is that they are too tied up in resolving immediate issues and conflicts: Hindu-Muslim problems arising out of the demolition of the disputed shrine at Ayodhya, for example, has taken hundreds of lives in sectarian riots. The sinews of the State have atrophied, incapable of lunging swiftly into action. Yet, with co-operation, there are chances of denting the most intractable of problems.

Without it, India, Bangladesh and even Myanmar are doomed to tangle with each other in a series of disputes that can escalate into large clashes.

By 2020, there will be 220 million Bangladeshis and one billion Indians competing for land and jobs. Without policies on population growth, migration, flood control and agricultural production, sharing of resources and better co-operation, they are fated to confront each other in savage conflicts. Should this happen, the civil wars in Bosnia, Somalia and Azerbaijan will be reduced to a shadow on the world's memory.

SECTION FOUR
Appendices

Appendix A (I)

Saadulla-Bardoloi-Chaudhury Accord

AGREEMENT ARRIVED AT AFTER DISCUSSION BETWEEN SIR SAADULLA REPRESENTING THE GOVT. AND SHRI GOPINATH BARDOLOI AND SHRI ROHINI KUMAR CHAUDHURY REPRESENTING THE OPPOSITION IN THE ASSAM LEGISLATIVE ASSEMBLY[*]:

After mutual discussion on the points raised in the letter dated 18th March '45 from Messrs G.N. Bardoloi and R.K. Chaudhury to Hon'ble Sir Mahammad Saadulla, Premier of Assam, and his reply thereto (contained in his letter dated 19-3-45) it is agreed as follows:

. Restoration of Civil Liberty:-

(a) Two third of the security prisoners now detained in jail should be released within April '45. All M.L.As and prominent Congressmen shall be released forthwith. The remaining security prisoners will be released as early as possible but not later than June, '45.

(b) Convicted politicals shall also be released forthwith except those convicted for offences of grave and heinous nature such as sabotage, but their cases also shall be revived and released after examination of their cases on merit.

(c) Ban on public meetings, assemblies and processions etc. shall be forthwith withdrawn from all places excepting protected areas and sadr subdivision of Lakshmipur District. But there will be no such ban on Dibrugarh town and Khowang area on the south bank and Sisi Dhemajion the North bank of the subdivision. There will however be no ban on any where against such meetings, assemblies and processions held in connection with elections to local bodies and legislature.

(d) Ban, if any, against Congress committees in the province shall be withdrawn.

(e) All restriction orders on M.L.As shall be forthwith withdrawn. So also

See, Gopinath Bardoloi Papers, Nehru Memorial Museum and Library, Delhi.

in cases of other politicals save in few cases requiring scrutiny.

II. Procurement and supply:-

The policy of Government in this matter shall be reviewed and revised wi
a view to provide adequate supplies to the people, remove corruption and to secu
more popular support and co-operation.

III. Land Settlement:-

(a) The policy of Land Settlement embodied in the Govt. resolution of 15
January '45 will be modified as follows:-

Paragraph (8) of the resolution shall be substituted by the following:-

In order to raise the standard of living of our cultivating classes the Gov
shall provide on application, land in the planned settlement area, an econom
holding which shall be at least 20 bighas for an applicant on a family of five perso
or less. In no case shall a family or an applicant get more than 30 bighas.

Para 4 shall be deleted:-

(b) In explanation of para 3 and 15 of the aforesaid resolution provisio
shall be inserted for the purpose of creating tribal blocks side by side with bloc
meant for other communities in planned settlement areas where the tribal peop
have their villages and homes.

(c) The last sentence in para 15 of the resolution shall be deleted.

(d) Paragraph 18(c) shall be rewritten as follows:-

(c) Subject to (a) and (b) above the professional grazing reserves shall b
kept intact, and the Deputy Commissioners will be directed to see that they ar
kept free of encroachment by eviction of trespassers, past, present or future. 'B
individual cases of hardship arising out of the policy of such eviction shall b
reported to Government for decision.'

(e) In order to carry out the Govt. policy thus revised and the spirit of th
memorandum submitted by leaders of parties, the consent of the leaders of th
Congress and Nationalist Co-alition party will be taken in the selection of th
member in charge of Revenue portfolio.

IV. Local Board Constituencies seats:-

The reconstituted Cabinet shall have the option of reopening the question
distribution of seats with a view to allay widespread criticism against it.

V. Reconstitution of the Cabinet:-

The present Cabinet will resign on the 23rd. March, 1945 and will b
reconstituted by Sir Mahammad Saadulla so that the members of the new Cabine
may take their seats in the House on the 24th. March '45 before prorogation.

(b) The cabinet shall be reconstituted in the following manner:

(i) 5 Muslims including the Premier, to be selected by Muslim members
Sir Mahammad Saadulla's party.

(ii) Five non-Muslims by the Opposition in the following manner:

Appendix A (I)

(1) 3 caste Hindus (2) 1 Plain Tribal (3) 1 Schedule Caste.

In selecting (2) opinion of the group shall prevail. The Schedule Caste representative will be taken from the members of the community either by selection or by election under the supervision of the Opposition.

(III) We wish that the Hills Tribal and Indian Christians are represented by a seat in the Cabinet to be selected by them, if an eleventh seat is available.

Shillong 22-3-45

Sd/ Syed M. Saadulla
Sd/ Rohini Kumar Chaudhury
Sd/ Gopinath Bardoloi

Appendix A (II)

Details of Land Settlement Changes

Land settlement policy changes, Government of Assam, January 1945, as a result of an All-Party conference on the issue and the leadership of Gopinath Bardoloi. (Sir Mohammad Saadulla was Premier of the State[*].)

1. In the districts of Goalpara, Kamrup, Darrang and Nowgong there should be systematic distribution of land for all landless people of all communities including the immigrants who came before 1938.

2. A family would not get more than 10 acres or 30 bighas of land.

3. If required land is not available in these four districts, in that case North Lakhimpur would be opened.

4. Those having land less than five bighas should be considered landless.

5. Reserved areas would be formed for the tribals. Its size would be double the size of the lands acquired by them at the present. Along with this, lands would be kept reserved for (their) future expansion also.

6. What was decided in 1940, according to this formula, was that at least 30% of the land of all districts, would be kept for future expansion. In the actual reserved grazing areas, even if they were found additional, no human settlements would be allowed. Of course, present settlers in these lands would not be evicted.

8. If any community failed to occupy fully the lands alloted to them within two years, in that case these lands would be distributed among other communities. Throughout the state and in the three main districts[**], advisory committees would be formed, one for each district, with representatives of all parties.

9. Same of the parts of the old scheme of the government with regard to the distribution of additional lands would be deleted.

[The August 1943 land proposals of Saadulla which created an uproar in

---

[*] See, an article by Nirode K. Barooah in the *Prantik* magazine, Guwahati, 1990, (translated from the Assamese by Arobindo Sarma).

[**] Darrang, Nowgong [or Nagaon] and Kamrup.

Assam declared that the grazing lands should be converted to lands for settlement (by immigrants) in the districts of Darrang, Nowgong and Kamrup; and in Sibsagar and Lakhimpur districts, the foothills were to be reclaimed by landless local people.]

Appendix B (I)

A Note On Assam's Stand vis a vis British Government Statement of 6th December, 1946[*]

APPEAL (TO CONGRESS WORKING COMMITTEE, MEMBERS OF ALL INDIA CONGRESS COMMITTEE AND MEMBERS OF THE CONSTITUENT ASSEMBLY FROM ASSAM PROVINCIAL CONGRESS COMMITTEE.)

On the very day of announcement by the British Cabinet Mission of their Statement of May 16, 1946, the Assam P.C.C., which was in session at Gauhati, sent a telegraphic message to the Congress Working Committee in session in New Delhi, intimating the universal feeling of apprehension of the people of Assam, and lodging emphatic protest against the Grouping clauses in the State Paper and Shri G.N. Bardoloi, who was then in New Delhi, was also instructed telegraphically to meet Congress Working Committee and represent Assam's case and acquaint the Committee with Assam's strong opposition and her refusal to accept the Grouping Plan.

Accordingly Shri G.N. Bardoloi met Congress Working Committee and submitted a Memorandum on 19th May, 1946.

On June 10, 1946, the Assam Congress Delegation headed by M. Tayyebulla, President A.P.C.C., met the Congress Working Committee at New Delhi where Mahatma Gandhi was also present, and submitted a Memorandum and urged upon Congress Working Committee to lend full support to Assam in her decision not to accept under any circumstances whatsoever, the provision of decision by simple majority of votes in Section 'C' in the matter of settling her constitution.

Maulana Abul Kalam Azad, the then Congress President, gave on behalf of the Congress Working Committee, full assurance of support and also conveyed

---

[*] See, Gopinath Bardoloi Papers, Nehru Memorial Museum and Library, Delhi.

through the Assam Delegation a message of sympathy and support to the people of Assam. This allayed, for the time being, to a great extent the anxiety of the people of the province.

In July, the Assam Legislative Assembly elected Assam's ten representatives to the Constituent Assembly including the three Muslim League members and gave a clear Mandate in a Resolution which was passed without division not to go into Section and accept the Group Plan of H.M.G. State Paper (Vide Annexure IV).

On September 25, 1946, the Assam P.C.C. President M. Tayyebulla and the A.I.C.C. Members of Assam met Mahatmaji and other Congress leaders at New Delhi during the A.I.C.C. session and obtained further assurances of strong support to Assam. Mahatmaji advised on the very line of his recently published Srirampur Note on 17th December, 1946, wherein he advised Assam not to go into the Section if full assurance is not given by the Congress (Vide Annexure III).

But H.M.G. Statement of December 6, 1946, which now seeks to alter and add to the 16th May State Paper fundamentally, has given a rude shock to the people of India in general and to the people of Assam in particular, by its interpretation of the Grouping Clause and thereby raised a deep universal feeling of alarm and resentment in the province. Assam finds herself in grave peril—facing a crisis indeed!

On December 9, 1946, Shri G.N. Bardoloi on behalf of the Assam Members of the Constituent Assembly, submitted a Memorandum to the Congress Working Committee in regard to the stand of Assam vis-a-vis H.M.G. Statement of December 6, and represented Assam's case fully (Vide Annexure I).

On December 10, 1946, President A.P.C.C. sent a telegraphic message to Congress President and the Members of the Working Committee and Mahatma Gandhi (at Srirampur) conveying Assam's decision not to accept under any circumstances whatsoever to submit to simple majority vote in Section C for the settlement of Assam's H.M.G. Statement and asked for assurances of support (Vide Annexure II)[*].

On December 17, Shri Bejoychandra Bhagavati, Secretary Assam P.C.C. and Shri Mahendra Mohan Choudhury, Secretary Assam Congress Parliamentary Party, were deputed to meet Mahatma Gandhi at Srirampur and seek his advice. Mahatmaji handed over to them a Note giving his advice, which was published in the Press on Dec. 23, 1946 (Vide Annexure III)[**].

Shri G.N. Bardoloi and prominent Assam Constituent Assembly Members thereupon met the Congress Working Committee at New Delhi and acquainted them of the new position of Assam and Gandhiji's advice in the matter of Grouping and Section.

On return from New Delhi, Shri G.N. Bardoloi made a full statement before

---

[*] Annexures I and II are excluded in this Appendix.
[**] Published as Appendix B (II) on p. 343.

the Provincial Congress Working Committee and Constituent Assembly. The Working Committee on Dec. 26, 1946, regarding the position of Assam obtaining in the counsels of the Congress Working Committee thereupon having reviewed the whole matter adopted a Statement which will speak for itself (Vide Annexure V).

To place the decision and point of view of the Assam P.C. Working Committee, contained in the Statement, Deputation was appointed to meet the Congress Working Committee at New Delhi during the A.I.C.C. session as well as to meet A.I.C.C. members and others and make all possible efforts to obtaining the fullest support and a final decision of the A.I.C.C. in the full satisfaction of the people of Assam.

The question of Assam, and of N.W.F.P. and the Sikhs, vis-a-vis Grouping and Section is today a vital issue of All India importance before the Indian National Congress and the whole country. The A.P.C.C., therefore, appeal to the Congress Working Committee, Members of the A.I.C.C. and the Members of the Constituent Assembly to lend their fullest support to the just and righteous cause of Assam in their hour of grave crisis in her national life when her very existence is in peril.

Appendix B (II)

GANDHIJI'S ADVICE TO ASSAM

Two Assam friends Shri Bijoy Chandra Bhagabati and Shri Mohendra Mohan Chaudhuri saw Gandhiji on the morning of 15-12-46 on behalf of Shri Bardoloi. They asked him what Assam was to do with regard to the question of grouping. It was a question of life and death for Assam. They did not wish to be grouped with Bengal. Some people told them that they would be helping the League if they stayed out. Assam could not be allowed to stand in the way of the progress of the rest of India and so on. They had asked the Working Committee. There did not seem to be any clear guidance from them. So they had come to him for advice. In reply Gandhiji said : 'I do not need a single minute to come to a decision for on this I have a mind. I am a Congressman to the very marrow, as I am mainly the framer of constitution of the Congress as it stands to-day. I told Bardoloi that if there is no clear guidance from the Congress Working Committee Assam should not go into the Sections. It should lodge its protest and retire from the Constituent Assembly. It will be a kind of satyagraha against the Congress for the good of the Congress.

'Rightly or wrongly the Congress has come to the decision that it will stand by the judgement of the Federal Court. The dice are heavily loaded. The decision of the Federal Court will go against the Congress interpretation of grouping as far as I can make out for the simple reason that the Cabinet has got legal advice which upholds their decision. The Federal Court is the creation of the British. It is a packed court. To be consistent the Congress must abide by its verdict whatever it may be. If Assam keeps quiet it is finished. No one can force Assam to do what it does not want to do. It must stand independently as an autonomous unit. It is autonomous to a large extent to-day. It must become fully independent and autonomous. Whether you have that courage, grit and the gumption, I do not know. You alone can say that. But if you can make that declaration it will be a fine thing. As soon as the time comes for the Constituent Assembly to go into sections you will say, "Gentlemen, Assam retires". For the independence of India it is the only condition. Each Unit must be able to decide and act for itself. I am hoping that in this, Assam will lead the way. I have the same advice for the Sikhs. But your position is much happier than that of the Sikhs. You are a whole province. They are a community inside a province. But I feel every individual has the right to act for himself, just as I have.'

Q. But we are told that the framing of the constitution for the whole of India cannot be held up for the sake of Assam. Assam cannot be allowed to block the way.

A. There is no need to do that. That is why I say I am in utter darkness. Why are not these simple truths evident to all after so many years! If Assam retires it does not block but leads the way to India's independence.

Q. The League has said that the Constitution framed by the Constituent Assembly cannot be imposed on unwilling Units. So if some parts do not accept it, the British Parliament won't accept it.

Gandhiji flared up at this question. 'Who is the British Government? If we think independence is going to descend on our heads from England or somewhere, we are greatly mistaken. It won't be independence, we will be crushed to atoms. We are fluctuating between independence and helpless dependence. The Cabinet Mission's plan lie in between. If we act rightly there will be the full blown flower of independence. If we react wrongly the blossom will wither away. Mind you, the League standpoint is quite correct. If they stand out the Constituent Assembly cannot impose its constitution on an unwilling party. The British Government has no say in the matter one way or the other.

'The British cannot interfere with the working of the Constituent Assembly. Supposing the vast majority including the Muslims and others form a constitution, you can defy the British Parliament if it seeks to interfere. Power is in your hands. Some such thing happened in Ireland only recently. And De-Valera is no non-violent fighter. The position of India is far better than that of Ireland. If we have not the penetration we will lose the advantage we have as it is apparently being lost to-day.

'If Assam takes care of itself the rest of India will be able to look after itself. What have you got to do with the constitution of the Union Government? You should form your own constitution. That is enough. You have the basis of a constitution all right even now.

'I have never despised the 1935 constitution. It is based on provincial autonomy. It has the capacity for fullest growth, provided the people are worth it. The hill people are with you. Many Muslims are also with you. The remainder can be too, if you act on the square.

'You will have to forget petty jealousies and rivalries and overcome your weaknesses. Assam has many weaknesses as it has strength, for I know my Assam.'

'With your blessing we can even go outside the Congress and fight,' the friends put in.

Gandhiji replied that in 1939 when there was the question of giving up the Ministry, 'Subhas Babu opposed it as he thought Assam's was a special case. I told Bardoloi that there was much in what Subhas Babu had said and although I was the author of that scheme of boycott I said Assam should not come out if it did not feel like it. But Assam did come out. It was wrong.'

The friends said 'Maulana Sahib had then said that exception could not be made in the case of Assam.'

Gandhiji said, 'Here there is no question of exception, Assam rebelled and that civilly. But we have that slavish mentality. We look to the Congress and then feel that if we do not follow it slavishly something will go wrong with it. I have said that not only a province but even an individual can rebel against the Congress and by doing so save it assuming that he is on the right. I have done so myself. Congress has not attained the present stature without much travail. I remember in 1918 I think there was the Provincial Conference of the Congress workers of Gujarat at Ahmedabad. The late Abbas Tyabjee Saheb was in the chair. All the old guards were there. Ali Brothers had not yet joined hands with me fully as they did later on. The Late Shri Patel was there, and I moved the non-co-operation resolution. I was a non-entity then. A constitutional question arose. Could a provincial conference anticipate the decision of the Congress? I said "Yes". A provincial conference and even a single individual could anticipate the Congress for its own benefit. Inspite of opposition of old hands, the resolution was carried. That paved the way for the Congress to pass a similar resolution at Calcutta. India was dumbfounded at the audacity of a provincial conference passing the resolution.

'We had formed a Satyagraha Sabha outside the Congress. It was joined by Horiman, Sarojini Devi, Shankarlal, Umar Sobhani, Vallabhbhai the mischief making Sardar. I was ill. The Rowlatt Act was passed. I shook with rage. I said to the Sardar I could do nothing unless he helped me. Sardar was willing. And the rest you know. It was rebellion but a healthy one. We celebrate the 6th of April, to the 13th. You have all these historical instances before you.

'I have given you all this time to steel your hearts, to give you courage. If you do not act correctly and now, Assam will be finished. Tell Bardoloi I do not want Assam to lose its soul. It must uphold it against the whole world. Else I will say that Assam had only mannikin and no men. It is an impertinent suggestion that Bengal should dominate Assam in any way.'

The friends asked if they could tell the people that they have rebelled against the Congress with Gandhiji's blessings.

'Talk of God's blessings,' said Gandhi, 'they are infinitely richer.'

Appendix C

The Naga-Akbar Hydari Accord

TRIBES REPRESENTED AT DISCUSSIONS ON THE 26TH, 27TH AND 28TH JUNE, 1947, AT KOHIMA[*]

Western Angamis.
Eastern Angamis.
Kukis.
Kacha Nagas (Mzemi).
Rengmas.
Semas.
Lothas.
Aos.
Sangtams.
Changs.

HEADS OF PROPOSED UNDERSTANDING

That the right of the Nagas to develop themselves according to their freely expressed wishes is recognized.

1. Judicial—All cases whether civil or criminal arising between Nagas in the Naga Hills will be disposed of by duly constituted Naga Courts according to Naga customary law or such law as may be introduced with the consent of duly recognized Naga representative organizations: save that where a sentence of transportation or death has been passed there will be a right of appeal to the Governor.

In cases arising between Nagas and non-Nagas in (a) Kohima and Mokokchung town areas, and (b) in the neighbouring plains districts the judge if not a Naga will be assisted by a Naga assessor.

---

[*] See, Bishnuram Medhi Papers, Nehru Memorial Museum and Library, Delhi.

2. Executive—The general principle is accepted that what the Naga Council is prepared to pay for the Naga Council should control. This principle will apply equally to the work done as well as the staff employed.

While the District Officer will be appointed at the discretion of the Governor Subdivisions of the Naga Hills should be administered by a Subdivisional Council with a full time executive President paid by Naga Council who would be responsible to the District Officer for all matters falling within the latter's responsibility, and to the Naga Council for all matters falling within their responsibility.

In regard to: (*a*) Agriculture—the Naga Council will exercise all the powers now vested in the District Officer.

(*b*) C.W.D.—the Naga Council would take over full control.

(*c*) Education and Forest Department—The Naga Council is prepared to pay for all the services and staff.

3. Legislative—That no laws passed by the Provincial or Central Legislature which would materially affect the terms of this agreement or the religious practices of the Nagas shall have legal force in the Naga Hills without the consent of the Naga Council. In cases of dispute as to whether any law did so affect this agreement the matter would be referred by the Naga Council to the Governor who would then direct that the law in question should not have legal force in the Naga Hills pending the decision of the Central Government.

4. Land—That land with all its resources in the Naga Hills should not be alienated to a non-Naga without the consent of the Naga Council.

5. Taxation—That the Naga Council will be responsible for the imposition, collection, and expenditure of land revenue and house tax and of such other taxes as may be imposed by the Naga Council.

6. Boundaries—That present administrative divisions should be modified so as (1) to bring back into the Naga Hills District all the forests transferred to the Sibsagar and Nowgong Districts in the past, and (2) to bring under one unified administrative unit as far as possible all Nagas. All the areas so included would be within the scope of the present proposed agreement. No areas should be transferred out of the Naga Hills without the consent of the Naga Council.

7. Arms Act—The Deputy Commissioner will act on the advice of the Naga Council in accordance with the provisions of the Arms Act.

8. Regulations—The Chin Hills regulations and the Bengal Eastern Frontier Regulations will remain in force.

9. Period of Agreement—The Governor of Assam as the Agent of the Government of the Indian Union will have a special responsibility for a period of 10 years to ensure the due observance of this agreement; at the end of this period the Naga Council will be asked whether they require the above agreement to be extended for a further period or a new agreement regarding the future of Naga people arrived at.

Appendix D

A Brief Note on NEFA, Manipur State, Naga Hill District (Kohima) and Lushai Hills (Aijal)[*]

The NEFA and the tribal areas in Assam and Manipur State are in many ways peculiar and different from other parts of India. Though most of these areas, particularly in the hills, are inhabited by so-called 'backward' tribes, the degree of their 'backwardness' varies considerably from tribe to tribe and from area to area. The general problem of the development of these areas presents many similar features, but their location, strategic importance, the extent to which they have been in touch with the rest of India and the degree to which they have advanced are important factors which necessitate a separate treatment of each area.

It might be useful however, to deal with some of the general aspects of the tribal question in these areas as a whole and then deal with each one separately later.

SHORT HISTORY AND BACKGROUND:

In *British days* they were called 'partially' or 'totally excluded' areas. No one was allowed to go to these areas except British officers and foreign missionaries. In some of the distant areas the British officers led only punitive expeditions from time to time and went occasionally to hold Durbars. Their authority was symbolic rather than effective. On the other hand since there was little or no contact with the rest of India and the world, these tribal folk were not inspired or influenced by India's national struggle for freedom. Various political and social movements in the rest of India and the world left these areas practically untouched. Thus during British rule, they were separate political areas. Historically also they were separate. Even economically they were cut off from the rest of the world for want of communications.

On the eve of India's independence some British officers and missionaries,

---

* See, Bishnuram Medhi Papers, Nehru Memorial Museum and Library, Delhi.

who did not like India becoming independent, encouraged separatist tendencies among some of the tribes, particularly the Nagas and the Lushais. They dubbed the new independent India as 'Hindu' India which belonged to an inferior culture and might swallow up the free and virile tribal folk. Thus was born the agitation for an independent Nagaland under the Naga National Council, and a movement for a Mizo Union to combine the Lushais living in Assam, Manipur, Tripura and across the border in Burma. Since, however, the Lushais were better educated than the Naga and were not so completely cut off as the Naga Hill District, this separatist movement did not make any deep impression among them. But among the Nagas, who are simpler and more primitive and, therefore, more gullible, the separatist tendencies gained some force, particularly in the Christian element among them.

In the *post-independence* years we were new to these areas and its problems; partly from ignorance and partly due to pre-occupation with other matters, we could not, perhaps, take immediate action to befriend these people. But a provision was made in the Sixth Schedule of our Constitution providing for the development of autonomous District Councils in the 'partially' excluded areas of Assam. The old 'totally excluded' areas were converted into the NEFA, to be administered by the Governor of Assam as the Agent of the President of India.

The *present position* is that the NEFA is directly under the External Affairs Ministry. While autonomous District Councils have been established in five out of the six tribal areas in Assam State, the sixth, namely, the Naga Hill District, has non-cooperated and not formed an autonomous council. Manipur State has been formed into a Part 'C' State under a Chief Commissioner and an Advisory Council is proposed to be set up there shortly.

COMMON PROBLEMS:

Because of partial or complete neglect of these areas during the British administration many problems in these areas today present certain common features, such as:-

1. Lack of communications.
2. Lack of educational facilities.

3. *Economic Backwardness*:

This varies from area to area. Except in the Angami Naga areas of the Naga Hill District, the practice of Jhumming (burning down forests and shifting cultivation from year to year) is denuding the forest wealth. Cottage Industries like weaving, basket making and fruit cultivation are dying out partly for want of a ready market and partly because of Partition, before which some of these products were sold in Sylhet and other Districts of East Pakistan.

4. *Social*:

Most of the tribal folk have social customs which may appear peculiar to a stranger at first but many of them are picturesque and perhaps worth preserving. Some, of course, like head hunting among the Nagas are bad, and are dying out. There is a community feeling and a group sense among most of the tribes which keeps them still together. Although each tribe differs from every other tribe (names like Nagas and Lushais do not really cover one single tribe but about a dozen each), they have a rich fund of folk art, folk songs, folk dances and a gay social outlook. They are much less inhibited than the plain's people. It would be worthwhile studying their social habits and customs and their cultural heritage and examining what should and can be preserved and how we can give them the benefits of modern culture without producing undesirable results.

5. *Religion*:

The influence of missionaries is very deep in some areas like the Lushai Hills and quite strong in certain other areas like the Naga Hills District. They have done some good work in the field of education and medical help, but they have imposed a new kind of narrow-minded missionary culture, (as distinct from a Christian culture, as in certain other parts of India), upon those whom they have converted. But this missionary culture is only skin deep and even the tribal converts still drink their Zhu (beer) when the missionary is out of sight, and sing their uninhibited love songs in their own language. About 80% of the people in the Lushai Hills have been converted to Christianity and about 30% in the Naga Hill District. In other areas the percentage varies between these two limits and is in some cases even less. In the NEFA, missionary activity is practically nil except in one or two places, and we have instead a vague form of Animism and nature worship. The question, as to what religion or culture should take the place of the existing foreign missionary or indigenous animistic culture is very important. Should we allow Indian missionaries of Christianity and other faiths to go and work among the simple tribal people or should we confine activities of even Indians to purely social and cultural work such as schools, dispensaries, etc? One point, however, seems to be clear that foreign missionaries should not be encouraged to go to any of these areas and even where foreign missions exist at present, their activities should be confined to medical and educational work rather than purely evangelical.

New China had to face this problem, not so much amongst their tribal folk but amongst the Han population. They have employed a new National Church in its place run by Chinese nationals who help the Government in their propaganda and other political work. In Russia, they did not have this problem of foreign missionaries, as the Russian orthodox church had always a strong hold on the Russian people. But even among their Muslim minorities, they have not done away with religion and minority culture but only took the anti-national sting out of it and made it a tool of the Government. At the same time, they developed the literature, languages and even evolved some scripts for their minorities.

Our problem is different from both that of China and Russia as (1) we have to deal with tribal people; (2) what religious activity exists in them is that of foreign missionaries; (3) their indigenous religion, if it can be called as such, is animism in its various forms and not likely to survive the development of education and modern culture among the tribes. We have, therefore, to be careful to see that we do not merely leave a vacuum in place of the old missionaries but create something positive in its place.

6. *Political*:

Apart from certain anti-Indian feelings which have been inculcated by foreign missionaries among the tribes, various degrees of tension exist between the plains' people and the hill tribes and among the hill tribes *inter se*. For instance, the Kukis and the Nagas of Manipur and the various sub-sections of the Nagas themselves have come into conflict in the past and may do so in the future if the feeling of oneness with the rest of India, which would supersede these separatist tendencies, is not created. Secondly, the main Indian political party, the National Congress, did not have a chance to work in these areas before and only started working after independence. There are in existence a number of tribal associations and unions but they are also in their formative stages. There is not much evidence of Communist influence in the hill areas, but if the situation is not properly watched and handled, these simple folk could be easily misled into Communism.

Since the greatest need of these areas is their economic, social and educational development, it would, perhaps, be best to gradually introduce some kind of village and district councils in each area, where the more educated and progressive leaders may be associated with the administration. This would, of course, vary from area to area. For instance, in the Naga Hill District where the Naga National Council has refused to cooperate, it has been suggested that a District Council of Nagas in service, some of their chiefs and loyal elements should be nominated. This is a point worth considering. So far as the NEFA is concerned, conditions there are not yet ripe for autonomous councils, but it would be desirable to train up some of the tribal people in administration and associate them with it, at the lower levels to start with. We may, even start nominated councils with limited powers to run their cooperative stores, agriculture stores and settle their petty disputes where conditions are suitable.

7. *Administration*:

This is one of the most important problems in all these areas. It has to be considered as to what steps should be taken to make the tribal people feel one with India. There should be no question of superiority or inferiority between plain's and tribal people. For this we need special types of officials and workers who will go and mix with them socially, live and eat with these and endear themselves to them by serving their real interests. The usual bureaucratic routine-minded officials will not do in these areas. It is, therefore, necessary to create a special cadre of officers carefully selected to meet the needs of these areas and we may have to relax the usual methods of recruitment, age limits, educational qualifications, etc., in their selection. At the same time, we have to make it attractive for such officers to offer their services in these areas since they will have to lead a very hard and arduous life and may have to run separate establishments for their families. We should make their emoluments attractive enough to induce them to go there.

We must also provide for a continuous flow of such people. For this it would be desirable to train a few people from among the tribal people themselves in the higher grades and put them through a course of training in various fields of administration. In the lower grades this training should be given in larger numbers and not in the plains but training schools should be started in the tribal areas concerned so that they do not get isolated from their own people and adopt ways and manners which are foreign to them. This creation and training of a special cadre from among the minorities has been tried with great success both in Russia and China, where they have set up special schools and colleges for training cadres from among the minorities to work in the minority areas.

Since most of these areas are difficult of access and communications take from three to six weeks in contacting Headquarters, it is important that the senior local official, like the District Officer, should have ample discretionary powers and some money grants at his disposal to utilize for the welfare of those people. Burma has started an experiment on a small scale of this nature by providing a welfare scheme and a welfare grant and a small band of welfare workers in each centre. Perhaps something of this nature could be tried in our hill districts also in addition to the large schemes we have in hand already. It is important to remember that the tribal people do appreciate quick, simple and easy remedies of their problems and have little faith in elaborate schemes which do not make a tangible and immediate appeal to them. We should, therefore, have both long term and short term plans for each area. While the former can be worked out in detail and thoroughly, the latter may be left to the discretion of the local official on the spot.

Until we are able to train the tribal folk themselves for subordinate jobs, we must offer at least subsistence wages to our subordinate staff. At present, a clerk in the P.W.D. and other Departments of the NEFA gets only Rs. 60/- including allowances and cannot possibly make a living on this. The result is that we get third-rate people who are rejected elsewhere and even they are discontented. We must, therefore ensure a minimum wage of at least Rs.100/- p.m. to our lowest subordinate staff. I am making separate recommendations regarding this.

Lastly, it is most important to bear in mind that all officials in each area must compulsorily learn the tribal language of that area within a specific period of say six months. Our administration in the NEFA has compiled small books giving useful sentences and words in some of the tribal languages and it is not really difficult to learn them if one is living with the people.

DEFENCE AND SECURITY:

Most of these areas lie on the frontiers of India and are vital to its security and defence. In the old British days when India was one country under a strong Central Government and even Burma was under the British, while China was a weak and divided country and had no hold over Tibet, the British could well afford to neglect these frontier areas. In fact, they deliberately did so. Conditions, however, have changed now and apart from other reasons which necessitate the development of these areas the security and defence of India urgently demand that we should make these areas reasonably secure. Geography undoubtedly is in our favour, but geography alone will not do. Our greatest security is the friendship of the tribal people and we must, therefore, take steps to make them feel that their welfare and prosperity depend upon their being a part of India. Since, however, the areas are under-developed and communications hardly exist, top priority must be given to the development of communications both in the shape of fair weather, jeepable roads and metalled roads, fair weather and all weather landing strips. Another measure which is worth considering is, whether we should not form a body of frontier scouts from among the tribes on the lines of an armed police force and/or guerrilla force who could be used for the defence of their villages and constructive work in peace-time and for jungle and guerrilla war-fare in times of emergency. The P.L.A. in China has trained a large body of such guerrillas numbering over 12-1/2 million. While I am not suggesting that we should compete with them, we could at least take a leaf from their book and make a start. This would incidentally also provide employment to a number of tribal youths who are otherwise likely to go astray.

FUTURE:

It is difficult to foresee with any degree of certainty what the future of these people and areas is likely to be, i.e., whether they should form an independent state directly under the Central Administration, or whether they should be merged into Assam when developed. The question has no immediate importance except that there seems to be a tendency among most of the lower officials and even in some of the higher officials, to Assamise these areas as the Assamese naturally predominate among the services. This can have both good as well as evil repercussions; if ultimately these areas are to merge with Assam, it might be a good thing; if not, this tendency may have to be curbed. In any case, it is important that the people should be made to feel Indians first and anything else afterwards. For instance, I was taken by surprise when I went to a Primary School under a thatched bamboo shed in village Balik, near Passighat in NEFA I asked the teacher who was an Assamese, whether he had taught the children any song. He made them sing a beautiful song which, I was told, was the 'Assamese National Anthem'. I asked the teacher whether he had taught them the 'Indian National Anthem' also and he replied in the negative. This is a small instance, but it is significant a feeling in some members of the Assam Government that the NEFA is being kept deliberately out of their influence. At the same time, suggestions were made by others that the Naga Hill District should be joined with the NEFA and taken out of Assam. All these problems, however, are not of immediate importance, but may be kept in mind with regard to the future of these areas. They should be examined from the point of view of the good of India, as a whole and the welfare of these areas in particular.

Sd/- T.N. Kaul.
21.4.1953

Appendix E

Chaliha Report

Secret report of Shri Bimala Prasad Chaliha, President, Assam Pradesh Congress Committee to the Assam Pradesh Congress Executive Committee on the present situation in the Naga Hills[*].

INTERVIEW WITH THE LEADERS

I found great difficulty in contacting the leaders as practically all of them are underground whether there by any warrant of arrest or not. By 'Leaders' I mean the members of the Executive Council of the Naga National Council. I could contact 4 of them including the Secretary. My meetings with them were in different dates at night and in fairly risky circumstances. They were however kind and courteous to me. An agreement as below could be reached and a paper was signed to that effect. I have given them words at their request not to disclose their names and further informations about the meetings and therefore I am not giving names: and the interesting and efficient arrangement made for the meetings.

THAT THERE SHOULD BE NO BLOODSHED IS RECOGNIZED

1. That the present impasse in Nagaland should be resolved.
2. That the differences should be settled amicably and peacefully by negotiations.
3. It being understood that the negotiations will take place if the Congress party accepts to discuss the Naga Independence Issue.
4. If the Naga leaders be agreeable to come to negotiations it will be the effort of the Assam Pradesh Congress Committee President, with the help of his organization, to move the proper authorities to create favourable conditions so that the leaders may participate.

Sd/ Illegible.   Sd/ Bimala Prasad Chaliha,
28.9.53   18.9.53
Secy. N.N.C.   President, A.P.C.C.

The present Secretary of the Naga National Council said, 'You see I am

* See, Bishnuram Medhi Papers, Nehru Memorial Museum and Library, Delhi.

definite that the Naga problem cannot be solved by a small man or small organization. Jawaharlal is a great leader he should be able to solve it. To you Mr. Chaliha this is an additional responsibility and you must discharge it. No organization other than the Congress can solve it.'

Further he said that if the principle of independence is accepted whether it is granted today or a few years later there may be some acceptable working arrangement for the interim period.

They have asked me to visit Naga Hills again in the 3rd week of October latest.

Appendix F

Government of Free Nagaland Kautaga

Secretary-General
United Nations
New York[*].

Your Excellency,
I have the honour to send you this letter again, hoping that it will reach you safely. Whether our previous letters and the message reached Your Excellency or not, we have no way to find out. The cable message was despatched on November 18, 1954, and a letter was sent the following day on the nineteenth. And, on November 30, 1954 (our Reference Number KKN52/KP1) we submitted the details of the case of Free Nagaland and the Chergee against the Government of India. We enclose herewith a copy of the same Note. In case the first copy did not reach you, please treat this one as original. For precautions, this same copy is being forwarded to Your Excellency through different routes.

The entry of the Government of India's troops into the territory of Free Nagaland is not simply an encroachment of certain portions of our border areas, but it is a full scale invasion of Free Nagaland. And, their presence in our State become intolerable. They shoot our people like games, torture the villagers, bomb and burn houses day after day, and killing off our cattles and other domestic animals and fowls not for their food alone, put with an intent to exterminate it, ultimately to starve our people.

After we submitted the details of our case, dated November 18, 1954, the following eight more villages were either bombed or burned down by Indian troops.

1. Dayangkhu   2. Mohn   3. Nokoon   4. Sanglao
5. Tobu   6. Tuongsang   7. Wih   8. Yangphang

Those that were not bombed were first looted and burned. In Noksen, the Church property and all the cash were first looted and burned, while in Tuengsang

---

* See, Bishnuram Medhi Papers, Nehru Memorial Museum and Library, Delhi.

(500 houses) the houses of the leaders and elders were burned.

Our people face acute starvation. We, the citizens of our own country, exist now in our own State not like human beings. If the United Nations could send us a mercy mission to look after the starving people of Free Nagaland, we shall be grateful. We refuse to leave our country, but we need someone's merciful assistance for our starving women and children who suffer through India-made famine.

We urge Your Excellency to intervene immediately—and request the Government of India to desist inhumanities in Free Nagaland and withdraw their troops from our territory. We do hope the United Nations will strongly uphold the cause of humanity and the right for the continued self existence of this ancient independent country of Free Nagaland.

Kautaga
Dated January 31, 1955

We are,
Yours most respectfully,

Hongkhin, for the KILONSERS
Government of the peoples sovereign
Republic of Free Nagaland Kautaga

Appendix G

SECRET & PERSONAL

No. 1116-PMH/56
New Delhi,
May 13, 1956

My dear Medhi[*],

This morning we had a conference to consider the Naga situation. Pantji and Dr. Katju were present among our Ministers and there were the senior officials of the External Affairs and Defence Ministries. Also our Army Chief of Staff, General Shrinagesh.

    2. Nothing special had happened to necessitate such a conference, but we wanted to clear our minds not only about the present situation but the future. From a military point of view, some progress is being made on our side and no doubt this will continue. You suggested in one of your recent letters that more armed forces were necessary. The view of our Army Staff is that during the monsoon there will be no advantage in sending more forces. In fact this may well be a liability because of the large scale arrangements necessary for maintaining them there. It may be that later it would be desirable to send more forces. We shall review the situation from time to time and, when it is necessary, we shall try to send more forces. As far as we can see, this will not be necessary or desirable during the monsoon.

    3. We recognise of course fully that this revolt of some of the Nagas has to be dealt with firmly and speedily. It is far better to restore law and order in these affected areas as quickly as possible than to allow the situation to drag on. But, as I have said above, even from a military point of view, we cannot do very much in the interior hills during the monsoon. Operations will certainly continue even during the monsoon and we shall be preparing for a large scale effort a little later.

    4. That is, as I understand it, the military appraisal of the situation. But there is something much more to it than merely the military approach. These Naga troubles and revolts have a larger significance for us in the international sphere and they give a handle to our opponents everywhere. More particularly, of course, Pakistan takes advantage of them. In view of our tense situation in regard to

---

*   See, Bishnuram Medhi Papers, Nehru Memorial Museum and Library, Delhi.

Pakistan, we have to be wary always and it is unfortunate that we should be tied up in the Naga Hills etc., where some other emergency might have to be faced by us.

5. But more important than all this is the question of the basic policy that we should pursue.

There can be no doubt that an armed revolt has to be met by force and suppressed. There are no two opinions about that and we shall set about it as efficiently and effectively as possible. But our whole past and present outlook is based on force by itself being no remedy. We have repeated this in regard to the greater problems of the world. Much more must we remember this when dealing with our own countrymen who have to be won over and not merely suppressed.

6. We have to remember that the operations in remote mountainous country without communications are always difficult. We have an example in Malaya where, it is said, that about 5000 or so rebels have held up large British forces and aircraft now for seven years. In Malaya they have dense jungles, here we have this mountain area. Both are difficult of access. We know that the Nagas are tough people and are very disciplined. It is therefore conceivable that even when we have succeeded completely in a military sense, small scale guerrilla tactics may continue giving us continuous headaches, apart from affecting our reputation both in India and abroad. How then are we to face this situation?

7. We shall of course use our armed forces to the fullest extent necessary. But we have always to remember that the real solution will require a political approach and an attempt to make the Nagas feel that we are friendly to them and that they can be at home in India. It may be that the present is no time for the political approach, because it may be construed as a sign of weakness. But anyhow our minds should be clear and even now onwards we should do nothing which will come in the way of that political approach and we should let it be known that we want to be friends with the Nagas unless they revolt against us.

8. In this morning's Times of India there is an article on the Nagas. This article is not a fair one I think and puts the blame entirely on our side. Even the facts are not correctly given. Nevertheless, there is some little truth in this article and I feel that we have not dealt with this question of the Nagas with wisdom in the past. We must not judge them as we would others who are undoubtedly part of India. The Nagas have no such background or sensation and we have to create that sensation among them by our goodwill and treatment. We shall have to think how we can produce this impression and what political steps may be necessary. This may come later of course, but the thinking part should begin from now onwards.

9. Unfortunately the Nagas have got a particular grouse against the Assam Government. Your Government may not be responsible for this and the mere fact that you have to deal with them led to this situation. But the fact remains that they are very dissatisfied with the present position. One of their grievances is that under our Constitution we split them up in different political areas. Whether it is possible or desirable to bring them together again is for us to consider. Also what measure

of autonomy we should give them so that they can lead their own lives without any sensation of interference.

10. I suppose this developing Naga situation is bound to have some effect on the other Hill tribes in Assam. This has also to be borne in mind.

11. I have tried to think loudly in this letter, so that I might let you have a glimpse of my mind and I want you to think also and to have talks with your new Governor who has a good deal of experience and can view these questions with some wisdom.

Shri B.R. Medhi,   Yours sincerely,
Chief Minister, Assam,   Sd/- J. Nehru
Shillong.

Appendix H

TOP SECRET
No. 459-PMO/57
New Delhi
June 12, 1957

My dear Fazl Ali[*],
Our Cabinet Committee on Oil met yesterday and sat for about three hours continuously discussing the question of the oil refinery, pipelines, etc. This discussion took place on a report from our Negotiating Committee who were dealing with the Assam Oil Company.

The Assam Oil Company had taken up a very difficult attitude and insisted on the refinery being near Calcutta. They said that they did not consider any other proposal economic and would not like to be made responsible for it. In other words, there was a deadlock between them and our Negotiating Committee. This was reported to us, and we had to consider what we should do in the circumstances.

One aspect of the question was how far we could undertake this work entirely from our own resources. These resources are totally inadequate in so far as trained personnel is concerned and, in view of our entanglement with the Assam Oil Company, all kinds of difficulties are likely to arise. Also, as you know, this is just the time when we are very hard put to find money for anything. In fact, we have introduced stringent economies everywhere. In other words, it was not possible for us to undertake this heavy burden by ourselves. At the same time, we saw no reason why we should be dictated to by the Assam Oil Company in this matter.

Then another aspect of this question came forcibly before us. Our Defence Chiefs having examined these various schemes said definitely that they could not undertake to protect the refinery if it was situated in Assam or the pipeline if it went to Calcutta along the Pakistan border. This strong and definite statement by those responsible for our defence and security could not be ignored. In fact, this statement came also in the way of the Assam Oil Company's proposal to run a pipeline along the Pakistan border to Calcutta. It was possible, of course, to take that pipeline some distance away from the border, but that would have extended

---

[*] See, Bishnuram Medhi Papers, Nehru Memorial Museum and Library, Delhi.

...om other consequences.

the length of it, reasons, we could not agree to the Assam Oil Company's
For *j* opinion was dead against it, apart from other reasons to which
proposals been made previously.

While it was not necessary for us to come to a final decision about every
...er at this stage, we could not leave this question in a state of deadlock. Some
opening had to be made for fresh consideration. And, for hours we discussed this
matter thoroughly from every point of view, so that we could continue our
negotiations with the Assam Oil Company or make some other arrangements if
they were feasible.

We were driven to the conclusion that the only feasible proposition was to
locate the refinery at Barauni to proceed with our discussions on this basis. The
refinery initially should be capable of dealing with one million five hundred
thousand tons of oil per annum, but there should be the possibility of its extension
if and when necessary. The pipeline would, to begin with, come to Barauni only.
This pipeline is likely to be of twenty inches to provide for future developments.
Later, that is in two or three years time, we might be in a position to see how far
there was surplus oil to be sent to Calcutta for export or for Visakhapatnam. If this
appears desirable, a pipeline would have to be constructed either from Barauni or
from somewhere else on the way to it to Calcutta.

Further we were of opinion that steps should be taken to develop the use of
natural gas in Assam for power and other purposes. The use of this can be expanded
in many ways and for various industries.

The refinery itself is not supposed to employ many people, just a few
hundreds, as the latest machinery is used.

We realised fully the disappointment that this would cause to our friends in
Assam. In fact, this matter was discussed, but we had no choice left except to give
up the scheme or delay it indefinitely, which was harmful to India and to Assam.
We were driven to our present conclusion, whatever the other reasons might have
been, and they were strong enough, the very definite and unequivocal attitude of
Defence left no other choice open to us. Personally, I think that the decision is a
correct one, not only from the point of view of the development of this oil, but
even of Assam. It is far easier and better to develop industries on natural gas and
start the exploitation of oil as soon as possible on an economic basis than to hold
up everything and to wait for some good fortune in the future. I have no doubt that
this oil is going to be of great benefit to Assam from the point of view of revenue
and industrial development. And, the sooner we get going with this, the better.

As I have indicated above, we are in the middle of negotiations and final
decisions depend upon many factors. We do not even know what the reaction of
the Assam Oil Company will be. They have been troublesome, but we have to
have some basis for future discussion as the old line did not work, and hence these
present decisions.

I am sending a copy of this letter to your Chief Minister, Medhi.

I am leaving day after tomorrow for Europe and shall b̶
With all good wishes to you.

̶r̶ a month.

Yours sᴎ̶
Shri Fazl Ali,   Sd. Jawaharlal Neᴎ̶
Governor of Assam,
Shillong

ARTICLE 7
The High Contracting Parties shall promote relations in the fields of art, literature, education, culture, sports and health.

ARTICLE 8
In accordance with the ties of friendship existing between the two countries each of the High Contracting Parties solemnly declares that it shall not enter into or participate in any military alliance directed against the other party.

Each of the High Contracting Parties shall refrain from any aggression against the other party and shall not allow the use of its territory for committing any act that may cause military damage to or constitute a threat to the security of the other High Contracting Party.

ARTICLE 9
Each of the High Contracting Parties shall refrain from giving any assistance to any third party taking part in an armed conflict against the other party. In case either party is attacked or threatened with attack, the High Contracting Parties shall immediately enter into mutual consultations in order to take appropriate effective measures to eliminate the threat and thus ensure the peace and security of their countries.

ARTICLE 10
Each of the High Contracting Parties solemnly declares that, it shall not undertake any commitment, secret or open, toward one or more States which may be incompatible with the present Treaty.

ARTICLE 11
The present Treaty is signed for a term of twenty five years and shall be subject to renewal by mutual agreement of the High Contracting Parties.

The Treaty shall come into the force with immediate effect from the date of its signature.

ARTICLE 12
Any differences in interpreting articles of the present Treaty that may arise between the High Contracting Parties shall be settled on a bilateral basis by peaceful means in a spirit of mutual respect and understanding.

DONE IN DACCA ON THE NINETEENTH DAY OF MARCH NINETEEN HUNDRED AND SEVENTY TWO.

Sd/- INDIRA GANDHI   Sd/-SHEIKH MUJIBUR RAHMAN
Prime Minister,   Prime Minister, For the
For the Republic of India   People's Republic of Bangladesh

Appendix J

Manifesto of the National Socialist Council of Nagaland

Nothing is more inalienable for a nation, big or small, than her sovereignty. No moment, either, is more challenging for a people than the time when their free existence is challenged. The Naga National Council has failed. The sovereign existence of Nagaland is more at peril than ever before. It is high time for the revolutionary patriots to declare their national principles, their views and their aims.

I. NAGALAND AND THE NAGA NATIONAL COUNCIL

We live in a world of constant change. But the forces causing the change are not always the same. They develop and perish according to the different given conditions, stages and times.

To us, the forces that defend the righteous cause of sovereign national existence and further the just cause of the people along the inevitable course are alone patriots and revolutionaries. All forces standing in opposition to this are traitors and reactionaries, in that they try to pull the wheels of history back. All the reactionary traitors lean upon one another; all revolutionary patriots stand as one, supporting one another; there is no via media.

The Naga National Council was the only authentic political organisation of the people of Nagaland. It was this council that boldly took up the historic national trust, that is, the safeguarding of the right of the sovereign existence of Nagaland. With all its resoluteness, the Council faced ups and downs and it was never deterred by setbacks here and setbacks there. It had withstood the bitter period of the past three decades or so, turning neither to the right nor to the left—although there had been marked degeneration in its integrity and vigour. Our country could exist and we owe it to the National Council and to the thousands of patriots who have unsparingly laid down their lives and to the unprecedented endurance of the people, thanks to the leadership Naga National Council had given to the people in their past trials and tribulations till the time of its failure to condemn the treacherous Ministry and the Accord of treason of 1975.

The sober reality, however, is that our country is still under heavy occupation of the enemy troops. What are we to do with this? The enemy will never withdraw of its own accord. In no circumstances should we allow ourselves either to count on the sensibleness of the enemy. Because it is always suicidal. History has sufficiently warned us against the possible repetition of such error. Politics is successful but only when backed by arms. We are safe so long as we fight to save ourselves. Therefore, we have to fight . . . If negotiations, however, would be indispensable, they should be done only from a position of strength. Any attempt, therefore, at negotiated settlement at the moment would undoubtedly mean doing away with oneself, if not, it is traitorous in motive.

Facts must be acknowledged in spite of whatever turn the world might take; people must be told the truth so that they may understand their country and know what is what. The enemy is superior, therefore, our war will have to be a protracted one. We are in the course of active defence. Who will lead us through this long war? It is the most decisive issue. Is this the Naga National Council still? It has got to be reasoned out.

True, facts must be admitted and it is a fact that the most ignominious sell-out in the history of Naga people ever since the time the first bullet of freedom was fired, is beyond dispute the notorious 'Shillong Accord.' That Accord deserved an outright official and open condemnation by the Ministry that surrendered arms and consented to such sell-out. This failure left the country in a dangerous political mess. Nationwide danger was thus brought about. Any earnest appeal in a time like this for guidance, and letters of determination to fight to the last were never vouchsafed; no imperative given. The helpless unyielding were left entirely to themselves . . . .

NAGALAND AND THE NATIONAL SOCIALIST COUNCIL

The world is changing fast but the Naga National Council has failed to keep pace with changing conditions. It has not understood the world and Nagaland; it has isolated itself from the people; it has not promised the people any future from the danger of the forces of domination, exploitation and assimilation. All the old forces have yielded and are drowned without a trace and any contrary claim is just a claim to save one's own face, and not to save the nation. All have fallen and Nagaland remains to be saved. Where is the way to save our nation now? Where is the Council that upholds the cause of the sovereign Nagaland and the salvation of the people?

We declare we are revolutionary patriots. Let no traitorous nor reactionary bounds be on us. To us the sovereign existence of our country, the salvation of our people in Socialism with their spiritual salvation in Christ are eternal and unquestionable. It is because life has meaning and that is in freedom alone. Only the revolutionary patriots are diametrically opposed to all the anti-national, anti-people forces. Because: We refuse Nagaland to be gotten for gold; we refuse Nagaland to be weighed in terms of silver, wine and women; we refuse Nagaland to be valued for one's status. Indeed, our Nagaland shall forever refuse to perish together with any leadership or organisation that has failed and betrayed her cause, that has no promise of future for her people. Time moves on, and we have to move along, although the Naga National Council does not, for we have to redeem Nagaland. Therefore, in this irreconcilable world, our National Socialist Council declares:

(a) *National existence*
We stand for the unquestionable sovereign right of the Naga people over every inch of Nagaland whatever it may be and admit of no other existence whatever.

(b) *Political institution*
We stand for the principle of people's supremacy, that is, the dictatorship of the people through the National Socialist Council and the practice of Democracy within the organization.

(c) *Economic system*
We stand for Socialism. Because it is the only social and economic system that does away with exploitation and ensures fair equality to all the people.

(d) *Religion*
We stand for the faith in God and the salvation of mankind in Jesus, the Christ, alone, that is 'NAGALAND FOR CHRIST.' However, the individual freedom of religion shall be safeguarded and the imposition of this faith on others is strictly forbidden.

(e) *Means*
We rule out the illusion of saving Nagaland through peaceful means. It is arms and arms alone that will save our nation and ensure freedom to the people.

(f) *Self-reliance and the policy of United Front*
We stand for the practice of the principle of self-reliance and for the policy of United Front with all the forces that can be united with.

SONS AND DAUGHTERS OF NAGALAND:
Ask not what the Maker has in store for us. In His righteousness, He has given us all that is ours. Let us understand our country and our freedom and hold them fast, for what have the people that doubt their freedom and that of their country? They are only fit to be ruled, nay, they are already ruled. They are the people to be pitied most. Without her freedom Nagaland too has nothing. Truly, when freedom falls, everything falls. Your country is challenged; your freedom is in peril. Arise and look! It is time, it is our today; we should never fail her, for no amount of sermons and lamentations can save her tomorrow. We have chosen Nagaland and her freedom forever; we will never part with them. Indeed, it is the war we have to

fight; it is the war we have to win. We shall accept no summons to bow down; our Nagaland shall never put her hands up. We shall live only in freedom. This alone is the way to our salvation. Praise the Lord! We hold the promises of history.

LONG LIVE NAGALAND!
LONG LIVE THE NATIONAL SOCIALIST COUNCIL OF NAGALAND.

Appendix K

Asia Watch Report on Assam, April 18, 1993

NO END IN SIGHT: HUMAN RIGHTS VIOLATIONS IN ASSAM (EXCERPTS)

Introduction

The Indian state of Assam, located south of Bhutan and east of Bangladesh, is geographically almost cut off from the rest of India, with its only physical link a narrow land corridor to West Bengal. Home to a number of tribes and ethnic groups, Assam has been the site of separatist movements and violent insurgencies since India's independence in 1947. The most serious has been the campaign waged by the United Liberation Front of Asom (ULFA) since 1979. In attempting to crush the ULFA organization and several other groups, the Indian government has launched counterinsurgency campaigns that have been fraught with widespread human rights violations.

The Indian army has conducted massive search-and-arrest operations in thousands of villages in Assam. Many victims of abuses committed during the operations are civilians, often relatives or neighbours of young men suspected of militant sympathies. Villagers have been threatened, harassed, raped, assaulted and killed by soldiers attempting to frighten them into identifying suspected militants. Arbitrary arrest and lengthy detention of young men picked up in these periodic sweeps, or at random from their homes and from public places is common, and detainees of the armed forces are regularly subjected to severe beatings and torture. Deaths in custody have occurred as a result of torture, and in alleged encounters and escape attempts.

Security laws that grant extraordinary powers to the armed forces provide the context for many of these abuses. Dissent is severely curtailed. Human rights activists and journalists have been arrested for reporting on human rights abuses in Assam or for criticizing the government's reliance on security legislation. Freed from normal legal restraints on arrests and detentions and on the use of force, the Indian army has had little reason to fear accountability for its abuses in Assam.

Militant groups have also engaged in violent abuses such as bombings, kidnapping and assassinations.

As is true in other parts of India, victims of army violations in Assam very often have been civilian men and women too poor and too powerless to get help from local authorities or to appeal to the courts. Amnesty International described similar conditions in its October 1990 report on human rights violations in Manipur during 'Operation Bluebird.'

'The testimonies cited . . . demonstrate that witnesses giving evidence in court face a real risk of repercussions. This is one of the reasons why victims have only rarely complained to the civilian courts, even though reports of human rights violations in the northeast have been frequent. Another reason is that the victims live in inaccessible regions with poor communications; the only contact many have with outsiders is the army. Many are illiterate, and they often do not know how to approach the courts, do not have funds to bring legal action and believe that petitions would not be accepted. Although villagers have complained to the civilian authorities such as the local police or deputy commissioner, these authorities have often said that they felt powerless to do anything about matters concerning the security forces that are controlled by the central government. Finally, . . . Section 6 of the Armed Forces Special Powers Act prevents citizens from bringing a case against the security forces without prior permission from the central government. Moreover, court cases often take years before a final ruling is given.' !*

Abuses by the army in Assam have included extrajudicial killings, illegal imposition of curfews, long periods of detention at army posts and camps, use of school and churches as detention or interrogation centers, and the molestation and rape of women. Civilians also reported large-scale looting of homes and granaries by army personnel, even after army operations had been called off in January 1992.

Torture has been widely used. Former detainees reported beatings with fists, wooden sticks, rifle butts and whips. Detainees were kicked, suspended from the ceiling, beaten on the soles of their feet, and burned with cigarettes. Use of chili powder and electric shocks, often applied to the face or genitals, was also common. Asia Watch also received reports of starvation and near-drowning as methods of torture. In many cases the victims of these abuses did not even speak the language of their interrogators and were therefore unable to answer their questions. In the words of one Assamese human rights group,

'Many of these procedures are adopted not only for interrogation but are done at random—because most of the times [sic] people were not

---

* See, Amnesty International, *India: 'Operation Bluebird'. A Case Study of Torture and Extrajudicial Executions in Manipur,* October 1990, p.59.

interrogated properly but nevertheless tortured. Torture acquires an independent existence—a momentum of its own and a sadistic, sinister underpinning. This makes it a tool for creating pure terror.'[*]

The hallmark of the Indian army's counterinsurgency efforts in Assam is the 'cordon and search operation,' involving massive raids and house-to-house searches in thousands of villages. The primary targets of these raids are young men suspected of militant sympathies, but their neighbors and family members also fall victim to army violence. During search operations, civilians are routinely subjected to threats, harassment and assaults. Rapes of family members are common. The primary goal of these raids appears to be to frighten villagers into identifying suspected militants. Once identified, suspects are detained in army facilities, and subjected to severe mistreatment. It should be noted that Asia Watch has documented similar abuses during operations in Punjab and Kashmir, and Amnesty International reported abuses of the same sort in Manipur in 1990[**].

Young men in Assam are regularly subjected to arbitrary arrest and lengthy detention. Picked up in markets and other public places, or taken from their homes, they are detained in army camps and interrogated. Often no charges are brought against them and they are released, sometimes, with life-threatening injuries resulting from beatings and other forms of torture. Torture in Indian army facilities is routine and is often used as a method of summary punishment. Methods of torture in Assam have included beating, kicking, administering electric shocks and starvation.

Asia Watch has also received reports of deaths in custody as the result of torture, and in alleged encounters and escape attempts. According to the US Department of State, human rights groups in Assam reported that as many as 40 people were killed in army custody in 1991 and early 1992.[+] Bypassing normal judicial channels in favour of summary justice with the help of security laws like the National Security Act (NSA) and the Terrorist and Disruptive Activities (Prevention) Act (TADA), the army in Assam and other parts of India regularly detains individuals against whom there is little evidence of wrongdoing.[++] Used in conjunction with the Disturbed Areas Act and the Armed Forces Special Powers

---

[*] See, MASS, *A Report on Human Rights Violations and State Terrorism in Assam during Operation Rhino,* September 1991, p.5.

[**] See, Asia Watch, *Kashmir Under Siege,* May 1991 and *Punjab in Crisis,* August 1991. See also, Amnesty International, *India: 'Operation Bluebird'. A Case Study of Torture and Extrajudicial Executions in Manipur,* October 1990.

[+] See, US Department of State, *Country Reports on Human Rights Practices for 1992,* p. 1136.

[++] See, Asia Watch, *Kashmir Under Siege. Human Rights in India,* May 1991, pp.1008–115. See also, *Punjab in Crisis,* August 1991, pp 152–157 and *Human Rights in India: Police Killings and Rural Violence in Andhra Pradesh,* pp. 15, 25–26.

Act, these laws free authorities from legal restraints on arrests and detentions and on the use of force. The Indian military uses them to weed out suspected militant sympathizers, intimidate critics and silence dissent; aggrieved civilians have little recourse. Human rights activists and journalists are discouraged from investigating abuses in Assam, and several have been charged under these security laws for attempting to report on human rights conditions or for criticizing the government's use of the laws themselves.

ULFA has also committed abuses. Since 1990 the group has engaged in assassinations and kidnappings of civilians, including police officers, businessmen and others. Also among its victims in 1992 were former ULFA members, or members of the faction that supported negotiations with the government[*]. In January 1993 ULFA militants kidnapped V.G. Raghavan, the chief executive of a large Indian corporation, Prag Bosimi Synthetics. They also killed three tribal youths whose bodies were found hanging in trees. The killings were apparently in retaliation for the youths' suspected role in the arrests of three of ULFA's Nagaon district leaders[**]

Cases of Abuse by the Security Forces

An Asia Watch consultant who travelled to Assam in March 1992 was harassed, questioned and followed by police throughout her ten-day stay. She nevertheless managed to visit Lakhimpur District, one of the hardest hit areas in the northern part of the state, where she interviewed several families affected by army violence. Her interviews exposed a pattern of severe abuse by military personnel, corroborating earlier reports by local human rights groups. She found evidence of similar acts of violence by members of ULFA, and spoke with relatives of victims in Guwahati who described severe violations by ULFA members. The cases described below are based on her investigation.

Bhanimai and Tarun Dutta

Mukuta Dutta, a resident of Kowadanga Village, in Naobaisa, North Lakhimpur, told Asia Watch that on October 16, 1991, at 3:00 p.m., members of the security forces arrived at his house in two trucks and four jeeps just as his fourteen-year-old daughter Bhanimai was returning from fetching water from a nearby well. The soldiers asked Dutta how many sons he had. He told them he had two sons and that the older, twenty-five-year-old Tarun, was in the village; twenty-year-old Babul was at home. The soldiers accused Tarun of having ULFA connections and began slapping Dutta. They then dragged Mukuta and his younger son Babul towards the jeeps. Dutta's wife Rakhada ran after the soldiers, pleading with them to stop. But the soldiers continued to beat Babul and his father, and then, leaving

---

[*] See, US Department of State, *Country Reports on Human Right Practices for 1992*, p.1136.

[**] See, *The Times of India*, 1 February 1993.

Mukuta Dutta lying on the ground, forced Babul into a waiting vehicle and drove away.

As his wife helped Mukuta return to the house, they saw three other members of the security forces leaving through the front door. Mukuta and Rakhada ran inside to find Bhanimai lying on the bed almost totally naked and unconscious. She was trembling violently, saliva dripping from the sides of her mouth.

Rakhada screamed for help and neighbors came running. Sumita Sut, a neighbor, 13, said she saw Bhanimai lying on the bed with bruising and bite marks all over her body. She said she tried to stop the trembling in Bhanimai's arms and legs by holding on to them, but Bhanimai died soon after.

Because government doctors were on strike at the time, the next day, on October 17, Bhanimai's uncle took her body to a private hospital for the postmortem, but the results of the autopsy were not released to the family.

On the day of the attacks, after the security forces left the Dutta house, the soldiers in army jeeps and trucks spotted Tarun crossing a bridge and picked him up. Although Babul was released soon after his arrest, Tarun was not released until March 10, 1992. According to his parents he had been tortured in army custody for two days and then jailed. His ribs and skull had been pressed between clamps, which caused him to lose his sense of balance and he had been given electric shocks. He had continuous tremors in his hands.

Although the state government initially tried to deny that Bhanimai Dutta was raped, a state minister, Bargoram Deuri, went personally to the Dutta home and promised her parents compensation of Rs. 100,000 ($3,300) and offered one of Mukuta's sons a government job. Four months later neither promise had yet been kept.

Babul Barua

Hamadhar Barua told Asia Watch that on October 12, 1991, at about 2.30 a.m., eight or nine members of the army arrived at his house in Bandadwa village and arrested his nephew, Babul Barua, 20, who had been visiting for a few days. The arresting soldiers said Babul was wanted in connection with the death of two people allegedly killed by ULFA and that he knew where the bodies were.

On October 15, 1991, at about 7:30 p.m., Babul was returned to the uncle's house by four soldiers, who were carrying him, and several policemen. Babul's arms and legs were bandaged and he was unable to move. When the bandages were removed, the family discovered that he could not walk and his shoulders had been dislocated. Biju Borua, Babul's fifteen-year-old cousin, and Sarbeswar Barua, his elder brother, told Asia Watch that Babul's body bore marks of severe beating and his urine contained large amounts of blood. A doctor who treated Babul said that Babul's kidneys had been ruptured. Due to a strike by local government doctors, and despite appeals to local officials, Babul Barua could not get the necessary medical help. He died on October 24, 1991. According to the soldiers who brought him back after the interrogation, he had been found innocent.

Dibakar Handique

At 2:30 p.m. on September 28, 1991, Dibakar Handique, 27, of Basapukhui Village in Dholpur Maiza, Narayanpur, North Lakhimpur, was playing *carrom* (a board game) with his friends at the house of his neighbor, Bogi Handique, when he was arrested by 10 or 12 soldiers deployed in the area. Bogi Handique, who witnessed the arrest, told Asia Watch that the soldiers accused Dibakar of being a member of ULFA. They tied Dibakar's hands behind his back and kicked him and beat him with rifle butts in the face, abdomen, and all over his body. The soldiers then took him to a paddy field and beat him again before kicking him into a nearby pond. The soldiers then dragged Dibakar out of the water and continued to beat him. Bogi saw blood pouring out of Dibakar's nose, and hair being pulled from his head. His sister Saranami Handique, stated that the soldiers finally carried Dibakar away, as he could no longer walk. She also said that a lot of his hair was gone.

Rupada Handique, Dibakar's sister-in-law, said that when she tried to stop the soldiers from taking Dibakar away, they laughed at her. Three or four other villagers were arrested along with Dibakar, but had been released after they were tortured. Dibakar was taken to Jorabari Army Camp.

On September 29, 1991, the body was handed over to Lakhimpur Civil Hospital and on September 30, 1991, at 9.00 a.m., the family was informed that he was dead. His eldest brother, Indrakanth Handique, went to the hospital to identify the body and Dibakar's body was brought home at 8:00 p.m., by army soldiers. Although the army did not permit relatives to inspect the body, they were able to see that his arms, legs and fingers appeared broken, and that the body bore the marks of severe beating.

According to Jogen Kanwar, a neighbor, other male members of the village were taken away and questioned before Dibakar's arrest. They were all asked whether Dibakar was a member of ULFA, and although Jogen denied it, he could not speak for the rest.

Numali Baniya

Numali Baniya, a widow, 40, said that at about midnight on October 21, 1991, three uniformed Indian army soldiers broke into her house in Jalukota village, Mermukh, Narayanpur, Lakhimpur, where she was asleep with her three daughters. While two soldiers kept guard in the bedroom where the girls were sleeping, the third dragged Numali out of the house and raped her at gunpoint.

The next day, Numali went to the Dhalpur government hospital for medical treatment and a certificate stating that she had been raped. But the doctor there refused to help her until she registered her case with the local police. Being too frightened to approach the police, Numali instead sought the help of the civil Sub-Deputy Collector R.K. Regu, hoping that he would help her register her case with the police, but he refused.

Conclusions and Recommendations

The pattern of abuse in Assam in strikingly similar to that found in Punjab Kashmir and elsewhere in India. As in these areas, the Indian government doe face a major security threat from militants. But the means used to address tha threat violate fundamental international standards and undermine respect for the rule of law. The persistent threat of violence by insurgent groups in Assam make it critical that India end this practice and demonstrate that it is not official policy India must discipline abusive troops and guarantee that all its forces are hel accountable for their actions. As part of this process, Asia Watch suggests that th government of India direct its newly formed National Commission on Huma Rights to investigate the cases documented in this report.

In previous reports Asia Watch has made a number of recommendation aimed at improving the human rights climate in India. Many of these recommendations focus on the need for investigation of all reported abuses and the amendment or repeal of abusive security regulations. We reiterate those concerns:

- The government of India should repeal the Terrorist And Disruptive Activities (TADA) Act as its provisions are so broad as virtually to criminalize legitimate political dissent.
- The government of India should amend the National Security Act to ensure that it cannot be used to curb legitimate political dissent.
- The government of India should establish independent, impartial commissions of inquiry into all reports of extrajudicial execution, torture, rape and assault carried out by members of the army and security forces. Members of the army and security forces found responsible for murder and other gross abuses should be prosecuted and punished. Family members should be paid compensation.
- The government of India should strengthen and enforce the safeguards existing in Indian law that protect detainees from torture, including requirements that all detainees be brought before a magistrate or other judicial authority empowered to review the legality of their arrest within 24 hours of arrest, that they be informed promptly of the charges against them, and that all detainees have immediate and regular access to lawyers, family members and medical care. A centralized register of detainees accessible to lawyers and family members should be established.
- Militant organizations should abide by the principles set forth in common Article 3 of the 1949 Geneva Conventions, which prohibit killings or other attacks on persons taking no part in hostilities. Asia Watch condemns all acts of violence against civilians.
- The International Committee of the Red Cross should be permitted to undertake the full range of its protection activities in Assam, and we urge the government of India and all militant groups operating in

Assam to extend their full cooperation to the ICRC.

In addition:
- The Armed Forces (Assam and Manipur) Special Powers Act should be amended to include an absolute time limit on its validity and should be required to undergo parliamentary review pending continuation.
- Article 4(a) of the Armed Forces (Assam and Manipur) Special Powers Acts should be repealed. The powers it grants the military regarding the use of deadly force are so broad as to contravene international standards.
- All military personnel should be required to file a full report on any incident in which deadly force is used. This report should include the circumstances under which the decision was made to use deadly force. All reports of civilian deaths should be promptly investigated and forces found guilty of gross human rights violations should be prosecuted.
- Section 6 of the Armed Force Special Powers Act should be repealed as it makes it virtually impossible for civilians to bring charges against errant military personnel.
- All members of the armed forces should be required to report and justify the destruction of buildings and other private property. Procedures must be developed which allow civilians to claim compensation for wrongful destruction of property, and to ensure prosecution of forces guilty of willful criminal behavior in this regard.
- Army personnel should be required to inform all detainees of the grounds of their arrest; all detainees should be provided with legal counsel; and all persons arrested by the military should be remanded to police custody within 24 hours.
- The Armed Forces Special Powers Acts should be amended to require warrants for search and seizure. Reports of violence against civilians including sexual abuse and rape, reports of intimidation and harassment, and property damage that occur during military search operations should be promptly investigated. Again, personnel found guilty of such abuses should be prosecuted and victims or their families paid compensation.
- The Armed Force Special Powers Act should be amended specifically to prohibit torture. The right to be protected against torture by agents of the state is inherent in the right to life and personal liberty guaranteed under Article 21 read with Article 14, 19(1), 20 and 22 of the Indian Constitution. Moreover, the use of torture to extract confessions is an offence under Section 330 of the Indian Penal Code.

- The Armed Force Special Powers Act should be amended to guarantee those arrested by Assam's security forces a fair trial. To promote due process, detainees arrested by the armed forces should be turned over to civil authorities as quickly as possible.

*

COPY OF EXPRESS LETTER NO. 26011/16/71-IC DATED 29-11-1971 OF THE UNDER SECRETARY TO THE GOVERNMENT OF INDIA ADDRESSED TO THE CHIEF SECRETARIES TO ALL STATE GOVERNMENTS AND UNDER TERRITORY ADMINISTRATION.

Sub: Grant of Indian Citizenship to refugees from East Bengal, who have crossed over to India after 25th March, 1971 Instructions that applications from such refugees for Indian Citizenship should not be entertained.

Refugees who have crossed over to India from East Bengal since the 25th March, 1971 on account of the situation in that area cannot be treated ordinarily resident in India.They are expected to return to their native places when the conditions permit. They should not be considered for registration as Indian citizens under section 5(I)(a) of the Citizenship Act, 1955, read with the Citizenship Rules, 1956. If such refugees make applications to the Collectors who are the prescribed authority for purposes of registration as Indian citizens under section 5(I)(a) of the Citizenship Act, such applications should be rejected. Enquiries on applications for registration under section 5(I)(a) of the Act should be made carefully to ensure that no refugee who has come after the 25th March, 1971 from East Bengal gets registered as Indian citizen by giving any false declarations claiming to be resident in India for long and from a date prior to 25th March, 1971. Suitable instructions may kindly be issued in the matter to all Registoring Authorities under your control immediately.

Select Bibliography

Azad, Maulana Abul Kalam, *India Wins Freedom*, Delhi: Orient Longman, 1988.

Barooah, Nirode, *Gopinath Bardoloi: Indian Constitution and Centre-Assam Relations*, Guwahati: Publications Board, 1990.

Barua, Hem, *The Red River and the Blue Hill*, Guwahati: Lawyers Book Stall, 1954.

Das, Amiya Kumar, *Assam's Agony*, Delhi: Lancer Publishers, 1982.

Dutta, Anuradha, *Assam in the Freedom Movement*, Calcutta: Darbari Prokashan, 1991.

Dutta, Arup Kumar, *Chai Garam!*, Delhi: Paloma Publication, 1992.

Franda, Marcus, *Bangladesh: The First Decade*, Delhi: South Asian Publishers, 1981.

Gandhi, Rajmohan, *Eight Lives: A Study of the Hindu-Muslim Encounter*, Delhi: Roli Books, 1986.

Gopalakrishnan, R., *Northeast India: Land, Economy and Peoples*, Delhi: Har Anand Publications, 1991.

Gordon, Leonard A., *The Nationalist Movement, 1876-1940*, Columbia: Columbia University Press, 1974.

Guha, Amalendu, *Planter Raj to Swaraj: Freedom Struggle and Nationalist Politics in Assam 1826-1946*, Delhi: People's Publishing House, 1977.

Hazarika, Sanjoy, *Bhopal: Lessons of a Tragedy*, Delhi: Penguin India, 1987.

Mansergh, Nicholas & Moon, Penderel, eds., *India: The Transfer of Power 1942-1947*, London: His Majesty's Stationery Office, 1980.

Meyase, Visier, *Essay on the Oral Traditions and History of Khonoma Village*, Nagaland [unpublished].

Moon, Penderel, ed., *Wavell: The Viceroy's Journal*, London: OUP, 1973.

Nibedon, Nirmal, *The Night of the Guerrillas*, Delhi: Lancer Publishers, 1978.

Nibedon, Nirmal, *The Ethnic Explosion*, Delhi: Lancer Publishers, 1987.

Rustomji, Nari, *Imperilled Frontiers: India's North Eastern Borderlands*, Delhi: OUP, 1983.

Sinha, A.C., *Bhutan: Ethnic Identity and National Dilemma*, Delhi: Reliance Publishing House, 1991.

Singh, B.P., *The Problems of Change*, Delhi: Vikas Publishing House, 1989.

Tendulkar, D.G., *Mahatma: Life of Mohandas Karamchand Gandhi*, Bombay: Vithalbhai Jhaveri, Vol. 7, 1953.

Tomlinson, B.R., *The Indian National Congress and the Raj: The Penultimate*

Phase 1929-1942, London: Macmillan Ltd., 1976.

Verghese, B.G., *Waters of Hope*, Delhi: IBH, 1991.

Weiner, Myron, *Sons of the Soil: Migration and Ethnic Conflict in India*, Princeton: Princeton University Press, 1978.

Census Reports: Assam, 1961, 1971, 1991; Tripura, 1961, 1971, 1981; West Bengal, 1961, 1971.

Sharifa Begum, "Birthrate and Deathrate in Bangladesh, 1951–1974", Dhaka, Bangladesh Institute of Development Studies, 1979.

Talukder Maniruzzaman, "The Future of Bangladesh", in A. Jeyaratnam Wilson and Dennis Dalton, *The States of South Asia: Problems of Integration*, London: C. Hurst and Co., 1982.

Agricultural Atlas of Assam, Faculty of Agriculture, Assam Agriculture University, Jorhat, 1983.

Atiur Rahman, "Impact of Riverbank Erosion: Survival Strategies of Displacees", Dhaka, Bangladesh Institute of Development Studies, 1985.

Mahabub Hussein, "Briefing Paper on Bangladesh", London, Overseas Development Institute, 1990.

Shaukat Hassan, "Environmental Security in South Asia", London, International Institute for Strategic Studies, 1990, Adelphi Paper, 262.

Sharifa Begum, "Population, Birth, Death and Growth Rates in Bangladesh: Census Estimates", Dhaka, Bangladesh Institute of Development Studies, 1990.

Centre for Science and Environment, "Floods, Flood Plains and Environmental Myths", Delhi, 1990.

Bangladesh Statistical Yearbook, Government of Bangladesh, Dhaka, 1990.

"Report of the Committee on Clause Seven of the Assam Accord", Planning Commission, Government of India, Delhi, 1990.

Statistical Outline of Assam, Government of Assam, Guwahati, 1990.

Life is Not Ours: Land and Human Rights in the Chittagong Hill Tracts, London, the Chittagong Hill Tracts Commission, 1992.

Sanjoy Hazarika, "Environmental Degradation, Migration and Ethnic Conflict: Bangladesh and Assam", Cambridge: American Academy of Arts and Sciences, Peace and Conflict Studies Program, University of Toronto, April 1993.

"Census of India 1991 and Paper 2 of 1992, Final Population Tables", Registrar-General of India, 1993.

Transfer of Power Papers, Nehru Memorial Museum and Library [hereafter NMML] and the India International Centre Library, Delhi.

Gopinath Bardoloi Papers, NMML, Delhi; Bishnuram Medhi Papers, NMML, Delhi; and Sir Syed Mohammad Saadulla Papers, NMML, Delhi.

Index

A

Acquired Immune Deficiency Syndrome (AIDS), 241, 320, 322
Abdullah, Farooq, 189
Advani, Lal Krishan, 196
Afghan mujahideen, 169, 172, 173
Ahmed, Fakhruddin Ali, 49
Ahmed, Ikram, 3
Ahmed, Khondakar, 277
Ahmed, Serajuddin, 22
Ahmed, Tajuddin, 278
Akali Dal, 148, 159
Alexander, A. V., 69
Ali, Amjad, 57
Ali, Moon, 218
All Assam Students Union (AASU), 137–139, 141–144, 148–150, 157, 168, 178, 182, 186, 211, 219, 221, 229, 233
All Bodo Students Union (ABSU), 153–155, 159, 160, 162, 165, 166
ABSU-Assam Government Accord, 166
All Burma Students Union (ABSU), 322
All India Congress Committee (AICC), 47
All India Dravida Munnetra Kazhagam (AIDMK), 150
All India Sikh Students Federation (AISSF), 139
All Party Hill Leaders Conference (APHLC), 127
All Tripura Tribals Front (ATTF), 125
Amnesty International, 116, 278, 313, 314
Ao, Longri, 107
Aram, M., 107
Arunachal Peoples Liberation Army, 134
Armed Forces (Special Powers) Act, 221
Asia Watch, 116
Asian Development Bank (ADB), 284
Assam, migration into, 34, 35, 38, 39–41, 58, 64–65, 66, 78–80, 83
Assam Accord, 148–151, 183, 211
Assam Association, 46

Assam Congress, 48, 65, 76, 77, 80
Assam Congress Parliamentary Party (ACPP), 76
Assam Muslim League, 26, 33
Assam Nationalist Coalition Party, 65
Assam Oil Company, 268
Assam People Liberation Army, 169
Assam Provincial Congress Committee (APPC), 39, 46, 47, 71
Assam Union Muslim League, 51
Asom Gana Parishad (AGP), 137, 150, 151, 153, 154–157, 159, 165, 169, 176, 178, 183–184, 186, 189–190, 192, 198, 200, 203, 210, 211, 223, 227, 267
Asom Gana Sangram Parishad, 137
Asom Jatiyabad Chattra Yuva Parishad, 167, 169
Asom Sahitya Sabha, 139
Autonomous Implementation Demand Committee, 246, 248
Azad, Maulana Abul Kalam, 55, 61, 68, 71–72, 76

B

Bahadur, Dev, 290–292, 308
Bahadur, Sher, 315
Bangladesh and environmental degradation, 13, 15–17, 22; and its drug policy, 15; and floods, 6, 13–14, 18–23
Bangladesh Mohajir Sangstha, 254
Bangladesh National Party (BNP), 287
Bangladeshi migrants, 4–9, 16–17, 27–33, 123, 125, 138–140, 141, 143–145, 148–150, 229, 232–233, 235, 250–255, 325–328, 330
Bank of Credit, Commerce and Industry (BCCI), 229
Barah, Sheikh, 4–6, 15
Bardoloi, Bolin, 163, 164
Bardoloi, Gopinath, 46–58, 69–69, 71–84, 97, 98, 126, 138, 151, 154, 162, 249,

255, 266
Bardoloi, Nabin Chandra, 46
Barooah, Hemen, 195
Barooah, Nirode, 49, 71, 75–76
Baruah, Goutam, 193–194
Barua, Hem, 42
Barua, Liladhar, 48
Barua, Maniram Dutta, 37
Barua, Paresh, 167, 169, 172–174, 178, 201, 203–204, 205, 214, 217, 219, 223–226, 229, 231, 232, 235, 238
Barua, Tapan Lal, 160, 222, 228
Basnet, R. D., 310
Bastola, Chakra, 315
Basu, Tarun, 148
Begum, Sharifa, 30–31
Bengal, partition of, 33, 46
Bezboruah, Arpan, 169
Bhagwati, Bijoy, 47, 55, 75–77
Bhanot, Deepak, 211, 216
Bharatiya Janata Party (BJP), 4, 6, 196, 254, 326
Bhasin, S. K., 239
Bhashani, Abdul Hamid, 26, 80
Bhattarai, Krishna Prasad, 309
Bhindranwale, Jarnail Singh, 159
Bhutan Congress Party, 303
Bhutan State Trading Corporation, 310
Bhutto, Zulfikar Ali, 26
Biseswar, 120–122
Bodo Accord, 160–162
Bodo Security Force (BSF), 159, 160–166, 246, 264
Bodo Volunteer Force, 165
Bombay Silk Mills, 269–270
Borgohain, Hemen, 193, 195
Borooah, Dev Kanta, 75, 142
Bose, Sarat Chandra, 75–76
Bose, Subas Chandra, 55, 56, 75, 77
Brahma, Prem Singh, 160, 162, 165
Brahma, Upendra, 155–158, 159, 165, 166
Brahma, Renukarani, 190
Brahma, Rupkumar, 153–154
Brahmachowdhury, Satyen, 154, 155, 159
Brar, K. S., 199–200
Bronson, Miles, 45
Brooke Bond, 197
Burmese Communist Party, 285, 321–322
Bwasumatari, Sugwai, 153–154, 155, 159, 160

C
Central Intelligence Agency (CIA), 158–159, 170, 172
Central Intelligence Department, 191, 199
Chaliha, Bimala Prasad, 88–89, 102, 113, 255
Chaliha, Kuladhar, 46
Chakma, Arnab Jyoti, 288
Chakma, Priti, 279, 285, 286, 287
Chakma, Upendra, 288
Chavan, S. B., 222–223, 252
Chetia, Arup, 167, 172, 214, 218, 221, 224–228, 231–232. *See also* Golap Barua
Chiang Kai-shek, 51
China and the Mizos, 116–117
China and the Nagas, 103–105, 116–117
Chittagong Hill Tracts (CHT), 8, 17, 117, 123, 124, 253, 278, 279, 280–290
Chou En-lai, 51
Choudhury, Mahendra Mohan, 75–77
Choudhury, Rohini Kumar, 47, 59, 65, 67
Chowdhury, Moinul Huq, 80
Civil Disobedience, 46, 47, 48
Communist Party of India (Marxist) [CPI(M)], 124–125
Congress Party, 3, 23, 36, 38, 44, 46, 48, 49, 54, 57, 58, 59, 61, 64, 66–68, 72–84, 118, 124, 137, 139, 140, 142, 143, 145–147, 150, 156, 171, 184, 190, 198, 211, 239, 243, 244, 249–250, 252, 254, 255, 277, 298
Cripps Mission, 59
Cripps, Stafford, 69, 71
Curzon, Lord, 33

D
Daimuri, Anjali, 164
Daimuri, Ranjan, 164, 165, 166, 246
Daimuri, Subodh, 164
Das, Amiya Kumar, 268
Das, Basanta, 54
Das, Haren, 194, 215
Das, Parag, 209, 248, 256
Das, Pushpa Lata, 75
Deb, Santosh Mohan, 142, 156
Desai, Morarji, 90–91, 137
Dewan, Gautam, 283
Disturbed Areas Act, the, 195, 209, 221
Dolie, Kevi, 100
Dorji, Chimi, 314
Dorji, Jigme, 297
Dorji, Kazi Ugen, 297
Dravida Munnetra Kazhagam (DMK), 150

Dunn, Mavis, 66
Dutta, Arup Kumar, 35–36
Dutta, B. B., 253
Dutta, Tapan, 193, 204

E

Eastern Indian Tribal Union, 111
Eastern Naga Revolutionary Council, 104
Elwin, Verrier, 130–131, 134
Emergency, the, 91, 109, 137, 198, 277
Ershad, H. M., 11, 253, 281, 284

F

Fernandes, George, 189, 277
Food and Agriculture Organization (FAO), 294
Franda, Marcus, 27–29, 33

G

Gandhi, Indira, 4, 23, 80, 88, 90–91, 101–102, 103, 109, 117, 137–139, 141–146, 147, 198, 251, 253, 277, 278, 279
Gandhi, M. K., 46, 47, 48, 56, 60–61, 64–65, 68, 71–72, 74–80, 97, 102
Gandhi Mission, the, 107
Gandhi, Rajiv, 117, 118, 147–148, 150, 156, 195–196, 205, 251, 253
Gandhi, Sanjay, 277
Gas Authority of India (GAI), 268
Ghising, Subhas, 299–300
Ghosh, Manash, 219
Gill, Kanwar Pal Singh, 170, 246–247
Glieck, Peter, 319–320
Gogoi, Samiran, 167, 172, 221–222, 224, 226–227. *See also* Pradip Gogoi
Gogoi, Tarun, 211
Gohain, Bhadreshwar, 169
Gohain, Chakra, 168, 231
Gopalakrishanan, R., 267
Goswami, Apu, 248
Gritchenko, Sergei, 212–213
Gulf War, the, 12, 267
Gurkha Liberation Organization, 300
Gurkha National Liberation Front (GNLF), 299–300
Gurung, Purna Bahadur, 306–308

H

Handique, Bijoy, 188
Harlalkar, Girdharilal, 169, 186
Hassan, Shaukat, 16–17

Hazarika, Jogendranath, 140
Hazarika, Manoj, 172
Hekmatyar, Gulbuddin, 172
Hezb-i-Islami, the, 172
Hindu-Muslim riots, 4, 16, 72, 75, 76, 234–235, 327
Hindustan Lever Limited (HLL), 195
Hitler, Adolf, 51
Hmar Peoples Convention, 106, 238–239, 246
Horam, H., 92
Hossein, Mahabub, 13
Hrangkhawl, Bijoy, 124–125, 185
Huire, Zashi, 109
Hydari, Akbar, 97–98, 101

I

Indian Oil Corporation (IOC), 268
Indian Peace Keeping Force (IPKF), 199, 205
Indian Tobacco Company (ITC), 194
Illegal Migrants (Determination by Tribunals) Act of Assam, 251
Intelligence Bureau (IB), 191, 192, 196, 199, 225, 229, 279
Inter Services Intelligence (ISI), 170, 171–175, 179, 225
Islam, Zahirul, 138, 140

J

Jacob, M. M., 254
Jain, L. C., 266
Jaitly, Jaya, 271–272, 273–274
Jamir, S. C., 107, 109
Jan Sangh, 76
Jana Sanghati Samiti, 278–279, 282
Janata Party, 4, 137–139
Jasokie, J. C., 108–109
Jinnah, Mohammad Ali, 23, 26, 53, 58, 59, 64, 66, 72, 79, 80, 81, 82, 255
Johnstone, Colonel, 94–95, 96
Jumla, Mir, 44

K

Kachin Independence Army (KIA), 103, 105, 109, 121, 166, 177, 178–180, 244, 320–321
Kampani, M. L., 102, 106–107
Kaul, T. N., 91, 103
Keane, Michael, 51, 52
Keishing, Rishang, 122
Kevichusa, Chalie, 241–242

Keyho, Biseto Medom, 107
Keyho, Thinsolie, 104–105
Khan, Liaquat Ali, 58, 65–66, 72, 76
Khan, Yahya, 27
Khaplang, S. S., 104, 110, 178–179, 180–182
Koirala, Girija Prasad, 299, 304, 305, 308, 309, 310, 312, 315
Konwar, Rajiv, 167. *See also* Arobindo Rajkhowa
Koza, 86
Kuki National Army (KNA), 243
Kuki National Front, 243
Kuki National Organization, 243
Kumar, Dinesh, 206

L

Labour Party, 241–242
Laldenga, 112–114, 116–119, 120, 171, 233–234
Land Settlement Policy, 58, 64, 66–67
Larma, Manobendra, 278, 279, 285–286, 288
Larma, Shanto, 278, 279, 286, 287, 288
Laxmi Chand Jain Committee, the, 260–261
Levor, Kevi, 86–87, 91
Liberation Tigers of Tamil Eelam (LTTE), 199, 205
Lipton, 197
Longowal, Harcharan Singh, 148
Luthra, P. N., 28

M

Macleod Russel, 193
MacNeil Magor, 193, 239
Mahaliya, Jones, 163–165
Mahanta, Hirakjyoti, 167–168, 169, 172, 217, 218–220, 221, 223, 231, 248, 256
Mahanta, Jugal Kishore, 179, 180–181, 204–207
Mahanta, Prafulla Kumar, 141, 143, 147, 149, 155–156, 183, 190, 194, 195, 198, 211–212
Manav Adhikar Sangram Samiti, 209–210
Manipuri Peoples Liberation Army, 180
Maniruzzaman, Talukder, 15
Mautam, 111–112
Medhi, Bishnuram, 47–48, 69, 84, 249–250
Meyase, Visier, 92, 96, 99–100
Military Intelligence, 191, 196
Mishra, Dwarka Prasad, 51
Mishra, Lokenath, 209, 210

Mitra, Asok, 32–33
Mizo Famine Front, 112
Mizo National Army, 117
Mizo National Front (MNF), 112–119, 171, 233–234
Mizo Union, 111
Muivah, Thuengaling, 103–106, 109–110, 121–122, 166, 174, 178–179, 180–182, 225–226, 229, 237, 243, 244, 245
Mukti Bahini, 11, 28, 159
Mullen, C.S., 7
Muslim Front, 251
Muslim League, 26, 49, 53, 57, 58, 61, 65, 68, 69, 71–84, 126, 142, 253
Myanmar and Northeast India, 121, 123, 134, 159, 165, 178–180, 182–183, 208, 237–238, 244

N

Naga National Council (NNC), 89, 91, 97
Naga Nationalist Organization, 108
Najibullah, 173
Namgyal, Ngawang, 295
Narain, Raj, 137–138
Narayan, Jaya Prakash 36, 86, 102, 198, 277
Nath, Sunil, 165, 172–174, 176, 204, 218, 220, 221–222, 224, 226, 231–232, 246. *See also* Siddharth Phukan
National Front (NF), 137, 157, 189–190, 195
National Security Act, 248
National Socialist Council of Nagaland (NSCN), 89, 91, 110, 122, 134, 159, 162, 165, 166, 174, 177, 178, 180, 181, 225, 237, 238–239, 242, 243, 244, 245, 246
National Socialist Council of Nagaland (K), 110
Nationalist Independent Group, 65. *See also* Assam Nationalist Coalition Party
Nayar, Kuldip, 195
Nehru, Arun, 195
Nehru, Braj Kumar, 102, 106, 238
Nehru, Jawaharlal, 46, 68, 71–74, 76, 78, 82–83, 99, 101, 107, 127, 158, 249–250, 255, 277, 281
Neog, Kalpajyoti, 218, 221, 226
Nepali Congress, 299
Nepali Congress Party, 299
Nibedon, Nirmal, 99, 105, 120
Nichols-Roy, J. J. M., 78, 126–127
Nichols-Roy, Stanley D. D., 127
Nobis, Munim, 169–170, 174–175, 179,

226–227, 231–232
Non-Co-operation movement, 46, 78–79
Non-violence, 64–65, 75

O

Oil and Natural Gas Commission (ONGC), 212, 268
Operation Bajrang, 174, 199–211, 215–216, 219
Operation Bluestar, 199
Operation Cloudburst, 216–217
Operation Jericho, 113
Operation Rhino, 172, 174, 211, 217–220
Osmani, A. F. Golam, 138, 140

P

Pakistan, and Assam, 61, 64, 68, 71, 73, 75, 84; and the Mizos, 117, 171; and the Nagas, 101, 103, 171; and ULFA, 169–175, 179
Pakistan Democratic Party, 26
Pakistan Peoples Party (PPP), 26
Partition, the, 24, 257–260, 281, 327
Patel, Vallabhbhai, 55, 68, 71, 73, 76, 83, 255, 281
Patwari, Hiralal, 137–138
Pegu, Ronesh, 233
People Liberation Army, 120–122
Peoples Revolutionary Party of Kanglepiak (PREPAK), 121–122, 180
Phizo, Angami Zapu, 85, 86–93, 95, 96, 97–99, 101, 103–104, 106–107, 109–112, 118–119, 178, 181, 240
Phookan, Tarun, 46–47, 48
Phukan, Anandaram Dhekiyal, 45
Phukan, Brighu Kumar, 141, 147, 149, 155, 183, 190, 211–212
Phukan, Siddharth, 165. *See also* Sunil Nath
Pilot, Rajesh, 160–162
Plains Tribal Council of Assam, 151, 155–156
Prabhakara, M. S., 220, 233–234
Pradhan, Ram, 149
Prag Bosimi, 269–273
Prasad, N. K., 209
Pyarelal, 64

Q

Quit India resolution, 57, 59

R

Radcliffe Award, the, 258, 281–282

Rajkhowa, Arobindo, 167, 169, 172, 204, 221, 224–228, 231, 232, 233–234. *See also* Rajiv Konwar
Rajkumar, T. L., 132
Raju, T. S., 212, 214
Rahman, Atiur, 22
Rahman, Sheikh Mujibur, 26–27, 253, 276, 277, 278, 279, 281
Rahman, Ziaur, 14, 253, 277, 279, 281
Ramyo, Z., 103, 107
Rao, Papa, 213, 230–231, 264, 273
Rao, P. V. Narasimha, 156, 159, 221–222, 231, 235, 251–253
Ratikhowa Sampradai, 43
Reddy, Neelam Sanjiva, 138
regrouping of villages, 113–115
Reid, Robert, 50, 52
Research and Analysis Wing (RAW), 156–157, 170, 175, 179, 191, 196–197, 218, 225, 279, 285–286, 288
Revolutionary Government of Manipur, 119
Rikhye, Ravi, 193–194
Rizal, Tek Nath, 312–314
Rodrigues, Alfred, 199
Rongpi, Jayanta, 246
Roy, Pabitra, 36–37
Rustomji, Nari, 89, 96–97, 114–115, 129–131, 132, 133, 134

S

Saadulla, Syed Mohammad, 33, 49–60, 64–67, 79–80, 82, 84, 126–127, 142, 154
Sabhajanik Sabha, 46
Sahay, Subodh Kant, 189–190, 196
Saikia, Ashok, 153, 184
Saikia, Hiteswar, 146–147, 148, 157, 160, 162, 165, 174, 206, 212–216, 218, 220–222, 227–231, 235, 251–252, 255–256, 269
Sailo, Thenphunga, 117–118
Sakhrie, T., 97, 98, 99
Salt Tax, the, 47–48
Sangma, Purno, 253
Sankardev, 43
Seshan, T. N., 210
Shaiza, Rano, 107
Shakdher, Sham Lal, 138–139, 141
Shanti Bahini, 279–280, 282, 285, 287–288
Sharma, Manabendra, 228
Sharma, O. P., 306
Shastri, Lal Bahadur, 277

Shekhar, Chandra, 192, 196, 198–199, 209, 277
Simon Commission, 153
Singh, Ajai, 198–200, 210, 215, 222, 227
Singh, Baldev, 72
Singh, B. P., 33, 40, 45
Singh, Charan, 137–138, 141
Singh, Lalan Prasad, 106–109, 140–141
Singh, Prakash, 213
Singh, V. P., 157, 189, 192, 196, 198
Singha, Purandhar, 37, 94
Sinha, Sarat Chandra, 140, 153
Small, G. A., 68
Sobhan, Farooq, 8, 252
South Asian Association for Regional Cooperation (SAARC), 309, 315
Special Branch, 191, 199
Special Services Bureau (SSB), 158
Srivastava, A. S., 212
Srivastava, P. P., 202
Stalin, Josef, 51
State Security Bureau, 191
Subba, Bhim, 302, 310, 315
Subramanium, S., 194
Subsidiary Intelligence Bureau (SIB), 191, 199
Suhrawardy, Husain Shahi, 26
Suu Kui, Aung San, 179
Swaraj, 46
Swarajya Party, 47
Swu, Isak, 109–110, 180, 225
Swu, Scato, 104

T
Tagore, Rabindranath, 26
Tarang, Holiram, 248
Tata, Jamset, 270
Tata Tea, 193
Tayyebulla, Mohammed, 76
Telugu Desam (TD), 150
Terrorist And Disruptive Activites (TADA) Act, 164
Thinley, Jigme, 311
Tripura National Volunteer Force (TNVF), 124–125, 185, 283
Tripura Volunteer Force (TVF), 124
Trivedi, H. P., 149
Tsultrun, Jigme, 301–302, 307–308

U
Unilever Brothers, 192, 195
United Democratic Front (UDF), 107–109
United Liberation Front of Asom (ULFA), 89, 110, 134, 141, 159, 162, 165–166, 167–236, 237–239, 246, 247–248, 250, 252, 256, 264, 267–268, 273, 283
United Minorities Front, 186
United Nations, the, 88, 102, 305
United Nations Development Programme (UNDP), 294
United Nations High Commission for Refugees (UNHCR), 288–289, 291, 301, 304, 310, 324
United Nations Population Front, 328
United Opposition Front, 26
United Peoples Forum of Assam, 247
United Peoples Manipur Liberation Army, 165
United Reservations Minority Communities of Assam, 233
Upadhyaya, Chabilal, 39

V
Vajpayee, Atal Bihari, 109
Vamuzo, 242
Venkataraman, R., 200
Verghese, B. G., 17–20, 275, 329
Vizol, 107–109
Vyas, Hemant, 269–273

W
Wajed, Sheikh Hasina, 276
Wangchuk, Jigme, 295
Wangchuk, Jigme Singye, 297, 308, 309, 310, 311–313, 315
Wangchuk, Ugyen, 295
Wavell, Lord, 59–60, 63, 72, 73
Weiner, Myron, 30–31, 41
World Health Organization (WHO), 15

Y
Yandaboo, Treaty of, 94
Yallay, Kevi, 107

Z
Zia, Begum Khalida, 11, 235–236, 252, 287
Zokunga, Joseph, 115